1987

OPERATING SYSTEM
DESIGN

OPERATING SYSTEM DESIGN - Volume II

Internetworking with Xinu

DOUGLAS COMER

Department of Computer Sciences
Purdue University
West Lafayette, IN 47907
and
AT&T Bell Laboratories
600 Mountain Avenue
Murray Hill, NJ 07974

Prentice-Hall, Inc., Englewood Cliffs, New Jersey 07632

Library of Congress Cataloging-in-Publication Data
(Rev. for vol. 2)

COMER, DOUGLAS.
    Operating system design.

    Includes bibliographies and indexes.
    Contents: [1] The Xinu approach—
    v. 2. Internetworking with Xinu.
        1. Xinu (Computer operating system)
2. System design.   I. Title.
QA76.76.063C65 1984   005.4'3   83-19270
ISBN   0-13-637539-1 (v. 1)
ISBN   0-13-637414-X (v. 2)

Cover design: Jim Kinstrey
Manufacturing buyer: Ed O'Dougherty

This book was typeset by the author on an Autologic APS-5 using TROFF and other UNIX text-processing software at AT&T Bell Laboratories, New Jersey.

LSI 11, PDP 11, and VAX are registered trademarks of Digital Equipment Corporation
Pronet is a trademark of Proteon Incorporated
UNIX is a registered trademark of AT&T

Printed in the United States of America

10 9 8 7 6 5 4 3 2 1

ISBN 0-13-637414-X 025

Prentice-Hall International (UK) Limited, *London*
Prentice-Hall of Australia Pty. Limited, *Sydney*
Prentice-Hall Canada Inc., *Toronto*
Prentice-Hall Hispanoamericana, S.A., *Mexico*
Prentice-Hall of India Private Limited, *New Delhi*
Prentice-Hall of Japan, Inc., *Tokyo*
Prentice-Hall of Southeast Asia Pte. Ltd., *Singapore*
Editora Prentice-Hall do Brasil, Ltda., *Rio de Janeiro*

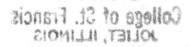

To the memory of my father

Contents

Chapter 15   A Syntactic Namespace   239

Chapter 16   User Interface Design   263

Bibliography   **553**

Index   **559**

Foreword

The design of an operating system is an exercise in the art of abstraction. The software of the operating system cloaks the raw hardware, and presents instead a more directly useful version of the system function. Consider the disk, which in its primitive form provides fixed size storage containers identified by an integer index. So much more useful is the abstract version of the disk, the file, which provides a variable size storage container identified by a meaningful character string name. In fact, a system is usually a sequence of abstractions: from the disk a file is made, from this a directory, and perhaps from this a data base. If the designer has practiced his art well, each of these abstractions will prove to be directly relevant to the task next at hand.

In this respect, a packet network is nothing new. The basic service provided by a network is certainly primitive, and is much more appealing when suitably cloaked in abstraction. The basic service is delivery of individual data containers of rather small maximum size, which may in transit be lost, damaged, reordered, or duplicated. But out of this the operating system software can build the illusion of a reliable byte stream, or a remote file system, or a global shared address space.

The designer who has fashioned these network abstractions may well feel pleased, but the implementor who must write the software is not likely to be so fortunate. Present experience suggests that the implementor who must fit network software into some existing operating system will have a hard time of it. The problem is that the network software makes demands on the operating system which the operating system is ill-equipped to meet. In other words, the operating system abstractions and the network abstractions do not mesh well.

To illustrate this problem, consider what happens within an operating system when a process suspends itself pending the completion of some input operation. A common system design is to divide such suspensions into "short" and "long". The "short" suspension might typically be waiting for a disk, which should take less than 100 milliseconds. A "long" wait might be for user input, which is unpredictable and might take minutes, or even hours. For a "short" suspension, it is reasonable to leave the process loaded and runnable in main memory, while for a "long" suspension the memory resources of the process are reclaimed by swapping the process to disk.

How should a network be fit into this scheme? A file transfer would tend to generate short waits, remote login long. If the scheduler knew what application protocol a process was running, it could select the correct mode of suspension for it, but the scheduling decisions are made at the very lowest levels of the system, and knowledge of the application is not available there; application software is at the highest level of network code. The result is that the programmer of the network code cannot make effective use of this sort of scheduler.

In a typical implementation, there will be many difficulties of this sort. It is therefore very important to understand the source of these problems. Perhaps the network abstraction has been designed and layered improperly. Or perhaps the operating system must be redesigned to match the needs of the network. What can we conclude?

It is very possible that the abstractions we propose today for networks will turn out to be wrong. When the disk was first invented, the designers saw it only as a tool to enhance the abstractions already at hand; the disk was a random access tape drive. Only over a decade did new ideas such as virtual memory evolve which depended on the particular characteristics of a disk. Exactly the same thing has happened with the network; it has been used to emulate an asynchronous terminal link, a disk, and most recently a procedure call. Only now are we beginning to see new proposals for network abstractions which are unique to networks and which model their distinctive characteristics.

If new abstractions are to replace the ones now proposed for networks, it is equally true that the result of these new abstractions may completely change the function and structure of operating systems, just as the concept of virtual memory did twenty years ago. It is in fact a very exciting time to be involved in the business of networking, because the current debates about abstraction will probably define the mature form of the network based operating system. Other parts of operating systems are very stable by comparison. While it is still possible to argue about the merits of a disk abstraction such as single level storage, no one has proposed a new abstraction for the disk in a long time. New network abstractions are being proposed every year.

The source of the implementation problems discussed above is thus that both the network abstraction and the operating system are not yet designed properly, and both will change in the next decade. None of this helps the poor implementor who must code the software for today's abstractions using today's operating system. The implementor must be concerned with seemingly more basic questions, such as, "How should the network software be modularized?" And even a simple question like this can prove surprisingly difficult.

The implementor might turn to the specification for the network software to help in modularizing it. For example, the International Standards Organization has given us a reference model for protocols, with seven levels of abstraction. Almost all protocol specifications reflect this layered approach in their structure, and many implementors, turning to this model for guidance, have implemented each layer as a procedure, perhaps in its own process. The results have generally been disastrous, with performance degradation of orders of magnitude over what was expected. This book, after only twenty eight pages, must observe that the layering suggested by the specification must be violated to insure efficient execution.

What went wrong? In fact, the seven layer reference model was intended to modularize the design process into subcommittees, not the software into processes. The committee structure has the obvious effect of producing specifications in layered form, since each layer comes from its own subcommittee. But it offers no real help to the implementor, and if the implementor cannot turn to the specification for support, there is nowhere left to turn. The implementor must go it alone, trying to blend together network abstraction and operating system abstraction which don't seem to fit well.

What is needed is a book which describes proper implementation practices for network code. And that is what this book is all about.

David D. Clark, MIT
DARPA Internet Architect

October, 1986

Preface

The art of designing communication software involves understanding how complex, autonomous computer systems can exchange information correctly and efficiently. Like an artist who composes a painting one brush-stroke at a time, the communication system designer considers details in small steps, composing individual components into larger and larger groups until recognizable forms take shape. Neither the artist nor the system designer can afford to proceed blindly if they hope to produce a masterpiece; both start with a vision of the ultimate goal and follow a careful plan to achieve it.

Most texts on networking survey hardware technologies and protocol standards without discussing an overall plan for communication system design. They discuss protocol software without considering how to integrate it into an operating system or how an operating system might use it. Such surveys, while useful at the introductory level, often leave students with the mistaken impression that communication is a field dominated by hardware, and that designing communication systems means choosing among appropriate technologies.

This text is unlike others because it focuses on the key abstraction in communication system design: internetworking. Internetworking is fundamental because it provides an architectural framework for building communication systems, as well as a basis for making software design decisions. It forms a common thread that runs through the entire text, and gives a central perspective around which each component fits.

Chapters 1–11 comprise a self-contained unit that covers the basics of internet communication. Each of the eleven chapters explores one component of internet protocol software, motivating and explaining how that component fits into the overall system design. The unit starts with a detailed examination of one network technology, the Ethernet, and moves on to consider the internet concept, address resolution, internet datagrams, routing, control messages, user datagrams, and datagram demultiplexing. Later chapters build on the basic communication system, examining client-server interaction, and remote file access, as well as a user interface and commands that manipulate both local and remote files.

This book is suitable for both undergraduate and graduate courses in operating systems or networks. Although no concept is difficult by itself, undergraduates may find it difficult to maintain a pace sufficient to cover the material in a single semester. At the graduate level, instructors can expect students to understand the basics well enough to explore subtleties and design consequences. Class time can be devoted to alternatives, and students can be asked to read pertinent journal articles.

Written as a continuation of *Operating System Design — The XINU Approach* (Comer [1984]), this text starts where the earlier one ends. The two volumes were written to support a two-semester course in systems design that encompasses operating systems and networks, with a blend of both operating systems and networks in both semesters. However, it is possible to use them in separate courses. A course in operating systems can use the chapters on naming and user interface from the second book in conjunction with the first book, and a course in networking can use the chapters on frame-level communication from the first book in conjunction with the second.

At Purdue University, my approach to teaching operating systems and networks has been experimental. I supplement lectures with required weekly laboratory† work in which students begin with their own copy of the Xinu software, and then modify, measure, and extend it. In addition to lab problems, students are assigned homework, journal papers to read, and additional programming. The student response to the formal labs has been extremely positive, and they seem to gain a much deeper appreciation for design possibilities and issues through the hands-on experience. More information on the lab can be found in Comer [1986].

To encourage other institutions to use the experimental approach, we make copies of the software available for a nominal charge. Prentice-Hall distributes machine readable copies of the programs from either book, using 1600 BPI UNIX tar tapes. For information contact:

> James Fegen, Jr.
> College Editorial
> Prentice-Hall Inc.
> Englewood Cliffs, NJ 07632

Information about other versions of the software can be obtained from:

> Xinu Librarian
> Computer Science Department
> Purdue University
> West Lafayette, IN 47907

Many people have contributed to the Xinu project over many years. Students in the advanced systems seminar provide a sounding board for new ideas and exercise code by experimenting with the software. Ralph Droms, Chris Kent, Steve Munson, Thomas Narten, and Ken Rodemann critiqued early designs of the Xinu Internet software; Ralph and Chris built their own Ethernet driver and UDP/IP software for an Intel 8086 system, and Chris helped diagnose the behavior of DEQNA hardware. Steve built the first version of the UNIX file server software from which the version in Chapter 13 was derived.

---

†The Xinu lab includes a dedicated VAX 11/785 running the 4.3BSD UNIX timesharing system, 16 work areas, each with a Wyse CRT terminal, as well as 7 LSI 11/2 and 8 LSI 11/23 PLUS microcomputers, each with an Ethernet interface and a console line (connected to the VAX). The lab also houses other microcomputers available for Xinu projects including several Microvax I, Microvax II, Intel 86/14, AT&T UNIX PC machines.

In other seminar projects, Raj Yavatkar and Steve Kennedy transported the basic Xinu software to SUN Microsystems 2/120. Andy Thomas and Marc Mengel transported it to an IBM PC. Raj and Santiago Zapata-Sauceda are currently working on Ethernet drivers for both the SUN and IBM PC versions for use in the Cypress network. Steve Chapin is currently working on a port for the AT&T UNIX PC.

Tom Stonecypher transported the software in this book to a Microvax I, then to a Microvax II, VAX 11/780, and finally to a VAX 8600, finding several subtle errors along the way. He is currently working to complete the Ethernet driver portion of the 780/8600 version. Tom also designed and implemented a resident loader for the VAX version that dynamically loaded a compiled program from a remote file and started a process executing it. Building on the Microvax version, Steve Kennedy and Cathy Privette each designed and implemented virtual memory software. Their work helped exercise the code further, and uncovered a few more subtle problems.

Santiago and Daryl Steen each built a version of the domain naming software, and helped me ferret out several small details of name server interaction, using the domain nameserver initially installed by Larry Peterson (and now maintained by the departmental facilities staff).

Dan Hachigian built the *VAX* side of the Ethernet downloader and tested my resident code.

Georgia Conarroe drew most of the figures using pic.

Many of the people mentioned above read and commented on early drafts of the text. Above all, I thank my wife, Christine, who provided several good suggestions and found more mistakes in the manuscript than anyone else.

I am indebted to Digital Equipment Corporation for grants that provided substantial discounts on laboratory equipment, and to Purdue University for supporting the Xinu work with lab space, equipment, and personnel for lab supervision and system maintenance.

I also thank AT&T Bell Laboratories for choosing to make Xinu part of their Academy for Computer Science and Engineering, for their support of the project, and for the use of their excellent typesetting facilities at the Murray Hill Lab.

1

Introduction and Overview

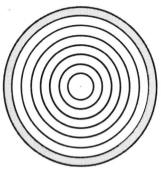

1.1 Introduction

Communication is a fundamental and exciting part of modern computer systems. It is exciting because it offers entirely new ways of computing in which processing is distributed among two or more machines that each handle part of the task. It is fundamental because the computational demands of users have overtaken the growth in power of single machines, forcing them to use multiple, interconnected machines to solve their computational problems. Indeed, some of the computations performed by multiple machines could not be handled by a single processor ten times more powerful than current machines.

Communication software does more than permit a program executing on one machine to interact with a program executing on another. It makes possible *sharing* of data and resources. More important, integrating the design of the operating system and the communication software allows the operating system itself to share resources with other systems.

Another form of communication occurs when a user interacts with a computer system to request computation or control processing. Usually, such interactions take the form of imperative commands issued by the user to the system. The interactive user interface software accepts commands and maps them to services supplied by the underlying system.

This book considers the design of both internetwork communication software that permits one computer system to communicate with another, and user interface software that permits a user to communicate with a computer system. The discussion focuses on design decisions and software organization, and examines how these two components fit into the overall operating system design.

1

1.2 Internetworking

The most important abstraction behind computer communication is a concept known as *internetworking*. It is a fundamental idea that pervades every design decision and influences every piece of communication software. In a sense, internetworking is the framework on which all communication software is built.

Physically, an internetwork (or *internet*) consists of a collection of networks connected together by special-purpose computers. The goal of internetworking is to hide the low-level architectural details from users, making the entire collection of networks appear to be a single, large, unified network. With internet software, communication among computers several networks away is as easy to achieve as communication among computers on a single local network. Users invoke one set of communication primitives and use one machine addressing format for both local and remote communication.

Communication system designers face an interesting challenge. They must provide internetwork communication using conventional processors and network technologies, hardware that was designed without regard for internetworking. They need to develop efficient mechanisms to translate operations in the high-level internet world into operations on low-level networks, and to map between abstract addresses assigned in the internet and physical addresses used by the hardware.

This book explores the design of basic internet software, and explains how such software allows machines to communicate without knowledge of underlying network architecture. It examines how internet software fits into a conventional operating system, and shows how the operating system uses internet software to share resources. The book uses the popular internet protocols developed by the Defense Advanced Research Project Agency (DARPA), and includes discussion of address resolution, routing, encapsulation, packet format, and demultiplexing.

1.3 Design Methodology

We will follow a hierarchical design methodology that starts with basic operating system primitives and adds, layer-by-layer, the pieces of internetworking software. The Xinu operating system serves as a base on which the software is built. Xinu is a small, elegant, hierarchically organized operating system that is easy to understand and easy to change. It is described in Comer [1984], which shows how the hierarchical design methodology works. The software described in this book begins at the Xinu device manager level, and extends through the user interface. It discusses an Ethernet device driver, and then adds network protocol software to support the DARPA Internet and User Datagram Protocols (IP/UDP). Later chapters add additional levels to the hierarchical design to provide a remote file system, naming system, and finally, a UNIX-like command interpreter. Thus, we start with a basic operating system and extend it.

1.4 Goals

The goals of this text are to explain the design of computer systems that make extensive use of communication networks, and to show how user interface software fits into the hierarchical operating system structure. To make the problem more concrete, we will identify a target system and build toward it, assuming the reader is already familiar with basic operating system components like the process manager. The target is a single user "diskless internetwork station", a computing system that supplies conventional computing capabilities, but relies on a remote machine for file storage. This chapter describes the target system in more detail, giving the reader examples of the user interface and system capabilities. The remainder of the text examines the internal structure of operating system components that make such a system possible, concentrating on the layers of network protocol software and the structure of user interface software.

1.5 A Target System

Imagine a small computer that connects to a high speed network, but has no secondary storage devices. One would like a program running on the diskless computer to be no different from a program on any machine: it should be able to open files by name, read data from them, and write data to them. A program executing on the diskless machine should also be able to use the network to communicate with programs on other diskless machines.

Because our imagined machine is diskless, files cannot be stored locally. They must reside instead on a remote system called a *file server*, with requests to read or write data passing over the network from the diskless computer to the file server, and replies from the file server returning over the same network.

1.6 User Interface

How will a user interface with the diskless machine? Like users on a typical time-sharing system, we imagine that users of our diskless system will interact with a command interpreter that accepts input from the terminal, allowing the user to invoke commands. When started, the diskless system will initialize the network software, use the network to obtain needed information like the time of day, ask the user to identify himself or herself by name and then begin running the command interpreter.

Our command interpreter will be a UNIX-like shell that accepts commands, one at a time. It repeatedly issues a prompt, reads an input line, and then executes the command named by the first word on the line (where "word" means contiguous string of nonblank characters). All words on the input line are passed as arguments to the command. For example, the *ps*[1] command prints a readable, formatted listing of the process table. When a user types

---

[1]many command names come from UNIX.

ps

to the shell, it produces output like:

pid	name	state	prio	stack range	stack length	sem	message
0	prnull	ready	0	157320-157777	62 / 304	-	-
3	ps	curr	20	152124-153027	308 / 452	-	-
4	UDPecho	wait	30	153030-153623	118 / 380	10	-
5	rwhod	sleep	20	153624-154277	80 / 300	-	-
6	rwho-in	wait	20	154300-154753	130 / 300	14	-
7	netout	wait	99	154754-155573	80 / 400	5	-
8	netin	susp	100	155574-156333	90 / 352	-	-
9	main	recv	20	156334-157317	96 / 500	-	-

The output contains one line for each process that includes the process id, name, state, priority, stack bounds, and current stack size. If the process is blocked, the output shows the semaphore id on which it is waiting.

The *ruptime* command provides information about machines on the network, showing how long each has been up, the number of users logged in, and the load averages[2] of the machine over the past 1 minute, 5 minutes and 15 minutes. Typing

ruptime

produces a listing with one machine per line:

```
xinu        up            3:13    1 users,    load 0.00,  0.00,  0.00
cypress1    up            8:23    2 users,    load 0.10,  0.09,  0.08
gareth      down          1:00
gawain      up      1 + 10:09    3 users,    load 0.13,  0.00,  0.00
merlin      up      9 +  0:58   10 users,    load 0.37,  0.78,  0.94
lucas       up     20 + 15:27    1 users,    load 0.00,  0.08,  0.00
bedivere    up      7 + 19:20    8 users,    load 0.26,  0.12,  0.01
blays       up      4 +  7:24    5 users,    load 4.12,  4.85,  5.26
mordred     up     16 + 11:10   29 users,    load 2.17,  2.30,  1.92
arthur      up      4 +  6:08   28 users,    load 1.32,  1.41,  1.42
gwen        up     12 + 11:11   10 users,    load 1.73,  1.58,  1.59
lancelot    up     14 +  5:23    4 users,    load 1.54,  1.32,  1.28
```

The names in the left column are names of machines in the Computer Science Department at Purdue University.

---

[2] the load average represents the average number of processes currently ready to use the CPU.

Another command, *mem*, prints statistics about the current memory allocation and the allocation at system startup. It might show something like this:

```
Memory: 57343 bytes real memory, 36082 text, 4738 data, 5944 bss
 initially: 10579 avail
 presently: 1052 avail,  2684 stack,  6843 heap
 free list:
   block at 150070, length  1052 (02034)
```

As the output shows, the Xinu system that was executing, including the communication software, remote file system, naming system, shell, and commands like *ruptime*, requires about 53K bytes of memory. At the time the command was executed, the free memory list contained only one block.

1.6.1 Other System Information Commands

Like *ps*, many Xinu commands give the user information about the operating system itself. The *routes* command displays information about the network routing cache. Typing

```
routes
```

produces output formatted as shown:

```
Routing cache: size=6, next=5
   0. Route=D, Dev= 1 IPaddr=128.010.002.075, Ether addr=0800.1100.834a
   1. Route=D, Dev= 1 IPaddr=128.010.002.009, Ether addr=aa00.0301.1483
   2. Route=D, Dev= 1 IPaddr=128.010.002.003, Ether addr=0800.2b02.2618
   3. Route=D, Dev= 1 IPaddr=128.010.002.002, Ether addr=0207.0100.27ba
   4. Route=D, Dev= 1 IPaddr=128.010.002.007, Ether addr=aa00.0301.27c0
   5. Route=D, Dev= 1 IPaddr=128.010.002.071, Ether addr=0800.1100.82fa
```

The exact meaning of each routing entry will become clear in Chapter 6; for now, it is enough to understand that each entry corresponds to a network route.

Another system information command, *dg*, displays information about the currently active network datagram devices. Typing

```
dg
```

produces output like:

```
Dev= 3: lport= 513, fport=    0, mode=002, xport=29 addr=192.5.48.3
Dev= 4: lport=   7, fport=    0, mode=001, xport=28 addr=0.0.0.0
Dev= 5: lport=2051, fport=2001, mode=042, xport=27 addr=192.5.48.3
```

The output contains one line per datagram device, that specifies the foreign address to which the device sends messages as well as the mode of operation and local identification number. The details will become clear in Chapter 11.

Finally, the *mount* command prints information from the Xinu syntactic namespace, which shows how file names correspond to devices. Typing

```
mount
```

with no arguments prints the current namespace table formatted as shown:

```
"Xinu/"                  -> (RFILSYS  ) "/usr/Xinu/"
"h/"                     -> (NAMESPACE) "Xinu/src/sys/h/"
"kernel/"                -> (NAMESPACE) "Xinu/src/sys/sys/"
"core11"                 -> (NAMESPACE) "kernel/core11"
"a.out"                  -> (NAMESPACE) "kernel/a.out"
"/dev/console"           -> (CONSOLE  ) ""
"/dev/null"              -> (RFILSYS  ) "/dev/null"
"/dev/"                  -> (SYSERR   ) ""
"/"                      -> (RFILSYS  ) "/"
"~/"                     -> (NAMESPACE) "Xinu/"
""                       -> (NAMESPACE) "Xinu/storage/"
```

When invoked with arguments, *mount* adds new entries to the table or replaces existing entries.

1.6.2 Background Processing

Because the Xinu shell has access to all the services supplied by the operating system, it can allow commands to execute concurrently. That is, it can start a process executing one command while it prompts the user and accepts others. The syntax is taken from UNIX. To start a command executing in the background, the user appends an ampersand (&) on the end of the command line. Thus, typing

```
ps &
```

causes the shell to start a process running the *ps* command in background. Background processing is uninteresting for commands like *ps*, but it can be quite helpful for commands with long execution times. For example, the *cp* command copies one file to another. Typing

```
cp /usr/dict/words /tmp/words
```

copies file *lusr/dict/words* to file *ltmp/words*. On one system, this command takes over a minute because *lusr/dict/words* is a large file that contains 25000 words from an English spelling dictionary. Typing

```
cp /usr/dict/words /tmp/words &
```

runs the copy process in background allowing the shell to read and interpret other commands while the copy activity proceeds. Thus, background processing provides a powerful way for users to specify concurrent activity.

1.6.3 Changing To Background

The Xinu interface provides another way to specify that a process should execute in background. Typing a control-B (for "background") to the shell forces the currently executing foreground process to be placed in background. Control-B is used mainly to regain control after starting a command that takes much longer than expected. For example, typing

```
sleep 60
```

causes the shell to execute the *sleep* command, which merely delays for 60 seconds. The user can type ahead while the *sleep* command executes, but the shell will not read the input until the *sleep* exits. Typing a control-B during the 60-second pause, however, causes the process executing *sleep* to go off in background, and returns the user to the shell prompt again where command interpretation resumes immediately. Control-B is especially helpful when users do not know in advance how long a command will take. The *cp* command is a good example. Copying small files takes almost no time, but copying large ones may take many minutes. Because users do not always know the sizes of files, they may not know how long copying will take.

1.6.4 I/O Redirection

The Xinu shell also allows I/O redirection, another idea found in UNIX. Each command has a standard input device and standard output device, which usually correspond to the user's terminal. Appending a greater than sign (>) followed by a name to any command will redirect the standard output from that command into the named file. Thus, typing

```
ps > xxx
```

runs the *ps* command and places its output in file *xxx* (instead of displaying it on the screen). Similarly, a less than sign (<) followed by a file name redirects input so that the command reads from the named file instead of from the terminal.

I/O redirection and background processing may be combined. For example, the command *cat* copies its input to its output. Typing

```
cat < xxx
```

redirects input but leaves output directed to the terminal, resulting in a copy from file *xxx* to the terminal display screen. Typing

```
cat < xxx > yyy
```

copies from file *xxx* to file *yyy* without affecting the terminal. Finally, typing

```
cat < xxx > yyy &
```

causes the shell to start a process copying from file *xxx* to file *yyy*, but runs the process in background. As soon as the background process starts, the shell continues issuing its prompt and executing commands.

1.6.5 Quoting

The need for quoting can be illustrated with a simple *echo* command. *Echo* merely prints its arguments, separating them by a blank. Thus,

```
echo a bbb    c
```

produces the output

```
a bbb c
```

The extra white space between *bbb* and *c* disappears because *echo* receives three arguments, and places exactly one blank between them on output. Typing

```
echo > xxx
```

redirects the output to file *xxx*. How can *echo* be used to print the greater than sign? Quoting provides the solution. Typing

```
echo '>' xxx
```

produces the output

```
> xxx
```

because the quotes tell the shell to take what lies inside them literally without interpreting special characters. As expected, blanks can be quoted, so typing

```
echo 'a bbb    c'
```

produces output

```
a bbb    c
```

1.7 Internetwork Communication

Although the remote file system provides a key motivation for network communication, the network communication software will not be built for the remote file system alone. Instead, the communication component will form a general purpose subsystem, with the remote file system as merely one application that uses it. For example, the network software will allow arbitrary processes on two machines to exchange messages analogous to the way in which processes on a single machine send and receive messages.

The communication software in our diskless machine will provide much more than interconnection across a single network. It will permit processes to communicate across an internet (a concatenated set of networks). The internet addressing mechanism allows senders to identify destinations on distant networks as well as local ones. Higher layers of network protocol allow senders to specify one of many possible recipients within the destination machine.

1.8 Design Plan

Our design will follow the hierarchical design pattern used in Xinu. We will begin with the device manager level of the operating system and add a device interface for a high-speed local area network (an Ethernet). The device driver software will provide a physical transport capable of moving frames from one machine on the network to another. On this physical transport, we will build address resolution protocols and internet protocol software (responsible for routing packets across the internet to their destination).

As Figure 1.1 shows, the next level of our system incorporates a key component of the design, a remote file system that uses internet communication software to access secondary storage. The remote file system will use a stateless, transaction-based protocol, and we will examine software for the file server that honors requests as well as software for the client that makes requests.

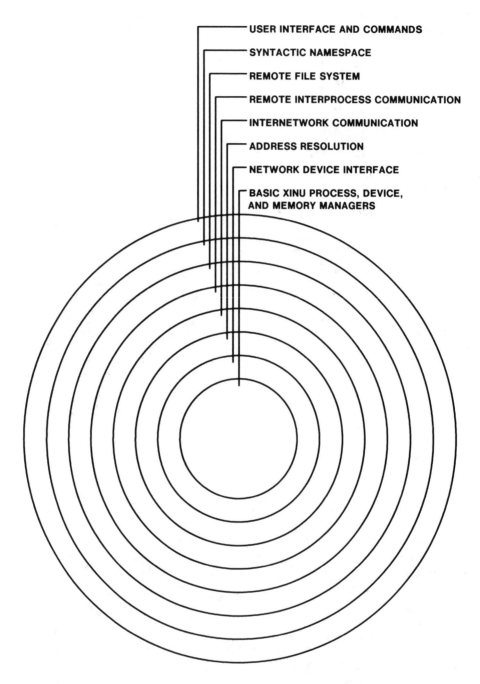

USER INTERFACE AND COMMANDS

SYNTACTIC NAMESPACE

REMOTE FILE SYSTEM

REMOTE INTERPROCESS COMMUNICATION

INTERNETWORK COMMUNICATION

ADDRESS RESOLUTION

NETWORK DEVICE INTERFACE

BASIC XINU PROCESS, DEVICE,
AND MEMORY MANAGERS

Figure 1.1 The hierarchical structure of Xinu internetworking software.

The level above the remote file system comprises a syntactic naming system that unifies all devices into a single naming hierarchy. The Xinu naming system is interesting because it provides a powerful naming scheme with little mechanism. It is important because it helps the reader distinguish between file systems and naming systems.

Finally, with the naming software in place, we will examine the highest level, a user interface (shell). Besides the shell itself, we will study a small set of commands to see how to handle I/O redirection and command-line arguments.

1.9 Summary

This book considers two fundamental components of an operating system: the internetwork protocol software, and the user interface. To help clarify the concepts, we specified a target system that we will design and build. The target consists of a diskless internet station that uses a remote file server for access to secondary storage. It has a command interpreter that supports concurrent background processing, I/O redirection, and quoting. While this chapter described the features and use of the diskless system, the remaining chapters will focus on the design and internal structure. We will begin with network hardware and add successively higher levels of software until the entire system has been built.

FOR FURTHER STUDY

Tanenbaum [1981] provides an excellent survey of communication network hardware, protocols, and terminology. Stallings [1985] contains a more recent view, while Abramson and Kuo [1973] and Frank and Frisch [1971] deal with older technologies. Local area networks are covered in more depth by Stallings [1984] and Franta and Chlamtac [1981]. Finally, McNamara [1982] provides low-level communication hardware details. References at the end of each chapter cite pertinent journal articles and reports. The view of internetworking presented in this text and the protocol standards are contained in Feinler *et. al.* [1985].

Although once found only in research laboratories, diskless workstations are now available in commercial products. For examples, contact Apollo Computing Corporation of Chelmsford Massachusetts, and SUN Microsystems of Mountain View, California.

EXERCISES

1.1 Log into a Xinu diskless station and try some of the commands shown in this chapter.

1.2 Build two processes that execute on separate machines but use the network software to send messages back and forth.

1.3 Try executing command *rf* with input redirected to file *ldevlnull* and with input redirected to file *ldevlconsole*. What can you tell about these files?

1.4 Create two background processes that sleep for *30* seconds and *15* seconds, and then run the *ps* command repeatedly to find them in the process table.

1.5 Contact workstation vendors to find the prices of diskless workstations and file servers, and compare to the cost of "equivalent" time-sharing systems.

1.6 List three disadvantages of using a diskless workstation.

1.7 Experiment with two diskless Xinu machines that use a common file server to determine if the machines buffer characters locally. That is, see if machine *B* can read characters from a shared file immediately after machine A writes them.

1.8 Look carefully at the stack memory occupied by the null process as listed in the output of *ps*, and then examine the stack size specified in the code that creates the null process. Can you explain the discrepancy?

2

An Overview of Network Hardware

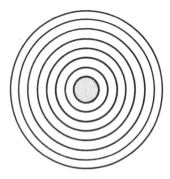

2.1 Introduction

An understanding of network communication begins with knowledge of network hardware technology. This chapter reviews packet-switched network technology, discussing only the most basic concepts and then examining Ethernet local area network hardware in more detail. While hardware technology plays only a minor role in the overall design, it is important to be able to distinguish between the low-level mechanisms provided by the hardware itself, and the higher-level facilities that the network protocol software provides, and to understand how packet-switched technology affects our choice of high-level abstractions.

2.2 Two Approaches To Network Communication

Whether they provide connections between one computer and another or between terminals and computers, communication networks can be divided into two basic types: *circuit-switched* and *packet-switched*. Circuit-switched networks operate by forming a dedicated connection (circuit) between two points. The U.S. telephone system uses circuit switching technology — a telephone call establishes a circuit from the originating phone through the local switching office, across trunk lines, to a remote switching office, and finally to the destination telephone. While a circuit is in place, no other traffic can travel over the wires that form the circuit. The advantage of circuit switching lies in its guaranteed capacity: once a circuit is established, no other network activity will decrease the capacity of the circuit. One disadvantage of circuit switching is cost: circuit costs are fixed independent of traffic. Thus, one pays the same rate for a phone call even when no one talks.

Packet-switched networks, the type usually used to connect computers, take an entirely different approach. In a packet-switched network, traffic on the network is divided into small segments called *packets* that are multiplexed onto high-capacity inter-machine connections. A packet, which contains only a few hundred bytes of data, carries identification that enables computers on the network to know whether it is destined for them, or how to send it on to its correct destination. For example, a file to be transmitted between two machines may be broken into many packets that are sent across the network one at a time. The network delivers the packets to the specified destination where network software reassembles them into a single file again. The chief advantage of packet-switching is that multiple communications among computers can proceed concurrently, with inter-machine connections shared by all pairs of machines that are communicating. The disadvantage, of course, is that as activity increases, a given pair of communicating computers can use less of the network capacity.

Despite the potential drawback of not being able to guarantee network capacity, packet-switched networks have become extremely popular. The motivations for adopting packet switching are cost and performance. Because multiple machines can share a network, fewer interconnections are required, and cost is kept low. Because engineers have been able to build high-speed network hardware, capacity is not a problem. So many computer interconnections use packet-switching, that throughout the remainder of this text the term *network* will refer only to packet-switched networks.

2.3 Long-Haul And Local-Area Networks

Packet-switched networks that span large geographical distances (e.g., the continental U.S.) are fundamentally different from those that span short distances (e.g., a single room). First, *long-haul networks* operate at slower speeds than *local-area networks*. Typical speeds for a long-haul network range from 9.6 to 56 Kbps (thousand bits per second), while local-area networks usually operate between 3 to 100 Mbps (million bits per second). Second, computers attach directly to local-area network media. Typically, each computer on a local-area network has a network device interface that connects directly to a passive interconnection media like coaxial cable or copper wire cable. Long-haul networks, on the other hand, usually consist of special purpose packet switching computers that are interconnected by leased lines. Connecting to the network means connecting to a packet switching computer. Third, long-haul networks introduce high delay between transmission and receipt of a packet, whereas local-area networks introduce little delay.

The goal of network protocol design is to hide the technological differences between networks, making interconnection independent of the underlying hardware technology. Thus, while we understand that many network technologies are available, and while we will consider one particular local-area network technology in more detail, it should soon become apparent that the differences between networks can be isolated at low levels, making most of the communication system independent of such details.

2.4 Ethernet Packet-Switched Network Technology

Ethernet is the name given to a popular local-area packet-switched network technology that was invented at Xerox PARC in the early 1970s, and the version described here was standardized by Xerox Corporation, Intel Corporation, and Digital Equipment Corporation in 1978. As Figure 2.1 shows, an Ethernet consists of a coaxial cable about 1/2 inch in diameter, and up to 500 meters in length. Resistance is added between the center wire and shield at each end to prevent reflection of electrical signals. Called the *ether*, the cable itself is completely passive; all the active electronic components that make the network function are associated with computers that are attached to the network.

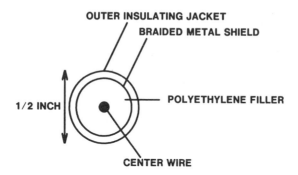

Figure 2.1 Coaxial cable used in an Ethernet

Ethernets may be extended with hardware devices called *repeaters* that relay electrical signals from one cable to another. Figure 2.2 shows a typical use of repeaters in an office building. Only two repeaters may be placed between any two connections, however, so the total length of a single Ethernet is still rather short (1500 meters).

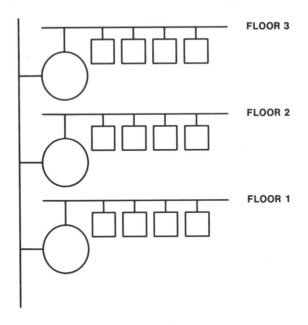

Figure 2.2 Repeaters used to join Ethernet cables in a building.

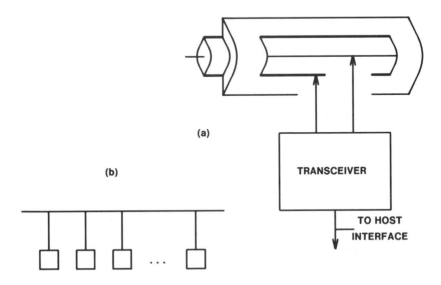

Figure 2.3 (a) A cutaway view of the cable showing the details of a tap, and (b) the schematic diagram of an Ethernet with many taps.

Connections to the ether are made by *taps* as Figure 2.3 shows. At each tap, a small hole in the outer layers of cable allows small pins to touch the center wire and the braided shield (some manufacturers' connectors require that the cable be cut and a "T" inserted). Each connection to an Ethernet has two major electronic components. A *transceiver* connects to the center wire and braided shield on the ether, sensing and sending signals on the ether. A *host interface* connects to the transceiver and communicates with the computer (usually through the computer's bus).

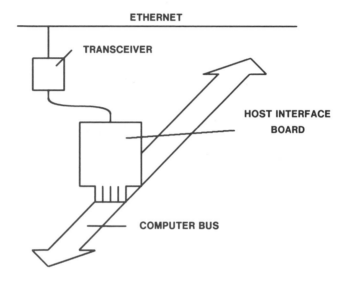

Figure 2.4 The connection between an Ethernet cable and a computer.

The transceiver is a small piece of hardware usually found physically adjacent to the ether. In addition to the analog hardware that senses and controls the ether, a transceiver contains digital circuitry that allows it to communicate with a digital computer. The transceiver can sense when the ether is in use, and can translate analog electrical signals on the ether to (and from) digital form. The transceiver cable that runs between the transceiver and host interface carries both power to operate the transceiver as well as signals to control its operation.

The host interface controls the operation of one transceiver according to instructions it receives from the computer. To the operating system, the interface appears to be an input/output device that accepts basic data transfer instructions from the computer, controls the transceiver to carry them out, interrupts when the task has been completed, and reports status information. While the transceiver is a simple hardware device, the host interface may be complex (e.g., may use a microprocessor to control transfers).

2.5 Properties Of An Ethernet

The Ethernet is a 10 Mbps broadcast bus technology with distributed access control. It is a *bus* because all stations lie along a single communication channel; it is *broadcast* because all transceivers receive every transmission. The method used to direct packets from one station to just one other station or a subset of all stations will be discussed later. For now, it is enough to understand that transceivers do not filter transmissions — they pass all packets onto the host interface that chooses packets the host should receive and filters out all others. Ethernet access control is distributed because, unlike some networks, there is no central authority granting access. The Ethernet access scheme is called *Carrier Sense Multiple Access* (*CSMA*) because multiple access points each sense a carrier wave to determine when the network is idle. Each host interface that wants to transmit a message listens to the ether to see if a message is being transmitted (i.e., performs carrier sensing). When no transmission is sensed, the host interface starts transmitting. Each transmission is limited in duration (because there is a maximum packet size), and there is a required minimum idle time between transmissions, which means that no single pair of communicating machines can use the network without giving other machines an opportunity for access.

2.6 Collision Detection And Recovery

When a transceiver begins transmission, the signal does not reach all parts of the network simultaneously. Instead it travels along the cable at approximately 80% of the speed of light. Thus, it is possible for two transceivers to both sense that the network is idle and begin transmission simultaneously. When the two electrical signals cross they become scrambled such that neither is meaningful. Such incidents are called *collisions*.

The Ethernet handles collisions in an ingenious fashion. Each transceiver monitors the cable while it is transmitting to see if a foreign signal interferes with its transmission. Technically, the monitoring is called *collision detect* (*CD*), and Ethernet is termed a *CSMA-CD* network. When a collision is detected, the host interface aborts transmission, waits for activity to subside, and tries again. Care must be taken or the network could wind up with all transceivers busily attempting to transmit and every transmission producing a collision. To help avoid such situations, Ethernet uses a binary exponential backoff policy where a sender delays 1 time unit after the first collision, 2 time units if a second attempt to transmit also produces a collision, 4 time units if a third attempt results in a collision, and so on. In addition, a sender adds a small random variation to its delay to prevent two transceivers from using exactly the same delay steps.

2.7 Ethernet Capacity

The standard Ethernet is rated at 10 Mbps, which means that data can be transmitted onto the cable at 10 million bits per second. This speed should not be thought of as the rate at which two computers can exchange data. Indeed, few computers are fast enough to supply or consume data continuously at Ethernet speed, which is close to the speed of a memory system. Network hardware speed is important, however, because it gives a measure of network total traffic capacity. Think of the network as a highway connecting multiple cities. High speeds make it possible to carry high traffic loads, while low speed means the highway cannot carry as much traffic. A 10 Mbps Ethernet, for example, can handle a few computers that generate heavy loads, or many computers that generate light loads.

When high capacity is not needed, the network can still use Ethernet-like technology, but operate at slow speed. The advantages are primarily economic. Lower speed means less complicated hardware, and lower cost. One reason cost is lower for slow-speed networks is that engineers can build entirely digital network interface hardware, completely avoiding analog transceivers. Single-chip drivers for slow-speed networks are already available, making the cost extremely low.

Costs can also be reduced when an Ethernet is used in an environment that is free from electrical interference and noise. In such environments, an Ethernet can be implemented with standard coaxial cable like that used for cable television. Called *thin-wire Ethernet*, the thin cable is inexpensive, but supports fewer connections and covers shorter distances than standard Ethernet cable.

2.8 Ethernet Addresses

An Ethernet host interface also provides an *addressing mechanism* that prevents a receiving computer from being overwhelmed with incoming data. Each computer attached to an Ethernet is assigned a 48-bit integer known as its *Ethernet address*. These addresses are assigned by vendors of Ethernet hardware, and are usually fixed in machine readable form on the host interface hardware. Because Ethernet addresses belong to hardware devices, they are sometimes called *hardware addresses* or *physical addresses*. Note the following important property of physical addresses

> *Physical addresses are associated with the interface hardware; moving the hardware interface to a new machine or replacing a hardware interface that has failed changes physical addresses.*

Knowing that Ethernet physical addresses can change will make it clear why higher levels of the network software are designed to accommodate such changes.

The 48-bit Ethernet address does more than specify a single hardware interface. It can be one of three types:

- The physical address of one network interface,
- The network *broadcast* address, or
- A *multicast* address.

Vendors purchase blocks of physical addresses and assign them in sequence as they manufacture Ethernet interface hardware. Thus, no two hardware interfaces have the same physical address. By convention, the broadcast address (all 1s) is reserved for sending to all stations simultaneously. Multicast addresses provide a limited form of broadcast in which a subset of the computers on a network agree to respond to a multicast address. Every computer in a multicast group can be reached simultaneously without affecting computers outside the multicast group.

To accommodate broadcast and multicast addressing, Ethernet interface hardware must recognize more than its physical address. A host interface usually accepts at least two kinds of transmissions: those addressed to the interface physical address and those addressed to the broadcast address. Some interfaces can be programmed to recognize multicast addresses or even alternate physical addresses. When the operating system starts, it initializes the Ethernet interface, giving it a set of addresses to recognize. The interface then scans each transmission, passing on to the host only those transmissions designated for one of the specified addresses.

2.9 Ethernet Frame Format

The Ethernet should be thought of as a link-level connection among machines. Thus, it makes sense to view the data transmitted as a *frame*†. Ethernet frames are of variable length, with no frame larger than 1536 bytes. As in all packet-switched networks, a frame must identify its destination. Figure 2.5 shows the Ethernet frame format that contains both the sender's physical address as well as the destination physical address.

In addition to identifying the source and destination, each frame transmitted across the Ethernet contains a *preamble, type field, data field*, and *Cyclic Redundancy Code* (*CRC*). The preamble consists of 64 bits of alternating *0*s and *1*s to help receiving nodes synchronize. The 32-bit CRC helps the interface detect transmission errors: the sender computes the CRC as a function of the data in the frame, and the receiver recomputes the CRC to verify that the packet has been received intact. Finally, higher levels of protocol use the 16-bit type field to identify frame contents and data format.

Preamble	Destination Address	Source Address	Packet Type	Data	CRC
8 octets	6 octets	6 octets	2 octets	46 to 1522 octets	4 octets

Figure 2.5 The Ethernet packet (frame) format.

---

†The term *frame* derives from communication over serial lines in which the sender "frames" the data by adding special characters before and after the transmitted data.

2.10 DEQNA Ethernet Interface

Now that we understand the general operation of an Ethernet, it is time to
consider an example interface device. Details of the interface hardware are included here primarily to enable the reader to understand the device driver presented in
Chapter 3. As you will see, this section only discusses the highlights of the device,
ignoring low level details whenever possible. Readers interested in further information should refer to the vendor's hardware manuals.

The Ethernet interface used in this text is a Digital Equipment Corporation
DEQNA (Digital Equipment Q-bus Network Adapter). To the host computer, the
DEQNA is an intelligent I/O device. The operating system can instruct the DEQ-
NA to read or write packets on the network. It can also interrogate the network or
DEQNA status, enable or disable device interrupts, or tell the DEQNA where to
deposit incoming packets.

The operating system interacts with the DEQNA in three ways. First, the
DEQNA has device control and status registers (CSR) assigned to an address on
the computer's bus. The operating system reads or writes values to the CSR addresses to control the device. Second, the operating system places data transfer
commands for the DEQNA in memory and informs the DEQNA where to find
them by storing their address in an appropriate DEQNA control register. Third,
the operating system assigns the DEQNA an interrupt vector so the DEQNA can
interrupt the CPU when it completes an operation.

2.10.1 DEQNA CSR

The DEQNA control and status registers (CSR) occupy 16 contiguous bytes in
the computer's address space, organized into eight 16-bit words as Figure 2.6
shows. When read, the first 6 words return the physical Ethernet address in the
low-order byte. The seventh and eighth words return the current interrupt vector
address, and the Control and Status Register (CSR). When written, the first two
registers have no meaning, but registers three through six are used by the operating
system to pass the addresses of input or output command lists in memory. Writing
a memory address to register pair 3-4 starts the DEQNA reading the command list
and performing the specified input operation; writing to register pair 5-6 starts an
output operation. Writing to register 7 sets the interrupt vector address, and writing to register 8 changes bits of the CSR.

Register	Meaning when read	Meaning when written
1	octet 0 of physical addr.	not used
2	octet 1 of physical addr.	not used
3	octet 2 of physical addr.	input command list address
4	octet 3 of physical addr.	bits 21:16 of above address
5	octet 4 of physical addr.	output command list address
6	octet 5 of physical addr.	bits 21:16 of above address
7	interrupt vector addr.	interrupt vector addr.
8	Control & Status (CSR)	Control & Status (CSR)

Figure 2.6 The eight DEQNA registers that occupy 16 contiguous bytes

2.10.2 The DEQNA CSR Bits

The 16 bits of the DEQNA CSR register each have a separate meaning. Figure 2.7 summarizes the meaning of the most important CSR bits, where bits are numbered right to left starting with zero.

Bit	meaning
15	Receive interrupt (set to 1 when read completes; operating system must clear)
13	Carrier (read as 1 if carrier present on the ether)
7	Transmit interrupt (set to 1 when transmit completes; operating system must clear)
6	Interrupt enable (enables interrupts whenever read or transmit operation completes).
5	Receive list invalid (set by DEQNA to indicate that it has exhausted the read command list)
4	Transmit list invalid (set by DEQNA to indicate that it has exhausted the write command list)
1	Reset (write 1 to reset device)
0	Receiver enable (must be set after power-up to enable packet reception)

Figure 2.7 Bits of the DEQNA CSR register.

Some of the DEQNA CSR bits require writing *1* to clear them; many require that neither *0* nor *1* be written while changing other bits. Before programming the device, consult the vendor's manuals for details and meanings of other register bits.

2.11 Format Of DEQNA Command Lists

When the operating system wants to start a transfer to or from the Ethernet, it must build a packet in memory, build a command list in memory, and then pass the DEQNA the address of the command list. The command list, called a *buffer descriptor list* by the vendor, consists of a list of 12-byte descriptors either linked together or physically contiguous in memory. Each descriptor in a command list has the format shown in Figure 2.8, and corresponds to one transfer operation.

Flag
Address Descriptor
Buffer Address (low-order 16 bits)
Buffer Length
Status Word 1
Status Word 2

Figure 2.8 Format of the buffer descriptor that the operating system and device share

Both the DEQNA and the operating system use the buffer descriptor. The DEQNA sets bit 15 in the *flag* word to show that it is performing the command, and writes results in the two *status* words when the operation is complete. The two status words are always written before the DEQNA interrupts the CPU to show that the operation is complete. The operating system uses the remaining three fields of the command structure to communicate requests to the DEQNA. The *buffer address* field contains the address of a buffer to use when reading or writing a packet, and the *buffer length* field gives the length of the buffer area. The *address descriptor* field tells the DEQNA whether the address field points to another buffer, another buffer descriptor, or is the last descriptor in the list. There is no field in the buffer descriptor that encodes whether the operation requested is input or output because the DEQNA uses separate lists for input descriptors and output descriptors.

2.12 Summary

This text deals with packet-switched computer communication networks. Such networks can be classified into two types: local-area networks used in one building or group of buildings, and long-haul networks that span large geographical distances.

We examined the Ethernet local-area network technology in some detail. The Ethernet consists of coaxial cable with taps on the cable connecting to transceivers that, in turn, connect to host interface hardware. Transmission on the Ethernet occurs in frames, where the size of a frame is bounded. Ethernet uses a CSMA-CD method of granting access; hosts detect collisions and back off giving others a chance to transmit.

Each Ethernet host interface has a 48-bit physical Ethernet address assigned to it by the vendor, but can be directed by the operating system to recognize multiple addresses. By convention, all host interfaces accept frames sent to the broadcast address (all *1*s).

FOR FURTHER STUDY

Early computer communication systems employed point-to-point interconnection, often using general-purpose serial line hardware that McNamara [1982] describes. Metcalf and Boggs [1976] introduced the Ethernet, with a 3 Mbps prototype version. Digital [1980] specifies the 10 Mbps standard adopted by most vendors, with IEEE standard 802 reported in Nelson [1983]. Shoch, Dalal, and Redell [1982] provides a historical perspective of the Ethernet evolution. Related work on the ALOHA network is reported in Abramson [1970], with a survey of technologies given by Cotton [1979].

Token passing ring technology, an alternative to the Ethernet, was proposed in Farmer and Newhall [1969]. Miller and Thompson [1982] as well as Andrews and Shultz [1982] give recent summaries. Another alternative, the slotted ring network was proposed by Pierce [1972]. For a comparison of technologies, see Rosenthal [1982].

EXERCISES

2.1   Explore network technologies that provide connections between terminals and computers. Are circuit-switched or packet-switched networks more popular?

2.2   Compare network access using CSMA-CD to token-passing schemes, listing the advantages and disadvantages of each.

2.3   Read about collision detection and recovery schemes, and compare p-persistent backoff with binary exponential backoff.

2.4   The Ethernet specification requires a 9.6 microsecond gap between packets. Assume a computer receives 1500 byte packets (plus 64 bit frame header) arriving at 10 Mbps with 9.6 microsecond inter-packet gap. At what speed will data be deposited in memory? What is the memory cycle time on your local computer?

2.5   Find out more about "thin wire" Ethernet. What are the restrictions? Costs?

2.6   What happens when you connect or disconnect Ethernet taps on an idle network? What happens when the network is in use?

2.7   Read about other vendor's Ethernet interface hardware. In what ways does it differ from the DEQNA?

2.8   Why does the hardware follow lists of transfer operations instead of allowing the operating system to control one operation at a time?

2.9 A *bridge* is a computer that connects two Ethernets by sending all packets from one to another and vice versa. An *adaptive bridge* monitors source and destination addresses in all packets it encounters, gradually building a table of addresses on each network so it knows whether transfer is needed. What problems might arise if more than one adaptive bridge is placed between a pair of Ethernets?

2.10 Multiple adaptive bridges (see previous exercise) can be used to join more than two Ethernets. For example, two bridges can be used to interconnect three Ethernets. Characterize the interconnection topologies that are allowed, and those that are not.

2.11 Find out about alternatives to the Ethernet offered by other computer vendors.

2.12 Research the history of your local computing facility. Try to determine the year in which a local area network was first used.

3

Physical Transport

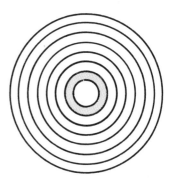

3.1 Introduction

At the lowest level, network communication consists of transferring a copy of data from one machine to another over a network to which both machines directly connect. This chapter discusses the component of network software responsible for such transfer, using as an example a device driver that controls transmission and reception of frames over an Ethernet. Later chapters show how higher levels of network protocols use this low-level physical transport facility, and how packet routing in an internet relates to frame transfer across a single network.

3.2 Blocks And Frames

We have been using the term *packet* in a broad sense to mean "a quantity of data sent across a packet-switched network." We now need to be more precise in distinguishing between the transmitted information as it appears when a user process passes it to the operating system, as it appears when the operating system passes it to the network interface device, and as it appears on the wires of a particular network. We start by defining a *frame* to be the form of data as it passes across the network. Each network technology has its own frame format, but frames are always capable of carrying a block of data from one machine to another.

As we saw in the previous chapter, Ethernet frames contain 6 fields that give the preamble, source and destination addresses, frame type, data, and CRC. Network interface hardware handles most of work involved in framing data for transmission over an Ethernet. The hardware accepts a frame for transmission, prepends the 64-bit preamble, appends the 16-bit CRC, and transmits the result.

Thus, the operating system stores frames without the preamble or CRC fields.

The hardware transmits each frame over the network as a single *Ethernet packet*. Although the frame format and contents depends on the particular network on which they are used, frames usually contain a destination address to which they have been addressed.

The component of the system that understands the details of frames is known as the *physical transport software*. It provides two abstract operations: one to send packets and one to receive them. In our design, the physical transport software consists of a device driver for the network interface device. A process writes to the network interface device to send a packet and reads from the network interface device to receive a packet.

Unlike usual devices, which use *read* or *write* to transfer only a single block of data, the physical transport software also requires the caller to specify a destination network address when writing data, and to obtain the sender's address when receiving data. There are two possible design choices. We could pass two arguments to the transmit routine, one that gives the destination address and one that gives the data, or we could store the destination address along with the data and pass the address of the aggregate to the transmit routine. The choice depends on our view of the network interface. Should the interface accept and deliver blocks of data, or should it accept and deliver frames already in the proper form expected by the network interface hardware?

The software we will examine accepts and delivers Ethernet frames, not just blocks of data. Dealing with frames has both advantages and disadvantages. The most striking disadvantage is that it forces higher layers of software to understand frame format and contents. One reason for dividing network protocols into layers was to isolate details so they did not propagate throughout the code. Making frame details available to higher layers violates the layered design principle, and makes it difficult to change the underlying frame format.

Transferring frames does have some advantages. Because the destination address is stored in the frame to be transmitted, the interface can follow the convention of using a *write* primitive with only three arguments:

write (ETHER, frame, length)

where *ETHER* is a symbolic constant for the Ethernet device, *frame* is the memory address of a frame to be sent, and *length* is the length of the frame in bytes.

Passing frames to the lowest network layer is more efficient than transferring data blocks because it avoids copying data into a form suitable for the network interface device. By carefully building upper layers of the network protocol, we can have them allocate a frame, fill it in, and then pass it to the physical transport level without copying data from one place in memory to another. Likewise, a process that wishes to receive a frame can allocate space and pass the address of the buffer to the low-level network input primitive using a conventional *read* operation:

read (ETHER, buffer, length)

where *buffer* is the address of a buffer into which a frame should be read, and *length* is the length of the buffer.

3.3 An Example Implementation Using Xinu

We have now made two important design choices: the lowest level of network software will transfer frames in a form suitable for the network interface hardware, and frame transfer primitives will be implemented with *read* and *write* operations. The next sections provide an example of Ethernet frame-level I/O routines that implement these decisions. They assume the reader is familiar with the device-independent I/O routines in Xinu, and Xinu device driver organization.

3.3.1 Ethernet And Interface Device Definitions

File *deqna.h* contains C language definitions for the DEQNA Ethernet hardware device. Recall from Chapter 2 that the DEQNA device registers occupy 8 contiguous words of the bus address space. Structure *dqregs* defines the layout of these registers. When read, the first six registers return the device physical address in the low-order byte.

```
/* deqna.h */

/* Definitions Digital equipment Corporation's DEQNA Ethernet interface */

/* Device register layout */

struct  dqregs  {                         /* deqna registers in I/O space */
        int     d_addr;                   /* when read, low order byte of */
        int     d_addr2;                  /*  these and next 4 regs give  */
                                          /*  6-byte Ethernet node address*/

        char    *d_rcmd;                  /* list of read cmds in memory  */
        char    *d_rcmdh;                 /* high order bits of d_rcmd    */
        char    *d_wcmd;                  /* list of write cmds in memory */
        char    *d_wcmdh;                 /* high order bits of d_wcmd    */
        char    *d_vect;                  /* interrupt vector address     */
        int     d_csr;                    /* control and status register  */
};

/* Bits in the Control and Status Register */

#define DQ_ENBL         0000001           /* Receiver enable                 */
#define DQ_REST         0000002           /* Software reset                  */
#define DQ_NXMI         0000004           /* Nonexistent memory interrupt */
#define DQ_BROM         0000010           /* Fetch boot/diagnostic ROM       */
#define DQ_XLI          0000020           /* Xmit list invalid               */
#define DQ_RLI          0000040           /* Receive list invalid            */
#define DQ_IEN          0000100           /* Interrupt Enable                */
#define DQ_XINT         0000200           /* Xmit interrupt                  */
#define DQ_ILOP         0000400           /* Internal loopback mode          */
#define DQ_ELOP         0001000           /* External loopback mode          */
#define DQ_TIME         0002000           /* Sanity timer enable             */
#define DQ_RES1         0004000           /* Vendor reserved                 */
#define DQ_FUSE         0010000           /* Fuse OK                         */
#define DQ_CARR         0020000           /* Carrier present on ether        */
#define DQ_RES2         0040000           /* Vendor reserved                 */
#define DQ_RINT         0100000           /* Receive interrupt               */

/* Command to device as it appears on buffer descriptor list in memory  */

struct  dcmd    {                         /* DEQNA command in memory       */
        int     dc_flag;                  /* flag word marked USED/UNUSED */
        int     dc_bufh;                  /* desc.+ high  buf. addr. bits */
        char    *dc_buf;                  /* buffer addr. (low order bits)*/
        int     dc_len;                   /* buffer length (see manual)   */
        int     dc_st1;                   /* Status word 1                */
```

```
        int     dc_st2;                     /* Status word 2              */
};


/* Bits in the flag word of dcm */

#define DC_NUSED        0100000       /* This dcmd entry not in use  */
#define DC_USED         0140000       /* DEQNA using this dcmd entry */


/* Bits in the descriptor word of dcm (i.e. in dc_bufh) */

#define DC_VALID        0100000       /* This is a valid buffer addr. */
#define DC_CADDR        0040000       /* This is a chain address      */
#define DC_ENDM         0020000       /* Xmit: end of message         */
#define DC_SETUP        0010000       /* Xmit: setup packet           */
#define DC_NORM         0000000       /* Xmit: non-setup packet       */
#define DC_ENDL         0000000       /* Last descriptor in list      */
#define DC_XRES         0007400       /* Vendor reserved              */
#define DC_LBIT         0000200       /* Buffer ends on odd address   */
#define DC_HBIT         0000100       /* Buffer starts on odd address */


/* Bits returned to first status word (dc_st1) */

#define DC_LUSE         0140000       /* LAST/USE bits (see manual)   */
#define DC_INIT         0100000       /* Initial value of status word */
#define DC_ERRU         0040000       /* ERROR/USED bit (see manual)  */
#define DC_LOSS         0010000       /* Xmit: lost carrier           */
#define DC_NCAR         0004000       /* Xmit: no carrier             */
#define DC_ST16         0002000       /* Xmit: timer enabled          */
#define DC_ABRT         0001000       /* Xmit: abort                  */
#define DC_FAIL         0000400       /* Xmit: heartbeat failure      */
#define DC_CCNT         0000360       /* Xmit: collision count        */
#define DC_ESET         0020000       /* Recv: setup packet           */
#define DC_DISC         0010000       /* Recv: discard packet         */
#define DC_RUNT         0004000       /* Recv: runt packet (too short)*/
#define DC_HLEN         0003400       /* Recv: bits 10:8 of rec. len. */
#define DC_LLEN         0000377       /* Recv: bits  7:0 of rec. len. */
#define DC_XLEN         60            /* manual says add 60 to len... */
#define DC_RRES         0000370       /* Recv: vendor reserved        */
#define DC_FRAM         0000004       /* Recv: frame alignment        */
#define DC_CERR         0000002       /* Recv: CRC error              */
#define DC_OVER         0000001       /* Recv: overflow error         */


/* Definitions of device setup packet (see manual for details) */

#define DQ_ROWS         16            /* setup has 16 rows            */
```

```
#define DQ_COLS        8          /* setup has 8 columns        */
#define DQ_SETD        8          /* displacement of 2nd copy   */
#define DQ_BCST        0377       /* broadcast address bytes    */

#define dqlen(x) (-(((x)+1)>>1))  /* buffer len: map byte length */
                                  /* to 2s compl. of word length */
```

Symbolic constants beginning *DQ_* are used to refer to individual bits in the device control and status register. Definitions for all bits have been included, even though not all bits need to be used by a device driver.

File *deqna.h* also defines structure *dcmd* which specifies the format of a DEQNA command in memory. Transfer operations require the operating system to build two lists of such structures, one for input and one for output, and pass the addresses of the lists to the DEQNA. The DEQNA then processes each list sequentially, sending frames according to the commands in the transmit list, and reading frames according to the commands in the receive list. Field *dc_len* specifies the length of the buffer. Because the hardware requires that the length be specified as the twos complement word length, an in-line function, *dqlen*, has been included in file *deqna.h* to convert byte lengths into the form expected by the hardware.

File *deqna.h* provides symbolic constants for bits in the command flag, descriptor, and status. How these values are used in the command list will become more apparent when we look at the code; full details can be found in the vendor's hardware manual.

3.4 Ethernet Definitions

Definitions for Ethernet constants and frame format are given in file *ether.h*, shown below. At this point three terms need explanation. The first is *octet*, networking jargon for "eight-bit unit of data". Many hardware vendors use the term *byte* instead of octet, and we will often interchange the two. The term *header* refers to all those pieces in a frame except the data. Thus, the destination address and frame type are considered part of the header. Calling such information a header makes sense because it usually precedes the data portion during transmission, making it lie at the "head" of the packet.

Throughout the code we refer to the header and data together as an *Ethernet packet*. Technically, we should distinguish between the frame as it exists in memory and the packet that the hardware transmits across the network. The notions of packets and frames have become blurred, however, because it is easiest for the operating system designer to ignore details and assume that the hardware transmits the frame to its destination exactly as it appears in memory.

```
/* ether.h */

/* Ethernet definitions and constants */

#define EMINPAK 64              /* minimum packet length              */
#define EMAXPAK 1266            /*  1536; cut here to conserve space) */
#define EHLEN   14              /* size of Ethernet packet header     */
#define EDLEN   EMAXPAK-EHLEN   /* length of data field in ether packet */
#define EPADLEN 6               /* number of octets in physical address */
typedef char    Eaddr[EPADLEN]; /* length of physical address (48 bits) */
#define EXRETRY 3               /* number of times to retry xmit errors */
#define EBCAST  "\377\377\377\377\377\377"/* Ethernet broadcast address */

struct  eheader {               /* format of header in Ethernet packet */
        Eaddr   e_dest;         /* destination host address           */
        Eaddr   e_src;          /* source host address                */
        short   e_ptype;        /* Ethernet packet type (see below)   */
};

#define EP_LOOP 0x0060          /* packet type: Loopback              */
#define EP_ECHO 0x0200          /* packet type: Echo                  */
#define EP_PUP  0x0400          /* packet type: Xerox PUP protocol    */
#define EP_IP   0x0800          /* packet type: DARPA Internet protocol */
#define EP_ARP  0x0806          /* packet type: Address resolution  " */
#define EP_RARP 0x8035          /* packet type: reverse  "  "       " */

struct  epacket {               /* complete structure of Ethernet packet*/
        struct  eheader ep_hdr; /* packet header                      */
        char    ep_data[EDLEN]; /* data in the packet                 */
};

/* Ethernet control block descriptions */

struct  etblk   {
        struct  dqregs *eioaddr;/* address of device csr              */
        Eaddr   etpaddr;        /* Ethernet physical device address   */
        int     etrpid;         /* id of process reading from ethernet */
        int     etwpid;         /* id of process writing to ethernet  */
        int     etrsem;         /* mutex for reading from the ethernet */
        int     etwsem;         /* mutex for writing to the ethernet  */
        int     etsetup;        /* DC_NORM or DC_SETUP for normal/setup */
        int     etwtry;         /* num. of times to retry xmit errors */
        struct  dcmd ercmd[2];  /* deqna read command descriptor plus */
                                /*  end-of-list                       */
        struct  dcmd ewcmd[2];  /* deqna write command descriptor plus */
```

```
                                    /*  end-of-list                    */
};

extern  struct  etblk   eth[];
```

3.5 Frame Format In Memory

Structure *epacket* describes the format of an Ethernet frame in memory. The frame consists of a header described by structure *eheader*, followed by data for that frame. The format of structure *epacket* differs from the format of packets transmitted on the Ethernet because the structure contains neither the Ethernet preamble nor CRC. Network interface hardware handles such low-level details, inserting or deleting the preamble and CRC automatically when sending or receiving packets. In memory, the frame header contains only the source and destination addresses, and packet type.

Because we decided to pass frames on to higher layers of network software, they must understand the frame layout, and be sure to fill in the data area and destination Ethernet address before handing the packet to the device driver for transmission. The device driver will assume responsibility for filling in the sender's Ethernet address.

3.6 The Ethernet Frame Type

Field *e_ptype* encodes the frame type, which specifies to the receiver the purpose and format of the data area. Higher layers fill in the frame type before passing the frame to the physical transport software. Symbolic constants beginning *EP_* in file *ether.h* give values for the most common frame types. Strictly speaking, software built at the Ethernet driver level should not understand higher levels of protocol. However, we have chosen to collect the definitions for frame type into one files along with other Ethernet definitions to make it easy to identify frame contents without searching multiple files.

3.7 Ethernet Device Control Block

Each Ethernet hardware interface device corresponds to a Xinu I/O device. The Ethernet device driver consists of procedures that implement *read* and *write* operations and a data area in memory used to coordinate the actions of upper-half driver routines with lower-half (interrupt) routines. Structure *etblk*, declared in file *ether.h*, describes the Ethernet device control block that comprises the shared data area.

Fields in the *etblk* structure define all the data kept by the device driver. Field *eioaddr* gives the bus address of the DEQNA device registers. The driver uses a simplistic access scheme with two semaphores providing mutual exclusion among processes reading or writing to the Ethernet; fields *etrsem* and *etwsem* contain the ids of these two semaphores. Once a process calls the upper-half read routine, it is blocked until a frame arrives. While a read is in progress, the process id of the requesting process is kept in field *etrpid* so the lower-half can know which process to start once the read completes. In our driver, the command lists for reading and writing are also kept in the Ethernet control block. Fields *ercmd* and *ewcmd* each contain space for a single command and a slot that marks the end of the command list. Finally, field *etwtry* counts retries when transmission fails. The driver counts only complete attempts to transmit; the host interface handles collisions and backoff.

3.8 Upper-Half Input Routine

Routines that implement *read*, *write*, and *init* operations comprise the upper half of the Ethernet driver. We begin by looking at the input routine, *ethread*, in file *ethread.c*.

```
/* ethread.c - ethread */

#include <conf.h>
#include <kernel.h>
#include <proc.h>
#include <network.h>

/*------------------------------------------------------------------------
 * ethread - read a single packet from the ethernet
 *------------------------------------------------------------------------
 */
ethread(devptr, buff, len)
struct  devsw   *devptr;
char    *buff;
int     len;
{
        char    ps;
        struct  etblk   *etptr;
        struct  dcmd    *dcmptr;

        etptr = (struct etblk *) devptr->dvioblk;
        wait(etptr->etrsem);
        disable(ps);
        etptr->etrpid = currpid;
        ethrstrt(etptr, buff, len);
        suspend(currpid);
        dcmptr = etptr->ercmd;
        if ( (dcmptr->dc_st1 & DC_LUSE) == DC_ERRU) {
                signal(etptr->etrsem);
                restore(ps);
                return(SYSERR);
        }
        len = (dcmptr->dc_st1 & DC_HLEN) | (dcmptr->dc_st2 & DC_LLEN);
        len += DC_XLEN;
        signal(etptr->etrsem);
        restore(ps);
        return(len);
}
```

Ethread is passed three arguments: a pointer to the device switch table entry
for the Ethernet device, the address in memory at which to place the next incoming
frame, and a maximum length to read, in bytes. After waiting on the mutual exclusion semaphore, the calling process is guaranteed that it is the only process performing an input operation. It calls procedure *ethrstrt* to start the hardware device
reading.

Procedure *ethrstrt*, found in file *ethrstrt.c*, starts the Ethernet device. It assumes that the receive command list in field *ercmd* contains two entries: an empty command structure to be filled in, and an entry that terminates the list. It sets *dcmptr* to the address of the first entry on the read command list, and then initializes that entry, using the buffer address and buffer length that the user specified. After the entry has been initialized, *ethrstrt* passes the address of the command list to the DEQNA to start an input operation.

```
/* ethrstrt.c - ethrstrt */

#include <conf.h>
#include <kernel.h>
#include <network.h>

/*------------------------------------------------------------------------
 * ethrstrt - start an ethernet read operation on the DEQNA
 *------------------------------------------------------------------------
 */

ethrstrt(etptr, buf, len)
        struct  etblk   *etptr;
        char    *buf;
        int     len;
{
        struct  dcmd    *dcmptr;
        struct  dqregs  *dqptr;

        dcmptr = etptr->ercmd;
        dcmptr->dc_bufh = DC_VALID;
        dcmptr->dc_buf  = (short) buf;
        dcmptr->dc_len = dqlen(len);
        dcmptr->dc_st1 = dcmptr->dc_st2 = DC_INIT;
        dcmptr->dc_flag = DC_NUSED;
        dqptr = etptr->eioaddr;
        dqptr->d_rcmd = (short) dcmptr;
        dqptr->d_rcmdh = (short) NULL;
        return(OK);
}
```

Procedure *ethrstrt* returns to *ethread* immediately after the device has been started, but before the operation completes. Back in *ethread*, the calling process leaves its process id in field *etrpid* of the device control block, and then suspends itself. We will see later how the lower-half resumes the receiving process when the read completes.

Once resumed, the upper-half process continues execution immediately follow-ing the call to *suspend* in *ethread*. It checks the status words that were deposited in the read command entry by the DEQNA. If an error occurs during packet re-ception, *ethread* returns *SYSERR* to its caller. Otherwise, it extracts the packet length from the command status words, and returns it. The DEQNA scatters the bits of the length into the two status words, so the driver must reassemble them. Also, the length that the hardware returns must be incremented by DC_XLEN be-fore it gives the true frame length.

3.9 Upper-Half Output Routine

The implementation of an upper-half Ethernet output routine closely parallels that of the upper-half input routine. Procedure *ethwrite* verifies that the frame be-ing sent meets the required minimum size required by the Ethernet, waits for ex-clusive access, and then calls procedure *ethwstrt* to start the output operation. In this implementation, *ethwrite* returns once the output operation has been started without waiting for it to complete. The code can be found in file *ethwrite.c*.

```
/* ethwrite.c - ethwrite */

#include <conf.h>
#include <kernel.h>
#include <proc.h>
#include <network.h>


/*------------------------------------------------------------------------
 *  ethwrite - write a single packet to the ethernet
 *------------------------------------------------------------------------
 */
ethwrite(devptr, buff, len)
struct  devsw   *devptr;
char    *buff;
int     len;
{
        struct  etblk   *etptr;

        if (len > EMAXPAK)
                return(SYSERR);
        if (len < EMINPAK)
                len = EMINPAK;
        etptr = (struct etblk *)devptr->dvioblk;
        blkcopy(((struct eheader *)buff)->e_src, etptr->etpaddr, EPADLEN);
```

```
            wait(etptr->etwsem);
            ethwstrt(etptr, buff, len, DC_NORM);
            return(OK);
    }
```

Procedure *ethwstrt* is responsible for building an output command list entry, and starting the device. It operates almost the same as the input start routine, with two notable exceptions. First, it copies the local Ethernet physical address into the source field of the frame. Second, it waits for the device to show that the transmit list pointer is not in use. Normally, the device finishes using the list pointer just as it interrupts to indicate that the operation has completed. Thus, we do not expect any delay. However the documentation does not guarantee an idle device, so the test must be made to be safe.

After finding the device ready, *ethwstrt* builds a command list entry in the transmit command list field, *ewcmd*. The argument *setup*, passed from whatever routine called *ethwstart*, makes it possible to use the same procedure to start output for normal and setup packets (setup packets will be discussed under "device initialization" below). The command list entry also contains fields that specify odd starting or ending buffer addresses. The driver sets bits in the *dc_bufh* field to show odd buffer endpoints, and increments the word count to include them. Our implementation assumes that buffers begin on even-byte boundaries (they will, because buffers are allocated by the Xinu buffer pool mechanism), and only sets the odd termination bit. Once the command list entry has been created, *ethwstrt* passes its address to the DEQNA and returns. Like the input routine, *ethwstrt* assumes that the second entry in the command list has been initialized to stop DEQNA output.

```
/* ethwstrt.c - ethwstrt */

#include <conf.h>
#include <kernel.h>
#include <proc.h>
#include <network.h>


/*------------------------------------------------------------------------
 *  ethwstrt - start an ethernet write operation on the DEQNA
 *------------------------------------------------------------------------
 */

ethwstrt(etptr, buf, len, setup)
        struct  etblk   *etptr;
        char    *buf;
        int     len;
        int     setup;
{
        register struct dcmd    *dcmptr;
        register struct dqregs  *dqptr;

        dqptr = etptr->eioaddr;
        while (! (dqptr->d_csr & DQ_XLI) )
                ;
        etptr->etwpid = currpid;
        etptr->etwtry = EXRETRY;
        dcmptr = etptr->ewcmd;
        dcmptr->dc_bufh = DC_VALID | DC_ENDM | (etptr->etsetup = setup);
        if (isodd(len))
                dcmptr->dc_bufh |= DC_LBIT;
        dcmptr->dc_buf  = (short) buf;
        dcmptr->dc_len = dqlen(len);
        dcmptr->dc_st1 = dcmptr->dc_st2 = DC_INIT;
        dcmptr->dc_flag = DC_NUSED;
        dqptr->d_wcmd = (short) dcmptr;
        dqptr->d_wcmdh = (short) NULL;
}
```

3.10 The Lower-Half Routines

So far, we have seen how the upper-half routines wait for access, build command entries, and start the device performing an input or output operation. This section considers lower-half processing by looking at the part of the device driver that handles interrupts.

The DEQNA interrupts whenever an I/O operation completes. If both input and output happen to complete at the same time, the DEQNA may issue only one interrupt. Thus, the lower-half must be designed carefully to examine all outstanding interrupts before it returns or reschedules.

Procedure *ethinter* implements the driver lower-half; it can be found in file *ethinter.c*.

```
/* ethinter.c - ethinter */

#include <conf.h>
#include <kernel.h>
#include <proc.h>
#include <network.h>

/*------------------------------------------------------------------------
 *  ethinter - ethernet interrupt processing procedure
 *------------------------------------------------------------------------
 */
INTPROC ethinter(etptr)
	struct   etblk   *etptr;
{
	struct   dqregs  *dqptr;
	register struct dcmd     *dcmptr;
	short    csr;
	int      pid;
	Bool     doresch;

	dqptr = etptr->eioaddr;
	dqptr->d_csr = csr = dqptr->d_csr;        /* clear RINT, XINT */

	/* check BOTH receive and xmit completion before resched */

	doresch = FALSE;
	if (csr & DQ_RINT) {
		dcmptr = etptr->ercmd;
		if ( (dcmptr->dc_st1 & DC_LUSE) != DC_ERRU) {
			if (proctab[etptr->etrpid].pstate == PRSUSP) {
				ready(etptr->etrpid, RESCHNO);
				doresch = TRUE;
			}
			etptr->etrpid = BADPID;
		} else {         /* error, so retry operation */
			dcmptr->dc_st1 = dcmptr->dc_st2 = DC_INIT;
			dcmptr->dc_flag = DC_NUSED;
```

```
                              dqptr->d_rcmd = (short) dcmptr;
                              dqptr->d_rcmdh = (short) NULL;
                       }
              }
              if (csr & DQ_XINT) {
                       dcmptr = etptr->ewcmd;
                       if ( (dcmptr->dc_st1 & DC_LUSE) != DC_ERRU) {
                              if (etptr->etsetup == DC_NORM) {
                                     freebuf( dcmptr->dc_buf );
                                     signal(etptr->etwsem);
                              }
                              doresch = FALSE;
                       } else if (etptr->etwtry-- > 0) { /* retry on error */
                              while (! (dqptr->d_csr & DQ_XLI) )
                                     ;
                              dcmptr->dc_st1 = dcmptr->dc_st2 = DC_INIT;
                              dcmptr->dc_flag = DC_NUSED;
                              dqptr->d_wcmd = (short) dcmptr;
                              dqptr->d_wcmdh = (short) NULL;
                       } else {
                              if (etptr->etsetup == DC_NORM) {
                                     freebuf(dcmptr->dc_buf);
                                     signal(etptr->etwsem);
                              }
                              doresch = FALSE;
                       }
              }
              if (doresch)
                       resched();
}
```

The interrupt dispatcher calls *ethinter* each time the Ethernet device interrupts, passing it the address of the device control block as an argument.

Ethinter first records the device control and status register (CSR), and then resets device interrupts. Once the device has been handled, *ethinter* examines the stored copy of the CSR to determine whether either or both of an input or output interrupt occurred. Input interrupts are checked first.

If an input operation completed, *ethinter* checks the status to see if the input was a valid packet or an error (e.g., electrical interference on the network). For a normal reception, *ethinter* resumes the upper-half process that was waiting. For an error, it restarts the operation. Notice that rescheduling, if necessary, is deferred until the driver has checked output completion.

Output completion interrupts may also report errors, so *ethinter* checks the returned status for these as well, retrying the operation if an error occurred, or signalling the output exclusion semaphore if the write completed successfully. Thus, a process waits on the output semaphore each time it calls the upper-half write routine, and the lower-half routine signals the semaphore whenever a write operation completes.

The output side assumes that the address it was passed is that of a buffer allocated from the buffer pool mechanism, and invokes *freebuf* to return the buffer to its pool once output completes. Normally, buffers are allocated from buffer pools, and such disposal is convenient. In those cases where it is not, the user must carefully copy the frame into a buffer before handing it to the driver for output.

3.11 Device And Driver Initialization

DEQNA initialization is cumbersome and involved. When power is supplied to the device, it changes to a mode called *internal loopback*, in which the device returns outgoing frames without sending them. The device is reset, so it will not receive frames from the network. Finally, the set of recognized addresses remains uninitialized.

To initialize the DEQNA, the device driver must reset the device, fetch the physical Ethernet address from the device control registers, write a special initialization frame to the device, wait for loopback of the initialization frame, and finally reset the mode. As might be expected, performing all these chores in exactly the correct order makes the initialization code tedious and long.

Procedure *ethinit* initializes the DEQNA. As shown in file *ethinit.c*, it fills in the Ethernet device control block, including creating mutual exclusion semaphores *etrsem* and *etwsem*. It initializes the read and write command lists by making the second entry in each list a list terminator. After it resets the hardware device, it reads the physical hardware address from the device registers, and builds the special address initialization frame in a local array, *setup*. It starts a read operation to recapture the setup packet, and then starts a write operation to send it. Once the setup frame has been sent to the device and returned, *ethinit* resets the device mode, leaving the device ready to send and receive frames from the network.

```
/* ethinit.c - ethinit */

#include <conf.h>
#include <kernel.h>
#include <network.h>

/*------------------------------------------------------------------------
 *  ethinit  -  initialize ethernet I/O device and buffers
 *------------------------------------------------------------------------
 */
ethinit(devptr)
        struct  devsw   *devptr;
{
        struct  etblk   *etptr;
        struct  dqregs  *dqptr;
        struct  dcmd    *dcmptr;
        short   *iptr;
        int     i, j;
        char    setup[DQ_ROWS][DQ_COLS];
        char    secho[sizeof(setup)+4];

        etptr = &eth[devptr->dvminor];
        devptr->dvioblk = (char *) etptr;
        iosetvec(devptr->dvnum, etptr, etptr);
        etptr->eioaddr = dqptr = (struct dqregs *) devptr->dvcsr;
        etptr->etrsem = screate(1);
        etptr->etwsem = screate(1);
        etptr->etrpid = etptr->etwpid = 0;

        /* establish read and write buffer descriptor lists */

        dcmptr = &etptr->ercmd[1];
        dcmptr->dc_flag = DC_NUSED;
        dcmptr->dc_bufh = DC_ENDL;
        dcmptr->dc_buf = (short) NULL;

        dcmptr = &etptr->ewcmd[1];
        dcmptr->dc_flag = DC_NUSED;
        dcmptr->dc_bufh = DC_ENDL;
        dcmptr->dc_buf = (short) NULL;
        dcmptr->dc_st1 = dcmptr->dc_st2 = DC_INIT;

        /* initialize device */

        dqptr->d_csr |= DQ_REST;
```

```
        dqptr->d_csr &= ~DQ_REST;
        dqptr->d_vect = devptr->dvivec;

        /* extract physical ethernet address and setup device for it    */

        for (iptr=(short *)dqptr ,i=0 ; i<EPADLEN ; i++)
                etptr->etpaddr[i] = LOWBYTE & *iptr++;

        for (i=0 ; i < (DQ_ROWS>>1) ; i++) {
                setup[i+DQ_SETD][0] = setup[i][0] = 0;
                setup[i+DQ_SETD][1] = setup[i][1] = i<EPADLEN ? DQ_BCST : 0;
                for (j=2 ; j<DQ_COLS ; j++)
                        setup[i+DQ_SETD][j] = setup[i][j] =
                                i<EPADLEN ? etptr->etpaddr[i] : 0;
        }
        ethrstrt(etptr, secho, sizeof(secho));
        ethwstrt(etptr, setup, sizeof(setup), DC_SETUP);

        /* poll device until setup processed */

        for (dcmptr=etptr->ercmd ; dcmptr->dc_st1 == DC_INIT ; )
                ;

        /* reset device, leaving it online */

        dqptr->d_csr |=  DQ_REST;
        dqptr->d_csr &= ~DQ_REST;
        dqptr->d_csr &= ~DQ_ELOP;
        dqptr->d_csr |= (DQ_ENBL| DQ_IEN | DQ_ILOP);
        return(OK);
}

#ifdef  Neth
struct  etblk    eth[Neth];
#endif
```

When *ethinit* constructs a setup frame, it specifies the addresses of frames that the DEQNA will receive. The driver shown here chooses only two addresses — the physical hardware address and the broadcast address. Thus, the hardware will ignore all packets except those directed to the individual machine or those sent to the broadcast address. The exercises consider an interesting alternative addressing scheme.

3.12 Ethernet Device Driver Configuration

To understand how the Ethernet device driver routines in this chapter fit together, consider the declarations of the device type *eth* and the *ETHER* device as they appear in a Xinu configuration file:

```
/* Ethernet using a DEQNA interface */
eth:
        on DEQ          -i ethinit     -o ioerr        -c· ioerr
                        -r ethread     -w ethwrite     -s ioerr
                        -n ioerr       -g ioerr        -p ioerr
                        -iint ethinter -oint ethinter
%
/* Physical ethernet raw packet interface */

ETHER   is eth  on DEQ           csr=0174440 ivec=0400 ovec=0400
```

The file declares that type *eth* supports the I/O operations *init*, *read*, and *write*. In addition it specifies that procedure *ethinter* handles both input and output interrupts. The declaration of the device *ETHER* follows the type declaration, and specifies the vendor's standard device address.

3.13 Summary

We have designed an Ethernet device driver that sends and receives frames. The primary I/O primitives available to upper levels of the network software are *read* and *write*; both transfer entire frame images. The sender supplies a frame with the destination address, type, and data fields assigned. The device driver fills in the source address and sends the frame. Once an output has started, the calling process is free to continue (processes attempting output to the Ethernet only block if a previously initiated transfer is still in progress). Input from the Ethernet returns the next available frame, with the input process blocking until a frame arrives.

We looked in detail at code that implemented our Ethernet device driver for the DEQNA Ethernet interface. While the code to read or write frames was straightforward, initialization code was cumbersome and tedious.

FOR FURTHER STUDY

More information on the computer bus can be found in the vendor's handbook *Microcomputers and Memories*. The vendor also publishes the *DEQNA Ethernet User's Guide* (EK-DEQNA-UG-001) that describes the device operation, registers, frame format, and programming in detail, as well as *The ETHERNET, A Local Area Network, Data Link Layer and Physical Layer Specification* (AA-K759A-TK) that gives Ethernet hardware specifications, and *H4000 Ethernet Transceiver Technical Manual* (EK-H4000-TM) that describes transceiver hardware.

EXERCISES

3.1 Modify *ethinter* to count the number of errors that occur, and measure the error rate for your local network.

3.2 Design an experiment to estimate what percent of the time the network is in use.

3.3 Revise the driver to allow a user to add a multicast address to the set of addresses being recognized.

3.4 What problems are introduced if the driver is modified to allow a long queue of buffer descriptors?

3.5 Can you make the device initialization code less cumbersome?

3.6 Experiment to see how fast the driver can accept packets. What happens if packets arrive faster than the driver can absorb them?

3.7 The DEQNA is designed to follow a list of commands in memory, enabling it to accept packets more quickly. Modify the driver to maintain a pool of five buffers and use a list of input commands. How much faster can the modified driver accept packets?

3.8 There are three LED indicators on the DEQNA board that can be controlled when a setup frame is written to the device. Modify the driver to turn off exactly one indicator light during device initialization.

3.9 Testing an Ethernet device driver can be tricky. Assume a site has three different types of machines on a single Ethernet, one of which runs the driver in this chapter, while programmers are building and testing Ethernet drivers for the other two. Devise a fixed set of processes that can execute on the Xinu machine throughout the testing. See if you can build the Xinu system such that it does not need to know the physical addresses of other machines. Hint: it is easiest to test packet reception before testing packet transmission.

4

Internetworking

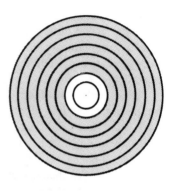

4.1 Introduction

So far we have looked at the low-level details of transmission across a single network, the foundation on which all computer communication is built. Knowing about networks makes it natural to visualize all communication in terms of the underlying interconnections: a message travels from machine *A* to machine *B* over one network, and from there to machine *C* over another.

Thinking of machines and interconnections among them may seem natural, but results in limited, cumbersome communication. The key to intelligent communication system design can be found in an abstract communication system concept known as *internetworking*.

The internetwork concept is as powerful as the process concept. It detaches the notions of communication from the details of network technologies, and hides low-level details from the user. More important, it drives all our design decisions, and explains how to handle physical addressing.

This chapter describes the high-level, abstract internetwork communication system. Later chapters show how to build the necessary layers of internet communication software on top of the physical transport mechanism described in Chapter 2, and how to use the resulting system.

4.2 Why An Internet?

Two observations are fundamental to the design of communication protocols:

- No single network can serve all users.
- Users desire universal interconnection.

The first observation is a technical one. Local area networks that provide the highest speed communication are limited in geographic span; long-haul networks span large distances, but cannot supply high-speed connections. Thus, no single network technology satisfies all needs.

The second observation should be selfevident. Ultimately, we would like to be able to communicate between any two points. In particular, we want to build a communication system that is not constrained by the boundaries of physical networks.

The goal is to build a unified, cooperative, interconnection of networks, the computers of which support universal communication service. Within each network, computers will use underlying technology-dependent communication primitives similar to the ones described in Chapter 2. Across the entire interconnection, however, higher-level software will hide the low-level details and make the collection of networks appear to be a single large network. Such a collection is called an *internetwork* or *internet*.

The idea of building an internet follows our pattern of system design: we imagine a high-level computing facility, and work from the available computing technology, adding layers of software until we have a system that efficiently implements the imagined high-level facility.

4.2.1 Properties Of The Internet

The notion of universal service is important, but it does not capture all the ideas we have in mind for a unified internet because there can be many implementations of universal services. For example, we want to hide the underlying internet architecture from the user. We want to reach all networks in the internet without having direct connections to them. We want to be able to send data across intermediate networks even though they are not connected to the source or destination machines.

Our notion of a unified internet also includes the idea of a network independence in the interface. That is, we want the set of operations used to establish communication or to transfer data to remain independent of the underlying network technologies or the destination machine. Certainly, a user should not have to understand the network interconnection topology when writing programs that communicate.

Finally, we want all machines in the internet to share a universal set of machine identifiers. Often, machine identifiers are classified as *names*, *addresses*, or *routes*. Shoch [1978] suggests that a name identifies *what* an object is, an address identifies *where* it is, and a route tells *how* to get there. Although these definitions are intuitive, they can be misleading. Names, addresses, or routes really refer to successively lower level ways to identify machines. We only insist on one globally honored method of identifying machines, but assume that all machines on the internet will understand how to map this identifier into a machine location.

4.3 The DARPA Internet

In this text we will study protocols used by the Defense Advanced Projects Research Agency (DARPA) Internet. The DARPA Internet, which was designed during the 1970's and early 1980's, includes a large long-haul network (the ARPANET) that spans the continental U.S., as well as a satellite-based network (SATNET), and many local area networks. The DARPA Internet consists of machines and networks at military and government establishments as well as networks and machines on campuses of some of the universities that engage in government funded research. Throughout the remainder of the text, we will use the terms *internet* and *DARPA Internet* interchangeably.

Computers connected to the DARPA Internet share a set of communication protocols commonly called the *DARPA protocol suite* or *TCP/IP*. These protocols define the universal identification of machines, and specify a common routing mechanism that sends packets toward their final destination on the internet.

This chapter considers the internet topology in more detail, and discusses the universal identification mechanism. Later chapters will return to specific DARPA protocols and show the design of protocol software. Eventually, we will have designed enough protocol software to support a remote file system for a diskless computer.

4.3.1 Internet Architecture

We have seen how machines connect to individual networks. The question arises, "How are networks interconnected to form an internet?" The answer has two parts. Physically, two networks can only be connected by a computer that attaches to both of them. A physical attachment does not provide the interconnection we have in mind, however, because such a connection does not guarantee that the computer will cooperate with machines that wish to communicate. To have a viable internet, we need computers that are willing to shuffle packets from one network to another. Such logical interconnections between networks are called *gateways*.

Consider an example consisting of two networks shown in figure 4.1. In the figure, machine *G* connects to both network 1 and network 2. For *G* to act as a gateway, it would need to transfer packets on network 1 destined for machines on network 2. It could capture such packets by reading them from network 1, and then sending them on network 2. Similarly, *G* could capture packets from network 2 that were destined for machines on network 1, and send them to their destination using network 1.

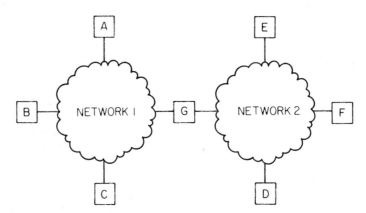

Figure 4.1 Two networks interconnected by a gateway G.

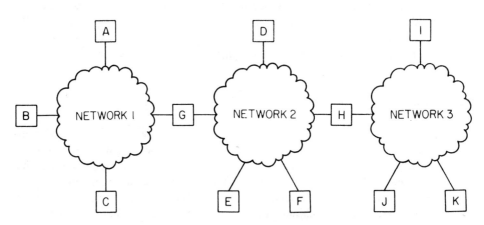

Figure 4.2 Three networks interconnected by two gateways.

4.3.2 Gateways

When internet connections become more complex, gateways need to understand about the internet topology beyond the networks to which they connect. For example, Figure 4.2 shows three networks interconnected by two gateways. In this example, gateway *G* must shuffle from network 1 to network 2 all packets destined for any of *D, E, F, I, J,* or *K*. As the size of the internet expands the list of machines for which packets must be shuffled expands.

You might suspect that gateways are large machines with enough primary or secondary memory to hold information about every machine in the internet. However, internet gateways are usually minicomputers; they often have little or no disk storage and limited main memories. The trick to building a small internet gateway lies in the following concept:

Gateways route packets among networks, not among machines.

If routing is based on networks, the amount of information that a gateway needs to keep is proportional to the number of networks in the internet, not the number of machines.

4.3.3 Internet Addressing

To base routing on networks, internet gateways must have an efficient method of binding a universal machine identifier to the network on which that machine lies. One clever solution encodes the network information in the universal identifier. Designers of the DARPA Internet adopted this method when they chose the *internet address* as their universal identifier.

Called a *host*, each machine connected to the DARPA Internet is assigned a 32-bit internet address that serves as its universal identifier. Internet addresses are not assigned at random, however, they are carefully chosen to make it easy to route packets. In particular, the bits of the internet addresses for all hosts on a given network share a common prefix.

Conceptually, an internet address is a pair (*netid, hostid*), where *netid* identifies a network, and *hostid* identifies a host on that network. In practice, internet addresses have three forms determined by the two high-order bits as shown in Figure 4.3. Class *A* addresses, which are used for the handful of networks that have more than 32768 hosts, devote 7 bits to netid and 24 bits to hostid. Class *B* addresses, which are used for intermediate size networks that have between 256 and 32768 hosts, allocate 14 bits to the netid and 16 bits to the hostid. Finally class *C* networks allocate 22 bits to the netid and only 8 bits to the hostid. Note that the internet address has been defined in such a way that it makes it possible to extract the hostid or netid portions in constant time. Gateways, which base routing on the netid, depend on such efficient extraction.

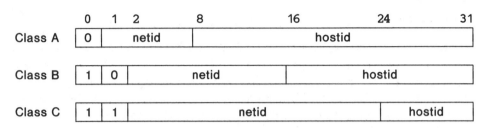

Figure 4.3 The three forms of Internet addresses.

Because internet addresses identify both the network and host, they do not specify a machine, but really a connection to a network. We have already cited the major advantage of naming connections: it makes possible efficient routing. Another advantage is that internet addresses can refer to networks as well as hosts. By convention, hostid zero is never assigned to an individual machine; instead, an internet address with hostid zero is used to refer to the network designated by the netid field.

Encoding network information in the internet address does have some disadvantages. First, if a machine moves from one network to another, its address must change. Second, a machine that connects to more than one network must have more than one internet address. More important, knowing one internet address for a machine may not be sufficient to reach it if network(s) are temporarily disconnected.

4.3.4 Network And Broadcast Addresses

Addresses in the DARPA Internet are assigned by a central authority. Local area networks like Ethernets are usually assigned Class C numbers because many local area networks are expected, but none has more than 255 hosts. Large networks, like the ARPANET, are assigned class A numbers because only a few such networks are expected.

Recall that, by convention, an internet address with hostid field set to zero is taken to be the address of a network, and not of a particular host. Convention also dictates that the hostid consisting of all 1s be reserved for broadcast. Of course, not all hardware technologies support broadcast; reserving an address for broadcast does not guarantee that broadcasting will be possible, it merely provides a way to specify broadcast if it is possible.

4.3.5 Dotted Decimal Notation

Internet addresses are usually written as four decimal integers separated by decimal points, where each integer gives the value of one octet of the internet address. Thus, the 32-bit internet address

$$10000000 \quad 0001010 \quad 00000010 \quad 00011110$$

is written

$$128.10.2.30$$

We will use the dotted decimal notation when expressing internet addresses.

4.3.6 The User's View

Remember that the Internet is designed to provide a universal interconnection among machines independent of the particular network to which they attach. Thus, we want the user to view the Internet as a single, virtual network to which all machines connect despite its physical connection. Figure 4.4 shows how thinking of the Internet instead of constituent networks simplifies the details and makes it easy for the user to conceptualize communication.

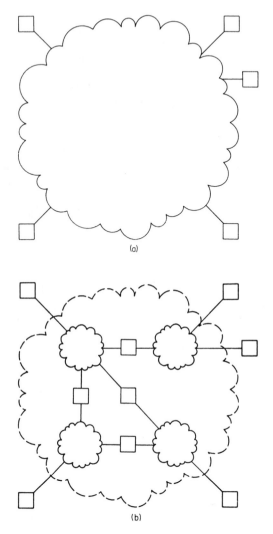

Figure 4.4 (a) The user's view of an Internet, and (b) the constituent networks.

4.3.7 An Example

To make the internet addressing scheme concrete, consider the example in Figure 4.5 that shows just a few of the connections and machines on the DARPA Internet at the Purdue University Computer Science Department.

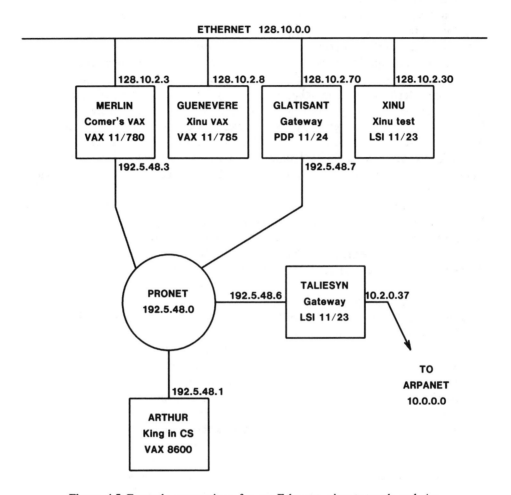

Figure 4.5 Example connections for an Ethernet, ring network and Arpanet.

The example shows three networks: the ARPANET (10.0.0.0), a Pronet[1], (192.5.48.0), and an Ethernet (128.10.2.0). In the figure, four hosts attach to these networks, labeled *Arthur, Merlin, Guenevere,* and *Xinu.* Machine *Taliesyn* serves as a gateway between the ARPANET and the Pronet, and machine *Glatisant* serves as a gateway between the Pronet and Ethernet. Host *Merlin* has connections to both the Ethernet and Pronet, so it can reach machines on either network without using a gateway. Although *Merlin* could also operate as a gateway, it is primarily a timesharing system in which any additional work reduces the amount of processing available to users (remember that the figure only shows a few

[1]Pronet is a 10 Mbps token-passing ring network.

of the departmental machines). Thus, the dedicated gateway, *Glatisant*, was installed to keep the gateway traffic load off the timesharing systems.

Both gateways examine every packet that arrives from any network connection, and determine whether to keep the packet or to *forward* the packet to another network. In the example, each gateway has two internet addresses, one for each of its network connections. When a packet arrives, the gateway first checks to see if its destination internet address matches any of the gateway's internet addresses. Packets not intended for the gateway must be forwarded on toward their destination. To forward a packet, the gateway first checks to see if the destination network is one of the networks to which there is a direct connection. If so, the gateway sends the packet directly to its final destination. If not, the gateway consults a routing table that gives, for each possible network in the internet, the "next hop" along a path toward that network.

Consider the next hop for a packet. We know that the gateway does not directly connect to the destination network (or the packet would have been sent directly to its final destination). We also know that a gateway can only send packets over networks to which it connects directly. So what machine can be used as the next hop? It must be another gateway, one that lies closer to the destination network.

In our example, gateway *Glatisant* at Purdue might receive a packet from machine *Xinu* destined for a network at the Massachusetts Institute of Technology (MIT). Since *Glatisant* at Purdue does not connect to the MIT network directly, its routing tables are set up to route the packet across the Pronet to gateway *Taliesyn*. *Taliesyn* directs the packet over the ARPANET to MIT. Notice that the two gateways share a common network, viz., the Pronet.

In a sense, the gateway routing tables describe a virtual communication system consisting of interconnected gateways. Two rules summarize the essence of internet routing. The first tells how packets travel across the virtual communication system.

> *Packets are routed among internet gateways based on destination network; only the final gateway along the path examines the host portion of the destination address and routes the packet to an individual host.*

The second rule tells how packets reach the gateway communication system.

> *A host sends packets directly to hosts on networks to which it connects directly; it sends other packets to the nearest gateway, which will forward them to their ultimate destination.*

It follows from what we have said that in an internet, each host must be able to reach a gateway. We will use both of these rules in building our routing mechanism.

4.4 Network Byte Order

To build an internetwork independent of any particular vendor's machine architecture or network hardware we must define a standard representation for data. Consider what happens, for example, when one machine sends a 32-bit binary integer to another. The physical transport hardware moves the sequence of bytes from the first machine to the second without changing the order. However, not all machines store 32-bit integers in the same way. On a Digital Equipment Corporation VAX computer, the lowest memory address contains the low-order byte of the integer. On an IBM machine, the lowest memory address holds the high-order byte. Thus, direct byte copying from one machine to another may change the value of the integer.

Standardizing byte-order is essential because the internet packets include binary data such as packet lengths that must be understood by both the sender and receiver. The DARPA Internet solves the problem by defining a *network standard byte order* that all machines must use for binary fields in internet packets. The host stores all binary items in network order before sending a packet, and converts from network order to the host-specific order when a packet is received. Naturally, the user data field in a packet is exempt from this standard — users are free to format their own data however they choose.

The Internet standard uses a highest-order byte first format for integers. Because the LSI 11 on which our software runs uses lowest-order byte first format, our network software will carefully translate between host-order and network-order for all binary fields in internet packets. To make the conversion clear, we will define a set of translation functions. For example, function *hs2net* maps from the host's *short* (16-bit binary integer) into a network short.

File *netutil.s* contains the translation functions.

```
/* netutil.s - hs2net, net2hs, hl2net, net2hl, vax2hl hl2vax */


/*------------------------------------------------------------------
/* Utility routines that map host data to/from network byte/word order
/* (needed because host is "Little Endian", network is "Big Endian")
/*------------------------------------------------------------------


        .globl  _hs2net, _hl2net, _net2hs, _net2hl
        .text
_hl2net:                                / Entry point that maps longs to/from
_net2hl:                                /  host/network byte order
        mov     4(sp),r1                / get high-order word and put in
        swab    r1                      /  network byte order

_hs2net:                                / Entry point that maps shorts to/from
_net2hs:                                /  host/network byte order
        mov     2(sp),r0                / pick up short argument
        swab    r0                      / swap bytes of result
        rts     pc                      / return to caller


/*------------------------------------------------------------------
/* auxiliary routines that map from host to/from VAX longword order
/*------------------------------------------------------------------


        .globl  _hl2vax, _vax2hl
        .text
_hl2vax:                                / Reverse order of shorts within long
_vax2hl:                                /  when mapping to/from VAX/PDP11 long
        mov     2(sp),r1
        mov     4(sp),r0
        rts     pc
```

In addition to functions that translate between host and network order, *netutil.s* includes functions that translate between the host and Digital Equipment VAX format because the file server runs on a VAX.

Include file *network.h* declares all the byte-order translation functions. It also contains *include* statements for all ten network include files because remembering the ten include files is difficult and makes programs messy.

```
/* network.h */

/* All includes needed for the network */

#include <deqna.h>
#include <ether.h>
#include <ip.h>
#include <icmp.h>
#include <udp.h>
#include <net.h>
#include <dgram.h>
#include <arp.h>
#include <fserver.h>
#include <rfile.h>
#include <domain.h>

/* Declarations data conversion and checksum routines */

extern   short        hs2net();        /* host to network short       */
extern   short        net2hs();        /* network to host short       */
extern   long         hl2net();        /* host-to-network long        */
extern   long         net2hl();        /* network to host long        */
extern   long         hl2vax();        /* pdp11-to-vax long           */
extern   long         vax2hl();        /* vax-to-pdp11 long           */
extern   short        cksum();         /* 1s comp of 16-bit 2s comp sum*/
```

Throughout the remainder of the text, procedures that deal with the network will include *network.h*.

4.5 Computing A Network Address

It will be necessary to extract the network portion of an internet address. Recall that internet addresses are divided into three classes, and that the network portion of the internet address occupies 1, 2, or 3 bytes of the address. To compute a network address, one merely needs to examine the bits that determine whether the address is type *A*, *B*, or *C*, and zero the appropriate host portion.

Procedure *netnum*, shown below in file *netnum.c*, performs the computation:

```
/* netnum.c - netnum */

#include <conf.h>
#include <kernel.h>
#include <network.h>


/*------------------------------------------------------------------------
 * netnum  -  obtain the network portion of a given IP address
 *------------------------------------------------------------------------
 */
netnum(netpart, address)
IPaddr  netpart;
IPaddr  address;
{
        blkcopy(netpart, address, IPLEN);
        switch (netpart[0] & IPTMASK) {
                case IPATYP: netpart[1] = '\0'; /* fall through */
                case IPBTYP: netpart[2] = '\0'; /* fall through */
                case IPCTYP: netpart[3] = '\0';
        }
        return(OK);
}
```

Netnum takes two arguments that are both pointers to internet addresses. It copies the host address from the second argument into the area specified by the first, and then extracts the network portion. Comments in the code remind the reader that individual cases within the *switch* fall through. Thus, *netnum* sets three bytes of a type *A* address to zero, two bytes of a type *B* address, and only one byte of a type *C* address.

4.6 The Unanswered Questions

Our sketch of internets leaves many unanswered questions. For example, you might wonder how internet addresses relate to the Ethernet physical hardware addresses used in Chapter 2. The next two chapters address this question, showing how hosts map physical Ethernet addresses to internet addresses, and how they map internet addresses to Ethernet addresses. You might also want to know exactly what a packet looks like when it travels through the internet, or what happens when packets arrive too fast for some host or gateway to handle them. Chapter 7 answers these questions. Finally, you might wonder how multiple processes on a single machine can send and receive packets to multiple destinations without becoming entangled in each other's transmissions. Chapters 9 and 10 answer this question, and Chapters 11 through 13 give examples of internet use including a remote file server.

The point is not merely to discuss networks, but to learn how to design and use internet protocol software. We have begun by establishing a physical transport layer on which the internet is built. Each of the next chapters will explore one piece of the internet software, and the result will be a working system that uses internet protocols for access to a remote file system.

4.7 Summary

An internet is more than a collection of networks interconnected by computers; it also implies that the interconnected systems agree to conventions that allow every computer to communicate with every other computer. In particular, the internet will allow two machines to communicate even if the communication path between them passes across a network to which neither connects directly. Such cooperation is only possible when computers agree on a set of universal identifiers and a set of procedures for moving data to its final destination.

Our software will use the DARPA Internet protocols, including 32-bit DARPA Internet addresses for host computers. The internet address encodes both a network id and a host id because internet routing is based on networks, not individual hosts.

In the internet, machines connected to two or more networks are called gateways; they are responsible for routing packets when the destination network does not directly connect to the gateway.

FOR FURTHER STUDY

Our model of an internetwork comes from Cerf and Cain [1983]. More information on the DARPA internet architecture can be found in Postel [1980], Postel, Sunshine, and Chen [1981], and in Hinden, Haverty, and Sheltzer [1983]. Shoch [1978] presents issues in internetwork naming and addressing. Boggs *et. al.* [1980] describe the internet developed at Xerox PARC, an alternative to the internet we will examine. Cheriton [1983] describes internetworking as it relates to the V-system.

EXERCISES

4.1   Complete Figure 4.5, adding a gateway to the ARPANET that connects to a local network at MIT as described in the text. Fill in the routing tables in each gateway.

4.2   Changing a gateway routing table can be tricky because it is impossible to change all gateways simultaneously. Investigate algorithms that guarantee to either install a change on all machines or install it on none.

4.3   In the DARPA Internet, gateways periodically exchange information from their routing tables, making it possible for a new gateway to appear and begin routing packets. Investigate the algorithms used to exchange routing information.

4.4   Read about The DARPA Exterior Gateway Protocol (EGP). How does it propagate information to gateways?

4.5   Compare the organization of the DARPA internet to the internet designed by Xerox Corporation.

4.6   What processors have been used as gateways in the DARPA Internet? Does the size and speed of the gateways surprise you?

5

Address Determination at Boot Time

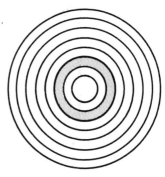

5.1 Introduction

We now know that physical network addresses are both low-level and hardware dependent, and we understand that each computer must be assigned a high-level internet address that internet gateways use when routing packets to it. Usually, a machine's internet address is kept on its secondary storage, where the operating system finds it at startup. This chapter explores how diskless machines, those that use a network to access secondary storage, determine their internet address.

When the operating system on a diskless machine first starts, it does not know its internet address. So, before attempting to use the internet, it must contact a remote server to obtain its internet address. The process sounds paradoxical: a machine communicates with a remote server to obtain an address used for communication.

The paradox is only imagined because the machine *does* know how to communicate. It can use its physical address to communicate over a single network. Thus, the machine must resort to physical network addressing temporarily in the same way that the operating systems use physical memory addressing to set up page tables that allow virtual addressing. Once the machine knows its internet address, it can communicate across the internet.

The idea behind finding an internet address is simple: the diskless machine broadcasts a request that identifies the machine, and waits until a server answers the request by supplying the needed internet address. Both the machine that issues the request and the machine that responds use physical network addresses during the brief communication.

What information can the operating system broadcast that will uniquely identify the machine on which it is executing? It can send the physical network address that it obtains from the network interface hardware. In practice, the request packet is a little more general than what we have just outlined: it allows one machine to ask about another as well as itself. It also allows for multiple types of physical networks. We will examine the details after considering how the diskless machine waits for a response.

5.2 A Mechanism For Timing Responses

After transmitting an internet address request, the operating system waits for a reply. How long should it wait? Network transmission delays and processing time required by the server mean that the response will not be instantaneous, and the requester must be willing to wait a short time for a response. Because packets may be lost (or discarded if they contain transmission errors), the requester must retry the operation after a reasonable time.

Although we could arrange to time responses by creating an additional process, timing responses from networks is important enough to justify inventing a permanent mechanism in the operating system. Our mechanism is an extension of the Xinu message passing mechanism. Usually, the Xinu primitive *receive* blocks the calling process until a message arrives for it, with the blocked process in the *RECEIVING* state. We will augment the message passing mechanism with a new primitive, *recvtim* (receive with timeout). *Recvtim* takes an integer argument *maxwait*. It blocks the calling process until a message arrives for it, but awakens the process after time *maxwait* if no message has arrived. *Recvtim* returns a message with value *TIMEOUT* if the time expired before some other message arrived.

The code for *recvtim* is found in file *recvtim.c*.

```
/* recvtim.c - recvtim */

#include <conf.h>
#include <kernel.h>
#include <proc.h>
#include <q.h>
#include <sleep.h>

/*------------------------------------------------------------------------
 * recvtim  -  wait to receive a message or timeout and return result
 *------------------------------------------------------------------------
 */
SYSCALL recvtim(maxwait)
        int     maxwait;
{
```

```
    struct   pentry  *pptr;
    int      msg;
    char     ps;

    if (maxwait<0 || clkruns == 0)
            return(SYSERR);
    disable(ps);
    pptr = &proctab[currpid];
    if ( !pptr->phasmsg ) {              /* if no message, wait      */
            insertd(currpid, clockq, maxwait);
            slnempty = TRUE;
            sltop = (int *)&q[q[clockq].qnext].qkey;
            pptr->pstate = PRTRECV;
            resched();
    }
    if ( pptr->phasmsg ) {
            msg = pptr->pmsg;            /* msg. arrived => retrieve it */
            pptr->phasmsg = FALSE;
    } else {                             /* still no message => TIMEOUT */
            msg = TIMEOUT;
    }
    restore(ps);
    return(msg);
}
```

As the code shows, a process passes its desired maximum delay time measured in clock ticks when it calls *recvtim*. *Recvtim* examines the process table entry, returning a message if one is waiting. If no message waits, the process is enqueued on the clock queue and placed in the timed receive process state. The process will be awakened by the clock routine *wakeup* when its time delay has expired, or by *send* if a message arrives. After awakening, *recvtim* examines its process table entry again, returning a message if one arrived, or the value *TIMEOUT* if no message has arrived.

To accommodate timed receives, procedure *send* must check the receiving process' state, and remove it from the clock queue if necessary. It calls procedure *unsleep* to gracefully remove a process from the sleep queue without affecting the delay of remaining processes. The code is a simple change of the Xinu *send* primitive, and follows in file *send.c*.

```
/* send.c - send */

#include <conf.h>
#include <kernel.h>
#include <proc.h>

/*------------------------------------------------------------------------
 * send  --  send a message to another process
 *------------------------------------------------------------------------
 */
SYSCALL send(pid, msg)
int     pid;
int     msg;
{
        struct  pentry  *pptr;          /* receiver's proc. table addr. */
        char    ps;

        disable(ps);
        if (isbadpid(pid) || ( (pptr= &proctab[pid])->pstate == PRFREE)
           || pptr->phasmsg) {
                restore(ps);
                return(SYSERR);
        }
        pptr->pmsg = msg;                /* deposit message             */
        pptr->phasmsg = TRUE;
        if (pptr->pstate == PRRECV)      /* if receiver waits, start it */
                ready(pid, RESCHYES);
        else if (pptr->pstate == PRTRECV) {
                unsleep(pid);
                ready(pid, RESCHYES);
        }
        restore(ps);
        return(OK);
}
```

5.3 Reverse Address Resolution Protocol (RARP)

RARP is a DARPA Internet protocol used to map a physical network address into an internet address. RARP is related to the Address Resolution Protocol (ARP) that is described in the next chapter; they share a common format for requests and replies as described in file *arp.h* below. Structure *arppak* gives the format of a RARP (or ARP) packet.

```
/* arp.h */


/* DARPA Internet Address Resolution Protocol  (see RFCs 826, 920) */

#define AR_HRD  1               /* Ethernet hardware type code         */
#define AR_PROT 0x0800          /* IP protocol address code            */
#define AR_HLEN 6               /* Ethernet physical address length    */
#define AR_PLEN 4               /* IP Protocol address length          */
#define AR_TAB  6               /* size of IP-to-Ether addr. cache (>1) */
#define AR_TIME 60              /* time to wait for reply in 1/10 secs */
#define AR_RTRY 2               /* num. of times to try an arp request */

/* Definitions of codes used in operation field of ARP packet */

#define AR_REQ  1               /* arp request to resolve address      */
#define AR_RPLY 2               /* reply to a resolve request          */
#define AR_RREQ 3               /* reverse ARP request (RARP packets)  */
#define AR_RRLY 4               /* reply to a reverse request (RARP ") */

struct  arppak  {               /* format of DARPA ARP packet          */
        short   ar_hrd;         /* type of hardware (Ethernet = 1)     */
        short   ar_prot;        /* format of proto. address (IP=0x0800) */
        char    ar_hlen;        /* hardware address length (6 for Ether)*/
        char    ar_plen;        /* protocol address length (4 for IP)  */
        short   ar_op;          /* arp operation (see list above)      */
        Eaddr   ar_sha;         /* sender's physical hardware address  */
        IPaddr  ar_spa;         /* sender's protocol address (IP addr.) */
        Eaddr   ar_tha;         /* target's physical hardware address  */
        IPaddr  ar_tpa;         /* target's protocol address (IP)      */
};

/* Format of the IP-to-Ethernet address resolution cache */

struct  arpent  {               /* format of entry in ARP cache        */
        char    arp_state;      /* state of this entry (see below)     */
        Eaddr   arp_Ead;        /* Ethernet address of this host       */
        IPaddr  arp_Iad;        /* IP address of this host             */
        int     arp_dev;        /* Xinu device for this host route     */
};

/* Definitions of table entry states */

#define AR_FREE         '\0'    /* Entry is unused (initial value)     */
#define AR_ALLOC        '\1'    /* Entry is used but route still unknown*/
#define AR_RGATE        '\2'    /* Entry is reachable only by gateway   */
```

```
#define AR_RSLVD          '\3'      /* Entry has been resolved to Eth. addr.*/

struct  arpblk  {                   /* all information about ARP cache       */
        struct arpent arptab[AR_TAB]; /* IP-to-Ethernet address cache        */
        int     atabsiz;            /* current entries in arptab             */
        int     atabnxt;            /* next position in arptab to use        */
        int     arpsem;             /* semaphore for access to ARP service   */
        int     arppid;             /* id of process waiting for ARP reply   */
        IPaddr  arpwant;            /* IP addr. process waiting to resolve   */
        int     rarppid;            /* id of process waiting for RARP reply  */
        int     rarpsem;            /* semaphore for access to RARP service  */
};

extern  struct  arpblk  Arp;
```

The RARP packet is sent from one machine to another in the data portion of the an Ethernet frame as illustrated in Figure 5.1.

| Frame Header | Complete RARP message treated as data |

Figure 5.1 A RARP message encapsulated in an Ethernet frame

An Ethernet frame carrying the RARP request has the usual preamble, Ethernet source and destination addresses, and packet type fields in front of the frame. The frame type contains a value that identifies the contents of the frame as a RARP message. The data portion of the frame contains the 28-octet message defined by structure *arppak*.

To make RARP useful on any physical network and not just Ethernet, the designers included field *ar_hrd* that defines the network hardware type. They also included fields *ar_hlen* and *ar_plen* that allow RARP to specify the length of physical and protocol internet addresses. Since we intend to use RARP and ARP only with Ethernet physical hardware addresses, and only with DARPA Internet addresses, structure *arppak* has been declared with fixed length fields.

RARP requests use the target hardware address field, *ar_tha*, to specify the physical address for which an internet address is desired. A RARP server answers the request by filling in the target protocol address field, *ar_tpa*, and sending the reply back to the requester. Requesters specify their own physical address in field *ar_sha*, so servers know where to send the reply. On an Ethernet, having a field for the sender's hardware address is redundant because the information is also contained in the frame header.

5.3.1 Sending A RARP Packet

Now that we understand the mechanics of RARP, it is time to look closely at an implementation. The code consists of three procedures, found in files *sndrarp.c*, *rarp_in.c*, and *mkarp.c*. A process calls procedure *sndrarp* to send a RARP request and wait for a reply.

```
/* sndrarp.c - sndrarp */

#include <conf.h>
#include <kernel.h>
#include <network.h>


/*------------------------------------------------------------------------
 *  sndrarp  -  broadcast a RARP packet to obtain my IP address
 *------------------------------------------------------------------------
 */
sndrarp()
{
        struct  epacket *mkarp();
        struct  epacket *packet;
        int     i;
        int     mypid;
        int     resp;
        IPaddr  junk; /* needed for argument to mkarp; not ever used */
        char    ps;

        mypid = getpid();
        for (i=0 ; i<AR_RTRY ; i++) {
                packet = mkarp(EP_RARP, AR_RREQ, junk, junk);
                if ( ((int)packet) == SYSERR)
                        break;
                disable(ps);
                Arp.rarppid = mypid;
                recvclr();
                write(ETHER, packet, EMINPAK);
                resp = recvtim(AR_TIME);
                restore(ps);
                if (resp != TIMEOUT)
                        return(OK);
        }
        panic("No response to RARP");
        return(SYSERR);

}
```

Making a RARP request is straightforward, but requires synchronization between the requesting process and the process that handles RARP replies. *Sndrarp* calls procedure *mkarp* to allocate and fill in a RARP request packet, and writes the packet to the Ethernet using the Ethernet device driver from Chapter 3. It uses the timeout mechanism, *recvtim* to await a response to its request for a timeout. Synchronization between the process calling *sndrarp* and the process handling RARP replies is carried out through the global data structure *Arp*. The sender leaves its process id in *Arp.rarppid* before calling *recvtim*. When a RARP reply arrives, the process receiving it checks *Arp.rarppid* to know whether the requester remains blocked waiting for a reply or whether time expired. As we will see soon, the process handling the reply sends a message to the process requesting RARP.

If a reply arrives before *AR_TIME* clock ticks, the call to *recvtim* will return the value *OK*. If no response arrives in *AR_TIME* ticks, *recvtim* returns *TIMEOUT*, causing *sndrarp* to transmit another request. After *AR_RTRY* attempts fail, *sndrarp* calls *panic* to stop the entire system.

The values for the retry counter and delay time have been carefully chosen. *Sndrarp* delays 6 seconds waiting for a RARP response, and only tries twice. A low retry count avoids flooding the network with unnecessary broadcast traffic. (Remember that every machine on a network must handle every broadcast request.) A large delay insures that servers had ample time to satisfy the request and return an answer. The two values chosen suggest that the operating system would rather wait patiently for a response and try only a few times than to make repeated requests.

5.3.2 Handling RARP Responses

Procedure *rarp_in*, found in file *rarp_in.c*, is called whenever a RARP packet arrives on the network. An incoming RARP packet may be a response to a previous RARP request, or it may be of no interest to us (e.g., a request being broadcast by some other system). If the packet is a reply to a request for the machine's internet address, *rarp_in* extracts the internet address, saving it in the global variable *Net.myaddr*.

```
/* rarp_in.c - rarp_in */

#include <conf.h>
#include <kernel.h>
#include <proc.h>
#include <network.h>


/*------------------------------------------------------------------
 * rarp_in - handle RARP packet coming in from Ethernet network
 *------------------------------------------------------------------
 */
```

```
rarp_in(packet, device)
struct   epacket *packet;
int      device;
{
        char    ps;
        int     pid;
        int     ret;
        struct  arppak  *apacptr;
        struct  etblk   *etptr;

        apacptr = (struct arppak *) packet->ep_data;
        if (net2hs(apacptr->ar_op) == AR_RRLY) {
                etptr = (struct etblk *)devtab[device].dvioblk;
                if ( blkequ(apacptr->ar_tha,etptr->etpaddr,EPADLEN) ) {
                        blkcopy(Net.myaddr, apacptr->ar_tpa, IPLEN);
                        netnum(Net.mynet, Net.myaddr);
                        disable(ps);
                        Net.mavalid = TRUE;
                        pid = Arp.rarppid;
                        if (!isbadpid(pid)) {
                                Arp.rarppid = BADPID;
                                send(pid, OK);
                        }
                        restore(ps);
                }
                ret = OK;
        } else
                ret = SYSERR;
        freebuf(packet);
        return(ret);
}
```

The details of *rarp_in* are not difficult to understand. Argument *packet* gives the address of a complete frame (i.e., it gives the address of a network buffer that contains the frame). *Rarp-in* first sets *apacptr* to the address of the data field within the frame, the location at which the RARP packet itself can be found. It then examines the packet operation code to see whether it is a reply. For a reply, *rarp_in* further verifies that the physical hardware address matches its physical hardware address, copying the internet address into *Net.myaddr* if they do. Finally, *rarp_in* checks to see if a process is blocked waiting for a RARP response. It sends the blocked process a message, permitting it to resume execution. Once *rarp_in* finishes processing the frame, it calls *freebuf* to return the buffer to the network buffer pool.

We have seen how a process that makes a RARP request blocks until an incoming RARP reply arrives or a timeout occurs. This section fills in the last
remaining details by showing procedure *mkarp* that *sndrarp* uses to create a valid
RARP packet. *mkarp* has been designed to work with both the *RARP* protocol
described in this chapter or the *ARP* protocol described in the next chapter (packet
formats are identical).

```
/* mkarp.c - mkarp */

#include <conf.h>
#include <kernel.h>
#include <network.h>

/*------------------------------------------------------------------------
 *  mkarp  -  allocate and fill in an ARP or RARP packet
 *------------------------------------------------------------------------
 */
struct  epacket *mkarp(typ, op, spaddr, tpaddr)
short   typ;
short   op;
IPaddr  spaddr;
IPaddr  tpaddr;
{
        register struct arppak  *apacptr;
        struct  epacket *packet;

        packet = (struct epacket *) getbuf(Net.netpool);
        if ( ((int)packet) == SYSERR)
                return((struct epacket *)SYSERR);
        blkcopy(packet->ep_hdr.e_dest, EBCAST, AR_HLEN);
        packet->ep_hdr.e_ptype = hs2net(typ);
        apacptr = (struct arppak *) packet->ep_data;
        apacptr->ar_hrd = hs2net(AR_HRD);
        apacptr->ar_prot = hs2net(AR_PROT);
        apacptr->ar_hlen = AR_HLEN;
        apacptr->ar_plen = AR_PLEN;
        apacptr->ar_op = hs2net(op);
        blkcopy(apacptr->ar_sha, eth[0].etpaddr, AR_HLEN);
        blkcopy(apacptr->ar_spa, spaddr, AR_PLEN);
        blkcopy(apacptr->ar_tha, eth[0].etpaddr, AR_HLEN);
        blkcopy(apacptr->ar_tpa, tpaddr, AR_PLEN);
        return(packet);
}
```

Mkarp is called to allocate and fill most of the fields in a RARP packet. The first two arguments of *mkarp* distinguish between ARP and RARP packets, and tell whether the packet is a request or a reply. The second two arguments give the host's internet address and target internet address; they are significant only in ARP packets.

Mkarp allocates a network buffer to hold the packet. The buffer is formatted as an Ethernet frame with the RARP (or ARP) packet in the data area. *Mkarp* initializes pointer *apacptr* to point to the data area of the frame, and then uses it to fill in the fields of the ARP packet. Once *mkarp* has filled in the packet, it returns the frame address to its caller.

Few remarks are needed because *mkarp* merely handles low-level details in a straightforward way. As always, binary integers must be mapped from the host's local format to the network byte order using procedure *hs2net*. Our operating system stores both physical and Internet addresses in the same order as the protocol needs, so no translation is required for them. Note that *mkarp* follows the convention of returning a pointer to an entire Ethernet frame, and not a pointer to the RARP portion.

5.4 Summary

In network protocol software, timing responses is a fundamental activity that justifies adding new primitives to the operating system. We extended Xinu's message passing facility by adding a "timed receive" operation, *recvtim*, and modifying the primitive *send* to cancel timeouts when sending a message.

At system startup, a diskless machine must contact a server to find its internet address before it can communicate on the Internet. We examined the RARP protocol that uses physical network addressing to obtain the machine's Internet address. The RARP mechanism supplies the machine's physical hardware address to uniquely identify the processor. Our implementation of RARP used the timeout mechanism to allow a process to broadcast a request and wait a specified time for a response.

FOR FURTHER STUDY

The details of RARP are given in Finlayson, *et. al.* [1984]. Croft and Gilmore [1985] propose an alternative bootstrapping protocol called BOOTP. Finlayson [1984] describes workstation bootstrapping using the TFTP protocol. The DEQNA described in Chapter 3 contains a bootstrap program that can be loaded into the host computer from ROM. However, the bootstrap program supplied with the board only works with the vendor's network protocols.

EXERCISES

5.1 Instrument *sndrarp* and *rarp_in* to measure the time it takes for a RARP response on
your local Ethernet. Is it ever over 2 seconds? If you reduce *AR_TIME*, the time the
system is willing to wait for a response, will it have noticeable effects?

5.2 Implement procedure *unsleep* without looking at the code.

5.3 Build a server that accepts RARP requests and issues replies based on a table of
Internet-to-Ethernet address bindings. Try to make the fewest possible changes to
Xinu (you may have to read a few chapters ahead).

5.4 A RARP server can broadcast RARP replies to all machines or transmit each reply
directly to the machine that makes the request. Can you imagine a system in which
broadcasting is beneficial?

5.5 RARP is a narrowly focused protocol in the sense that replies only contain one piece of
information (i.e., the requested internet address). When diskless machines boot, they
usually want to know at least the time, their internet address, and their machine name.
Extend RARP to supply the additional information.

5.6 How much larger will the Ethernet frames become when information is added to
RARP as described in the previous exercise?

5.7 Consider adding a backup RARP server to a network. If both servers respond to all
requests, they generate twice as much traffic as necessary. Devise a simple scheme in
which the backup server responds *only* if the main server is down.

6

Address Resolution at Run Time

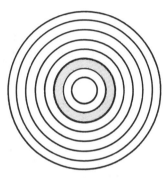

6.1 Introduction

We have described the internet routing scheme in which gateways forward packets toward their final destination. We also know how two machines that share a physical network can communicate by sending frames from one to the other *provided they know each other's physical network address*. What we have not mentioned is how two machines that share a common physical network map internet addresses into physical hardware addresses.

Consider, for example, a gateway that receives a packet destined for a host on a network to which the gateway directly connects. The gateway knows the internet address of the network, and the internet address of its connection on that network. However, knowing the internet address of some other host on that network does not tell the gateway how to send to that host. More important, the physical hardware address of the destination machine may change frequently (e.g., when host interface hardware fails and must be replaced), while the internet address of the machine tends to remain constant.

We call the problem of mapping internet addresses to physical network addresses the *address resolution problem*. This chapter considers a creative solution to the address resolution problem, one that exploits the network and does not require maintenance of a centralized database.

6.2 ARP: An Address Resolution Protocol

The DARPA Internet Address Resolution Protocol (ARP) provides the mapping between internet addresses and physical hardware addresses dynamically. The essential idea is simple: host A wants to send a packet to host B, using a network to which both hosts attach. Host A broadcasts a packet that supplies the internet address of B and requests B's physical address. Host B receives the request and sends a reply that contains its physical hardware address. When A receives the reply, it uses the physical hardware address to send the internet packet directly to B.

Although we will depend on ARP to map between internet and physical addresses, the reader should realize that ARP represents only one way to solve the problem. For example, we could store tables of internet-to-physical-address bindings at every host on the network. More important, ARP would be completely unnecessary if we could make all network interfaces understand their internet address. Thus, ARP merely imposes a new addressing scheme on top of whatever low-level addressing mechanism the hardware uses. The idea can be summed up:

> *ARP is a low-level protocol that hides the underlying network physical addressing, permitting us to assign internet addresses of our choosing to every machine. We think of it as part of the physical network system, and not as part of the internet protocol.*

To be useful, ARP must be efficient. Because it uses broadcast to find a target machine, ARP is far too expensive to be used every time one machine needs to transmit a packet to another. To reduce the cost, hosts that use ARP maintain a cache of recently acquired internet-to-physical address bindings. When the host receives an ARP reply, it saves the result in the cache for successive lookups. When transmitting a packet, the host looks in its cache for a binding before sending an ARP request. If a host finds the desired binding in its cache, it need not use the network. Experience shows that most network communication involves more than one packet transfer, and that even a small cache is worthwhile.

6.2.1 Refinements

Several refinements of ARP are possible. First, observe that if host A is about to use ARP because it needs to send to B, there is a high probability that host B will need to send to A in the near future. If we anticipate B's need, we can avoid extra network traffic by arranging for A to include its internet-to-physical address binding in its request. Second, when a new machine appears on the net (e.g., when an operating system reboots), we can avoid having every other machine run ARP by broadcasting the new pair of internet address and physical address.

The following rule summarizes refinements:

> *The sender's internet-to-physical address binding is included in every ARP broadcast; receivers add the internet-to-physical address binding information to their cache before processing an ARP packet.*

6.3 ARP Implementation

Functionally, ARP is divided into two parts. One determines physical addresses when sending a packet, and the other answers requests from other machines for the local physical address. Our implementation partitions responsibility in a slightly different way, dividing duties into three procedures: *arp_in*, *getpath*, and *arpfind*. Procedure *arp_in* is called whenever an ARP packet arrives, procedure *getpath* is called when a process wants to bind an internet address to a physical address, and procedure *arpfind* manages the cache, finding an existing entry or an empty slot when a new binding is needed.

6.3.1 Finding A Physical Address

Before looking at the code, the reader is advised to look again at file *arp.h* in the previous chapter. Note that structure *arpent* defines entries in the ARP cache.

The code for *getpath* is shown below in file *getpath.c*. A process calls *getpath* when it needs to know the physical address of a machine. Argument *faddr* contains the internet address for which the caller desires a physical address. *Getpath* returns to the caller the index in the ARP cache of an entry for the destination address. Usually, the entry specifies both the internet address and physical address for the destination machine. However, if the destination cannot be reached directly, the physical address portion of the entry identifies a gateway to which the packet should be routed.

```
/* getpath.c - getpath */

#include <conf.h>
#include <kernel.h>
#include <proc.h>
#include <network.h>

/*------------------------------------------------------------------------
 * getpath - find a path (route table entry) for a given IP address
 *------------------------------------------------------------------------
 */
getpath(faddr)
IPaddr  faddr;
{
        int     i;
        int     arindex;                /* route table entry index     */
        int     mypid;                  /* local copy of my process id */
        IPaddr  myaddr;                 /* my IP address               */
        char    ps;
        register struct arpent  *arpptr;
        register struct arppak  *apacptr;
        struct  epacket *packet, *mkarp();

        wait(Arp.arpsem);
        arpptr = &Arp.arptab[ arindex = arpfind(faddr) ];
        if (arpptr->arp_state != AR_ALLOC) {
                signal(Arp.arpsem);
                return(arindex);
        }

        /* Use ARP to obtain and record IP-to-Ether binding */

        getaddr(myaddr);
        mypid = getpid();
        for (i=0 ; i < AR_RTRY ; i++) {
                packet = mkarp(EP_ARP, AR_REQ, myaddr, faddr);
                blkcopy(Arp.arpwant, faddr, AR_PLEN);
                disable(ps);
                Arp.arppid = mypid;
                recvclr();
                write(ETHER, packet, EMINPAK);
                restore(ps);
                if (recvtim(AR_TIME) == OK)
                        break;
        }
```

```
Arp.arppid = BADPID;
signal(Arp.arpsem);
return(arindex);
}
```

Getpath first calls *arpfind* to locate the desired entry in the ARP cache. Each entry in the cache has a state field that tells whether the entry is valid or unused. We will see that *arpfind* always returns the index of a cache entry, leaving a freshly allocated entry in state *AR_ALLOC* to show that the entry has been allocated, the internet address field has been filled in, but the physical address is unknown. *Getpath* examines the state, to see whether the desired mapping is already in the cache. If the mapping is available from the cache, *getpath* returns the index of the cache entry to its caller.

If *getpath* cannot find the desired mapping in the ARP cache, it sends an ARP request, and then waits for a response before returning to its caller. *Getpath* uses *mkarp* to create an ARP request packet, and the low-level Ethernet driver to broadcast the packet on the Ethernet. The process that broadcasts an ARP request needs to delay, waiting for a response. It leaves its process id and the internet address for which it searches in global variables *Arp.arppid* and *Arp.arpwant*, and uses *recvtim* to await a response. As usual, ARP retries its request if time expires before a response returns.

6.3.2 Searching The ARP cache

Procedure *arpfind* takes as an argument an internet address and returns the index in the ARP cache where the entry for that address can be found. The code works in the obvious way, searching the entire table one entry at a time.

```
/* arpfind.c - arpfind */

#include <conf.h>
#include <kernel.h>
#include <proc.h>
#include <network.h>

/*------------------------------------------------------------------------
 * arpfind  -  find or insert entry in ARP cache and return its index
 *------------------------------------------------------------------------
 */
arpfind(faddr)
IPaddr  faddr;
{
        int     i;
        int     arindex;
        struct  arpent  *atabptr;

        for (arindex=0; arindex<Arp.atabsiz; arindex++) {
                atabptr = &Arp.arptab[arindex];
                if (blkequ(atabptr->arp_Iad, faddr, IPLEN)
                        && atabptr->arp_state != AR_FREE)
                        return(arindex);
        }
        if (Arp.atabsiz < AR_TAB) {
                Arp.atabsiz++;
        }
        arindex = Arp.atabnxt++;
        if (Arp.atabnxt >= AR_TAB)
                Arp.atabnxt = 0;
        atabptr = &Arp.arptab[arindex];
        atabptr->arp_state = AR_ALLOC;
        blkcopy(atabptr->arp_Iad, faddr, IPLEN);
        for(i=0 ; i<EPADLEN ; i++)
                atabptr->arp_Ead[i] = '\0';
        atabptr->arp_dev = -1;
        return(arindex);
}
```

If no matching entry can be found, *arpfind* creates a new table entry for the specified internet address. Two cases exist. First, if not all table entries are in use, *arpfind* allocates an unused entry. Otherwise, it uses a roving global pointer, *Arp.atabnxt*, to select an existing entry and replace it. *Arpfind* clears the physical address field of newly allocated entries, and marks their state *AR_ALLOC*, which means "allocated but not yet valid." Finally, *arpfind* returns the index of the new cache entry.

6.3.3 Handling Incoming ARP Packets

We have seen how a machine finds a physical hardware address either by consulting the cache or by broadcasting an ARP request. To complete the implementation, we need to update the cache from incoming ARP responses, and to respond to ARP requests sent to our machine by others. Procedure *arp_in* performs both of these tasks. The code can be found in file *arp_in.c*.

```c
/* arp_in.c - arp_in */

#include <conf.h>
#include <kernel.h>
#include <proc.h>
#include <network.h>

/*------------------------------------------------------------------------
 * arp_in  -  handle ARP packet coming in from Ethernet network
 *------------------------------------------------------------------------
 */
arp_in(packet, device)
struct  epacket *packet;
int     device;
{
        char    ps;
        int     pid;
        short   arop;
        struct  arppak  *apacptr;
        struct  arpent  *atabptr;
        struct  etblk   *etptr;

        etptr = (struct etblk *) devtab[device].dvioblk;
        apacptr = (struct arppak *) packet->ep_data;
        atabptr = &Arp.arptab[arpfind(apacptr->ar_spa)];
        if (atabptr->arp_state != AR_RSLVD) {
                blkcopy(atabptr->arp_Ead, apacptr->ar_sha, EPADLEN);
                atabptr->arp_dev = device;
                atabptr->arp_state = AR_RSLVD;
        }
        arop = net2hs(apacptr->ar_op);
        switch (arop) {

            case AR_REQ:        /* request - answer if for me */
                if (! blkequ(Net.myaddr, apacptr->ar_tpa, IPLEN)) {
                        freebuf(packet);
                        return(OK);
                }
                apacptr->ar_op = hs2net(AR_RPLY);
                blkcopy(apacptr->ar_tpa, apacptr->ar_spa, IPLEN);
                blkcopy(apacptr->ar_tha, packet->ep_hdr.e_src, EPADLEN);
                blkcopy(packet->ep_hdr.e_dest, apacptr->ar_tha, EPADLEN);
                blkcopy(apacptr->ar_sha, etptr->etpaddr, EPADLEN);
                blkcopy(apacptr->ar_spa, Net.myaddr, IPLEN);
                write(device, packet, EMINPAK);
```

```
                    return(OK);

            case AR_RPLY:          /* reply - awaken requestor if any */
                disable(ps);
                pid = Arp.arppid;
                if (!isbadpid(pid)
                    && blkequ(Arp.arpwant, apacptr->ar_spa, IPLEN)) {
                        Arp.arppid = BADPID;
                        send(pid, OK);
                }
                freebuf(packet);
                restore(ps);
                return(OK);

            default:
                Net.ndrop++;
                freebuf(packet);
                return(SYSERR);
        }
}
```

A process calls *arp_in* each time an ARP packet arrives, passing a pointer to the frame and the device id of the network device as arguments. As with *rarp_in* the frame address is the address of a network buffer into which the frame has been copied. *Arp_in* uses *arpfind* to find or allocate a cache entry for the packet's sender, and copies in the sender's physical hardware address. It then processes the packet.

Two packet types must be handled. A request, marked *AR_REQ*, must be examined to see if it requests information about the local machine. If so, *arp_in* fills in the physical address, and writes a reply.

Arp_in examines ARP replies to see if a process is blocked waiting for the reply. The code is careful to compare the internet address in the reply to the internet address for which the blocked process is waiting. If they match, *arp_in* sends a message to the blocked process, allowing it to continue execution.

Like the RARP input procedure, *arp_in* receives responsibility for the network buffer passed as an argument. It must either pass responsibility on (e.g., by writing the buffer to the Ethernet device), or explicitly call *freebuf* to return the buffer to the network buffer pool.

6.4 ARP And RARP Initialization

The ARP subsystem must be initialized before it can be used. Procedure *arpinit* contains the initialization code.

```c
/* arpinit.c - arpinit */

#include <conf.h>
#include <kernel.h>
#include <proc.h>
#include <network.h>

/*------------------------------------------------------------------------
 * arpinit  -  initialize data structures for ARP processing
 *------------------------------------------------------------------------
 */
arpinit()
{
        struct  arpent  *atabptr;
        int     i, j;

        Arp.atabsiz = 0;
        Arp.atabnxt = 0;
        Arp.arpsem = screate(1);
        Arp.rarpsem= screate(1);
        Arp.arppid = Arp.rarppid = BADPID;
        for (i=0 ; i<AR_TAB ; i++) {
                atabptr = &Arp.arptab[i];
                atabptr->arp_state = AR_FREE;
                for (j=0 ; j<EPADLEN ; j++)
                        atabptr->arp_Ead[j] = '\0';
                atabptr->arp_dev = -1;
        }
}

struct  arpblk  Arp;
```

Initialization consists of creating the mutual exclusion semaphores for ARP and RARP, and clearing the ARP cache. Note that our initialization routine does not send a RARP broadcast. It merely initializes the data structures, making them ready for ARP and RARP traffic.

6.5 Summary

Internet addresses are assigned independent of the physical hardware address. However, high-level network software that uses internet addresses must ultimately map them into physical hardware addresses when delivering packets to their final destination. The ARP protocol uses only the low-level network communication system to resolve physical addresses dynamically, permitting machines to resolve addresses without keeping a permanent record of bindings.

A machine uses ARP to find the hardware address of another machine by broadcasting an ARP request that contains the internet address for which it searches. Each machine responds to requests for its physical hardware address, and sends replies that contain the needed binding.

To make ARP efficient, each machine caches internet-to-physical address bindings. Because internet traffic tends to consist of a sequence of interactions between pairs of machines, the cache eliminates most of the ARP broadcast requests.

FOR FURTHER STUDY

The address resolution protocol used here is given by Plummer [1982], and has become a DARPA Internet standard. Dalal and Printis [1981] describe the relationship between Ethernet and internet addresses, and Clark [1982] discusses addresses and bindings in general.

EXERCISES

6.1 Our cache replacement policy uses a roving global pointer when choosing an entry to replace. Modify the algorithm to replace the least-recently-used entry and compare the results.

6.2 Our implementation of ARP is nonstandard in that it does not update the cache if an old entry already exists. Explain how this can cause problems. Can you guess why the nonstandard version was chosen?

6.3 Modify *arp_in* to update an entry every time it receives an ARP packet, and measure the difference in performance.

6.4 Modify *arp_in* so that it only adds entries when they respond to a request. Do you notice any difference?

6.5 Our implementation of ARP can fail when used on a network that has many hosts and much ARP traffic. Explain how.

6.6 It is clear why a diskless machine needs to use RARP before it can send an internet packet. Explain why a diskless machine must use RARP before it can receive an internet packet.

7

The Internet Protocol and Routing

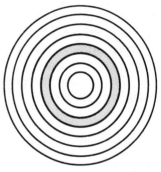

7.1 Introduction

We have been assembling pieces of network software that make internet communication possible, starting with the physical transport layer and adding address resolution. This chapter tackles the design of internet software, showing the format of internet datagrams, and a simple routing mechanism.

7.2 A Virtual Network

Chapter 4 discussed the architecture of an internet in which gateway machines connect multiple physical networks. Looking at the architecture may be misleading, because the focus should not be on the interconnection technology, but on the interface that the internet provides to a user.

> *A user thinks of the internet as a single virtual network that interconnects all hosts, and through which communication is possible; its underlying architecture is both hidden and irrelevant.*

In a sense, the internet is an abstraction of real networks.

7.3 Internet Datagram

The analog between a physical network and the internet is strong. On a physical network, the unit of transfer is a frame that consists of header and data fields,
where the header gives the source and destination physical network addresses. The
internet calls its basic transfer unit a *datagram*. Like the frame, a datagram is divided into a header and a data area. Like the frame header, the datagram header
contains the source and destination addresses, which are expressed as internet addresses.

7.3.1 Datagram Length And Fragmentation

How large can a datagram be? Unlike physical network frames that must be
recognized by hardware, datagrams are handled by software. They can be of any
length we choose. We know that physical networks transport datagrams to their final destination. As datagrams move from one machine to another, they must always be transported in physical frames.

Knowing that datagrams travel in frames might lead us to choose a maximum
datagram such that the datagram fits into a network frame, as shown in Figure 7.1

frame header	complete datagram treated as data in the frame

Figure 7.1 The obvious encapsulation of an internet datagram in a frame

But which frame size should we use? After all, a datagram might travel across
many networks as it moves from gateway to gateway, from a gateway to its destination host. Choosing the minimum of all network frame sizes makes datagrams
much too small (only a few bytes of data could be transferred). Allowing datagrams to be larger than the maximum frame size means that a single datagram
may not always fit into a physical frame.

The choice should be obvious: the point of the internet is to hide underlying
network technologies, and make communication convenient for the user. Thus, instead of designing datagrams that adhere to the constraints of physical networks,
we will choose a convenient datagram size and arrange a way to divide large datagrams into small pieces called *fragments*, so they can be shipped across a physical
network and *reassembled* into a complete datagram.

7.3.2 Datagram Format

Now that the basic datagram content has been described, we will look at the fields
in more detail. Datagrams have the format described by structure *ip* in file *ip.h*
below.

```
/* ip.h */

/* DARPA Internet Protocol (IP)  Constants and Datagram Format */

#define IPLEN    4           /* IP address length in bytes (octets) */
typedef char     IPaddr[IPLEN];  /* DARPA internet address          */
#define IPTMASK 0300         /* Mask for IP type in top byte of addr */
#define IPATYP  0000         /* IP Class A address (1st 2 bits)     */
#define IPBTYP  0200         /* IP Class B address (1st 2 bits)     */
#define IPCTYP  0300         /* IP Class C address (1st 2 bits)     */
#define IPHLEN  20           /* IP datagram header length in bytes  */
#define IMAXLEN 1200         /* Maximum IP datagram length (Notes:  */
                             /*  1) hosts & gateways only required  */
                             /*  to recognize 576 bytes. 2) must be */
                             /*  less than EMAXPAK for our network  */

/* Assigned Protocol numbers */

#define IPRO_ICMP    1       /* protocol type for ICMP packets      */
#define IPRO_UDP    17       /* protocol type for UDP packets       */

struct  ip      {            /* Format of DARPA Internet datagram   */
        char    i_verlen;    /* IP vers.(0x40) + hdr len in longs (5)*/
        char    i_svctyp;    /* service type (0 => normal service)  */
        short   i_paclen;    /* packet length in octets (bytes)     */
        short   i_id;        /* datagram id (to help gateways frag.) */
        short   i_fragoff;   /* fragment offset (0 for 1st fragment) */
        char    i_tim2liv;   /* time to live in gateway hops (10)   */
        char    i_proto;     /* IP protocol (UDP is assigned 17)    */
        short   i_cksum;     /* 1s compl. of sum of shorts in header */
        IPaddr  i_src;       /* IP address of source                */
        IPaddr  i_dest;      /* IP address of destination           */
        char    i_data[1];   /* IP datagram data area               */
};

/* Datagram field constants used by simple IP software */

#define IVERLEN         0x45     /* current version length field value  */
#define ISVCTYP         '\0'     /* service type for normal service     */
#define IFRAGOFF        0        /* Fragment offset (0 => no fragment)  */
#define ITIM2LIV        10       /* Initial time-to-live value          */

extern  int     ipackid;        /* Internet datagram id                */
```

Structure *ip* describes a complete datagram, with field *i_data*, containing the data portion, and the remaining fields describing the header. Fields *i_src* and *i_dest* specify the source and destination internet addresses, and field *i_tim2liv* contains the *time to live* counter. A gateway decrements the time to live counter when it receives a datagram, and discards the datagram if its counter reaches zero. Thus, datagrams do not travel around the internet forever, even if routing tables become corrupt and point in circles.

Field *i_proto* is analogous to the type field in an Ethernet frame. Higher level protocols use *i_proto* to specify the format and contents of the data by identifying the high-level protocol type. The mapping between a high level protocol and the integer value used in *i_proto* to identify it must be administered by a central authority to guarantee standardization across the entire internet.

Field *i_cksum* ensures data integrity. It contains the IP checksum, which is formed by taking the ones complement of the ones complement sum of the 16-bit integers in the header. (For purposes of computing the checksum, the *i_cksum* is assumed to be zero.) File *cksum.s* contains the code for computing the IP checksum.

```
/* cksum.s - cksum */

/ Compute the ones complement of the 16 bit ones complement checksum of
/   an array of 16 bit words.  Adapted from a version by Noel Chiappa
/
/ C Calling sequence:
/
/        check = cksum(buf, nwords)
/
/ where arguments and return value are declared as:
/
/        int     buf[];          /* array of words to be summed   */
/        int     nwords;         /* number of 16-bit words in buf */
/        int     check;          /* returned value                */
/
/
         .text
         .globl   _cksum
_cksum:
         mov     r2,-(sp)           / Save register 2
         mov     4(sp),r1           / Get address of buffer in r1
         mov     6(sp),r2           / Get count of words in r2
         clr     r0                 / Clear r0 for collecting sum

1:       add     (r1)+,r0           / add in next word
         adc     r0                 / add in carry bit
```

```
        sob     r2,1b                    / decrement count and continue

        mov     (sp)+,r2                 / restore r2
        com     r0                       / take 1s complement of result
        rts     pc                       / return to caller
```

Normally, a machine computes the checksum before sending a datagram, and verifies the checksum after receiving one. Interestingly, the IP checksum covers only the information in the datagram header, and not the data in the packet (a separate checksum must be used to ensure that the data arrives intact). Because the checksum includes the time to live field, a value that changes at each gateway, the checksum must be recomputed often (at least once per gateway).

Only a few of the remaining fields in *ip* are important to the simplest internet protocol implementations. Field *i_paclen* carries the packet length in octets (bytes). Each datagram carries the internet protocol version number and header length in field *i_verlen*, and a service type in *i_svctyp*.

Two fields control fragmentation of datagrams. Field *i_fragoff* gives the relative offset in the original datagram of the fragment contained in the current datagram. The top three bits of *i_fragoff* inform the receiver whether this is the last fragment (i.e., fragment with highest offset). Field *i_id* contains an identification assigned by the sender. Each datagram is assigned an id so that fragments can be grouped together for reassembly.

7.4 Sending An IP Datagram

Sending an IP datagram consists of filling in the IP packet structure and then selecting a route. We will look at routing after considering the implementation of the header generator, *ipsend*. Procedure *ipsend* accepts an IP datagram that has data stored in it, fills in the internet header information, and then passes the datagram on to the routing software for transmission.

The code for *ipsend*, shown below in file *ipsend.c*, accepts three arguments. Argument *faddr* gives the destination internet address to which the datagram should be sent. Argument *packet* is a pointer to a complete Ethernet frame containing the datagram, while argument *datalen* gives the length of the datagram data area.

```
/* ipsend.c - ipsend */

#include <conf.h>
#include <kernel.h>
#include <network.h>

/*-------------------------------------------------------------------------
 * ipsend  -  fill in IP header and send datagram to specified address
 *-------------------------------------------------------------------------
 */
ipsend(faddr, packet, datalen)
IPaddr  faddr;
struct  epacket *packet;
int     datalen;
{
        register struct ip *ipptr;

        packet->ep_hdr.e_ptype = hs2net(EP_IP);
        ipptr = (struct ip *) packet->ep_data;
        ipptr->i_verlen = IVERLEN;
        ipptr->i_svctyp = ISVCTYP;
        ipptr->i_paclen = hs2net( datalen+IPHLEN );
        ipptr->i_id = hs2net(ipackid++);
        ipptr->i_fragoff = hs2net(IFRAGOFF);
        ipptr->i_tim2liv = ITIM2LIV;
        ipptr->i_cksum = 0;
        getaddr(ipptr->i_src);
        blkcopy(ipptr->i_dest, faddr, IPLEN);
        ipptr->i_cksum = cksum(ipptr, IPHLEN>>1);
        return( route(faddr, packet, EHLEN+IPHLEN+datalen) );
}
```

Ipsend initializes each field in the datagram header and then calls procedure *cksum* to compute the checksum. Note that the checksum field is assigned zero before the checksum is computed.

7.5 Routing

Once the datagram header has been filled in, control passes to a procedure that is responsible for routing the datagram to its final destination. Routing can be difficult, especially in a gateway, where the routing code must select a network connection over which to send the datagram. Ideally, the routing software would examine such things as network load, datagram length, or the type of service (as specified in the datagram header) when selecting the best path. Most routing software is much less sophisticated, and uses static routes.

There are two possible types of routes. A route is *direct* if the destination can by reached using only one network. That is, the sender and destination both connect to a single network. A route that requires intermediate gateways to relay the datagram to its destination is *indirect*.

7.5.1 Direct Routing

Direct routes are the easiest to derive. We assume that each machine knows the internet address of its network interfaces. To determine whether a datagram can be routed directly over one of these interfaces, the routing procedure simply compares the network id portion of the destination address to the network id portion of each of the machine's interface address(es). If a match occurs, the router knows which network interface to use. The router finds the physical network address of the destination by using the Address Resolution Protocol described in Chapter 6.

7.5.2 Indirect Routing

Indirect routing is more difficult than direct routing because the sender must identify a gateway to which the datagram can be sent. The gateway will then forward the datagram on toward its destination network. How can a host know which gateway to use for a given destination? Usually the algorithm that selects a route employs an *internet routing table* that consists of pairs (N, G), where N is an internet network address, and G is the internet address of a gateway to which to send datagrams destined for network N.

Information in the routing table can be *static* or *dynamic*. Static routing information is placed in the routing table when a machine starts, usually by reading it from disk. Often, the system administrator bases static routes on knowledge about network capacity and the expected traffic load. Dynamic routing updates come from gateway machines, which usually know more about internet connectivity and traffic than individual hosts. Whenever a gateway receives a datagram, it looks at the source and destination addresses to see if the host has chosen the best possible route. If not, the gateway uses the DARPA Internet Control Message Protocol (ICMP) to ask the host to change its routes.

Because incorrect entries in the routing table can prevent communication, care must be taken when building it. In particular, a routing table entry must always route to a gateway that is directly reachable from the host. Thus, once the routing software maps a destination into a gateway's internet address, the host can use the Address Resolution Protocol (ARP) to find the gateway's physical network address.

Whether the route is direct or indirect, the routing software ultimately produces a physical network address to which the datagram is sent. The correspondence between destination internet address and physical network address can be summarized:

> *Internet routing software maps a destination internet address, D, into a physical network address, P. If D can be reached directly, P is its physical address. Otherwise, P is the physical address of a gateway that will route the datagram toward its final destination.*

Thinking about this another way, we see that gateways receive two kinds of datagrams: datagrams addressed to the gateway itself, and datagrams that the gateway must forward to their final destination.

7.5.3 Simplified Routing For Single Connections

Hosts with multiple network connections can function as gateways if they are willing to forward datagrams from one network to another. It is not difficult to arrange for such hosts to forward datagrams because their internet routing tables contain the necessary routing information. Fortunately, hosts with a single network connection can avoid much of the complexity in routing. They need not maintain a routing table because all outgoing datagrams must be sent over a single network. They need not forward datagrams because a singly-connected host cannot serve as a gateway.

Consider, for example, our sample router implemented with procedure *route*, shown below in file *route.c*. *Route* accepts a datagram along with its destination internet address, and sends the datagram out over the only available network.

```
/* route.c - route */

#include <conf.h>
#include <kernel.h>
#include <network.h>

/*------------------------------------------------------------------------
 *  route  -  route a datagram to a given IP address
 *------------------------------------------------------------------------
 */
route(faddr, packet, totlen)
IPaddr  faddr;
struct  epacket *packet;
int     totlen;
{
        int     result;
        int     dev;
        struct  arpent  *arpptr;
        IPaddr  mynet, destnet;
```

```
        /* If IP address is broadcast address for my network, then use  */
        /* physical broadcast address.  Otherwise, establish a path to   */
        /* the destination directly or through a gateway                 */

        getnet(mynet);
        netnum(destnet, faddr);
        wait(Net.nmutex);
        /* NOTE: This code uses host 0 as broadcast like 4.2bsd UNIX */
        if ( blkequ(mynet, faddr, IPLEN) ) {
                dev = ETHER;
                blkcopy(packet->ep_hdr.e_dest, EBCAST, EPADLEN);
        } else {
                if ( !blkequ(destnet, mynet, IPLEN))
                        faddr = Net.gateway;
                arpptr = &Arp.arptab[ getpath(faddr) ];
                if (arpptr->arp_state != AR_RSLVD) {
                        arpptr->arp_state = AR_RGATE;
                        arpptr = &Arp.arptab[getpath(Net.gateway)];
                        if (arpptr->arp_state != AR_RSLVD) {
                                panic("route - Cannot reach gateway");
                                freebuf(packet);
                                signal(Net.nmutex);
                                return(SYSERR);
                        }
                }
                dev = arpptr->arp_dev;
                blkcopy(packet->ep_hdr.e_dest, arpptr->arp_Ead, EPADLEN);
        }
        result = write(dev, packet, totlen);
        signal(Net.nmutex);
        return(result);
}
```

Procedure *route* considers only three possibilities. First, if the destination internet address specifies broadcast on the local network, *route* copies the physical network broadcast address into the frame header before sending the packet. Second, *route* checks the destination network address to see if it matches the local network address. If so, *route* calls procedure *getpath* to find the destination physical address, and then copies it into the frame header before sending the packet. Third, *route* assumes that all other packets must be sent to a gateway. It uses *getpath* to determine the physical address of the gateway, and then copies the address into the frame header. Once *route* has selected a physical address and filled in the frame header, it writes the packet to the appropriate network.

7.6 Summary

The internet protocol software is responsible for filling in the datagram header, including the source and destination internet addresses, and for routing the datagram. Routing involves mapping the destination internet address into a physical network address. The route is direct if the destination and sending machines both connect to a common network; the route is indirect if the datagram must be sent to a gateway for delivery.

We have seen that routing in a singly connected machine requires little complexity. The example implementation honored three types of routes: direct, broadcast, and indirect through a gateway. Our router mapped the Internet broadcast address to the broadcast physical address. It used ARP to obtain physical addresses for other destinations on the net to which it attached, and sent other packets to a gateway.

FOR FURTHER STUDY

Postel [1980] discusses possible ways to approach internet protocols, addressing, and routing. In later publications, Postel [1981] gives the standard for the DARPA Internet Protocol and Hornig [1984] specifies the standard for the transmission of Internet datagrams across an Ethernet, both of which are used in this chapter. In addition to the packet format, DARPA also specifies many constants needed in their network protocols. These values can be found in Reynolds and Postel [1985]. An alternative internet protocol suite known as *xns*, is described by Boggs *et. al.* [1980].

Routing is an important topic. Frank and Chou [1971] discuss routing in general. Fultz and Kleinrock [1971] analyze adaptive routing schemes, and McQuillan, Richer, and Rosen [1980] describe the ARPANET adaptive routing algorithm.

EXERCISES

7.1 Redesign procedure *cksum* by unrolling the loop and measure the difference in performance.

7.2 What is the single greatest advantage of having the IP checksum cover only the datagram header and not the data? What is the disadvantage?

7.3 Under what circumstances might a gateway request a host to redirect datagrams to another gateway? Could singly-connected hosts receive such a request?

7.4 Change the Xinu IP routing mechanism so that it can handle ICMP *redirect* requests.

7.5   Is it ever necessary to use an IP checksum when sending packets over an Ethernet?

7.6   Write a C procedure to compute the IP checksum and measure the difference in performance between the assembler version and the C version. Hint: use long arithmetic.

7.7   Argue that the Xinu routing code hides an important conceptual level of routing.

8

Internet Control Messages

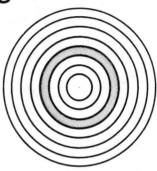

8.1 Introduction

Internet routing tables usually remain static over long periods of time. Hosts initialize them from a disk file at system startup, and system administrators seldom make routing changes during normal operations. Network interconnections do change, however, leaving the routing tables in a particular host out of date. The changes can be temporary (e.g., when hardware needs to be repaired), or permanent (e.g., when a new site is added to the network). Gateways exchange routing information periodically to accommodate network changes and keep their routes up to date. Thus, a gateway usually knows better routes than hosts. When a gateway detects that some host is using a non-optimum route, or when the gateway detects an unusual condition like network congestion that affects the host, the gateway needs to instruct the host to take action to avoid or correct the problem. For example, if a particular network connection becomes inoperative, the gateway may ask senders to reroute datagrams around the faulty hardware. This chapter examines a protocol that gateways use to pass such requests to hosts.

8.2 Extranormal Communication

Usually, packets sent across the internet contain user data preceded by an internet header that specifies the source and destination hosts. As we will see later, the header contains other information that the network software uses to select a user process to which the packet is directed. Control messages sent from gateways to hosts fall outside the normal communication mechanism because the messages are directed to the network software itself, not to a particular user process. However, such messages rely on the internet to deliver them because they may travel across several networks to reach their final destination. Thus, they cannot be delivered by the physical transport alone.

8.3 Internet Control Message Protocol

This chapter examines the Internet Control Message Protocol (*ICMP*), a special-purpose protocol that gateways use to communicate with the network software in hosts. In addition to routing information, ICMP messages provide ways to notify hosts when a datagram's destination is unreachable or when a datagram is destroyed because its time-to-live field reaches zero. ICMP messages travel in the data field of an IP datagram, as Figure 8.1 shows.

IP Datagram Header	Complete ICMP Message Treated as Data

Figure 8.1 The encapsulation of an ICMP message in an IP datagram.

However, ICMP should not be considered a higher-level protocol — it is a required part of IP.

8.3.1 ICMP Messages

Each ICMP message has its own format, but they all begin with three fields: an 8-bit integer message *type* field, an 8-bit *code* field that provides further information about the message type, and a 16-bit *checksum* field (ICMP uses the same checksum algorithm as IP, but the ICMP checksum only includes the ICMP message).

The ICMP type field defines the meaning of the message and the format of the rest of the packet. The type codes include:

Type Code	ICMP Message Type
0	Echo Reply
3	Destination Unreachable
4	Source Quench
5	Redirect (change a route)
8	Echo Request
11	Time Exceeded for a Datagram
12	Parameter Problem on a Datagram
13	Timestamp Request
14	Timestamp Reply
15	Information Request
16	Information Reply

The four most commonly used ICMP messages are: *echo request*, *echo reply*, *redirect*, and *source quench*. The next three sections describe these messages in more detail, giving details of the message format and its meaning.

8.3.2 ICMP Echo Request And Reply Messages

A host or gateway sends an echo request message to test whether a destination host is alive. Any hosts that receives an echo request must formulate an echo reply and return it to the host that sent the request. Echo requests include a type field (8 for echo request, 0 for echo replies), code field (always 0), and checksum, as well as an arbitrary amount of data. The reply must contain the same data as was sent in the request.

8.3.3 ICMP Redirect Messages

A gateway, G, sends an ICMP redirect message to a host, H, to request H to change its routing tables. The redirect message contains, in addition to the requisite type, code, and checksum fields, a 32-bit internet address field, and a datagram prefix field. The internet address field contains the address of a gateway $G2$ to use instead of G, and the datagram prefix field contains a prefix of the IP datagram that triggered gateway G to send the redirect message. The datagram prefix includes the IP header plus the next 64 bits of the datagram. A host receiving an ICMP redirect examines the datagram prefix to determine the datagram's destination address, D.

The code field of an ICMP redirect message further specifies which datagrams a host should redirect. Again assume that host H receives a redirect request that is triggered by a datagram with destination D. In the redirect request, code 0 means that datagrams for any host on the same network as D should be redirected to the gateway specified in the redirect message. Code 1 means that only those datagrams destined for host D itself should be sent to the new gateway address. Code 2 means that datagrams sent to hosts on the same network as D, and using the same type-of-service should be redirected to the specified gateway. Finally, code 3 means that datagrams for host D using the same IP type-of-service should be sent to the specified gateway. In any case, a gateway always forwards the original IP datagram on toward its destination even if the datagram triggers an ICMP redirect message to the originating host.

8.3.4 ICMP Source Quench

Gateways or hosts send source quench requests when datagrams arrive too quickly. Usually, one source quench is sent for every datagram that must be discarded. There is no ICMP message to reverse the effect of a source quench. Instead, a host that receives source quench messages lowers the rate at which it sends datagrams until it stops receiving source quench requests; it then gradually increases the rate as long as no further source quench is received.

Source quench messages contain, in addition to the type, code, and checksum fields, an unused 32-bit field, and a datagram prefix field. As with the redirect request, the datagram prefix field contains a prefix of the datagram that caused the source quench request.

8.4 An Implementation Of ICMP

We will build a skeleton implementation of ICMP that handles echo requests, and leave it to the reader to extend our implementation for other message types. File *icmp.h*, shown below, defines the ICMP echo request message format and defines symbolic constants for ICMP message types.

```
/* icmp.h */

/* Internet Control Message Protocol Constants and Packet Format */

#define ICRPECH 0               /* Echo reply                    */
#define ICDESTU 3               /* Destination unreachable       */
#define ICSRCQN 4               /* Source quench                 */
#define ICREDIR 5               /* Redirect message type         */
#define ICRQECH 8               /* Echo request                  */
#define ICTIMEX 11              /* Time exceeded                 */
#define ICPARMP 12              /* Parameter Problem             */
#define ICTIMST 13              /* Timestamp message             */
#define ICTIMRP 14              /* Timestamp reply               */
#define ICRQINF 15              /* Information request           */
#define ICRPINF 16              /* Information reply             */

/* ICMP packet format (part of the packet that follows the IP header)   */

struct  icmp    {               /* ICMP packet                   */
        char    ic_typ;         /* type of message (see above)   */
        char    ic_code;        /* code (often zero)             */
        short   ic_cksum;       /* checksum of icmp header+data  */
        short   ic_id;          /* for echo type, a message id   */
        short   ic_seq;         /* for echo type, a seq. number  */
        char    ic_data[1];     /* data area of ICMP message     */
};
```

Note that although the type and code fields, *ic_typ* and *ic_code* contain numeric values, they are declared as *char*. Also observe that fields *ic_id* and *ic_seq* have been declared separately from the rest of the data area because the official protocol document mentions them. In practice, an echo reply duplicates all information following the checksum.

8.4.1 ICMP Message Input Processing

We will see in Chapter 10 exactly how ICMP packets arrive from the network. At present, it is sufficient to understand that whenever an ICMP packet arrives, it is passed to procedure *icmp_in* for processing. The implementation of *icmp_in* is shown in file *icmp_in.c* below.

```
/* icmp_in.c - icmp_in */

#include <conf.h>
#include <kernel.h>
#include <network.h>


/*-------------------------------------------------------------------------
 *  icmp_in  -  handle ICMP packet coming in from the network
 *-------------------------------------------------------------------------
 */
icmp_in(packet, icmpp, lim)
struct  epacket *packet;
int     icmpp;
int     lim;
{
        struct  ip      *ipptr;
        struct  icmp    *icmpptr;
        int     len;

        ipptr = (struct ip *)packet->ep_data;
        icmpptr = (struct icmp *) ipptr->i_data;
        if (!Net.mavalid || icmpptr->ic_typ != ICRQECH) {
                freebuf(packet);
        } else {
                icmpptr->ic_typ = (char) ICRPECH;
                blkcopy(ipptr->i_dest, ipptr->i_src, IPLEN);
                len = net2hs(ipptr->i_paclen) - IPHLEN;
                if (isodd(len)) {
                        ipptr->i_data[len++] = NULLCH;
                }
                icmpptr->ic_cksum = 0;
                icmpptr->ic_cksum = cksum(icmpptr, len>>1);
                if (pcount(icmpp) < lim)
                        psend(icmpp, packet);
                else
                        freebuf(packet);
        }
        return(OK);
}
```

Icmp_in begins by setting *ipptr* to the address of the internet header within the
packet. It then assigns *icmpptr* the address of the icmp message, which resides in
the data field of the internet datagram.

Icmp_in examines the ICMP type field, and immediately discards packets other than ICMP echo requests. Having determined that the message is an echo request, *icmp_in* proceeds to change the type to make the packet an echo response, copies the source internet address to the destination internet address, and recomputes the ICMP checksum.

Once the checksum has been recomputed, the echo response is ready to go out. *Icmp_in* merely deposits the packet on Xinu port *icmpp* for the network output process to receive and send it.

8.5 Summary

Normal communication across the internet involves sending messages from a user process on one host to a user process on another host. Gateways may need to communicate directly with the network software on a particular host to report abnormal conditions, or to send the host new routing information.

The Internet Control Message Protocol provides for extranormal communication among gateways and hosts in the DARPA Internet, including source quench messages that retard the rate of transmission, redirect messages that request a host to change its routing tables, and echo request/reply messages that are used to determine whether a host can be reached. An ICMP message travels in the data area of an internet datagram, and has three fixed-length fields at the beginning of the message: an ICMP message type field, a code field, and an ICMP checksum field. The message type determines the format of the message as well as its meaning.

We looked at a skeletal implementation of ICMP, one that handled only echo request messages. To process an echo request, the receiving machine reverses the internet source and destination fields, changes the ICMP type to specify an echo response, recomputes the checksum, and sends the packet back to the original source.

FOR FURTHER STUDY

Both Tanenbaum [1981] and Stallings [1985] discuss control messages in general, and relate them to various network protocols. The central issue is not how to send control messages, but when. Grange and Gien [1979], as well as Driver, Hopewell, and Iaquinto [1979] concentrate on a problem for which control messages are essential, namely, flow control. Gerla and kleinrock [1980] compare flow control strategies analytically.

The Internet Control Message Protocol described here is a DARPA standard defined by Postel [1981a], and includes many more message types than we have discussed. Nagle [1984] discusses ICMP source quench messages, and how gateways should use them to handle congestion control.

EXERCISES

8.1 Revise *icmp_in* to keep a count of the various types of ICMP messages received.

8.2 Experiment to see if Xinu can send packets through a gateway fast enough to trigger an ICMP source quench message.

8.3 Read the official description of ICMP carefully [DARPA]. Do you expect the version of IP in the previous chapter to ever receive an ICMP redirect message? Why?

8.4 In network jargon, the verb *to ping* means "send an ICMP echo request and wait for an ICMP echo reply to see if a host is alive". Build a Xinu program that lets you ping a specified host.

8.5 If you connect to the DARPA internet, try to ping host *xinu.cs.purdue.edu*.

8.6 Should a gateway give ICMP messages priority over normal traffic? Why or why not?

8.7 Consider an Ethernet that has one conventional host, *H*, and 12 gateways connected to it. Find a single (slightly illegal) frame that, when sent by host *H*, causes *H* to receive exactly 24 packets.

9

User Datagram Protocol

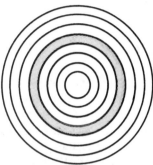

9.1 Introduction

Previous chapters described an internet capable of transferring IP datagrams among host computers. Internet protocol software in each machine sends and receives IP datagrams based on the source and destination Internet addresses, using the address resolution protocol to translate internet addresses into physical network addresses. At the internet level, the destination address identifies a host computer; no further distinction is made regarding which process on that computer will receive the datagram. This chapter extends the internet protocol suite by adding a mechanism that further distinguishes the datagrams arriving at a host, and passes them to the appropriate user process.

9.2 Identifying The Ultimate Destination

Thinking of the ultimate destination of an IP datagram as a process on a particular machine is somewhat misleading. First, senders seldom know enough to identify a particular process on another machine. Second, we would like to be able to replace processes that receive datagrams without informing all senders (e.g., rebooting a machine may change process ids, but rebooting should not require senders to learn about the changes). Third, we need to identify destinations based on the functions they implement without knowing the process that implements the function (e.g., to allow a sender to contact a mail server without knowing which process on the destination machine implements the mail server function).

Instead of thinking of processes as the ultimate destination, we will imagine that each machine contains a set of abstract destination points called *protocol ports*.† Typically, each protocol port is identified by a positive integer, and accessed by a synchronous interface. Packets arriving for a particular port are queued until a process extracts them, and processes waiting at a port are blocked until packets arrive.

To communicate with a port, a sender needs to know both the internet address of the destination machine and the protocol port number of the destination within that machine. With each message, the sender will supply a port number on the source machine to which replies should be addressed, making it possible for a recipient to reply to messages.

9.3 The Important Concept Of Unreliable Delivery

Before examining a mechanism that allows a sender to specify a particular recipient on the destination machine, we need to understand an important property of an internet. The property, known as *unreliable delivery*, tells how the internet passes messages, and makes us aware of the type of service that we can expect.

An understanding of unreliable delivery begins with a look at the network hardware. At the lowest level of a packet-switched network, the hardware offers only "best effort" delivery. Electrical interference, congestion, or physical disconnection may cause transmission failures that result in lost packets. If the device driver attempts to retry transmission when it senses errors, it may inadvertently duplicate packets. Duplicate packets may also arise if a packet switch senses congestion and tries an alternate route. Finally, if a packet switch runs out of space or cannot keep up with the arrival of packets, it may discard them.

Even with network hardware that guarantees reliable delivery, internetworks exhibit fundamentally unreliable message transport. Gateways in an internet misbehave in exactly the same ways as packet switches on a long-haul network. Lack of buffer space may cause them to discard packets. They may also drop packets if the traffic load exceeds the gateway's capacity. Because gateways choose among possible routes, they may inadvertently duplicate packets or deliver them out of order.

The internet protocols have no provision for recovering from any of these problems; they must all be solved by higher levels of network software.

> *Internet protocols provide unreliable delivery because messages can be lost, duplicated, or delivered out of order.*

When building upper levels of software that use unreliable delivery, designers take responsibility for handling the consequences.

---

† the use of the term "port" here should not be confused with the Xinu port mechanism.

9.4 DARPA User Datagram Protocol

In the DARPA protocol suite, the *User Datagram Protocol* or *UDP* provides the mechanism that senders use to distinguish among multiple recipients on a single machine. In addition to the data sent by a user process, each UDP message contains both a destination port number and source port number, making it possible for a recipient to send a reply.

UDP provides unreliable delivery. UDP depends on the underlying Internet Protocol to transport a UDP message from one machine to another. UDP does not use acknowledgements to make sure messages arrive, nor does it order incoming messages. Thus, UDP messages can be lost, duplicated, or arrive out of order.

Each UDP message (datagram) consists of two parts as Figure 9.1 shows: a UDP header and UDP data area.

| UDP header | UDP data area |

Figure 9.1 A UDP message (datagram) with header and user data

The UDP header is divided into four 16-bit fields that contain the source and destination port numbers, the UDP length, and the UDP checksum. The length is a byte count of the UDP message including the UDP header as well as the user data.

9.4.1 The Relationship Between Packet Layout And Protocol Software

As shown in Figure 9.2, a complete UDP message, including the UDP header and data, is encapsulated in an IP datagram as it travels across the internet.

| IP header | Complete UDP datagram treated as data by IP |

Figure 9.2 A UDP datagram encapsulated in an IP datagram

The encapsulation of UDP messages in IP datagrams is not an accident. It results from the division of responsibilities among layers of network protocols. The division of duties is rigid and clear: the IP layer is responsible only for transferring data between hosts on the internet, while the UDP layer is responsible only for differentiating among multiple sources or destinations *within* one host. Thus, only the IP header identifies the source and destination hosts; only the UDP layer identifies the source or destination ports within a host. Assigning these responsibilities to two layers of software isolates the implementations and makes it easier to understand or modify one layer.

Conceptually, the network software consists of many layers, with each layer providing more services than lower layers. For example, Figure 9.3 shows the network layers we have explored.

User Program
User Datagram Protocol (UDP)
Internet Protocol (IP) and Routing
Physical Transport (Ethernet)

Figure 9.3 The Layers of Network Software

Layering is a powerful technique for keeping protocol software manageable. On output, the data to be written is given to the highest layer of protocol software. The highest layer passes it down through the next layer, and so on, until it reaches the network output device. Each layer treats the information received from a higher layer as data, and forms a message by encapsulating the data. For the DARPA protocols we have examined, encapsulation means prepending a header to what is received from the higher layer. Once the data reaches the physical transport level, it travels from one machine to another.

On input, a packet arrives at the lowest layer of network software, and begins its ascent through successively higher layers. Each layer removes one header before passing the message on, so that by the time the highest level passes data to the receiving process, all headers have been removed.

Layering in the protocol software differs from the hierarchical ordering of components in an operating system in two ways. First, while our hierarchical organization organizes software components to make them understandable, the hierarchical ordering disappears after the design has been completed. Users see the result as a set of independent operations; they need not understand the relationships among the components. Second, in a hierarchically designed operating system, control can pass from higher levels to lower levels without passing through intermediate levels. In network protocols, however, each procedure in a given layer can only call procedures in the next lower layer.

The key to understanding layered protocol software lies in realizing that the layers follow an invariant:

> *The data passed from layer i to the next higher layer in the receiving machine is exactly the data that was passed to layer i on the sending machine.*

Thus the data that UDP delivers to a user process on the receiving machine should be exactly the data that a user process passed to UDP on the sending machine. Similarly, the data passed from the IP layer to UDP layer on the receiving machine

should be exactly the data that was passed from the UDP layer to the IP layer on
the sending machine.

9.4.2 UDP Declarations

File *udp.h* contains declarations pertinent to UDP.

```
/* udp.h */

/* DARPA User Datagram Protocol (UDP) constants and formats */

#define UHLEN    8                  /* UDP header length in bytes          */
#define UMAXLEN IMAXLEN-IPHLEN-UHLEN /* Maximum data in UDP packet          */

struct  udp      {                  /* Message format of DARPA UDP          */
        short   u_sport;            /* Source UDP port number               */
        short   u_dport;            /* Destination UDP port number          */
        short   u_udplen;           /* Length of UDP data                   */
        short   u_ucksum;           /* UDP checksum (0 => no checksum)       */
        char    u_data[UMAXLEN];    /* Data in UDP message                  */
};

/* UDP constants */

#define UPROTO           (char)17/* IP protocol type (17 => UDP)            */
#define ULPORT           2050    /* Initial UDP local "port" number         */

/* Assigned UDP port numbers */

#define UECHO            7       /* echo server                             */
#define UDISCARD         9       /* discard packet                          */
#define UUSERS           11      /* users server                            */
#define UDAYTIME         13      /* day and time server                     */
#define UQOTD            17      /* quote of the day server                 */
#define UCHARGEN         19      /* character generator                     */
#define UTIME            37      /* time server                             */
#define UWHOIS           43      /* who is server (user information)         */
#define UDNAME           53      /* darpa domain name server                */
#define UTFTP            69      /* trivial file transfer protocol server*/
#define URWHO            513     /* remote who server (ruptime)             */
```

Structure *udp* defines the format of UDP messages including the four header fields
and the data area. Fields *u_sport* and *u_dport* give the source and destination datagram port identifiers. Field *u_udplen* gives the length in bytes of the entire UDP

datagram, and field *u_ucksum* gives the UDP checksum. A checksum of zero means that no checksum was computed by the sender.

9.4.3 Sending User Datagrams

Sending a user datagram consists of filling in the header and data areas, and passing the result to the IP software for transmission. As usual, our software will allocate a network frame when it wants to transmit a user datagram, leaving space for the frame header, the IP header, and the UDP header. Once the data portion of the user datagram has been filled, the frame is passed to procedure *udpsend*, shown below in file *udpsend.c*, for transmission.

```
/* udpsend.c - udpsend */

#include <conf.h>
#include <kernel.h>
#include <network.h>


/*------------------------------------------------------------------------
 * udpsend  -  send one UDP datagram to a given (foreign) IP address
 *------------------------------------------------------------------------
 */
udpsend(faddr, fport, lport, packet, datalen)
IPaddr  faddr;
short   fport;
short   lport;
struct  epacket *packet;
int     datalen;
{
        register struct udp     *udpptr;
        register struct ip      *ipptr;

        /* Fill in UDP header; pass to ipsend to fill in IP header */

        ipptr = (struct ip *) packet->ep_data;
        ipptr->i_proto = IPRO_UDP;
        udpptr = (struct udp *) ipptr->i_data;
        udpptr->u_sport = hs2net(lport);
        udpptr->u_dport = hs2net(fport);
        udpptr->u_udplen = hs2net(UHLEN+datalen);
        if (isodd(datalen))
                udpptr->u_data[datalen] = (char)0;
        udpptr->u_ucksum = 0;
        return( ipsend(faddr, packet, UHLEN+datalen) );
}
```

Udpsend takes five arguments that specify the destination internet address, the destination UDP port id, the sender's UDP port id, the frame address, and the length of the UDP data area. After calculating the locations of the UDP header and IP header within the frame, *udpsend* fills in the UDP header. It assigns the source and destination UDP port id fields according to the arguments it received, and then assigns the UDP message length field the sum of the UDP data length plus the length of the UDP header.

The UDP protocol specifies that the checksum field of a message can be either a valid checksum for the message (using the same checksum algorithm as IP) or zero if no checksum has been computed. For communication over a single network, checksum computation is usually unnecessary because the network hardware computes its own checksum and detects corrupted packets. The code shown avoids the overhead of checksum computation by assigning zero to the checksum field. One of the exercises suggests adding the checksum computation and measuring the cost.

9.4.4 Assigning The IP Packet Type

Although the packet type field was defined as part of the IP layer, it must always be set by a higher layer of the network software because the higher layers know how the IP datagram is being used. Procedure *udpsend* sets the IP type field to specify that the packet contains a message in UDP format. In the code, constant *IPRO_UDP* has the preassigned packet type code for UDP datagrams.

9.4.5 Passing A User Datagram To Lower Layers

Once the entire UDP datagram has been filled in and the packet type has been assigned, *udpsend* passes the packet, as well as the destination internet address received as an argument, to *ipsend* for transmission. Procedure *ipsend* will return *OK* if it sends the datagram, and *SYSERR* if it finds an error. *Udpsend* returns to its caller whatever *ipsend* returns to it. Because the internet software layer will treat the entire UDP message, including the header, as data, the data length specified in the call to *ipsend* includes the UDP header length as well as the length of the UDP data.

9.5 Summary

The internet software described in previous chapters provided a mechanism that transferred data from one machine to another across the internet. This chapter considered the DARPA User Datagram Protocol, UDP. Although each UDP message travels across the internet in an IP datagram, UDP adds additional functionality by distinguishing among several sources or destinations within a host. UDP identifies a destination within a machine by assigning it a UDP port number. In the example implementation, procedure *udpsend* handled UDP messages by supplying a UDP header and then passing the result to procedure *ipsend* for transmission.

FOR FURTHER STUDY

Tanenbaum [1981] contains a comparison of the datagram and virtual circuit models of communication. Ball *et. al.* [1979] describe message-based systems without discussing the message protocol. The UDP protocol described here is standard for the DARPA Internet, and is defined by Postel [1980a].

EXERCISES

9.1 Modify *udpsend* to correctly compute a UDP checksum and measure the difference in time required to transfer a large file.

9.2 Why is the UDP checksum separate from the IP checksum? Would you object to a protocol that used a single checksum for the complete IP datagram including the UDP message?

9.3 Not using checksums can be dangerous. Explain how a single corrupted ARP packet broadcast by machine *P* can make it impossible to reach another machine, *Q*.

9.4 UDP provides datagram communication because it does not guarantee delivery of the message. Devise a reliable datagram protocol that uses time-outs and acknowledgments to guarantee delivery. How much does reliability cost?

9.5 *Name Registry.* Suppose you want to allow arbitrary pairs of user processes to establish communication with UDP but you do not wish to assign them fixed UDP port identifiers. Instead, you would like potential correspondents to be identified by a character string of 64 or fewer characters. Thus, a process on machine *A* might want to communicate with the "funny-special-long-id" program on machine *B* (you can assume that a process always knows the internet address of the host with which it wants to communicate). Meanwhile, a process on machine *C* wants to communicate with the "comer's-own-program-id" on machine *A*. Show that you only need to preassign one UDP port to make such communication possible by designing software on each machine that allows (a) a local process to pick a fresh UDP port id over which it will communicate, (b) a local process to register the 64-character name to which it responds, and (c) a foreign process to use UDP to establish communication using only the 64-character name and destination internet address.

9.6 Implement name registry software from the previous exercise.

10

Network Input and Protocol Demultiplexing

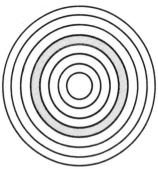

10.1 Introduction

So far, we have discussed internet communication without considering how a host processes network input. This chapter describes input processing, showing a process that reads frames from the network device and delivers them to the appropriate destination within the host. It provides the crucial link between the physical transport mechanism and procedures that handle incoming packets, and illustrates how input processing must be isolated from network output.

10.2 A Network Input Process

The need for a process to handle network input arises because of two earlier design decisions. First, recall that the lowest layers of network software cast physical transport in a device paradigm, using operations *write* and *read* to send and receive frames. Because devices are passive objects they require a process to start data transfer operations. Second, recall that the address resolution protocol required hosts to accept and respond to ARP requests even when no user process on the host is engaged in network communication. Thus, we need to invent a special process that continually reads a frame from the network and then processes it.

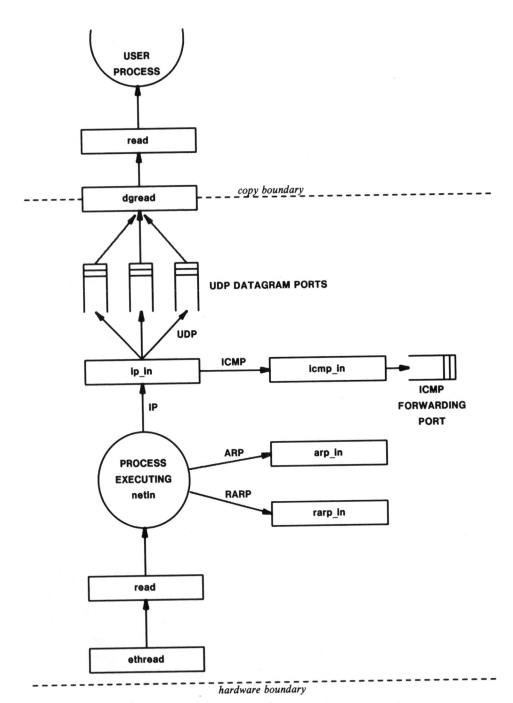

Figure 10.1 The flow of an arriving datagram as the network input process demultiplexes it.

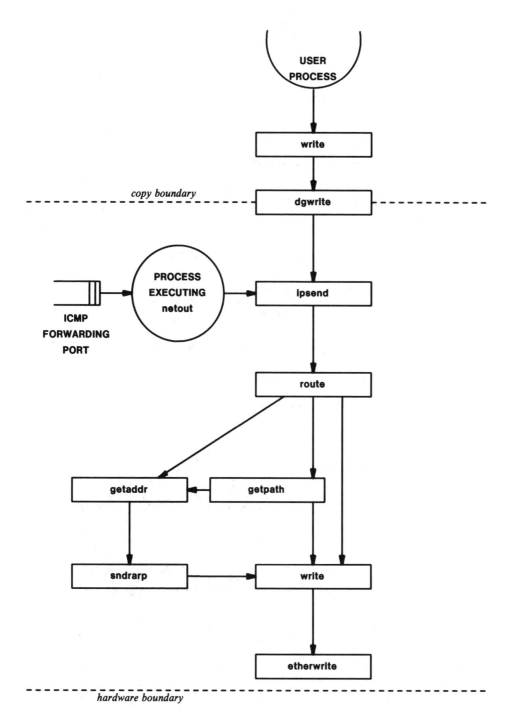

Figure 10.2 The flow of an outgoing ICMP echo reply or datagram from a user process.

10.3 Demultiplexing

The network input process reads frames one at a time, and processes each frame as it arrives, using the frame type field to determine how the frame should be handled. The central idea is *demultiplexing*, as Figure 10.1 shows. Frames from many sources are combined, or *multiplexed*, onto a single network during output. The input process must separate, or *demultiplex*, frames that arrive over a single network, depending on their contents and purpose.

The frame type field controls demultiplexing. The sender sets the frame type to record the purpose and format of the frame; the input process examines the frame type to determine which procedure handles the frame. For example, frames that carry ARP messages have frame type *EP_ARP*; the network input process must pass them to procedure *arp_in*, as seen in Chapter 6.

Demultiplexing continues at higher levels of protocol. For example, the network input process passes all frames that contain IP datagrams to a procedure *ip_in* that we will see shortly. *Ip_in* demultiplexes further based on the IP packet type field. Finally, UDP packets must be demultiplexed based on the UDP destination port id.

10.4 Implementation Of The Network Input Process

10.4.1 General Network Declarations

The code for the network input process will help clarify the notion of demultiplexing, and make the link between the physical transport layer and the lowest-level protocols apparent. We will begin by looking at file *net.h* which contains declarations for many network variables and constants.

```
/* net.h */

/* High-level network definitions and constants */

#define NETBUFS       5                  /* number of network buffers      */
#ifndef Ndg
#define NETQS         1                  /* number of xinu ports used to */
#else                                    /*   demultiplex udp datagrams    */
#define NETQS         Ndg
#endif
#define NETQLEN       3                  /* size of a demux queue          */
#define NETFQ         3                  /* size of input-to-output queue*/
#ifndef NETNLEN
#define NETNLEN       24                 /* length of network name         */
#endif
```

```
/* Commands for the network pseudo device control call */

#define NC_SETGW          1               /* set gateway IP address      */

/* Network input and output processes: procedure name and parameters */

#define NETIN           netin           /* network input daemon process */
#define NETOUT          netout          /* network output process       */
extern  int             NETIN(), NETOUT();
#define NETISTK         350             /* stack size for network input */
#define NETOSTK         400             /* stack size for network output*/
#define NETIPRI         100             /* network runs at high priority*/
#define NETOPRI          99             /* network output priority      */
#define NETINAM         "netin"         /* name of network input process*/
#define NETONAM         "netout"        /* name of network output   "   */
#define NETIARGC          1             /* count of args to net input   */
#define NETOARGC          2             /* count of args to net output  */

/* Mapping of external network UDP "port" to internal Xinu port */

struct  netq    {                       /* UDP demultiplexing info      */
        Bool    valid;                  /* is this entry in use?        */
        short   uport;                  /* local UDP "port" number      */
        int     pid;                    /* pid of process if one waiting*/
        int     xport;                  /* Corresponding Xinu port on   */
};                                      /*  which incoming pac. queued  */

struct  netinfo {                       /* info and parms. for network  */
        int     netpool;                /* network packet buffer pool   */
        struct  netq netqs[NETQS];      /* UDP packet demux info        */
        Bool    mnvalid;                /* is my host name field valid? */
        Bool    mavalid;                /* is my network address valid? */
        char    myname[NETNLEN];        /* domain name of this machine  */
        IPaddr  myaddr;                 /* IP address of this machine   */
        IPaddr  mynet;                  /* Network portion of myaddr    */
        IPaddr  gateway;                /* IP address of gateway to use */
        int     nxtprt;                 /* next available local UDP port*/
        int     nmutex;                 /* output mutual excl. semaphore*/
        int     npacket;                /* # of packets processed       */
        int     ndrop;                  /* # of packets discarded       */
        int     nover;                  /* # dropped because queue full */
};

extern  struct  netinfo Net;            /* All network parameters       */
```

Many of the declarations in *net.h* pertain to the UDP datagram demultiplexing mechanism that we will consider in the next section. For now, it is enough to observe that the declarations of many variables have been collected together under a single variable *Net*, which is defined to be a structure of type *netinfo*.

10.4.2 The Network Input Procedure

The system creates a process at startup to execute procedure *netin*, found in file *netin.c*, below.

```
/* netin.c */

#include <conf.h>
#include <kernel.h>
#include <proc.h>
#include <network.h>


/*-------------------------------------------------------------------------
 * netin - initialize net, start output side, and become input daemon
 *-------------------------------------------------------------------------
 */
PROCESS netin(userpid)
int     userpid;                                /* user process to resume        */
{
        register struct epacket *packet;
        struct  epacket *getbuf();
        int     icmpp;

        arpinit();
        netinit();
        icmpp = pcreate(NETFQ);
        resume(create(NETOUT, NETOSTK, NETIPRI-1, NETONAM,
                        2, userpid,icmpp));

        for (packet = getbuf(Net.netpool) ; TRUE ;) {
                Net.npacket++;
                if ( read(ETHER,packet,sizeof(*packet)) == SYSERR ) {
                        Net.ndrop++;
                        continue;
                }
                switch (net2hs(packet->ep_hdr.e_ptype)) {

                    case EP_ARP:
                        arp_in(packet, ETHER);
```

```
                    packet = getbuf(Net.netpool);
                    break;

            case EP_RARP:
                    rarp_in(packet, ETHER);
                    packet = getbuf(Net.netpool);
                    break;

            case EP_IP:
                    ip_in(packet, icmpp, NETFQ);
                    packet = getbuf(Net.netpool);
                    break;

            default: /* just drop packet */
                    Net.ndrop++;
            }
        }
}
```

Procedure *netin* performs three tasks. First, it calls *arpinit* and *netinit* to initialize the variables used by ARP and the other variables used by the network. Second, it creates a network output process. Third, it becomes the network input process, repeatedly reading frames from the network and demultiplexing them based on frame type.

Demultiplexing is easiest to understand, and should be studied first. In the *for* loop, *netin* reads a packet from the Ethernet, and then uses the packet type field in a *switch* statement to select one of four possible actions. If the frame contains an ARP message, *netin* passes the frame to procedure *arp_in*, along with an argument that specifies the Ethernet device id. Similarly, *netin* passes RARP messages to procedure *rarp_in*. It passes *IP* datagrams to procedure *ip_in*, and discards any other type of frame.

Netin always reads a frame into a network buffer allocated from buffer pool *Net.netpool*. It allocates the first buffer in the initialization part of the *for* statement. When control passes to *arp_in*, *rarp_in*, or *ip_in*, they take responsibility for the buffer, returning it to the buffer pool after using it. Thus, after calling one of these routines, *netin* must allocate a new buffer for the next iteration. In the default case, the frame is not a recognized type. *Netin* discards the frame without processing by merely keeping the same buffer for the next input.

10.4.3 Network Initialization

Having studied the frame demultiplexing code, we can go back to the beginning of *netin* and look at initialization. *Netin* calls procedure *arpinit* which, as we have seen in Chapter 6, initializes the ARP cache. It also calls procedure *netinit* to

initialize variables in the *Net* structure. Code for *netinit* can be found in file
netinit.c.

```
/* netinit.c - netinit */

#include <conf.h>
#include <kernel.h>
#include <sleep.h>
#include <network.h>

/*------------------------------------------------------------------------
 *  netinit  -  initialize network data structures
 *------------------------------------------------------------------------
 */
netinit()
{
        struct  netq    *nqptr;
        int     i;

        /* Initialize pool of network buffers and rest of Net structure */

        if (clkruns == FALSE)
                panic("net: no clock");
        Net.netpool = mkpool(EMAXPAK, NETBUFS);
        for (i=0 ; i<NETQS ; i++) {
                nqptr = &Net.netqs[i];
                nqptr->valid = FALSE;
                nqptr->uport = -1;
                nqptr->xport = pcreate(NETQLEN);
        }
        Net.mnvalid = Net.mavalid = FALSE;
        dot2ip(Net.gateway, GATEWAY);
        Net.nxtprt = ULPORT;
        Net.nmutex = screate(1);
        Net.npacket = Net.ndrop = Net.nover = 0;
        return(OK);
}

struct  netinfo Net;
```

Procedure *netinit* checks to make sure there is a clock because packet timeout will
not work correctly without one. It then creates the network buffer pool and initializes the array *netqs* by marking each entry unused. As we will see in the next section, each entry in *netqs* corresponds to one UDP datagram port. Finally, *netinit*

creates the network mutual exclusion semaphore, and assigns miscellaneous variables like the counters for packets received, dropped, and overflowed.

10.4.4 Output By The Network Input Process

Recall from Chapter 8 that the Internet Control Message Protocol included messages for echo request and reply. When the network input process reads an IP packet that contains an ICMP echo request, it passes the packet to procedure *ip_in*, which eventually calls procedure *icmp_in*. If you recall from Chapter 8, *icmp_in* did not call output procedures like *ipsend* directly. Instead, it formed a response and enqueued the response on a Xinu port for output. Now we can understand why *icmp_in* was not free to call *ipsend* directly: if *ipsend* needed to resolve an internet address it might call the ARP software. ARP cannot resolve addresses unless the network input process remains ready to read and handle incoming ARP packets. Thus, the network input process cannot be blocked because it may be needed to handle ARP requests.

> *The network input process must remain ready to execute during*
> *datagram output because sending a single IP datagram may*
> *trigger low-level protocols like ARP to send and receive frames.*

To help the reader remember this requirement, we have adopted the convention of adding "_in" to the names of procedures invoked by the network input process.

We can finally understand the remaining initialization code in procedure *netin*. To handle IP output, *netin* creates a separate process and a Xinu port that serves as a queue between the two. In the code, the process is referred to as the network output process, but the name may be slightly misleading because it only handles output from the network input process. *Netin* creates the port first, and then passes the port id as an argument to the network output process.

Netin also passes its argument *userpid* to the network output process at creation. *Userpid* is the process id of a process the operating system created at startup time to execute the user's main program. The operating system leaves the process suspended because it cannot permit a user process to execute until *netin* has initialized the network and is ready to handle packets.

10.4.5 Implementation Of Network Output Process

The network output process completes network initialization by performing chores that require the network input process to be running. It then repeatedly accepts and sends IP datagrams for the network input process. The code is found in file *netout.c*, below:

```
/* netout.c - netout */

#include <conf.h>
#include <kernel.h>
#include <network.h>

/*------------------------------------------------------------------------
 * netout  -  start network by finding address and forward IP packets
 *------------------------------------------------------------------------
 */
PROCESS netout(userpid, icmpp)
int     userpid;
int     icmpp;
{
        struct  epacket *packet;
        struct  ip      *ipptr;
        long    tim;
        int     len;
        IPaddr  addr;

        getaddr(addr);
        gettime(&tim);
        resume(userpid);
        while (TRUE) {
                packet = (struct epacket *) preceive(icmpp);
                ipptr = (struct ip *) packet->ep_data;
                blkcopy (addr, ipptr->i_dest, IPLEN);
                len = net2hs(ipptr->i_paclen) - IPHLEN;
                ipsend(addr, packet, len);
        }
}
```

Initialization consists of calling procedures *getaddr* and *gettime*, both of which use UDP to acquire information. (Code for these routines appears in Chapter 12.) After initialization, *netout* starts (resumes) the user process, and then repeatedly iterates through a cycle of acquiring a packet and sending it. Each iteration waits for a packet on the Xinu port specified by argument *icmpp*, extracts the destination internet from the packet, and calls *ipsend* to route the packet to its destination. Although extracting the address may seem awkward, it is necessary because *ipsend* requires that the destination address be passed as a separate argument. Storing the destination address in the packet while passing it between the network input and output processes makes it possible to use a Xinu port.

10.5 The Details Of Datagram Demultiplexing

So far we have seen how the network input process reads incoming frames and demultiplexes them according to frame type. We still need to arrange demultiplexing of packets that contain user datagrams. Because UDP messages travel in IP packets, *netin* passes them to procedure *ip_in* (as it does all frames that contain IP datagrams). Procedure *ip_in*, shown below in file *ip_in.c*, further demultiplexes the packet based on the IP type field.

```
/* ip_in.c - ip_in */

#include <conf.h>
#include <kernel.h>
#include <proc.h>
#include <network.h>

/*------------------------------------------------------------------------
 * ip_in - handle IP packet coming in from the network
 *------------------------------------------------------------------------
 */
ip_in(packet, icmpp, lim)
struct  epacket *packet;
int     icmpp;
int     lim;
{
        struct  udp     *udpptr;
        struct  ip      *ipptr;
        struct  netq    *nqptr;
        int     dport;
        int     i;
        int     to;
        char    ps;

        ipptr = (struct ip *)packet->ep_data;
        switch (ipptr->i_proto) {

        case IPRO_ICMP:             /* ICMP: pass to icmp input routine */
                return(icmp_in(packet, icmpp, lim));

        case IPRO_UDP:              /* UDP: demultiplex based on UDP "port" */
                udpptr = (struct udp *) ipptr->i_data;
                dport = net2hs(udpptr->u_dport);
                for (i=0 ; i<NETQS ; i++) {
                        nqptr = &Net.netqs[i];
```

```
                        if (nqptr->uport == dport) {
                                /* drop instead of blocking on psend */
                                if (pcount(nqptr->xport) >= NETQLEN) {
                                        Net.ndrop++;
                                        Net.nover++;
                                        freebuf(packet);
                                        return(SYSERR);
                                }
                                psend(nqptr->xport, packet);
                                disable(ps);
                                to = nqptr->pid;
                                if ( !isbadpid(to) ) {
                                    nqptr->pid = BADPID;
                                    send(to, OK);
                                }
                                restore(ps);
                                return(OK);
                        }
                }
                break;

        default:
                break;
        }
        Net.ndrop++;
        freebuf(packet);
        return(OK);
}
```

Ip_in handles only two types of IP packets. It passes ICMP messages to procedure *icmp_in*, sends UDP messages to the appropriate datagram port, and ignores all other IP packets.

To demultiplex a UDP datagram, *ip_in* extracts the udp destination datagram port, and then searches array *netqs* looking for an entry with that datagram port id. Each entry in *netqs* corresponds to a single UDP datagram port id as specified by field *uport*. The queue of datagrams is kept in a Xinu port (the use of "port" by UDP and Xinu is an unfortunate coincidence; Xinu ports are merely queues with blocking operations to enqueue and dequeue objects). Because the network input process must remain running to handle low-level protocols like ARP, it cannot block while waiting to deposit a datagram. To avoid blocking, *ip_in* examines the count of packets already waiting in the Xinu port and discards the current packet if the Xinu port is full (i.e., the call to *psend* would block).

10.5.1 Datagram Timeout

Often, processes need to limit the time they are willing to wait for a datagram to arrive. To handle such timeouts, our datagram demultiplexing mechanism uses the *recvtim* primitive from Chapter 5. A process wishing to time out while waiting for a datagram leaves its process id in field *pid* of the *netqs* entry, and calls *recvtim*. When a datagram arrives, *ip_in* checks field *pid* in the *netqs* entry to see if a process is timing reception. If a process is, *ip_in* sends message *OK* to the process. In the code, interrupts must be disabled while *netin* tests the process id field and sends the message to avoid having a process register its id after *ip_in* examines the id field.

10.6 The Needed Interface

Although the *netqs* array adequately provides queues for arriving datagrams, it is only useful internally within the operating system. We still need to devise a convenient way for user processes to send and receive datagrams without knowing about the internal queueing mechanism or the network input process. The next chapter describes just such a mechanism.

10.7 Summary

A network input process repeatedly reads frames from the network and demultiplexes them. Once a frame has been read, the network input process extracts the frame type field, and uses it to determine whether to call the ARP frame handler, the RARP frame handler, and so on. IP frames must be further demultiplexed based on the IP packet type, which could specify ICMP, UDP, or other types. UDP packets are demultiplexed based on UDP port id; separate queues are kept for each UDP port id. ICMP packets may require a reply; the network input process passes them to the network output process through a queue.

Because the network input process must remain running to handle low-level protocols like ARP, it cannot send IP datagrams directly. Thus, we arranged a separate network output process and used a Xinu port between the two to allow procedures executed by the input process to send IP datagrams. Our implementation has the network input process initialize network data structures and start the network output process. The network output process finishes network initialization, and starts the process that executes the user's program.

FOR FURTHER STUDY

Multiplexing and demultiplexing are common themes that run through all networking protocols. Stallings [1984] covers multiplexing at the hardware level, while both Tanenbaum [1981] and Stallings [1985] describe protocol hierarchies with implicit multiplexing and demultiplexing at each protocol level.

EXERCISES

10.1   Our demultiplexing code is *static* in the sense that the possible frame types are compiled into the network input process and the procedures it calls. Modify the demultiplexing code to make it *dynamic*, by providing a routine *setdemux* that takes two arguments: a frame type code, *T*, and a procedure to call when frames of type *T* arrive. Then base all demultiplexing on a table filled in by *setdemux*.

10.2   Refer to the previous exercise. What is the chief advantage of dynamic demultiplexing? Of static demultiplexing?

10.3   Use the counters in structure *netinfo* to determine what percentage of incoming packets are dropped.

10.4   Devise an experiment to determine the lengths of datagram queues by rapidly transmitting packets to a given UDP port id and observing the packet overflow count. Hint: command *netstat* prints packet drop count statistics.

10.5   Give two advantages of having short datagram queues. (Try to think of how higher-level protocols behave).

11

Device Interface for Datagram Communication

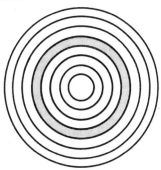

11.1 Datagram Interface And Copying

The mechanism for user datagram demultiplexing described in Chapter 10 implements the datagram port concept by providing a set of queues for incoming datagrams, where each queue corresponds to one UDP port id. The mechanism is extremely efficient because it avoids copying data. The network input process allocates a buffer that the physical transport level device driver fills directly with a frame from the network. The network input process then demultiplexes the frame based on the frame type field, and passes a pointer to the entire frame on to the next level. When processing an IP packet, the highest-level procedure further demultiplexes the packets based on UDP port number, but again leaves the data in the original buffer and enqueues only a pointer to the entire frame.

Where does frame passing end? Can user processes send and receive UDP datagrams without knowing frame formats? This chapter answers these questions by defining an interface that stands between the frame-passing routines built so far and user processes that use them. We need to isolate user level processes from the low-level network protocol routines for two reasons. First, we need to hide frame and packet encapsulation details so they can be changed without changing user programs. For example, if we add a new field to the internet protocol header, user programs should not be affected (they should not even have to be recompiled). Second, there is a finite set of buffers that hold frames, and running out of buffers will cause network communication to cease. We want to retain control of all the software that allocates, passes, or releases such buffers so we can understand how many buffers are needed, and guarantee that every buffer that we allocate is ultimately returned to its buffer pool.

Retaining control of the buffer allocation is essential; building a system that never runs out of buffers is subtle. If you think back, you will see that we have carefully designed each piece of the protocol software to use only a finite number of buffers. Even the datagram queues have finite size. Thus, it is possible to bound the number of buffers needed to keep the network running. An exercise suggests that you take time to think of where incoming packets might be found and add up the maximum possible buffers in the system.

Because our user interface will provide the boundary between routines that handle frames and those that handle only user data, it defines a *copy boundary*. When a user sends a message, the interface will allocate a frame, copy the user's message into the UDP data area, and then call procedure *udpsend* to send the message. Similarly, when the user accepts a message from some UDP datagram port, the interface copies data into the place specified by the user and returns the frame to its buffer pool.

11.2 Data Or Datagram Oriented User Interface

Designing the interface between user processes and the protocol software requires one to decide between a datagram-oriented or data-oriented paradigm. As with lower levels of network software, using a datagram-oriented approach means storing destination addresses contiguous with data. Unlike lower levels of protocol software that require the designer to use a standard datagram format that can be understood by all machines in the internet, the interface between user processes and the network software is operating system specific. Thus, the designer is free to choose an entirely new datagram format, one that is convenient for users. The other alternative, a data-oriented approach, keeps information like destination addresses separate from the data being transferred.

Which interface approach is best? It depends on the application. Sometimes the user would like to establish information like the destination address once, and then begin sending and receiving data messages by specifying only the location of data and its length. In other applications, the destination information must change for each message sent, making it more convenient for users to form a datagram that contains both the data and destination information. The design issue concerns binding time:

> *A network interface that binds destination addresses early makes sending or receiving messages efficient because only the data needs to be transferred; a late binding network interface provides flexibility because it permits a process to specify the destination of each message independently.*

Because no single interface design satisfies all needs, we will design parameterized interface software that permits each application to choose between the two basic approaches. The next section describes the datagram interface software, showing the details of how parameters distinguish between early and late address binding.

11.3 Datagram Pseudo-Device Interface

Like many operating systems, Xinu uses a device-based datagram interface. A user process calls *open* for the *INTERNET* pseudo-device, giving it arguments that specify the foreign and local UDP ports. *Open* returns the device descriptor of a datagram pseudo-device that can be used in calls to *read* and *write* to receive or send messages.

Hidden below operations like *open*, *read*, and *write* are device driver routines that implement these operations for a specific device. This chapter will explore the underlying driver routines for the *INTERNET* and datagram devices, as well as the data structures they use. We begin by considering the form of data as it passes between a user process and the datagram driver.

By default, datagram pseudo-devices expect the user to read and write structures known as *xinugrams*. A xinugram consists of two parts: a header and a data area. The header differs from most headers we have seen because it specifies *foreign* address and *local* address instead of *source* and *destination*. The single greatest advantage of using a foreign/local specification is that it permits a user process to read a xinugram, change the data area, and then write the xinugram without exchanging source and destination fields in the header.

11.4 Datagram Pseudo-Device Implementation

Looking at the datagram pseudo-device implementation will clarify the concepts. Declarations of the xinugram format as well as the pseudo-device control block can be found in file *dgram.h,* shown below.

```
/* dgram.h */

/* Datagram pseudo-device control block */

struct  dgblk   {                       /* Datagram device control block*/
        int     dg_dnum;                /* device number of this device */
        int     dg_state;               /* whether this device allocated*/
        int     dg_lport;               /* local datagram port number   */
        int     dg_fport;               /* foreign datagram port number */
        IPaddr  dg_faddr;               /* foreign machine IP address    */
        int     dg_xport;               /* incoming packet queue         */
        int     dg_netq;                /* index of our netq entry       */
        int     dg_mode;                /* mode of this interface        */
};

/* Datagram psuedo-device state constants */

#define DG_FREE         0               /* this device is available     */
#define DG_USED         1               /* this device is in use        */


#define DG_TIME         30              /* read timeout (tenths of sec) */

/* Constants for dgm pseudo-device control functions */

#define DGM_GATE        11              /* Set the default gateway      */

/* Constants for dg pseudo-device control functions */

#define DG_SETMODE      1               /* Set mode of device           */
#define DG_CLEAR        2               /* clear all waiting datagrams   */

/* Constants for dg pseudo-device mode bits */

#define DG_NMODE        001             /* normal (datagram) mode       */
#define DG_DMODE        002             /* data-only mode               */
#define DG_TMODE        040             /* timeout all reads            */

/* Structure of xinugram as dg interface delivers it to user */

struct  xgram   {                       /* Xinu datagram (not UDP)      */
        IPaddr  xg_faddr;               /* foreign host IP address      */
        int     xg_fport;               /* foreign UDP port number      */
        int     xg_lport;               /* local UDP port number        */
        char    xg_data[UMAXLEN];       /* maximum data to/from UDP     */
};
```

```
#define XGHLEN  8        /* error in ( (sizeof(struct xgram)) - UMAXLEN) */

/* Constants for port specifications on INTERNET open call */

#define ANYFPORT         (char *)0       /* Accept any foreign UDP port  */
#define ANYLPORT         0               /* Assign a fresh local port num*/


extern  struct  dgblk   dgtab[Ndg];
```

Structure *xgram* declares the format of a xinugram as delivered to a user process. The foreign address includes both the foreign machine's IP address (field *xg_faddr*) as well as the foreign UDP port id (field *xg_fport*), while the local specification includes only the local UDP port id (field *xg_lport*). Note that, as defined, xinugrams have only 8 bytes of header, whereas an IP-encapsulated UDP message has at least 28 bytes of header.

Structure *dgblk*, also declared in file *dgram.h*, defines the data needed by each datagram pseudo-device driver. Field *dg_dnum* holds the device number, and field *dg_state* specifies whether the device is in use. The mode, given by field *dg_mode*, specifies whether to transfer xinugrams or just data to the user, and whether to timeout reads. In data transfer mode, fields *dg_fport* and *dg_faddr* hold the foreign machine address. Field *dg_netq* specifies the entry in *netqs* that receives incoming datagrams for this pseudo-device. Finally, *dg_xport* tells the Xinu port on which incoming datagrams will be enqueued.

11.4.1 Datagram Pseudo-device Initialization

Procedure *dginit*, shown below in file *dginit.c*, initializes the datagram pseudo-devices at system startup.

```
/* dginit.c - dginit */

#include <conf.h>
#include <kernel.h>
#include <network.h>

/*------------------------------------------------------------------------
 *  dginit  -  initialize datagram protocol pseudo device marking it free
 *------------------------------------------------------------------------
 */
dginit(devptr)
struct   devsw   *devptr;
{
        struct   dgblk   *dgptr;

        devptr->dvioblk = (char *) (dgptr = &dgtab[devptr->dvminor]);
        dgptr->dg_dnum = devptr->dvnum;
        dgptr->dg_state = DG_FREE;
        return(OK);
}


#ifdef  Ndg
struct  dgblk   dgtab[Ndg];                    /* dg device control blocks    */
#endif
```

As the code shows, each datagram pseudo-device begins with its state field set to
DG_FREE, showing that the device is not currently in use.

11.4.2 Utility Procedures

Before we can understand the code that opens a datagram device, we need to
look at three utility procedures it uses. The first, *dgalloc*, is found in file *dgalloc.c*.
It allocates a free datagram pseudo-device by searching through the control block
array, *dgtab*, until it finds an entry with the state field marked free. Once such an
entry has been found, *dgalloc* marks the entry as in use, and returns its index to
the caller.

```
/* dgalloc.c - dgalloc */

#include <conf.h>
#include <kernel.h>
#include <network.h>


/*------------------------------------------------------------------------
```

```
 *  dgalloc  -  allocate a datagram psuedo device and return descriptor
 *-------------------------------------------------------------------------
 */
dgalloc()
{
        struct  dgblk    *dgptr;
        int      i;
        char     ps;

        disable(ps);
        for (i=0 ; i<Ndg ; i++) {
                dgptr = &dgtab[i];
                if (dgptr->dg_state == DG_FREE) {
                        dgptr->dg_state = DG_USED;
                        restore(ps);
                        return(i);
                }
        }
        restore(ps);
        return(SYSERR);
}
```

A second utility program used when opening a datagram pseudo-device, *dgparse*, scans a string of the form

$$digits.digits.digits.digits:digits$$

converting each group of digits into a binary integer, and placing the results in the datagram device control block. *Dgparse* assumes that the first four groups of digits give, in dotted decimal notation, a foreign IP address. It also assumes that the final group of digits give, in decimal, a UDP port number on the foreign machine.

```
/* dgparse.c - dgparse */

#include <conf.h>
#include <kernel.h>
#include <network.h>
#include <ctype.h>

/*------------------------------------------------------------------------
 * dgparse  -  parse foreign address specification; get IP and port #s
 *------------------------------------------------------------------------
 */
dgparse(dgptr, fspec)
struct  dgblk    *dgptr;
char    *fspec;
{
        int     i, byte;
        char    ch;
        char    *ipptr;

        if (fspec == ANYFPORT) {
                dgptr->dg_fport = 0;
                return(OK);
        }

        /* parse forms like 192.5.48.30:3 into (ip-address,udp-port) */

        ipptr = (char *) dgptr->dg_faddr;
        for (i=0 ; i<4 ; i++) {
                byte = 0;
                while ( isdigit(ch = *fspec++) )
                        byte = 10*byte + (ch - '0');
                if (byte > 256 || (i<3 && ch!='.') )
                        return(SYSERR);
                *ipptr++ = (char)byte;
        }
        if (ch != ':')
                return(SYSERR);
        i = 0;
        while ( isdigit(ch = *fspec++) )
                i = 10*i + (ch - '0');
        if (i==0 || ch!='\0')
                return(SYSERR);
        dgptr->dg_fport = i;
        return(OK);
}
```

In addition to recognizing a string in dotted decimal notation, *dgparse* also recognizes the special constant *ANYFPORT*. It sets field *dg_fport* to 0, to specify that any foreign port is allowed.

The third utility procedure, *nqalloc*, allocates an entry from the *netqs* array. The code, found in *nqalloc.c*, is straightforward.

```
/* nqalloc.c - nqalloc */

#include <conf.h>
#include <kernel.h>
#include <proc.h>
#include <network.h>

/*------------------------------------------------------------------------
 * nqalloc  -  allocate a network demultiplexing queue
 *------------------------------------------------------------------------
 */
nqalloc()
{
        int     i;
        struct  netq    *nqptr;
        char    ps;

        disable(ps);
        for (i=0 ; i<NETQS ; i++) {
                nqptr = &Net.netqs[i];
                if ( !nqptr->valid) {
                        nqptr->valid = TRUE;
                        nqptr->uport = -1;
                        nqptr->pid = BADPID;
                        restore(ps);
                        return(i);
                }
        }
        restore(ps);
        return(SYSERR);
}
```

Nqalloc searches sequentially through array *netqs* until it finds an unused entry (one with field *valid* set to *FALSE*). Before returning the index of the entry it finds, *nqalloc* carefully marks the entry valid and clears the process id as well as the UDP port field to prevent the UDP demultiplexing code from using the entry. Thus, *nqalloc* returns the index of a valid, but temporarily inactive entry in *netqs*.

11.4.3 Opening A Datagram Pseudo-Device

With the above three utility routines in place, it is possible to build the datagram master pseudo-device driver open routine, *dgmopen*. The master datagram
pseudo-device, usually named *INTERNET* is the one users specify in the call to
open. *Dgmopen* selects an unused datagram pseudo-device, sets it up for communication, and returns its device id, *D* to the caller. The caller uses *read* and *write*
operations on device *D* to carry out communication, and then calls *close* to make
device *D* available again. The code for *dgmopen* can be found in file *dgmopen.c*:

```
/* dgmopen.c - dgmopen */

#include <conf.h>
#include <kernel.h>
#include <network.h>

/*------------------------------------------------------------------------
 * dgmopen  -  open a fresh datagram pseudo device and return descriptor
 *------------------------------------------------------------------------
 */
dgmopen(devptr, forport, locport)
struct  devsw   *devptr;
char    *forport;
int     locport;
{
        struct  dgblk   *dgptr;
        struct  netq    *nqptr;
        int     slot;
        int     nq;
        int     i;
        char    ps;

        disable(ps);
        if ( (slot=dgalloc()) == SYSERR) {
                restore(ps);
                return(SYSERR);
        }
        dgptr = &dgtab[slot];
        if (locport == ANYLPORT)
                locport = udpnxtp();
        else {
                for (i=0 ; i<NETQS ; i++)
                        if (Net.netqs[i].valid &&
                                Net.netqs[i].uport == locport) {
```

```
                                  dgptr->dg_state = DG_FREE;
                                  restore(ps);
                                  return(SYSERR);
                          }
                  }
          if (dgparse(dgptr,forport)==SYSERR || (nq=nqalloc())==SYSERR ) {
                  dgptr->dg_state = DG_FREE;
                  restore(ps);
                  return(SYSERR);
          }
          nqptr = &Net.netqs[nq];
          nqptr->uport = dgptr->dg_lport = locport;
          dgptr->dg_xport = nqptr->xport;
          dgptr->dg_netq = nq;
          dgptr->dg_mode = DG_NMODE;
          restore(ps);
          return(dgptr->dg_dnum);
  }
```

Opening a datagram pseudo-device consists of calling *dgalloc* to allocate a free datagram device, using *dgparse* to help assign local and foreign port addresses, and allocating an entry in *netqs* that can be used to hold incoming datagrams. *Dgmopen* first uses *dgalloc* to find a free device. It then sets *dgptr* to the address of the device control block, and begins filling in fields. For example, if the user requested that the system choose a local UDP port id (by passing constant *ANYLPORT* in argument *locport*), then *dgmopen* calls *udpnxtp* to obtain a fresh port id, and uses the result to fill in field *dg_lport*.

Dgmopen searches the entire *netqs* array to make sure that the local datagram port it chose is not in use. Preventing duplicates is essential because our UDP input software demultiplexes on destination UDP port, it would have no way to distinguish among multiple destinations that use the same UDP port id.

Once *dgmopen* has checked for duplicate UPD ports ids, it can call *nqalloc* to allocate an entry in *netqs*. *Dgmopen* fills in the remainder of the device control block as well as the necessary fields of the *netqs* entry, and then returns the device number of the datagram pseudo-device to the caller.

11.4.4 Closing A Datagram Pseudo-Device

Once a user process finishes sending and receiving messages, it closes the datagram pseudo-device. Procedure *dgclose*, shown in file *dgclose.c*, carries out the operations necessary to close a datagram device and deallocate the corresponding entry in *netqs*. The code is straightforward.

```
/* dgclose.c - dgclose */

#include <conf.h>
#include <kernel.h>
#include <proc.h>
#include <network.h>


/*------------------------------------------------------------------------
 * dgclose  -  close a datagram pseudo device, making it available again
 *------------------------------------------------------------------------
 */
dgclose(devptr)
struct  devsw   *devptr;
{
        char    ps;
        struct  dgblk   *dgptr;
        struct  netq    *nqptr;
        int     nq;

        dgptr = (struct dgblk *) devptr->dvioblk;
        disable(ps);
        nq = dgptr->dg_netq;
        nqptr = &Net.netqs[nq];
        nqptr->valid = FALSE;
        nqptr->uport = -1;
        nqptr->pid = BADPID;
        dgptr->dg_state = DG_FREE;
        restore(ps);
        return(OK);
}
```

11.4.5 Data Transfer Operations

Before building code for data transfer operations, we must decide, in principle, how they operate. Remember that the datagram pseudo-device forms an interface between the user and the underlying network protocols. To provide the user with as much control over message exchange as possible, we will make *read* and *write* operations correspond to UDP message transfer. Each write operation on a datagram pseudo-device will cause one UDP message to be sent, and each read operation will transfer the contents of one incoming UDP message to the user. The device will not buffer output or retain unread message pieces. Thus, if the user does not read the entire UDP data field, the device will discard the remainder. Similarly, a user must understand that each call to *write* will transfer the data specified, even if it means that the UDP message consists of only one character.

11.4.6 Modes Of Transfer

Datagram devices operate in two basic modes: *normal* mode and *data* mode. In normal mode, the transfer operations *read* and *write* use xinugram format. In data mode, *read* and *write* copy only data to or from the user. When *dgmopen* allocates a datagram pseudo-device, it leaves the device in normal mode by setting the mode field to *DG_NMODE*. Like most devices in Xinu, our driver uses the *control* operation to permit users to change the driver parameters. Thus, the user program must call *control* to change from normal mode to data mode.

In normal mode, input produces the expected result but output poses a problem. If the arguments to *dgmopen* specify a particular foreign IP address and foreign UDP port number, these may be present in the datagram device control block. However, a particular xinugram may also specify a foreign IP address and UDP port id. To which foreign address should the outgoing datagram be sent? We will follow the simple rule:

> *In normal mode, the foreign address specified when opening a datagram device overrides the address specified in the xinugram header.*

Thus, the address in the xinugram header will be used only if no address was specified when the device was opened.

The datagram devices can also operate in *data mode*, which means that they transfer only data to or from the user. A datagram pseudo-device cannot be used for writing in data mode unless it has been opened with a specific foreign address. Reading in data mode causes the device to transfer to the user only the data portion of the next UDP message it receives.

11.4.7 Implementation Of Datagram Write

Procedure *dgwrite*, shown in file *dgwrite.c*, accepts a xinugram from the user and writes it according to the address selection rule stated above.

```
/* dgwrite.c - dgwrite */

#include <conf.h>
#include <kernel.h>
#include <network.h>

/*------------------------------------------------------------------------
 * dgwrite - write one datagram to a datagram protocol pseudo-device
 *------------------------------------------------------------------------
 */
dgwrite(devptr, buff, len)
struct  devsw   *devptr;
struct  xgram   *buff;
int     len;
{
        struct  epacket *packet;
        struct  ip      *ipptr;
        struct  udp     *udpptr;
        struct  dgblk   *dgptr;
        int     dstport;
        char    *dstIP;

        if (len < 0 || len > UMAXLEN)
                return(SYSERR);
        dgptr = (struct dgblk *) devptr->dvioblk;
        packet = (struct epacket *) getbuf(Net.netpool);
        ipptr = (struct ip *) packet->ep_data;
        udpptr = (struct udp *) ipptr->i_data;
        dstport = dgptr->dg_fport;
        dstIP = (char *) dgptr->dg_faddr;
        if ( (dgptr->dg_mode & DG_NMODE) != 0) {
                if (dstport == 0) {
                        dstport = buff->xg_fport;
                        dstIP = (char *) buff->xg_faddr;
                }
                blkcopy(udpptr->u_data, buff->xg_data, len);
        } else {
                if ( dstport == 0) {
                        freebuf(packet);
                        return(SYSERR);
                }
                blkcopy(udpptr->u_data, buff, len);
        }
        return( udpsend(dstIP, dstport, dgptr->dg_lport, packet, len) );
}
```

Writing consists of allocating a buffer to hold the frame, copying data into the UDP data area, and calling *udpsend* to send the frame. *Dgwrite* uses fields *dg_faddr* and *dg_fport* in the device control block as the destination address. If they do not contain a valid address, normal mode output extracts the destination address from the xinugram header.

11.4.8 Implementation Of Datagram Read

Procedure *dgread*, shown in file *dgread.c*, implements the *read* operation for datagram devices. Reading is complicated by a timeout mechanism that allows a process to limit the time it waits for a datagram. Many protocols use timeout to recover from errors or lost transmissions; building it into the datagram mechanism is much more efficient than using additional processes for timing.

```
/* dgread.c - dgread */

#include <conf.h>
#include <kernel.h>
#include <proc.h>
#include <network.h>


/*------------------------------------------------------------------------
 * dgread - read one datagram from a datagram protocol pseudo-device
 *------------------------------------------------------------------------
 */
dgread(devptr, buff, len)
struct  devsw   *devptr;
struct  xgram   *buff;
int     len;
{
        struct  dgblk   *dgptr;
        struct  epacket *packet;
        struct  udp     *udpptr;
        struct  ip      *ipptr;
        struct  netq    *nqptr;
        int     datalen;
        char    ps;

        disable(ps);
        dgptr = (struct dgblk *)devptr->dvioblk;
        if (dgptr->dg_mode & DG_TMODE) {
                nqptr = &Net.netqs[dgptr->dg_netq];
                if ( !isbadpid(nqptr->pid) ) {
                        restore(ps);
                        return(SYSERR);
                }
                if (pcount(dgptr->dg_xport) <= 0) {
                        nqptr->pid = getpid();
                        if (recvtim(DG_TIME) == TIMEOUT) {
                                nqptr->pid = BADPID;
                                restore(ps);
                                return(TIMEOUT);
                        }
                }
        }
        packet = (struct epacket *) preceive(dgptr->dg_xport);

        /* copy data into user's buffer & set length */
```

```
ipptr = (struct ip *) packet->ep_data;
udpptr = (struct udp *)ipptr->i_data;
datalen = net2hs(udpptr->u_udplen) - UHLEN;
if (dgptr->dg_mode & DG_NMODE) {
        if ( (datalen+XGHLEN) > len) {
                freebuf(packet);
                restore(ps);
                return(SYSERR);
        }
        blkcopy(buff->xg_faddr, ipptr->i_src, IPLEN);
        buff->xg_fport = net2hs(udpptr->u_sport);
        buff->xg_lport = dgptr->dg_lport;
        blkcopy(buff->xg_data, udpptr->u_data, datalen);
} else {
        if (datalen > len)
                datalen = len;
        blkcopy(buff, udpptr->u_data, datalen);
}
freebuf(packet);
restore(ps);
return(datalen);
}
```

As the code shows, *dgread* provides timeout with the timed receive primitive described in Chapter 5. When the mode field of the datagram pseudo-device control block has bit *DG_TMODE* set, all reads are timed. To time a read, *dgread* places the id of the executing process, *p*, in the appropriate *netqs* entry, and then calls *recvtim*. If a datagram arrives, the network input process passes it to procedure *ip_in*, which both enqueues the datagram and sends a message to process *p*. So, the call to *recvtim* returns *OK* if a datagram arrived, and *TIMEOUT* if the timer expired. If the timer expires, *dgread* returns *TIMEOUT* to its caller.

Timeout should be independent of the form in which the user process receives data. So, unlike normal mode and data mode, which are mutually exclusive, the timeout mode bit, *DG_TMODE*, can be set or cleared independently. The duration of the timeout, however, is fixed across all datagram pseudo-devices by constant *DG_TIME* (an exercise suggests relaxing this restriction).

If *dgread* acquires a datagram, it must extract the message. Like *dgwrite*, *dgread* honors the control block mode field to determine whether to deposit a xinugram or only the data in the user's buffer. In either case, *dgread* verifies that the information fits in the buffer, and then copies the appropriate information from fields in the IP datagram. Finally, *dgread* calls *freebuf* to return the network buffer to its buffer pool.

The code clearly shows the copy boundary between the network protocol software and user processes. Note that only the datagram pseudo-device driver accepts network buffers, and it carefully returns them once they have been emptied. User processes receive a copy of information from network buffers, but never the buffers themselves.

11.4.9 Datagram Device Control Functions

How can the user specify the mode for a particular datagram pseudo-device? Of course, we could allow user programs to examine and change the device control block. However, such access is inconvenient. Since we have cast the datagram interface in the device paradigm, it makes sense to use the *control* function to handle chores like changing mode.

Procedure *dgcntl*, shown below in file *dgcntl.c*, provides a simple mechanism for mode control.

```
/* dgcntl.c - dgcntl */

#include <conf.h>
#include <kernel.h>
#include <network.h>


/*------------------------------------------------------------------------
 * dgcntl  -  control function for datagram pseudo-devices
 *------------------------------------------------------------------------
 */
dgcntl(devptr, func, arg)
struct  devsw   *devptr;
int     func;
int     arg;
{
        struct  dgblk   *dgptr;
        int     freebuf();
        char    ps;
        int     ret;

        disable(ps);
        dgptr = (struct dgblk *)devptr->dvioblk;
        ret = OK;
        switch (func) {

                case DG_SETMODE:            /* set mode bits */
                        dgptr->dg_mode = arg;
                        break;
```

```
                    case DG_CLEAR:                  /* clear queued packets */
                            preset(dgptr->dg_xport, freebuf);
                            break;

              default:
                            ret = SYSERR;
        }
        restore(ps);
        return(ret);
}
```

Dgcntl recognizes only two operations: *DG_SETMODE*, which allows the user to set the mode field in the device control block, and *DG_CLEAR*, which allows the user to clear all datagrams that have arrived for a given device. (The exercises suggest several improvements to this code).

11.5 Datagram Pseudo-Device Interface Configuration

We have examined the details of procedures that comprise the datagram pseudo-device interface. To help see how the procedures fit together, consider how they are declared in the Xinu configuration file:

```
/* Datagram interface (master pseudo device) */
dgm:
        on ETH           -i ionull        -o dgmopen       -c ioerr
                         -r ioerr         -w ioerr         -s ioerr
                         -n dgmcntl       -g ioerr         -p ioerr
                         -iint ioerr      -oint ioerr      -csr 0
                         -ivec 0          -ovec 0


/* Datagram "connection"  (pseudo-device returned by dgopen) */
dg:
        on ETH           -i dginit        -o ioerr         -c dgclose
                         -r dgread        -w dgwrite       -s ioerr
                         -n dgcntl        -g ioerr         -p ioerr
                         -iint ioerr      -oint ioerr      -csr 0
                         -ivec 0          -ovec 0
%
/* Datagram network interface (master pseudo-device) */

INTERNET         is dgm  on ETH


/* Pseudo-device slots for datagram "connections" */

DGRAM1           is dg   on ETH
DGRAM2           is dg   on ETH
DGRAM3           is dg   on ETH
DGRAM4           is dg   on ETH
```

The device *INTERNET* is a master datagram device for which only the *open* operation is defined. Opening *INTERNET* produces the device id of a *DGRAMi* device, which can be read or written to receive or send datagrams.

11.6 Summary

Although network software must follow standard message formats when sending packets, the interface between the network software and user programs is operating system specific. This chapter has considered the design of a datagram interface for Xinu that uses a pseudo-device. The interface defines a copy boundary below which the system uses frame buffers for all packets, and above which user programs send and receive messages. Our interface operates in one of two modes based on a mode field in the device control block. The mode field allows processes to choose whether to send and receive messages in xinugram format or in data-only format. To help minimize overhead when timing datagram reads, the datagram input primitive has a timeout mechanism built into it.

FOR FURTHER STUDY

Many operating systems handle the general problem of multiplexing object access among processes with a method similar to the one described here. The 4.3BSD version of UNIX from Berkeley incorporates a mechanism called *sockets* that allows a user to specify a peer and then send and receive messages. The V-system (described in Cheriton [1984]) illustrates another popular alternative in which operating system message passing primitives can be used for either local or remote communication. In sharp contrast, Hoare [1978] gives a programming language notation for message-passing primitives called *CSP*.

EXERCISES

11.1 Explain the circumstances under which *dgmopen* can return an error when called with arguments *ANYFPORT* and *ANYLPORT*.

11.2 Compute an upper bound on the number of network buffers required for your local version of Xinu by adding up the number of buffers that could be enqueued and the maximum number in use by the network input process. Remember to count ICMP echo requests and low-level protocols like ARP.

11.3 Modify the datagram pseudo-device driver to allow the timeout to vary from device to device.

11.4 Modify the *DG_SETMODE* function in *dgcntl* to check for valid modes.

11.5 Add new control functions to *dgcntl* that permit a user to change modes but do not permit a user to store arbitrary values in the mode field.

11.6 What happens when two processes attempt to concurrently read from a timed datagram device? What happens when the device is not timed?

11.7 Compare the Berkeley 4.3BSD UNIX *socket* interface to the Xinu datagram pseudo-device interface.

12

The Client-Server
Interaction Paradigm

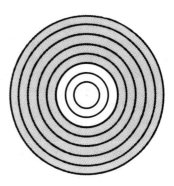

12.1 Introduction

Our design of internet protocol software culminated in the datagram pseudo-device interface discussed in the previous chapter. The primitives described there permit a process to specify a foreign destination (*open*), send a message (*write*), and receive a response (*read*). Although we have said much about internet protocols and the mechanisms that processes use to interact with them, we have avoided discussing how the internet should, or should not, be used.

This chapter examines, in some detail, examples of processes that profit from cooperative use of an internet. While the examples are both practical and interesting, they do not comprise the main focus. Instead, focus rests on the pattern of interaction among the communicating processes. The primary pattern of interaction, known as the *client−server* paradigm, forms the basis of most network communication; it is fundamental because it helps us understand the foundation upon which distributed algorithms are built. Throughout the chapter, each example further clarifies the relationship between client and server, paving the way for the next chapters that use the client−server pattern in a remote file system.

12.2 The Client-Server Model

The term *server* applies to any process that offers a service that can be reached over the network. Servers accept requests that arrive over the network, perform their service, and return the result to the requester. Usually, each request arrives in a single internet packet.

An executing process becomes a *client* when it sends a request to a server and waits for a result. Because the client-server model is a convenient and natural extension of interprocess communication on a single machine, many programs adopt it.

Servers can perform simple or complex tasks. For example, a *time-of-day server* merely returns the current time whenever a client sends it a packet. A *file server* receives requests to perform operations that store or retrieve information from a file; the server performs the operation, and returns the result.

Because a server is a process, it can execute on any computing system that supports internet communication. Thus, the server process for a particular service may execute on a timesharing system along with other processes. Multiple servers may offer the same service, even if they execute on multiple machines. In fact, it is common to replicate copies of a given server onto physically independent machines to increase reliability. If a machine's primary purpose is to support a particular server process, the term "server" may be applied to the machine as well as to the server process. Thus, one hears statements like "that machine is the file server".

12.3 UDP Echo Server

Our examination of client–server interaction begins with a simple service, namely, UDP datagram echo. The mechanics of an echo-server are straightforward. At one site, a UDP *echo server process* begins by establishing a UDP port id that it will use to accept echo requests. We call this the UDP *echo port*. The echo server process waits for a datagram to arrive at the echo port, reverses the source and destination addresses (including internet addresses and UDP port ids), and then returns the datagram to its original sender. At another site, a UDP *echo-client* process invokes the echo server by sending it a datagram and awaiting the reply. The client expects to receive back exactly the same data as it sent.

Who would use an echo service? Certainly not an average user. However, systems programmers who design, implement, measure, or modify network protocol software often use echo servers in testing. Echo servers can also be used to determine if it is possible to connect to a remote machine.

12.4 Echo Server Implementation

The datagram interface from Chapter 11 makes implementation of an echo server process especially easy, as shown by the code in file *udpecho.c*:

```
/* udpecho.c - udpecho */

#include <conf.h>
#include <kernel.h>
#include <network.h>

#define MAXECHO 600            /* maximum size of echoed datagram   */
static   char     buff[MAXECHO];  /* here because the stack may be small */

/*------------------------------------------------------------------------
 * udpecho  -  UDP echo server process (runs forever in background)
 *------------------------------------------------------------------------
 */
PROCESS udpecho()
{
        int    dev, len;

        if ( (dev=open(INTERNET, ANYFPORT, UECHO)) == SYSERR) {
                printf("udpecho: open fails\n");
                return(SYSERR);
        }
        while ( TRUE ) {
                len = read(dev, buff, MAXECHO);
                write(dev, buff, len);
        }
}
```

The server process must open a datagram pseudo-device that accepts incoming echo requests, and then respond to each incoming datagram. What UDP port id should it use? Fortunately, the DARPA UDP protocol definition reserves some port ids; one of them is reserved for the echo service. In the code, constant *UECHO* gives the reserved port id for the echo service. Its definition can be found, along with other predefined UDP port ids, in file *udp.h* (Chapter 9).

Because the echo server wants to accept echo requests from any source, it specifies *ANYFPORT* as the foreign address when calling *open*. Recall from Chapter 11 that *open* leaves the datagram pseudo-device in normal mode, so *read* and *write* operations transfer xinugrams to and from the user. Thus, each call to *read* creates a xinugram in the buffer, *buff*, complete with a header that includes the foreign sender's internet address and UDP port id.

The utility of the xinugram format should now be clear. If our datagram interface created headers with *source* and *destination* fields, the UDP echo process would need to reverse the fields to send the message back. Having *foreign* and *local* fields in the header eliminates the need to reverse source and destination. You might suspect that using *foreign* and *local* just moves the problem into the device driver. We know, however, that the device driver must copy the fields anyway, because it needs to assemble a UDP datagram. So, using the *foreign* and *local* format costs no more than using the *source* and *destination* format.

12.5 Time And Date Service

Now that we understand how a server operates, we can examine a client in more detail. Instead of concentrating only on the client code in isolation, we will examine several pieces that fit together to solve an important problem. The problem is to have the operating system provide the date and time-of-day on a machine that has no time-of-day hardware clock.

Many systems solve the problem with a real-time clock. They ask the user to set the time and date, and then measure time passing by counting ticks of the real-time clock. Later, when a user process asks for the date or time, the system adds the accumulated ticks to the time originally specified.

Now consider computing the time and date on a computer that connects to a network. If any machine on the network knows the correct time, it should be possible for all of them to learn it automatically by exchanging messages.

At first, it might seem that if the operating system had access to an internet it could obtain the date and time from a server whenever the need arose. Using an internet for each time or date request introduces long processing delays, and makes the operating system totally dependent on the server. To reduce such dependency, we will use a compromise in which the operating system obtains the current date and time from a server at system startup, but then maintains the correct time locally.

12.5.1 Representation For The Date And Time

How should an operating system maintain the date and time-of-day? Ideally, it should have a time-of-day hardware clock that operates independent of the CPU. When the machine does not have time-of-day hardware, the operating system can simulate it by counting ticks of its real-time clock.

In practice, most operating systems count seconds instead of clock ticks. Because many real-time ticks occur each second, counting ticks produces larger integers than counting seconds. Keeping the time-of-day accurate to the nearest second suffices for most applications, and permits a convenient representation.

One useful representation stores the time and date as the count of seconds since an epoch date. For example, UNIX uses the zeroth second of January 1, 1970 as its epoch date, while the DARPA Internet protocols use the zeroth second of January 1, 1900 as an epoch date. Both use 32-bit integers to store dates, a representation that accommodates any date in the near future.

Keeping the date as the time in seconds since an epoch makes the representation compact, and allows easy comparison. It ties together the date and time of day, and makes it possible to measure time by incrementing a single binary integer.

12.5.2 Maintaining The Time-of-Day In Xinu

In Xinu, procedure *clkint* serves as the real-time clock interrupt dispatcher that is called for each clock interrupt. Modifying it to maintain the time of day is trivial. It consists of introducing global variables *count10* and *clktime*. Variable *count10* converts Xinu's ten-per-second tick rate into a one-per-second increment rate. *Count10* cycles from ten down to zero, counting 10 clock ticks before taking action. On the tenth tick, *clkint* resets *count10* and increments the time-of-day counter, *clktime*.

Besides the addition of code to increment *clktime* once per second, *clkint* remains unaltered. The entire procedure, found in file *clkint.s*, has been included here.

```
/* clkint.s -  clkint */


/*------------------------------------------------------------------------
/* clkint  --  real-time clock interrupt service routine
/*------------------------------------------------------------------------
        .globl  _clkint
_clkint:
        dec     _count6             / Is this the 6th interrupt?
        bgt     clret               /  no => return
        mov     $6,_count6          /  yes=> reset counter&continue
        dec     _count10            / Is this 10th tick?
        bgt     clckdef             /  no => process tick
        mov     $10.,_count10       /  yes=> reset counter&continue
        add     $1,2+_clktime       / increment time-of-day clock
        adc     _clktime
clckdef:
        tst     _defclk             / Are clock ticks deferred?
        beq     notdef              /  no => go process this tick
        inc     _clkdiff            /  yes=> count in clkdiff and
        rtt                         /          return quickly
notdef:
        tst     _slnempty           / Is sleep queue nonempty?
        beq     clpreem             /  no => go process preemption
        dec     *_sltop             /  yes=> decrement delta key
        bgt     clpreem             /        on first process,
        mov     r0,-(sp)            /        calling wakeup if
        mov     r1,-(sp)            /        it reaches zero
        jsr     pc,_wakeup          /        (interrupt routine
        mov     (sp)+,r1            /         saves & restores r0
        mov     (sp)+,r0            /         and r1; C doesn't)
clpreem:
        dec     _preempt            / Decrement preemption counter
        bgt     clret               /   and call resched if it
        mov     r0,-(sp)            /   reaches zero
        mov     r1,-(sp)            /        (As before, interrupt
        jsr     pc,_resched         /        routine must save &
        mov     (sp)+,r1            /        restore r0 and r1
        mov     (sp)+,r0            /        because C doesn't)
clret:
        rtt                         / Return from interrupt
```

12.5.3 Local And Universal Time

When a user process asks for the time, the operating system delivers a single integer that represents the seconds that have elapsed since the epoch. What should we choose as the epoch, and exactly what time zone does the count represent? We have chosen to follow UNIX, making the epoch January 1, 1970. As for time zone, at least two representations are convenient. Most programs run locally; they prefer a system that reports the local time. When systems communicate across great distances, they need to agree on a standard time zone to keep values for date and time comparable. Usually, the time zone is selected to be GMT, now called *universal time*.

Although we must decide whether *clktime* represents local or universal time, we can accommodate users' needs by building two interface procedures that return the date. One procedure, *gettime*, takes as an argument the address of a long (32-bit) integer, and stores in that integer the local time as a count of seconds since the epoch. Another procedure, *getutim*, also takes the address of a long integer as an argument, but stores in that long integer a count representing the current universal time (GMT).

The code for *gettime*, shown in file *gettime.c*, reveals that *gettime* obtains the universal time from *getutim*, and then uses procedure *ut2ltim* to convert from universal time to local time.

```
/* gettime.c - gettime */

#include <conf.h>
#include <kernel.h>
#include <date.h>

/*------------------------------------------------------------------------
 * gettime - get local time in seconds past Jan 1, 1970
 *------------------------------------------------------------------------
 */
SYSCALL gettime(timvar)
long    *timvar;
{
        long    now;

        if (getutim(&now) == SYSERR)
                return(SYSERR);
        *timvar = ut2ltim(now);                     /* adjust for timezone */
        return(OK);
}
```

In this version, function *ut2ltim* is defined in file *date.h* along with several constants that pertain to date manipulation:

```
/* date.h - net2xt, xt2net, isleap, ut2ltim */

/* Xinu stores time as seconds past Jan 1, 1970 (UNIX format), with      */
/* 1 being 1 second into Jan. 1, 1970, GMT (universal time).  The        */
/* Internet uses seconds past Jan 1, 1900 (also GMT or universal time)   */

#define net2xt(x)       ((x)-2208988800L)  /* convert net-to-xinu time   */
#define xt2net(x)       ((x)+2208988800L)  /* convert xinu-to-net time   */

/* Days in months and month names used to format a date */

struct  datinfo {
        int     dt_msize[12];
        char    *dt_mnam[12];
};

extern  struct  datinfo Dat;

/* Constants for converting time to month/day/year/hour/minute/second    */

#define isleap(x)       ((x)%4==0)       /* leap year? (1970-1999)        */
#define SECPERDY        (60L*60L*24L)    /* one day in seconds            */
#define SECPERHR        (60L*60L)        /* one hour in seconds           */
#define SECPERMN        (60L)            /* one minute in seconds         */

/* date doesn't understand daylight savings time (it was built in        */
/*      Indiana where we're smart enough to realize that renumbering     */
/*      doesn't save anything). However, the local time zone can be      */
/*      set to EST, CST, MST,or PST.                                     */

#define ZONE_EST        5               /* Eastern Standard time is 5     */
#define ZONE_CST        6               /*  hours west of England        */
#define ZONE_MST        7
#define ZONE_PST        8
#define TIMEZONE        ZONE_EST         /* timezone for this system      */

/* In-line procedure that converts universal time to local time          */

#define ut2ltim(x)      ((x)-TIMEZONE*SECPERHR)

#ifndef TSERVER
#define TSERVER         "128.10.2.3:37"
#endif
```

12.5.4 Obtaining The Time

Procedure *getutim* contains the network client code used to initialize the date. Usually, it takes as an argument the address of a long integer, and copies into that long integer the system's internal time counter, *clktime*. However, *getutim* also uses the network to initialize *clktime* if needed.

To understand *getutim* we should first look at the clock initialization routine, *clkinit*, to see that it starts the local time counter *clktime* at zero:

```
/* clkinit.c - clkinit */

#include <conf.h>
#include <kernel.h>
#include <sleep.h>

/* real-time clock variables and sleeping process queue pointers        */

#ifdef  RTCLOCK
int     count6;                 /* counts in 60ths of a second 6-0       */
int     count10;                /* counts in 10ths of a second 10-0      */
int     clmutex;                /* mutual exclusion for time-of-day      */
long    clktime;                /* current time in seconds since 1/1/70  */
int     defclk;                 /* non-zero, then deferring clock count  */
int     clkdiff;                /* deferred clock ticks                  */
int     slnempty;               /* FALSE if the sleep queue is empty     */
int     *sltop;                 /* address of key part of top entry in   */
                                /* the sleep queue if slnempty==TRUE     */
int     clockq;                 /* head of queue of sleeping processes   */
int     preempt;                /* preemption counter. Current process   */
                                /* is preempted when it reaches zero;    */
                                /* set in resched; counts in ticks       */
int     clkruns;                /* set TRUE iff clock exists by setclkr   */
#else
int     clkruns = FALSE;        /* no clock configured; be sure sleep    */
#endif                          /*   doesn't wait forever                */

/*
 *-------------------------------------------------------------------------
 * clkinit - initialize the clock and sleep queue (called at startup)
 *-------------------------------------------------------------------------
 */
clkinit()
{
        int *vector;
```

```
        vector = (int *) CVECTOR;      /* set up interrupt vector       */
        *vector++ = clkint;
        *vector = DISABLE;
        setclkr();
        preempt = QUANTUM;             /* initial time quantum          */
        count6 = 6;                    /* 60ths of a sec. counter       */
        count10 = 10;                  /* 10ths of a sec. counter       */
        clmutex = screate(1);          /* semaphore for tod clock       */
        clktime = 0L;                  /* initially a low number        */
        slnempty = FALSE;              /* initially, no process asleep  */
        clkdiff = 0;                   /* zero deferred ticks           */
        defclk = 0;                    /* clock is not deferred         */
        clockq = newqueue();           /* allocate clock queue in q     */
}
```

Understanding *getutim* also depends on remembering that the network output process calls it to force initialization of the clock just after startup. Thus, we expect the first call to occur when *clktime* has an extremely small value.

As shown below, *getutim* uses the value in the local clock counter, *clktime*, to determine whether it should obtain the time locally or remotely. If *clktime* has a small value, *getutim* becomes a client of the network time service, obtaining and storing the current time. Otherwise, it assumes that the current value of *clktime* is accurate.

```
/* getutim.c - getutim */

#include <conf.h>
#include <kernel.h>
#include <sleep.h>
#include <date.h>
#include <network.h>


/*------------------------------------------------------------------------
 * getutim  --  obtain time in seconds past Jan 1, 1970, ut (gmt)
 *------------------------------------------------------------------------
 */
SYSCALL getutim(timvar)
long    *timvar;
{
        int     dev;
        int     len;
        int     ret;
        long    now;
```

```
long     utnow;
char     *msg = "No time server response";

wait(clmutex);
ret = OK;
if (clktime < SECPERHR) {         /* assume small numbers invalid */
        if ((dev=open(INTERNET, TSERVER, ANYLPORT)) == SYSERR ||
                control(dev,DG_SETMODE,DG_TMODE|DG_DMODE) == SYSERR) {
                panic(msg);
                ret = SYSERR;
        }
        write(dev, msg, 2);       /* send junk packet to prompt */
        if (read(dev,&utnow,4) != 4) {
                panic(msg);
                ret = SYSERR;
        } else
                clktime = net2xt( net2hl(utnow) );
        close(dev);
}
*timvar = clktime;
signal(clmutex);
return(ret);
}
```

The code, found in file *getutim.c*, reveals how a client of the standard UDP time server operates. To begin, *getutim* forms a string that contains the IP address of the host from which the service is sought, and UDP port id assigned to the date service. Constant *TSERVER* gives the server's IP address and the time server's UDP port id. *Getutim* opens a datagram pseudo-device for the destination, specifying that it is willing to use any local port id.

Once it has opened a datagram pseudo-device, *getutim* calls *control* to change the device into data mode and timeout mode. If either opening the device or setting the mode fails, *getutim* calls *panic*.

Once the datagram pseudo-device has been established, *getutim* performs the actions required of a UDP timeserver client. It sends an empty datagram to the server, and then immediately calls *read* to await the reply. Sending a datagram to a time server is equivalent to making a request for the current time. The server responds by returning a datagram that contains the current time. If the client receives a response, it converts the binary value from network byte order into the local host byte order, then converts the resulting time from network epoch to the host's epoch, and finally stores the result in *clktime*.

The client code in *getutim* uses a mutual exclusion semaphore to prevent multiple processes from sending to the server simultaneously. The semaphore, which has initial count of 1, allows at most one process to enter *getutim*. Thus, at most one process on a given machine will interact with the time server at any time.

12.6 RARP Client

So far, all our examples of client-server interaction require the client to know the complete address of the server. The RARP protocol from Chapter 5 provides an example of client-server interaction with a slightly different twist. Recall that when a diskless machine boots, it uses RARP to find its internet address. Instead of having the client communicate directly with a server, RARP clients broadcast their requests. One or more machines executing RARP server processes respond, each returning a packet that answers the query.

We have already seen both pieces of the RARP client. A process calls procedure *sndrarp* to broadcast a RARP request and then wait for a response. The network input process calls procedure *rarp_in* when a response arrives. What remains to be seen is how the operating system calls these underlying mechanisms in the first place.

Several designs are possible. We have chosen to build a procedure, *getaddr*, that returns to its caller the local machine's internet address. *Getaddr* becomes a RARP client, if necessary. Like the date mechanism built earlier, *getaddr* maintains the internet address locally once it has been acquired. Thus, the first call to *getaddr* invokes RARP, but successive calls do not. Here is the code:

```
/* getaddr.c - getaddr */

#include <conf.h>
#include <kernel.h>
#include <network.h>

/*------------------------------------------------------------------------
 *  getaddr  -  obtain this system's complete address (IP address)
 *------------------------------------------------------------------------
 */
SYSCALL getaddr(address)
IPaddr  address;
{
        wait (Arp.rarpsem);
        if ( !Net.mavalid)
                sndrarp();
        signal(Arp.rarpsem);

        if ( !Net.mavalid)
                return(SYSERR);
        blkcopy(address, Net.myaddr, IPLEN);
        return(OK);
}
```

A companion to *getaddr*, procedure *getnet*, returns only the network portion of the machine's internet address (i.e., the internet address with the host part set to zero). It can be useful when comparing internet addresses for routing purposes. File *getnet.c* contains the code:

```
/* getnet.c - getnet */

#include <conf.h>
#include <kernel.h>
#include <network.h>

/*------------------------------------------------------------------------
 * getnet  -  obtain the network portion of this system's IP address
 *------------------------------------------------------------------------
 */
SYSCALL getnet(address)
IPaddr  address;
{
        if ( !Net.mavalid && getaddr(address) == SYSERR)
                        return(SYSERR);
        blkcopy(address, Net.mynet, IPLEN);
        return(OK);
}
```

At startup, *netinit* calls *getaddr* after calling *gettime*. Knowing that each of these acts as a network client the first time it is called should explain why *netinit* invokes them.

12.7 The ICMP Echo Server And Client-Server Model

Chapter 8 discussed ICMP, the DARPA Internet Control Message Protocol, and showed software that answered ICMP echo requests. In a sense, the ICMP software follows the client-server model. A client process sends an echo request and awaits a response. However, there is no identifiable server process to answer the request. Instead, the network input and output processes cooperate to handle the request and response. The network input process calls procedure *ip_in*, which then calls procedure *icmp_in*. Once a response has been generated, *icmp_in* passes it to the network output process for transmission.

Many client-server implementations operate like the ICMP echo mechanism. Either the lower-half of the network device driver or the network input process formulates a response to a query. Depending on the system, it may be possible to enqueue output directly at interrupt time without using an output process.

12.8 Alternatives To The Client-Server Model

What are the alternatives to client-server interaction, and when might they be attractive? This section gives at least one answer to those questions by showing an *information-propagation* style of interaction.

In the client-server model, processes usually act as clients when they need information. As the RARP example shows, it may be wise to cache answers to improve the efficiency of later queries. Thinking about the date example shows that it may even be wise to expend local computational resources to maintain the cache once an initial value has been obtained over the network.

Caching improves the performance of client-server interaction in cases where the recent history of queries is a good indicator of future use. In the RARP server, a given machine always emits the same query (to find its own address). Furthermore, the answer to RARP queries is unlikely to change except over long periods of time (i.e., when the machine is moved to a new site or to a new network). Thus, the answer can be cached to avoid using the network for successive requests.

Although caching improves performance, it does not change the essence of client-sever interaction. The essence lies in our assumption that processing must be driven by demand. We have assumed that a process executes until it needs information, and then acts as a client to obtain the needed information. Taking a demand-driven view of the world is natural, and arises from experience. Caching helps alleviate the cost of obtaining information by lowering the retrieval cost for all except the first process that makes a request.

How can we lower the cost of information retrieval for the first request? In a distributed system, it may be possible to have concurrent background activities that collect and propagate information *before* any particular user requests it, making retrieval costs low even for the initial request. More important, precollecting information can allow a given system to continue executing even though other machines or the networks connecting them fail.

12.9 A Machine Status Service

As an example, consider a machine status service like that reported by the *ruptime* command shown in Chapter 1. When invoked, *ruptime* reports the CPU load and time since system startup for each machine on the network. We want to design a mechanism that supports an efficient version of *ruptime*. In the client-server model, each machine would run a status server that answered requests by giving that machine's status load. To find a machine's status, the user would invoke a client that had to send a message to the server, wait for a response, and then print the information for the user.

Polling a machine's server could take longer than a user is willing to wait, especially under heavy network load; polling all the machine servers one at a time is likely to be intolerable. More to the point, if a machine is down, no information would be available at all. One way to avoid taking too long is to have machines propagate and collect status information continuously, so that a user could quickly find the most recent status information without using the network at all. We refer to this style of interaction as an *information-propagation* system.

12.10 Implementation Of The Machine Status Service

12.10.1 Rwho Packet Format

Having described the basic ideas of our status service, we turn attention to implementation details. The basic protocol and packet format come from 4.3BSD UNIX, where it is called the *rwho protocol* (*rwho* stands for Remote Who, and is the UNIX command users invoke to find the names of users who are logged into various machines on the network). File *rwho.h* contains the declarations of *rwho* packet formats and the global data structure used to hold information:

```
/* rwho.h */

/* Data structures and constants for RWHO packet processing */

#define RMACLEN         16              /* length of machine name       */
#define RWNLOAD         3               /* number of "load averages"    */
#define RWNLEN          8               /* name length in rwho packet   */
#define RWCSIZ          8               /* size of rwho cache           */
#define RWMAXP          600             /* max packet length accepted   */
#define RWMINP          60              /* size of rwho pac, no users   */
#define RWDELAY         60              /* delay for output in seconds  */
#define RWCDOWN         120             /* consider down if this old    */
#define RWMAXDT         (60L*60L*24L*7L) /* maximum down time before     */
                                        /* machine removed from cache   */
#define RWIN            rwhoind         /* Rwho input process code      */
#define RWISTK          300             /* Rwho input process stack     */
#define RWIPRIO         20              /* Rwho input process priority  */
#define RWINAM          "rwho-in"       /* Rwho input process name      */
#define RWIARGS         0               /* Rwho input process arguments */
#define RWOUT           rwhod           /* Rwho output process code     */
#define RWOSTK          300             /* Rwho output process stack    */
#define RWOPRIO         20              /* Rwho output process priority */
#define RWONAM          "rwhod"         /* Rwho output process name      */
#define RWOARGS         0               /* Rwho output process arguments*/

extern  int     RWIN(), RWOUT();

struct  rwent   {                       /* rwho cache entry             */
        char    rwmach[RMACLEN];        /* Name of machine that is up   */
        long    rwboot;                 /* when machine was booted      */
        long    rwlast;                 /* Local time last packet recvd */
        long    rwslast;                /* Sender's time in last packet */
        int     rwload[3];              /* Load averages as in uptime   */
        int     rwusers;                /* Number of users logged in    */
};

struct  rwinfo  {                       /* all rwho information         */
        struct  rwent   rwcache[RWCSIZ];/* cache of received info       */
        int     rwnent;                 /* number of valid cache entries*/
        Bool    rwsend;                 /* send out rwho packets?       */
        long    rwbtime;                /* time I was booted            */
        char    rbuf[RWMAXP];           /* to hold input packets        */
};

extern  struct  rwinfo  Rwho;
```

```
/* Declarations that describe the format of rwho packets on the net    */

struct  rwhopac {                         /* format of rwho packet       */
        char    rw_vers;                  /* protocol version number     */
        char    rw_type;                  /* packet type                 */
        char    rw_pad[2];
        long    rw_sndtim;                /* sender's time stamp         */
        long    rw_rtim;                  /* receiver's time stamp       */
        char    rw_host[32];              /* sending host's name         */
        long    rw_load[3];               /* load averages               */
        long    rw_btim;                  /* boot time of sender         */
        struct  rw_who  {
                char    rw_tty[RWNLEN]; /* UNIX tty name                 */
                char    rw_nam[RWNLEN]; /* user's name                   */
                long    rw_ton;         /* time user logged on           */
                long    rw_idle;        /* user's idle time              */
        } rw_rww[1024 / sizeof(struct rw_who)];
};


#define RWVERSION       1                 /* protocol version number     */
#define RWSTATUS        1                 /* host status                 */
```

Structure *rwent* describes entries in a local table of status information. Each entry corresponds to one machine on the network, and contains that machine's name, boot time, time of last information update, CPU load average, and number of users. The load averages represent the average CPU load over the last five seconds, the last five minutes, and the last 15 minutes.

Structure *rwhopac* describes the format of an *rwho* packet as it travels across the network encapsulated in a UDP datagram. Most of the information is expected. The host specifies its name, load, boot time, and fills in array *rw_rww*, giving, for each active user, the user's name, the name of the terminal on which that user logged in, and the idle time on that terminal. Field *rw_rtim* is reserved for the receiver's time stamp; the sender does not fill it in.

The remaining declarations in *rwho.h* define the external variable *Rwho* to be an *rwinfo* structure. In *Rwho*, field *rwcache* holds the array of information entries, one per machine, as well as a count of valid entries in field *rwnent*. Another field in *Rwho*, *rbuf*, is the buffer area into which *rwho* packets are read.

12.10.2 Rwho Information Collection Daemon

Each machine collects incoming *rwho* packets, extracting and storing the information it needs. In our implementation, a process executing procedure *rwhoind* handles *rwho* input. Using UNIX terminology, we call the process a *daemon*. In general, the term "daemon" refers to a background utility process automatically created by the operating system. Many daemons execute forever; others are created whenever work appears and are designed to exit when they exhaust the set of requests.

Procedure *rwhoind* contains the code for the rwho input daemon process. It can be found in file *rwhoind.c*:

```
/* rwhoind.c - rwhoind */

#include <conf.h>
#include <kernel.h>
#include <network.h>
#include <rwho.h>


/*------------------------------------------------------------------------
 * rwhoind - rwho daemon to record info from incoming rwho packets
 *------------------------------------------------------------------------
 */
PROCESS rwhoind()
{
        int     dev;
        int     len;
        int     i;
        long    now;
        char    ps;
        struct  rwhopac *rpacptr;
        struct  rwent   *rwptr;

        if ( (dev=open(INTERNET, ANYFPORT, URWHO)) == SYSERR ||
            control(dev, DG_SETMODE, DG_DMODE) == SYSERR)
                panic("rwho_in: cannot open rwho port");
        while (TRUE) {
                if ( (len = read(dev,Rwho.rbuf,RWMAXP)) == SYSERR )
                        continue;
                rpacptr = (struct rwhopac *) Rwho.rbuf;
                for (i=0 ; i<Rwho.rwnent ; i++) {
                        rwptr = &Rwho.rwcache[i];
                        if (strncmp(rpacptr->rw_host, rwptr->rwmach,
                            RMACLEN) == 0)
                                break;
                }
                if (i >= Rwho.rwnent) {
                        disable(ps);
                        if (Rwho.rwnent >= RWCSIZ) {
```

```
                              restore(ps);
                              continue;
                    }
                    rwptr = &Rwho.rwcache[Rwho.rwnent++];
                    strncpy(rwptr->rwmach, rpacptr->rw_host, RMACLEN);
                    restore(ps);
            }
            rwptr->rwboot = net2hl(rpacptr->rw_btim);
            gettime(&now);
            rwptr->rwlast = now;
            rwptr->rwslast = net2hl(rpacptr->rw_sndtim);
            for (i=0 ; i<RWNLOAD ; i++)
                    rwptr->rwload[i] = net2hl(rpacptr->rw_load[i]);
            rwptr->rwusers = (len-RWMINP)/sizeof(struct rw_who);
    }
}
```

The code is cumbersome because it handles many details. After opening a datagram pseudo-device to receive *rwho* packets, and changing it to data-only mode, *rwhoind* enters an infinite loop, reading *rwho* packets, and extracting the information. For each packet that arrives, *rwhoind* searches the local cache until it finds the record for that machine, and then copies into the record, information like load averages.

12.10.3 Clock Consistency

Each *rwho* packet contains a field that gives the time at which the sender's system started. A problem arises if the receiver's clock and the sender's clock disagree because the receiver will be unable to interpret the sender's timestamp. For example, suppose that according to the sender's clock the time is 1 AM January 1, 1986, while according to the receiver's clock the time is 2:30 AM, January 1, 1986. If the sender specifies startup time in an *rwho* packet, the receiver will interpret the time relative to its own clock, and incorrectly report a time 1.5 hours later.

Rwho uses a simple technique to avoid gross misinterpretation of timestamps. It requires the sender to record its clock value in the packet just before transmission, and has the receiver record its clock value when the packet is received. Assuming negligible network delays, having both the sender's and receiver's clock values allows the receiver to adjust all other time fields to its local clock.

The *rwho* daemon does something better than convert all times to local clock times. It stores values for the two clocks in fields *rwslast* and *rwlast* of the stored information, and leaves the interpretation of time fields to whatever procedure uses the data. Why is this better than converting all times to the local clock time? For one thing, processes using the information may want to know whether the clocks disagreed, and if so, by how much. An exercise suggests another reason.

12.10.4 Rwho Output Daemon

In addition to collecting machine status from other systems, each machine must also propagate its own status information. A daemon process that propagates *rwho* information executes procedure *rwhod* in file *rwhod.c*:

```
/* rwhod.c - rwhod */

#include <conf.h>
#include <kernel.h>
#include <network.h>
#include <rwho.h>
#include <shell.h>


/*------------------------------------------------------------------------
 * rwhod - Periodically clean cache and (optionally) send rwho packets
 *------------------------------------------------------------------------
 */
PROCESS rwhod()
{
        int     i, j;
        struct  rwent   *rwptr;
        struct  rwent   *myptr;
        struct  rwhopac *rpacptr;
        struct  rw_who  *rwwptr;
        struct  epacket *packet;
        IPaddr  mynet;
        long    now;
        int     len;
        char    ps;

        /* Initialize rwho information */

        Rwho.rwnent = 1;
        Rwho.rwsend = TRUE;
        getutim(&Rwho.rwbtime);
        myptr = &Rwho.rwcache[0];
        getname(myptr->rwmach);
        myptr->rwboot = myptr->rwlast = myptr->rwslast = Rwho.rwbtime;
        for (i=0 ; i<3 ; i++)
                myptr->rwload[i] = 0L;
        myptr->rwusers = 1;

        getnet(mynet);
```

```
for( ; TRUE ; sleep(RWDELAY) ) {
        getutim(&now);
        myptr->rwlast = myptr->rwslast = now;
        disable(ps);
        for (i=0 ; i<Rwho.rwnent ; i++) {
                rwptr = &Rwho.rwcache[i];
                if (now - rwptr->rwlast > RWMAXDT) {
                        Rwho.rwnent--;
                        for (j=i-- ; j<Rwho.rwnent ; j++)
                                Rwho.rwcache[j] = Rwho.rwcache[j+1];
                }
        }
        restore(ps);
        if ( !Rwho.rwsend)
                continue;
        packet = (struct epacket *)getbuf(Net.netpool);
        rpacptr = (struct rwhopac *)
                ((struct udp *)
                (((struct ip *)packet->ep_data)->i_data))->u_data;
        rpacptr->rw_vers = RWVERSION;
        rpacptr->rw_type= RWSTATUS;
        rpacptr->rw_sndtim = hl2net(now);
        rpacptr->rw_rtim = 0L;
        getname(rpacptr->rw_host);
        for (j=0 ; j<RWNLOAD ; j++)
                rpacptr->rw_load[j] = 0L;
        rpacptr->rw_btim = hl2net(Rwho.rwbtime);
        len = RWMINP;
        if ( marked(Shl.shmark) && Shl.shused ) {
                rwwptr = &rpacptr->rw_rww[0];
                strcpy (rwwptr->rw_tty, "Console");
                strncpy(rwwptr->rw_nam, Shl.shuser, RWNLEN);
                rwwptr->rw_ton = hl2net(Shl.shlogon);
                rwwptr->rw_idle = hl2net(now - Shl.shlast);
                len += sizeof(struct rw_who);
        }
        udpsend(mynet, URWHO, URWHO, packet, len);
    }
}
```

Again, the code is conceptually simple, but cluttered with many details. After initializing the *Rwho* data structure, *rwhod* enters an infinite loop, awakening once every *RWDELAY* seconds to check the cached information and propagate its own *rwho* packet (As defined in *rwho.h*, *RWDELAY* is 60 seconds).

Each time the daemon awakens, it prunes out-of-date entries from the cache. An entry is considered out-of-date if the last information packet arrived more than *RWMAXDT* seconds ago. Thus, if a machine is moved to another network, or if its name is changed, *rwhod* will purge the original cache entry after one week, making room for new machine information.

After pruning stale entries from the cache, *rwhod* propagates an *rwho* packet if *Rwho.rwsend* is *TRUE*. Because Xinu does not keep load information, this version of the software simply reports load averages of zero. It obtains information about user logins from the Xinu shell data structure, *Shl*. For now, all you need to know to understand the daemon is that *Shl* contains information about the user logged in as well as the time the user last typed a command to the user interface (field *shlast*). Once the packet has been assembled, *rwhod* passes it to *udpsend* to broadcast.

Note that *rwhoind* used the datagram pseudo-device interface to the network while *rwhod* allocates a network buffer and calls *udpsend* directly. The two procedures represent two styles of network use that each have advantages and disadvantages. The exercises suggest alternatives and ask you to think about the two approaches.

12.10.5 Rwho Subsystem Startup

Procedure *rwho*, found in file *rwho.c* starts the *rwho* input and output daemons.

```
/* rwho.c - rwho */

#include <conf.h>
#include <kernel.h>
#include <network.h>
#include <rwho.h>


/*------------------------------------------------------------------------
 *  rwho  -  Initialize rwho subsystem and start daemon processes
 *------------------------------------------------------------------------
 */
rwho()
{
        resume( create(RWIN,  RWISTK, RWIPRIO, RWINAM, RWIARGS) );
        resume( create(RWOUT, RWOSTK, RWOPRIO, RWONAM, RWOARGS) );
}


struct  rwinfo  Rwho;              /* all globals used by rwho subsystem   */
```

12.11 Summary

Processes that use network communication often fall into a pattern of use called the client-server model. Server processes await requests, and perform an action based on the request. The action may include sending a response. Clients usually formulate a request, send it to the server, and then await a reply.

We have seen examples of clients and servers, and found that some of them use direct communication while others communicate by broadcasting information. Broadcast is especially useful when a single machine needs to supply information to many others.

FOR FURTHER STUDY

Tanenbaum [1981] provides an excellent discussion of the client-server paradigm as well as alternatives. Our UDP echo server obeys the DARPA standard specified in Postel [1983], and our *rwho* system follows the conventions of the 4.3BSD UNIX rwho mechanism. Feinler *et. al.* [1985] specifies many standard DARPA Internet server protocols not discussed here, including discard, character generation, day and time, active users, and quote of the day.

EXERCISES

12.1   What happens when you send a datagram containing exactly *MAXECHO* bytes of data to the UDP echo server?

12.2   Build a UDP echo client that sends a datagram to a specified echo server, awaits a reply, and compares it to the original message.

12.3   As time passes, the local clock may "drift" from an accurate count (especially if the real-time clock is slightly inaccurate or the processor misses real-time clock interrupts because it operates with interrupts disabled too long). Measure Xinu clock drift.

12.4   Devise a scheme that periodically uses the network to correct clock drift.

12.5   Find out the rules for daylight savings time, and rewrite *ut2ltim* so it can handle daylight savings.

12.6   What might happen if you removed the mutual exclusion semaphore *clmutex* from *getutim*?

12.7   Why does *clmutex* exclude processes from all parts of procedure *getutim* instead of excluding them just from the code that accesses the network?

12.8   Servers can be implemented by separate processes, as we have seen in this chapter, or by building server code into low-level network protocols, as in the *RARP* server of Chapter 5. What are the advantages and disadvantages of having a process per server?

12.9 Note that *ruptime* reports only relative times (e.g., how long a machine has been running, but not the exact date and time it started). Write a program that prints, for each machine in *Rwho.rwcache*, the exact day and time it was bootstrapped. What does your program print if a machine on the network has its clock incorrectly set one hour behind all others.

12.10 Modify *rwhod* to use the datagram pseudo-device interface. How many datagram pseudo-devices do you need to allocate for all the *rwho* daemons?

12.11 Adding procedures that allocate and free network buffers after the network software has been designed may be dangerous. Why?

12.12 Move all the *rwho* initialization code into *rwho.c*.

12.13 Build a shared memory service that reserves n bytes of memory on each machine for sharing (preferably, at the same address), and uses procedures *fetch* and *store* that fetch bytes from the shared area or store them in the shared area. Use broadcast to inform other machines of changes. Redesign the *rwho* service to use shared memory.

13

A Stateless File Server

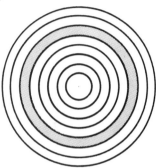

13.1 Introduction

The previous chapter introduced the client-server model of process interaction, and gave several simple examples. This chapter extends the study in two directions. First, it introduces the fundamental notion of *statelessness* in servers, and explains why stateless servers are easier to design, implement, and maintain. Second, it expands the set of examples by showing how the client-server model applies to a remote file access system.

This chapter deals only with the server software; the next chapter discusses the companion client. Both the client and server share an interface defined by the set of messages the server recognizes and the set of replies it generates. As we will see, the design of the server affects the message interface profoundly, and therefore affects the design of the client.

13.2 Remote Files Vs. Remote Disks

Like most computer systems, a diskless station needs access to large permanent file storage. Usually, several diskless machines all share a server that provides access to secondary storage as Figure 13.1 shows:

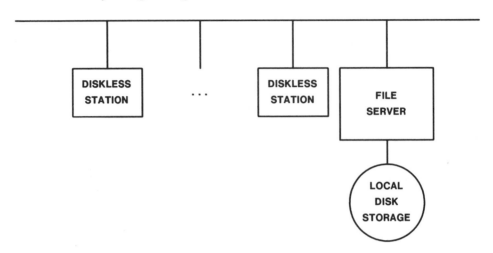

Figure 13.1 A network with many diskless machines and one storage
              server

There are two possible designs. In the first design, the server provides each
diskless machine with a small *virtual disk*, providing primitives that allow the diskless machine to *read* and *write* blocks on its virtual disk. In the second design, the
server provides access to files, allowing the diskless machines to *open* a file by
name, *read* and *write* to the file, and then *close* the file.

Each design has its advantages. A *remote disk server* is simpler and makes it
easier to isolate and protect data belonging to a machine. Furthermore, because
the disk server only sends and receives blocks, the diskless station is free to use the
disk however it chooses (e.g., it can build a complete file system with an index, or
treat the entire virtual disk as a randomly accessible data structure). A file server
introduces the higher-level notion of *files*, makes sharing easier, and reduces network traffic (and delays) because it handles housekeeping chores like index maintenance locally.

We will build a server that provides access to files, not merely to disk blocks.
Our design choice is motivated by a desire for file sharing, and a desire to place the
software that understands disk layouts and file indexing on the server.

13.3 The Property Of Statelessness In Servers

As described so far, a server is a process that handles requests, one at a time. Neither the type of request nor the information provided in the response has been specified or constrained. However, not all servers behave the same way. Some servers use a descriptor mechanism: the client contacts the server to obtain a *descriptor*, and then uses the descriptor each time it contacts the server. Usually, descriptors are unique integers or character strings chosen by the server. When the client informs the server that the interactive "session" has ended, the server invalidates the descriptor.

Descriptor-based interaction should be familiar to the reader. Consider, for example, the way in which a process interacts with the the datagram pseudo-device software of Chapter 11. A process opens the *NETWORK* device and obtains a device descriptor (small integer) to use. It then passes the descriptor to *read* or *write* when transferring information. Finally, the process passes the descriptor to *close* when it finishes using the pseudo-device.

Using the descriptor-based form of interaction over a network poses problems because requests or replies can be lost. If the server's reply to an initial request is lost, the descriptor it allocated may never be used. However, the server cannot release resources needed for that descriptor because the server cannot know whether the client has finished using it. More important, if the server maintains information about requests, and interprets each request relative to that information, it may incorrectly respond to requests.

To further understand the subtle ways in which servers can give incorrect information, consider a file server. Suppose the client opens a file, receiving a descriptor for that file. The client then issues *read* requests to the server to retrieve data from the file. If the server maintains a notion of file position, and each request specifies only the number of bytes to read, losing a reply causes trouble. After some time, the client, having failed to receive a reply, will send the *read* request again. The server, having responded to the first *read* request, will have updated its notion of file position, and will respond to the second *read* request by sending new data. Similar problems occur whenever the server maintains information about requests and makes responses depending on previous requests.

We seek to build servers that work correctly even when the internet loses packets or delivers them out of order. To help achieve this goal, we will make our servers *stateless*. That is, knowing it is impossible to accommodate network failure if the server maintains information about requests, we will carefully design the possible requests and responses so the server can respond to a request without keeping local information. The key point can be summarized:

> *A server is stateless if the response to a request does not depend in any way on the history of previous requests. Only stateless servers work correctly over a communication channel that destroys packets, loses packets or delivers packets out of order.*

13.4 Statelessness In A File Server

How can a file server be stateless? In one sense it cannot. After all, the client expects the server to maintain data that is written to the file and return the same data when the file is read later. One must distinguish, however, between the data held in files and information the server keeps about interactions with clients. While a stateless file server stores data in files, it does not keep any history of requests or other information about currently active clients. Thus, it maintains the minimum amount of state information needed to function.

The idea of minimizing state information comes from the observation that keeping state information introduces problems whenever messages are lost or delivered out of order. We can formulate the argument more precisely in the *state minimization principle*:

> *The less state a server keeps, the more robust it will be in the face of packet duplication, loss, or out-of-order delivery.*

13.5 File Requests And Responses

The state minimization principle helps us choose the contents of request and reply messages, and alerts the designer to potential problems in cases where the server maintains some state. For example, consider designing request and response messages for a file server. We know that the basic operations performed on files include: *open*, *read*, *write*, and *close*. To minimize the state information kept by the server, each request should be self-contained. In particular, servers should not pass clients file descriptors. Slightly less obvious, but equally important, the server should not maintain any notion of "current" or "default" directory. Thus, we will design the interface between clients and the server so that each request will contain a complete (absolute or unabbreviated) name for the file being accessed. Also, because the server should not maintain information about file position, we will choose to have each request contain an absolute position in the file at which the operation should occur. Finally, we realize that requests must contain a field that encodes which of the possible file operations (e.g., *read* or *write*) the client is requesting.

Like requests, responses can be lost. They, too, should contain all the information necessary to interpret them without requiring the client to keep a history of responses. For example, each response message should carry the file name and position information back to the client along with the results of the operation.

13.6 Efficient, Stateless File Access

A file server process usually executes on a general purpose computer system. Thus, it must contact its local operating system to *open*, and *read* or *write* files, as requested by the clients. However, the state minimization principle says that the file server should not maintain state information. One obvious implementation forces the server to wait for a request, *open* the local file specified in the request, *read* or *write* the file according to the requested operation, *close* the file, and then send the response back to the client. Opening a file for every request may be inefficient, however, especially when only a few clients are active. Ideally, the server should open the local file only once, perform all operations needed, and close the file when the client finishes using it.

Are stateless servers necessarily inefficient? Can we match our desire for a stateless server with the local operating system's descriptor-based processing? Fortunately, we can build an efficient, stateless file server. The key lies in realizing that:

> *The file server can depend on the state of its local operating system even though it should not pass that state information out to clients.*

In a file server, for example, the server can maintain its own set of open files internally, using the operating system's descriptor-based mechanism, while providing only stateless interactions externally.

Caching is the key to understanding how a server efficiently accommodates stateless requests. The server maintains a table of open files that include the file's full name (i.e., the representation used by clients when making requests), as well as the file descriptor (i.e., the representation that the server uses to access the file locally). When requests arrive, the server searches its table to see if the file is already open, and avoids the cost of opening it again. Once the server opens a file, it enters a record in the table to record the file descriptor for future use. Thus, the table represents a *cache* of all open files.

Most operating systems limit the number of files that a process can open simultaneously. If the server executes forever, it eventually reaches its limit, and must close an existing file before it can open a new one. Which open file should it choose to close? Obviously, it should choose a file that will no longer be needed. To be more precise, it should choose the file that will be needed the farthest in the future. Because the server cannot know exactly which file to close, it chooses the file that had activity the longest time ago. Choosing the least recently used file does not guarantee to minimize opening files, but experience shows that it performs well on the average. One advantage of choosing the least recently used file to close is that it helps the server reallocate resources after a client machine fails. Consider, for example, the case where a machine opens a file, *F*, begins reading, and then crashes. As other machines continue to run, they access files while *F* receives no activity. Under the policy that closes least recently used files, *F* quickly becomes a candidate for closing, allowing the server to reallocate local file resources to handle other requests.

To be able to decide which file is least recently used, the server must keep a record of the time at which each file is accessed. It might, for example, reserve a field in the file table for a *timestamp*, and replace the timestamp with the current time whenever a request specified the file. Alternatively, the server might keep entries in the table linked together on a list, and move an entry to the front of the list whenever it was accessed (our software will use this method).

13.7 UNIX Implementation Of A File Server

Having discussed the design of a stateless file server, we are ready to examine a particular implementation. Our implementation will operate under the 4.3BSD UNIX operating system, not under Xinu. Although the code includes UNIX system and library calls, the reader should be able to follow the ideas without outside references. Readers interested in knowing the exact form of arguments to all procedures should refer to the 4.3BSD *UNIX Programmer's Manual*.

To understand the code, some explanation of UNIX file names is needed. We will review only the rudiments of UNIX file names; details can be found in Ritchie and Thompson [1974].

UNIX employs a tree-structured directory scheme to name files, with / as the name of the root. Paths in the tree begin with /, and each /-separated component specifies the name of a file or subdirectory. Thus, */usr/dec/Xinu* is either a file or directory three levels down from the root. The root directory contains subdirectory *usr* which, in turn, contains subdirectory *dec*. The last component of the name, *Xinu*, specifies either a file or subdirectory within *dec*, but one cannot tell from the name alone which it is.

UNIX also permits files to be named with respect to a current working directory, but such names do not concern us because the file server will accept only full path names (i.e., names that begin with a */*).

13.7.1 Server Declarations

Our examination of the file server code begins with file *fs.h* that contains declarations for the major data structures used by the program, including the open file information cache. All the programs we will examine include *fs.h*.

```
/* fs.h */

#include "../../sys/h/kernel.h"        /*** Xinu include files ***/
#include "../../sys/h/file.h"
#include "../../sys/h/fserver.h"
#undef   EOF                           /*** remove conflicts ***/
```

```
#undef    NULL
#include <sys/file.h>                          /*** UNIX include files ***/
#include <sys/types.h>
#include <sys/socket.h>
#include <sys/stat.h>
#include <net/if.h>
#include <netinet/in.h>
#include <stdio.h>
#include <strings.h>
#include <errno.h>
#include <netdb.h>
#include <pwd.h>
#include <grp.h>
#include <signal.h>


/* Defines for miscellaneous constants */

#define PORTNAME        "wizard"        /* UDP port name server uses    */
#define FILEMODE        0664            /* protection mode for new files*/
#define DIRMODE         0775            /* protection mode for new dirs */
#define MAXNFILES       15              /* maximum number of open files */
#define NOFILE          MAXNFILES       /* last file entry is not a file*/
#define FHDRLEN         sizeof(struct fphdr)/* request/reply header only*/


/* Declaration of file table entry format */

struct  filent  {                       /* entry in table of files      */
        char    name[RNAMLEN];          /* file's name                  */
        int     fd;                     /* UNIX file descriptor to use  */
        int     mode;                   /* mode of file                 */
        long    currpos;                /* current offset for this file */
        int     prev;                   /* link to previously opened fl */
        int     next;                   /* link to next file opened     */
};
extern  struct  filent  fcache[];       /* table of open files          */
extern  int     freelst;                /* first free entry in fcache   */
#define NEWEST  fcache[MAXNFILES].prev  /* youngest file in file table  */
#define OLDEST  fcache[MAXNFILES].next  /* oldest file in file table    */


/* Declaration of the request-to-handler mapping */

struct  reqmap  {                       /* request-to-procedure mapping */
        int     req;                    /* request (e.g., FS_OPEN)      */
        int     (*reqproc)();           /* procedure to handle request  */
};
```

```
extern  struct  reqmap  rq[];                /* array of request mappings    */
extern  int     fsopen(), fsclose(), fsread(), fswrite(), fsunlink(),
                fsrename(),fsrmdir(),fsmkdir(),fsaccess(),fstrans();
extern  int     errno;                       /* UNIX's error code return var.*/
extern  int     port;                        /* UDP port number to use or -1 */
extern  char    *pname;                      /* UDP port name to use         */
```

Because the server references declarations in many .h files, they have all been collected together in *fs.h*. Among the referenced files, three are from Xinu and the rest from UNIX. *Fs.h* defines constants used throughout the server, and declares server data structures. Among the server data structures, *fcache* is perhaps the most important. *Fcache* is an array that holds the open file cache. Each entry consists of a *filent* structure that contains the name of a file, a local descriptor for that file, the access mode for which it has been opened, and current file position. Fields *prev* and *next* form a linked list in the *fcache* table, with files on the list ordered by time of last access. The last entry in *fcache*, which has index *NOFILE*, does not correspond to a file at all. Instead, it forms the head of a circularly linked list, with only the *next* and *prev* fields used. *fcache[NOFILE].next* gives the index of the oldest file in the cache (i.e., the one accessed least recently), and *fcache[NOFILE].prev* gives the index of the youngest file. The definitions of *OLDEST* and *NEWEST* reflect this convention.

The second data structure defined in *fs.h* consists of an array, *rq*, that maps a request code into a procedure to handle that request.

13.7.2 Xinu Include Files

The three Xinu .h files included at the beginning of *fs.h* contain constant declarations used throughout the file server. File *kernel.h*, shown below, defines basic constants like *SYSERR*.

```
/* kernel.h - disable, enable, halt, restore, isodd, min */

/* Symbolic constants used throughout Xinu */

typedef char            Bool;           /* Boolean type                 */
#define FALSE           0               /* Boolean constants            */
#define TRUE            1
#define NULL            (char *)0        /* Null pointer for linked lists*/
#define NULLCH          '\0'             /* The null character           */
#define NULLSTR         ""               /* Pointer to empty string      */
#define SYSCALL         int             /* System call declaration      */
#define LOCAL           static          /* Local procedure declaration  */
#define COMMAND         int             /* Shell command declaration    */
#define BUILTIN         int             /* Shell builtin " "            */
```

```
#define INTPROC         int           /* Interrupt procedure  "     */
#define PROCESS         int           /* Process declaration        */
#define RESCHYES        1             /* tell ready to reschedule    */
#define RESCHNO         0             /* tell ready not to resch.    */
#define MININT          0100000       /* minimum integer (-32768)   */
#define MAXINT          0077777       /* maximum integer            */
#define LOWBYTE         0377          /* mask for low-order 8 bits  */
#define HIBYTE          0177400       /* mask for high 8 of 16 bits */
#define LOW16           0177777       /* mask for low-order 16 bits */
#define SP              6             /* reg. 6 is stack pointer    */
#define PC              7             /* reg. 7 is program counter  */
#define PS              8             /* proc. status in 8th reg. loc */
#define MINSTK          40            /* minimum process stack size */
#define NULLSTK         300           /* process 0 stack size       */
#define DISABLE         0340          /* PS to disable interrupts   */
#define MAGIC           0125252       /* unusual value for top of stk */

/* Universal return constants */

#define OK              1             /* system call ok             */
#define SYSERR          -1            /* system call failed         */
#define EOF             -2            /* End-of-file (usu. from read) */
#define TIMEOUT         -3            /* time out  (usu. recvtim)   */
#define INTRMSG         -4            /* keyboard "intr" key pressed */
                                      /* (usu. defined as ^B)       */

/* Initialization constants */

#define INITSTK         500           /* initial process stack      */
#define INITPRIO        20            /* initial process priority   */
#define INITNAME        "main"        /* initial process name       */
#define INITARGS        1,0           /* initial count/arguments    */
#define INITRET         userret       /* processes return address   */
#define INITPS          0             /* initial process PS         */
#define INITREG         0             /* initial register contents  */
#define QUANTUM         10            /* clock ticks until preemption */

/* Miscellaneous utility inline functions */

#define isodd(x)        (01&(int)(x))
#define min(a,b)        ( (a) < (b) ? (a) : (b) )
#define disable(ps)     asm("mfps ~ps");asm("mtps $0340")
#define restore(ps)     asm("mtps ~ps") /* restore interrupt status  */
#define enable()        asm("mtps $000")/* enable interrupts         */
#define pause()         asm("wait")   /* machine "wait for interr."  */
#define halt()          asm("halt")   /* machine halt instruction    */
```

```
extern    int        rdyhead, rdytail;
extern    int        preempt;
```

The second Xinu *.h* file included by *fs.h* defines the meaning of bits in a file access
mode specification. Clients always specify access modes using the Xinu notion of
mode bits as defined in *file.h*. Thus, the server uses constants from *file.h* to define
the mapping from Xinu mode bits to UNIX mode bits.

```
/* file.h */

#define FLREAD          001          /* file mode bit for "read"        */
#define FLWRITE         002          /* file mode bit for "write"       */
#define FLRW            003          /* file mode bits for read+write*/
#define FLNEW           010          /* file mode bit for "new file"  */
#define FLOLD           020          /* file mode bit for "old file"  */


/* Definition of characters in the mode argument to open */


#define FLOMODE         'o'          /* Old  => file exists             */
#define FLNMODE         'n'          /* New  => file does not exist   */
#define FLRMODE         'r'          /* Read => open read-only          */
#define FLWMODE         'w'          /* Write=> open for writing        */


/* Universal file control functions (additional args in parentheses)   */


#define FLREMOVE        3001         /* remove file (name)              */
#define FLACCESS        3002         /* test access (name, mode)        */
#define FLRENAME        3003         /* change file name (old, new)     */
```

The third Xinu include file, *fserver.h*, contains declarations and constants for the
server request and reply messages as well as the message format. In essence,
fserver.h defines the interface between the server and clients that access it.

```
/* fserver.h */

#ifndef RSERVER
#define RSERVER             "128.10.2.3:2001"/* remote file server address   */
#endif


/* Definitions of remote file server constants and packet format */


/* Codes for operations */
```

```
#define FS_ERROR        -1              /* returned for error on op.    */
#define FS_OPEN          0              /* open a file                  */
#define FS_CLOSE         1              /* close a file                 */
#define FS_READ          2              /* read data from a file        */
#define FS_WRITE         3              /* write data to a file         */
#define FS_UNLINK        4              /* unlink a file from directory */
#define FS_RENAME        5              /* change the name of file (data*/
                                        /*   area in packet is new name) */
#define FS_MKDIR         6              /* make a directory (count=mode)*/
#define FS_RMDIR         7              /* remove a directory           */
#define FS_ACCESS        8              /* determine file accessibility */
#define FS_TRANS         9              /* other transaction            */

#define RDATLEN          512            /* Maximum bytes transferred    */
#define RNAMLEN          80             /* Maximum bytes in file name    */
#define RCLOSED          -1             /* server device not opened     */

struct  fphdr   {                       /* Format of server packet hdr  */
        long    f_pos;                  /* byte position in file        */
        short   f_count;                /* count of data bytes          */
        short   f_op;                   /* Operation requested          */
        char    f_name[RNAMLEN];        /* Name of remote file          */
};


struct  fpacket {                       /* Format of packet to/from rfs */
        struct  fphdr   fp_h;           /* packet header                */
        char    fpdata[RDATLEN];        /* data sent to/from server     */
};

#define FPHLEN  sizeof(struct fphdr)    /* size of server packet header */
#define FPPLEN  sizeof(struct fpacket)  /* size of server packet        */
```

Both the Xinu-based client and the UNIX-based server use *fserver.h*. Beside the
format of requests (and replies), *fserver.h* defines the set of possible operations the
server handles, using constants of the form *FS_x*, where *x* names a file operation.
We assume that all integer fields of the request/response packet travel across the
network in network byte order.

13.7.3 Utility Procedures

Before looking at the server organization and the procedures that carry out specific requests, we will examine a set of utility procedures from which the server is built. These procedures perform tasks like opening and closing files on the server machine, being careful to maintain the file cache table.

Reading the server code can be tricky because names reappear in many places. For example, we know that the ultimate user invokes file operations like *read* on the client machine, and that the client will send a message to the server requesting that it "read" from the file. The server contains several utility procedures that help it maintain a table of information about open files. Ultimately, the server must invoke the underlying UNIX routines like *open* and *read*. To understand the implementation, one must remember at which level each routine occurs. We begin by reviewing three utility procedures that are used just above the UNIX file system primitives. Although they perform the same function as their underlying UNIX counterpart, these utility routines have the side effect of updating the information that the server keeps about local files. By convention, each of the utility routines is named like its UNIX counterpart except that it begins with an upper-case letter.

13.7.4 Closing A File

When the server closes a file, it must add the cache table entry to the free list, making the entry available again. Procedure *Close*, shown below in file *Close.c* handles closing files. It takes as an argument the index of the cache table entry for the file being closed, calls the UNIX *close* routine, passing it the file descriptor for the file, and then adds the entry to the free list.

```
/* Close.c - Close */

#include "fs.h"

/*------------------------------------------------------------------------
 * Close - close a file given its index in the file cache table
 *------------------------------------------------------------------------
 */
Close(rfd)
int     rfd;
{
        if (close(fcache[rfd].fd) < 0)
                return(SYSERR);
        fcache[rfd].name[0] = NULLCH;
        fcache[fcache[rfd].prev].next = fcache[rfd].next;
        fcache[fcache[rfd].next].prev = fcache[rfd].prev;
        fcache[rfd].prev = NOFILE;
```

```
        fcache[rfd].next = freelst;
        freelst = rfd;
        return(OK);
}
```

In the code, constant *NOFILE* gives the index in *fcache* of the list head entry. The free list can be followed starting at the entry with index *freelst* and following *next* fields.

13.7.5 Seeking In A File

For efficiency, the server maintains, in its *fcache* table, the current position for each open file. Procedure *Seek*, shown in file *Seek.c*, moves a file to a new file position. *Seek* uses the UNIX routine *lseek* to set the actual file position and records the new position in the *fcache* entry for the file.

```
/* Seek.c - Seek */

#include "fs.h"

/*-------------------------------------------------------------------------
 * Seek - seek in a file given its index in the file cache table
 *-------------------------------------------------------------------------
 */
Seek(rfd, newpos)
int     rfd;
long    newpos;
{
        long    lseek();
        long    pos;

        if ( (pos=lseek(fcache[rfd].fd, newpos, 0)) < 0)
                return(SYSERR);
        fcache[rfd].currpos = pos;
        return(OK);
}
```

Like *Close*, *Seek* takes as an argument the index in *fcache* of the file to be changed, and a new position within that file. It invokes the underlying UNIX command that moves a file to a new position, returning *SYSERR* if an error results, *OK* otherwise.

13.7.6 Removing A File

Procedure *rmfile* removes (destroys) a file given its name. The code is shown in file *rmfile.c*. *Rmfile* calls the UNIX routine *unlink* to detach the file. It then works backward through the path name, removing any empty directories that were left behind. For example, when removing file *lusrldeclXinu*, *rmfile* first removes the file, and then checks to see if it can remove the directory *lusrldec*. If removing *lusrldec* succeeds, *rmfile* checks to see if directory *lusr* can be removed.

```
/* rmfile.c - rmfile */

#include "fs.h"

/*------------------------------------------------------------------------
 *  rmfile  -  remove a file given its name and delete cache entry
 *------------------------------------------------------------------------
 */
rmfile(name)
char    *name;
{
        char    fname[RNAMLEN];
        char    *subdir;

        if (unlink(name) < 0)
                return(SYSERR);
        strncpy(fname, name, sizeof(fname));
        fname[sizeof(fname)-1] = NULLCH;
        while ( (subdir=rindex(fname,'/')) != NULL && subdir != fname) {
                *subdir = NULLCH;
                if (rmdir(fname) < 0)
                        return(OK);
        }
        return(OK);
}
```

UNIX does not usually remove empty directories that are left behind when a file is removed. Having the file server remove empty directories makes sense only because we intend to have our open routine create directories when needed.

13.7.7 Opening A UNIX file

Procedure *openfile* is responsible for opening a UNIX file and returning a UNIX file descriptor for it. *Openfile* differs from the usual UNIX *open* routine because it creates intermediate directories if they do not exist. Thus, opening *lusrldeclXinu* may have the side-effect of creating directory *lusrldec* if it did not exist. The code for *openfile* can be found in file *openfile.c*.

```c
/* openfile.c - openfile */

#include "fs.h"

/*------------------------------------------------------------------------
 * openfile  -  open a file given its name and Xinu mode; return UNIX fd
 *------------------------------------------------------------------------
 */
openfile(name, xmode)
char    *name;
int     xmode;
{
        int     umode;
        int     fd;
        char    *subdir;
        char    fname[RNAMLEN];

        umode = fmode(xmode);
        if (xmode & FLOLD)
                return(open(name, umode, FILEMODE));
        for (subdir=index(name+1, '/') ; subdir != NULL ;
                subdir=index(subdir+1,'/')) {
                strncpy(fname, name, subdir - name);
                fname[subdir - name] = NULLCH;
                if (mkdir(fname, DIRMODE) < 0 && errno != EEXIST)
                        return(SYSERR);
        }
        if ((fd=open(name, umode, FILEMODE)) >= 0)
                return(fd);
        return( open(name, umode&~O_CREAT, FILEMODE) );
}
```

Openfile expects an argument that specifies the mode of the file to open. It uses procedure *fmode* to convert the mode from the Xinu format (see *file.h*) to UNIX format. The code for *fmode*, shown below in file *fmode.c*, may seem confusing, especially to readers who do not have access to UNIX documentation. It is only important to understand that *fmode* can convert each combination of Xinu mode bits into equivalent UNIX mode bits.

```
/* fmode.c - fmode */

#include "fs.h"

/*------------------------------------------------------------------------
 * fmode  -  convert Xinu file protection mode to analogous UNIX mode
 *------------------------------------------------------------------------
 */
fmode(xmode)
int     xmode;
{
        int     umode;                  /* UNIX file mode bits          */

        if ((xmode&FLREAD) && (xmode&FLWRITE)) /* Xinu Read + Write      */
                umode = O_RDWR;
        else if (xmode & FLREAD)        /* Xinu read only               */
                umode = O_RDONLY;
        else if (xmode & FLWRITE)       /* Xinu write only              */
                umode = O_WRONLY;
        else                            /* Xinu neither of RW specified */
                umode = O_RDWR;

        if (xmode & FLNEW)              /* Xinu says a new file OK       */
                umode |= O_CREAT | O_EXCL;
        else if (! (xmode & FLOLD))
                umode |= O_CREAT;       /* Xinu says create if needed   */
        return(umode);
}
```

13.7.8 Checking The Cache For Open Files

Recall that the server needs to maintain information in its cache about all open files. Procedure *Open*, found in file *Open.c*, takes as an argument the name of a file to be opened, and handles two tasks associated with the open. First, it checks the cache to see if the specified file is already open (and has the correct read/write mode). Second, if it must call *openfile* to open a file not in the cache, it records the file name and local descriptor. *Open* returns to its caller the index in the file cache of the open file.

```
/* Open.c - Open */

#include "fs.h"

/*------------------------------------------------------------------------
```

```
 *  Open - open a file given its name and Xinu mode; return cache index
 *-------------------------------------------------------------------------
 */
Open(name, mode)
char    *name;
int     mode;
{
        int     rfd;
        long    lseek();

        if (*name == NULLCH)
                return(SYSERR);
        for (rfd = 0; rfd < MAXNFILES; ++rfd)
                if (strcmp(fcache[rfd].name, name) == 0)
                        break;
        if (rfd < MAXNFILES && (fcache[rfd].mode & mode & FLRW) ==
                (mode&FLRW)) {  /* file already opened appropriately   */
                fcache[fcache[rfd].prev].next = fcache[rfd].next;
                fcache[fcache[rfd].next].prev = fcache[rfd].prev;
        } else {
                if (rfd < MAXNFILES)     /* file must be reopened        */
                        Close(rfd);
                if (freelst == NOFILE)
                        Close(OLDEST);
                rfd = freelst;
                if ((fcache[rfd].fd = openfile(name, mode)) < 0)
                        return(SYSERR);
                if ((fcache[rfd].currpos=lseek(fcache[rfd].fd,0L,1))<0) {
                        close(fcache[rfd].fd);
                        return(SYSERR);
                }
                strcpy(fcache[rfd].name, name);
                fcache[rfd].mode  = mode;
                freelst = fcache[freelst].next;
        }
        fcache[rfd].prev = NEWEST;
        fcache[rfd].next = NOFILE;
        fcache[NEWEST].next = rfd;
        NEWEST = rfd;
        return(rfd);
}
```

13.7.9 Removing Cached Information

Procedure *Uncache*, shown in file *Uncache.c*, takes as an argument the name of a file, and clears the cache entry for that file if one exists. *Uncache* searches the cache for the named file, and calls *Close* to close the file and link the cache entry into the free list.

```
/* Uncache.c - Uncache */

#include "fs.h"

/*------------------------------------------------------------------------
 * Uncache - remove the cached entry for a file and close the file
 *------------------------------------------------------------------------
 */
Uncache(name)
char    *name;
{
        int     rfd;

        for(rfd=0 ; rfd<MAXNFILES ; rfd++) {
                if (strcmp(name, fcache[rfd].name) == 0) {
                        Close(rfd);
                        return(OK);
                }
        }
        return(SYSERR);
}
```

13.7.10 Organization Of The Server

So far, we have described many utility routines that maintain the file cache when they perform chores like opening or closing files. Now, it is time to examine the overall organization of the server program, which can be found in file *fs.c*. After looking at *fs.c* we will consider the routines that it calls.

```
/* fs.c - main */

#include "fs.h"

struct  filent  fcache[MAXNFILES + 1];  /* Table of all open files    */
int     freelst;                        /* pointer to fcache free list */
int     port;                           /* UDP port. (if <0 use pname) */
```

```
char      *pname;                           /* UDP port name if port < 0    */

/* Areas to hold incoming request packet and address of sender */

struct  fpacket req;                        /* actual request/reply packet  */
struct  sockaddr_in      faddr;             /* sender's address saved here   */
int     flen;                               /* length of sender's address    */

struct  reqmap  rq[] = {                    /* table  of requests & handlers*/
        FS_OPEN,        fsopen,
        FS_CLOSE,       fsclose,
        FS_READ,        fsread,
        FS_WRITE,       fswrite,
        FS_UNLINK,      fsunlink,
        FS_RENAME,      fsrename,
        FS_MKDIR,       fsmkdir,
        FS_RMDIR,       fsrmdir,
        FS_ACCESS,      fsaccess,
        FS_TRANS,       fstrans};
#define NREQS           (sizeof(rq)/sizeof(struct reqmap))

/*------------------------------------------------------------------------
 *  main  -  4.2bsd UNIX-based file server for Xinu V7  Diskless Node
 *------------------------------------------------------------------------
 */
main(argc, argv)
int     argc;
char    *argv[];
{
        int     len;                        /* length of request            */
        int     sndlen;                     /* length of reply or zero       */
        int     reqop;                      /* operation in latest request  */
        int     i;                          /* index of request in rq        */
        int     sock;                       /* Internet datagram socket      */

        sock = finit(argc, argv);
        while (TRUE) {
                flen = sizeof(faddr);
                if ( (len=fgetreq(sock, &req, &faddr, &flen)) == SYSERR)
                        continue;
                reqop = req.fp_h.f_op;
                for (i=0 ; i<NREQS ; i++) {
                        if (rq[i].req == reqop)
                                break;
                }
```

```
        if (i >= NREQS || req.fp_h.f_name[0] != '/') {
                req.fp_h.f_op = FS_ERROR;
                sndlen = FHDRLEN;
        } else {
                sndlen = (*rq[i].reqproc)(&req, len);
        }
        if (sndlen > 0)
                fsndrply(sock, &req, sndlen, &faddr, flen);

    }
}
```

As shown, file *fs.c* contains the main program executed by the file server process. The server calls *finit* to initialize data structures and open a UNIX *socket*. Sockets are the UNIX equivalent of Xinu's datagram pseudo-device; they are used to send and receive UDP messages. Once a socket has been established, the server repeatedly awaits a request (*fgetreq*), looks up the requested operation in table *rq*, calls the appropriate procedure to handle the request, and sends a reply (*fsndrply*).

Notice that the main program checks each request to be sure it contains a valid operation, and to be sure that the specified file name begins with a slash (*/*). If the server detects an error, it changes field *f_op* in the request to *FS_ERROR*, and then sends the packet back to the client. In general, each request handler will work the same way. It receives as an argument the address of the request message. The handler reads the request, alters it, and sends it back to the client. Handlers usually report errors to the client by sending value *FS_ERROR* in the field *f_op* of the returned request message.

13.7.11 Acquiring A Request

Procedure *fgetreq*, shown below in file *fgetreq.c*, is responsible for receiving a message from the server's socket, and converting the integer fields from network byte order to host byte order. Because UNIX delivers the data and address into separate buffers, *fgetreq* takes four arguments. They specify the socket from which to receive, the data buffer area, the address buffer area, and the address length area. *Fgetreq* calls the UNIX primitive *recvfrom* to read the message and deposit it in memory. It then converts integer fields to host byte order, and returns the message length to its caller.

```
/* fgetreq.c - fgetreq */

#include "fs.h"

/*------------------------------------------------------------------------
 * fgetreq  - read a request packet from network and return its length
```

```
 *-------------------------------------------------------------------------
 */
fgetreq(sock, fpacptr, fromptr, fromlen)
int     sock;
struct  fpacket *fpacptr;
struct  sockaddr *fromptr;
int     *fromlen;
{
        int     len;
        struct  fphdr   *fptr;

        fptr = &fpacptr->fp_h;
        while ( (len=recvfrom(sock, fpacptr, sizeof(*fpacptr), 0,
                fromptr, fromlen)) < 0)
                if (errno != EINTR)
                        return(SYSERR);

        /* Convert from network byte order to host byte order */

        fptr->f_pos = ntohl(fptr->f_pos);
        fptr->f_op = ntohs(fptr->f_op);
        fptr->f_count = ntohs(fptr->f_count);

        return(len);
}
```

13.7.12 Sending Replies

Sending a reply consists of converting binary fields from host order to network order and sending the message to the server's socket. Given a socket, data buffer address, length, address buffer, and address length, procedure *fsndrply* sends a reply. Looking back at the main program reveals that the address buffer and address length passed to *fsndrply* is exactly the address buffer that *fgetreq* filled in when the message arrived.

```
/* fsndrply.c - fsndrply */

#include "fs.h"

/*------------------------------------------------------------------
 * fsndrply - send a reply packet to a  specified foreign address
 *------------------------------------------------------------------
 */
fsndrply(s, fptr, len, toaddr, tolen)
int     s;                              /* socket on which to write   */
struct  fpacket *fptr;                  /* data to write              */
int     len;                            /* length of data to write    */
struct  sockaddr *toaddr;               /* send to this Internet address*/
int     tolen;                          /* length of address field    */
{
        /* Convert inetgers from host byte order to network byte order  */

        fptr->fp_h.f_op = htons(fptr->fp_h.f_op);
        fptr->fp_h.f_pos = htonl(fptr->fp_h.f_pos);
        fptr->fp_h.f_count = htons(fptr->fp_h.f_count);

        if (sendto(s, fptr, len, 0, toaddr, tolen) < 0)
                return(SYSERR);
        return(OK);
}
```

Using the same buffer space for requests and replies is no accident. Our server has been designed so that normal replies often contain the same contents as their corresponding requests. For example, if the client sends a *close* request, the server returns exactly the same message to indicate success, including the operation code *FS_CLOSE* in field *f_op*. The server indicates failure by changing field *f_op* to *FS_ERROR* before returning the message.

13.8 Handlers For File Operations

13.8.1 Mapping Requests To Handlers

Each incoming request contains, in field *f_op*, a code that specifies the requested operation. The possible values for *f_op* are listed in file *fserver.h* above as constants of the form *FS_operation*. For each possible operation, the server has a procedure that handles the operation and forms a reply.

The main program, shown in file *fs.c*, uses array *rq* to map incoming requests to appropriate handler procedures. It extracts the operation code from field *f_op* of the incoming request, and compares it to field *req* in each element of array *rq*. Once it finds a match, the server invokes the procedure specified by field *reqproc*, passing the address of the request message and its length as arguments.

Using an array to map requests to operations makes it easy to add or delete entries, and allows the installer to configure the server for a particular subset of requests easily. Initialization code for the *rq* array occurs at the beginning of file *fs.c*, shown previously.

Each request handler must formulate its response in the message buffer, and return the length, where a length of zero suppresses a response. As an example, consider the *transaction* request. Because this version of the server does not handle the transaction operation, its handler is extremely simple. It changes field *f_op* in the request to indicate an error, and then returns it as a response. The code is found in file *fstrans.c*:

```
/* fstrans.c - fstrans */

#include "fs.h"

/*------------------------------------------------------------------------
 *  fstrans  -  handle transaction request and prepare reply
 *------------------------------------------------------------------------
 */
fstrans(fpacptr, flen)
struct  fpacket *fpacptr;
int     flen;
{
        struct  fphdr   *fptr;
        int     rfd;

        fptr = &fpacptr->fp_h;
        fptr->f_op = FS_ERROR;                  /* presently, no transactions */
        return(FHDRLEN);
}
```

How did the designer specify that the transaction operation mapped to procedure *fstrans*? Look back at the beginning of file *fs.c*. There, the declaration of *rq* includes initialization. It lists, among others, the pair (*FS_TRANS, fstrans*). The next sections show the code for other procedures listed in the *rq* initialization.

13.8.2 Handling The Close Operation

The client sends operation code *FS_CLOSE* to close a file; the server calls *fsclose* to handle closing:

```
/* fsclose.c - fsclose */

#include "fs.h"

/*------------------------------------------------------------------
 * fsclose  -  handle request to close a file
 *------------------------------------------------------------------
 */
fsclose(fpacptr, flen)
struct  fpacket *fpacptr;
int     flen;
{
        struct  fphdr    *fptr;
        int      rfd;

        fptr = &fpacptr->fp_h;
        if (Uncache(fptr->f_name) == SYSERR)
                fptr->f_op = FS_ERROR;
        return(FHDRLEN);
}
```

13.8.3 Handling The Access Operation

Like operation *FS_TRANS*, this server does not provide the *access* operation, *FS_ACCESS*. Thus, its handler, shown in file *fsaccess.c*, merely returns an error packet:

```
/* fsaccess.c - fsaccess */

#include "fs.h"

/*------------------------------------------------------------------
 * fsaccess  -  handle access request and prepare reply
 *------------------------------------------------------------------
 */
fsaccess(fpacptr, flen)
struct  fpacket *fpacptr;
int     flen;
```

```
{
        struct  fphdr    *fptr;
        int      rfd;

        fptr = &fpacptr->fp_h;
        fptr->f_op = FS_ERROR;
        return(FHDRLEN);
}
```

13.8.4 Handling The Unlink Operation

Clients send an *FS_UNLINK* request to destroy a file (i.e., permanently remove it from the file server). The server calls *fsunlink* to handle the request. *Fsunlink* uses procedure *rmfile* to remove the file (and any empty directories that result) from the UNIX file system. It then calls procedure *Uncache* to close the file and remove it from the open file cache table. File *fsunlink.c* contains the code.

```
/* fsunlink.c - fsunlink */

#include "fs.h"

/*------------------------------------------------------------------------
 * fsunlink  -  handle unlink request and prepare reply
 *------------------------------------------------------------------------
 */
fsunlink(fpacptr, flen)
struct  fpacket *fpacptr;
int     flen;
{
        struct  fphdr    *fptr;
        int      rfd;

        fptr = &fpacptr->fp_h;
        if (rmfile(fptr->f_name) < 0) {
                fptr->f_op = FS_ERROR;
        } else {
                Uncache(fptr->f_name);
        }
        return(flen);
}
```

13.8.5 Handling The Open Operation

A client uses operation *FS_OPEN* to open a file before its first use. As we will see, the stateless server must automatically open files for reading or writing whenever such a request arrives, so it may seem that having *open* requests are redundant. However, the *open* request permits a client to test whether a file can be opened without transferring data.

To minimize traffic, our server passes the file size back to the client in the response to an *open* request. The code is found in file *fsopen.c*:

```
/* fsopen.c - fsopen */

#include "fs.h"

/*-----------------------------------------------------------------------
 * fsopen  -  handle open request and prepare reply
 *-----------------------------------------------------------------------
 */
fsopen(fpacptr, flen)
struct  fpacket *fpacptr;
int     flen;
{
        struct  stat    stinfo;
        struct  fphdr   *fptr;
        int     rfd;

        fptr = &fpacptr->fp_h;
        if ((rfd=Open(fptr->f_name, fptr->f_count)) < 0 ||
                fstat(fcache[rfd].fd, &stinfo) < 0)
                fptr->f_op = FS_ERROR;
        else
                fptr->f_pos = stinfo.st_size;
        return(FHDRLEN);
}
```

After *fsopen* calls *Open* to open the file and update the cache, it uses the UNIX procedure *fstat* to obtain information about the file, and copies the file size into field *f_pos* of the response message.

13.8.6 Handling The Read Operation

With the utility procedures covered earlier in this chapter, implementing basic transfer operations becomes easy. For example, procedure *fsread*, shown below in file *fsread.c*, handles client's requests for file input.

```
/* fsread.c - fsread */

#include "fs.h"

/*------------------------------------------------------------------------
 *  fsread  -  handle read request and prepare reply
 *------------------------------------------------------------------------
 */
fsread(fpacptr, flen)
struct  fpacket *fpacptr;
int     flen;
{
        struct  fphdr   *fptr;
        int     rfd;
        int     n;

        fptr = &fpacptr->fp_h;
        if ((rfd=Open(fptr->f_name, FLOLD|FLREAD)) < 0
                || Seek(rfd, fptr->f_pos) < 0
                || (n=read(fcache[rfd].fd, fpacptr->fpdata,
                        fptr->f_count)) < 0) {
                fptr->f_op = FS_ERROR;
                return(FHDRLEN);
        }
        fcache[rfd].currpos = fptr->f_pos += fptr->f_count = n;
        return(n + FHDRLEN);
}
```

Before the server reads data from the specified file, it must make sure that the file is open for input and positioned as specified in the read request. *Fsread* uses procedures *Open* and *Seek* to open and position the file. As a side-effect, these procedures update the file cache.

Once the file has been opened successfully, *fsread* calls the UNIX *read* procedure to acquire data from the file and place it in the response packet. Finally, it updates the file position and count fields of the response as well as the file position information in the file cache, and returns the length of the response.

13.8.7 Handling The Write Operation

The server handles write requests similar to the way it handles read requests. As shown below, procedure *fswrite* calls *Open* and *Seek* to be sure the file has been opened for writing and positioned as specified in the request. It then invokes the UNIX *write* procedure to transfer data from the request packet to the specified file. Finally, it updates the transfer count in the response packet and the file posi-

tion in both the response packet and the file cache. After the transfer completes,
fswrite sends the packet header back to the client as a response.

```
/* fswrite.c - fswrite */

#include "fs.h"

/*------------------------------------------------------------------------
 * fswrite  -  handle write request and prepare reply
 *------------------------------------------------------------------------
 */
fswrite(fpacptr, flen)
struct   fpacket *fpacptr;
int      flen;
{
         struct   fphdr   *fptr;
         int      rfd;

         fptr = &fpacptr->fp_h;
         if ((rfd=Open(fptr->f_name, FLOLD|FLWRITE)) < 0
                 || Seek(rfd, fptr->f_pos) < 0
                 || (fptr->f_count=write(fcache[rfd].fd,
                         fpacptr->fpdata, fptr->f_count)) < 0) {
                 fptr->f_op = FS_ERROR;
         } else {
                 fcache[rfd].currpos = fptr->f_pos += fptr->f_count;
         }
         return(FHDRLEN);
}
```

13.8.8 Handling The Mkdir Operation

As we have seen, the server automatically creates intermediate directories as
needed when opening a file. Clients may know specific directories on the server's
file system, however, and may want to create or remove directories without opening
files in them. To make it possible to manipulate directories, our server honors two
directory commands: *FS_MKDIR*, and *FS_RMDIR*. Procedure *fsmkdir* handles
directory creation requests:

```
/* fsmkdir.c - fsmkdir */

#include "fs.h"

/*------------------------------------------------------------------------
 * fsmkdir  -  handle mkdir request and prepare reply
 *------------------------------------------------------------------------
 */
fsmkdir(fpacptr, flen)
struct  fpacket *fpacptr;
int     flen;
{
        struct  fphdr   *fptr;
        int     rfd;

        if (mkdir(fptr->f_name, fptr->f_count) < 0)
                fptr->f_op = FS_ERROR;
        else
                Uncache(fptr->f_name);
        return(FHDRLEN);
}
```

Fsmkdir uses the UNIX routine *mkdir* to create a directory. The name of the directory and its protection mode must be specified. The server takes the directory name from field *f_name* of the request, and the UNIX protection mode from field *f_count*. After the directory has been created, *fsmkdir* calls *Uncache* to remove any previously opened occurrence of the name from the file cache.

13.8.9 Handling The Rmdir Operation

Clients send operation code *FS_RMDIR* to the server to remove a named directory. Procedure *fsrmdir* handles directory removal by calling the UNIX procedure *rmdir* and then calling *Uncache* in case the name appeared in the open file cache.

```
/* fsrmdir.c - fsrmdir */

#include "fs.h"

/*------------------------------------------------------------------
 *  fsrmdir  -  handle rmdir request and prepare reply
 *------------------------------------------------------------------
 */
fsrmdir(fpacptr, flen)
struct  fpacket *fpacptr;
int     flen;
{
        struct  fphdr   *fptr;

        fptr = &fpacptr->fp_h;
        if (rmdir(fptr->f_name) < 0)
                fptr->f_op = FS_ERROR;
        else
                Uncache(fptr->f_name);
        return(FHDRLEN);
}
```

13.8.10 Handling The Rename Operation

The file server must translate requests to *rename* files (operation code
FS_RENAME) into actions appropriate for the system on which it runs. In
UNIX, for example, changing the name of a file changes the file's location in the
directory. Depending on the mapping of directories onto disks, such a change may
require a UNIX-based server to create the new file, copy the file contents, and then
remove the old file.

Our server calls procedure *fsrename*, shown in file *fsrename.c*, to handle file
renaming.

```
/* fsrename.c - fsrename */

#include "fs.h"

/*------------------------------------------------------------------
 *  fsrename  -  handle rename request and prepare reply
 *------------------------------------------------------------------
 */
fsrename(fpacptr, flen)
struct  fpacket *fpacptr;
int     flen;
```

```
{
        struct  fphdr    *fptr;
        int     rfd;
        int     len;
        int     from, to;                /* for copying, from & to files */
        char    buf[4096];               /* file copy buffer area        */

        fptr = &fpacptr->fp_h;
        if (rename(fptr->f_name, fpacptr->fpdata) < 0) {
                if (errno != EXDEV) {
                        fptr->f_op = FS_ERROR;
                        Uncache(fptr->f_name);
                        Uncache(fpacptr->fpdata);
                        return(FHDRLEN);
                }
                /* Copy the data to target file system */
                if ((from=openfile(fptr->f_name, FLOLD|FLREAD)) < 0) {
                        fptr->f_op = FS_ERROR;
                        return(FHDRLEN);
                }
                if ((rmfile(fpacptr->fpdata) < 0 && errno != ENOENT) ||
                        (to=openfile(fpacptr->fpdata, FLWRITE)) < 0) {
                        fptr->f_op = FS_ERROR;
                        close(from);
                        return(FHDRLEN);
                }
                while ((len=read(from, buf, sizeof(buf))) > 0)
                        if ((len=write(to, buf, len)) < 0)
                                break;
                close(from);
                close(to);
                if (len != 0) {          /* error transferring data      */
                        fptr->f_op = FS_ERROR;
                        rmfile(fpacptr->fpdata);
                        return(FHDRLEN);
                }
                if (rmfile(fptr->f_name) < 0) {
                        fptr->f_op = FS_ERROR;
                        rmfile(fpacptr->fpdata);
                        return(FHDRLEN);
                }
                Uncache(fptr->f_name);
                Uncache(fpacptr->fpdata);
                return(FHDRLEN);
        }
}
```

```
        return(flen);
}
```

Requests to rename a file contain the original file name in field *f_name* of the request header, as usual, and the new file name in field *fpdata*. If the UNIX routine *rename* succeeds, it means that the file does not need to be copied, and *fsrename* can return the request unaltered to indicate success. Otherwise, *fsrename* undertakes a sequence of steps to change the name by copying the file. It opens *from* and *to* files, and then enters a while loop to copy data, using the local variable *buf* as a temporary buffer. Once the copy completes, *fsrename* closes the files it was using, and removes the old file from the system. If at any step an error occurs, *fsrename* recovers by closing the temporary files, and returns an error message to the client.

Because renaming may destroy old files and copying may invalidate cached position information, *fsrename* carefully removes any occurrence of either the old or new names from its cache.

13.9 Server Initialization

13.9.1 Command Line Arguments

The UNIX command interpreter does more than recognize commands. It collects the remaining non-blank strings on the command line and makes them available to the program at execution time. The first two arguments of any UNIX main program describes the command line by which it was invoked. Refer to the declaration of *main* in file *fs.c* (shown previously). The first argument, *argc*, tells the number of words on the command line, and the second argument, *argv*, points to an array of *argc* entries, each of which is a pointer to a null-terminated character string.

Our server is usually invoked by typing

```
fs
```

to UNIX. If nothing else appears on the command line, the server opens a default UDP port and begins work. However, we have designed the server to work on an arbitrary UDP port number, and allow the invoker to specify the port on the command line. Thus, if the user types:

```
fs -p3000
```

the server should open UDP port 3000. In addition, UNIX permits sites to define names for UDP ports, and offers a way to open a datagram connection by name. So, we will allow the user to type

```
fs -pxinuport
```

to specify that the server should open the UDP connection using the name *xinu-port*.

13.9.2 Extracting Arguments At Run-Time

Remember that command line information is passed to the main program with two arguments, *argc* and *argv*. Figure 13.2 shows the storage for command line information at run-time.

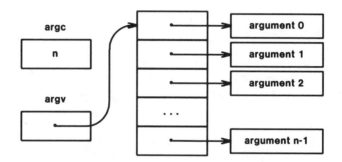

Figure 13.2 The run-time storage for command line arguments.

Our server passes both *argc* and *argv* to procedure *finit*, shown below, which passes them to procedure *fgetargs*. *Fgetargs*, which appears in file *fgetargs.c* below, examines *argc* and *argv* to see whether a UDP port was specified on the command line.

```
/* fgetargs.c - fgetargs, fexit */

#include "fs.h"

/*-------------------------------------------------------------------------
 * fgetargs - parse arguments to file server and record information
 *-------------------------------------------------------------------------
 */
fgetargs(argc, argv)
int      argc;
char     *argv[];
{
        char     ch;
        pname = PORTNAME;
        port = -1;
        if (argc == 1)
                return(OK);
        if (argc > 2 || strncmp(argv[1],"-p",2)!=0)
                fexit();
        argv[1]+=2;
        if ((ch= *argv[1]) >= '0' && ch <= '9') {
                if ((port = atoi(argv[1])) <= 0)
                        fexit();
        } else {
                pname = argv[1];
        }
        return(OK);
}


/*-------------------------------------------------------------------------
 * fexit - print use message and exit
 *-------------------------------------------------------------------------
 */
fexit()
{
        printf("fs: proper use is fs [-pPORT]\n");
        exit(1);
}
```

Fgetargs begins by setting the external integer *port* to -1, and the external string pointer to the constant *PORTNAME*, indicating that the server should open the socket by name. It then checks to see if a command line argument was supplied, and if so, whether it begins with the characters, $-p$. If it finds a command line string that begins with *-p*, *fgetargs* checks the next character to determine whether

the remainder of the string contains digits. If it finds a digit, *fgetargs* calls the
UNIX library routine *atoi* to convert it to an integer and places the converted value
in the external variable *port*. Otherwise, it assigns the address of the string to
pname and leaves *port* set to −1.

13.9.3 Server Initialization

Procedure *finit* contains the remainder of the server initialization code.

```
/* finit.c - finit */

#include "fs.h"

/*------------------------------------------------------------------------
 * finit  -  initialize data structures  for file server; return socket
 *------------------------------------------------------------------------
 */
finit(argc, argv)
int     argc;
char    *argv[];
{
        int     pid;
        int     i;
        int     sock;
        struct  servent *servptr;
        struct  servent *getservbyname();
        struct  sockaddr_in     sockadr;

        freelst = 0;
        fgetargs(argc, argv);
        sock = socket(AF_INET, SOCK_DGRAM, 0);
        if (port < 0) {
                if ( (servptr=getservbyname(pname, "udp")) == NULL)
                        exit(2);
                port = servptr->s_port;
        } else
                port = htonl(port);
        sockadr.sin_family = AF_INET;
        sockadr.sin_port = port;
        if (bind(sock, &sockadr, sizeof(sockadr)) < 0)
                exit(3);
        NEWEST = OLDEST = NOFILE;
        umask(0);
```

```
        /* Initialize open file information cache */

        for (i=0 ; i<MAXNFILES ; i++) {
                fcache[i].prev = NOFILE;
                fcache[i].next = i==MAXNFILES ? NOFILE : i+1;
        }
        if ( (pid=fork()) < 0 )            /* if fork fails, abort        */
                exit(4);
        else if (pid > 0)                  /* let parent exit so child can */
                exit(0);                   /*  run in background          */
        return(sock);
}
```

After calling *fgetargs*, *finit* creates a socket. It then examines the external variable *port* to decide whether it needs to convert a port name into a port number. Once a UDP port number has been chosen and placed in network byte order, *finit* calls the UNIX routine *bind* to give the operating system a UDP port number to use with the socket.

Finit also initializes the file cache, linking all entries onto the free list, and making all the *prev* fields point to the list head. It initializes the list head *next* and *prev* pointers to point back to the head.

The server uses the UNIX primitive *fork* to spawn a new process. The new process begins executing exactly the same code with exactly the same values for variables except that the process id returned by *fork* differs. The parent process immediately terminates itself by calling the UNIX routine *exit*. Meanwhile, the child process continues executing, and the call to *finit* returns. This maneuver may seem useless, but it has an interesting effect: it forces the server to execute in background. The command interpreter thinks that the command has finished because the process it creates to execute the command *has* finished (even though it has started a new process that continues to execute in the background).

13.10 Summary

The file server examined in this chapter provides another example of the client-server model. Clients send the server requests to *open*, *read*, or *write* files, and the server responds after attempting to honor the request. Problems like loss of packets, delivery of duplicate packets, or delivery out-of-order can produce incorrect results when a server tries to maintain information about clients and the history of their requests. To minimize such problems, the server should be *stateless*. To keep our server stateless, we forced each request to contain the full file name, operation, and position in the file at which the operation is to be performed. Thus, requests can be duplicated or delivered out of order without danger.

Statelessness does not imply inefficiency. In fact, the example file server maintained considerable state information in its internal cache of open files. The internal state information was never passed to clients, but merely used on receipt of a request to avoid unnecessary computation. In most circumstances, our server will leave a file open until the client finishes using it. Moreover, if a single client reads a file sequentially, the server will leave the file positioned in such a way that successive requests can be satisfied without adjusting the file position.

FOR FURTHER STUDY

The idea of providing file access across a network is not new, but has received much attention in the past decade. Mitchell and Dion [1982] compare two file servers. Brownbridge, Marshall, and Randall [1982] present a network file server for UNIX built from user-level processes. Weinberger [1985] reports on a recent UNIX network file system built in the operating system kernel. In other recent work, Mullender and Tanenbaum [1985] discusses an interesting file server design that uses version management. Brown, Kolling, and Taft [1985] consider a file server designed for storing databases. Fridrich and Older [1981] and Swinehart, McDaniel, and Boggs [1979] also report interesting work with file servers.

EXERCISES

13.1   Build a remote disk server and compare it to the remote file server. Which of the two takes less space? Which performs faster?

13.2   Modify the file server to accept an optional argument -*uxxx*, where *xxx* denotes a user login id, and execute as if owned by that user.

13.3   Add transaction processing to the file server by expanding *fstrans*. Define the data area of transaction requests to contain a type of transaction and data, and have *fstrans* return results in the data field. For example, add a date transaction that returns the current time and date, and a host-to-address transaction that accepts a host name and returns that host's internet address.

13.4   All programmers expect their file system to guarantee the following fundamental property: *(Data Preservation) Read operations return the data written by the most recent write operation.* Under what conditions might our file server fail to guarantee data preservation.

13.5   What response does a client receive to a successful *rename* operation? Be careful.

13.6   Remove the cache and build a version of the file server that opens a file, performs a transfer, and closes the file, for every request. Compare the two versions for speed.

13.7   Enhance the file server to allow each client to add ownership information, access modes, and authentication to its requests, making it possible for one client to create files that another cannot read.

13.8 Study permission in the UNIX file system. When the server runs, what files can it read? What files can it write?

13.9 Modify the server to add a client-dependent prefix to every file name, forcing each client to access files in a separate subtree. For example, if a client with internet address 192.5.48.33 sends a request with file name *la/b*, replace the file name with */tmp/192.5.48.33/a/b* before accessing the file.

13.10 Modify the server to change its UNIX userid and groupid when it starts. Under what userid do you choose to execute? What userids do other servers use? Why?

13.11 Without looking ahead, write a Xinu client that uses the file server to read and write files.

13.12 Write a UNIX client for the file server.

13.13 Suppose you wanted to have the server write a log record into a file each time it received a request or sent a reply. What server procedure would you use to open the log file? Why?

13.14 Build a new version of the file server that only supports *open*, *read*, *write*, and *close* requests. How much smaller is your new version than the original (a) when measured in lines of code? (b) when measured in space required at run-time?

14

Remote File Access

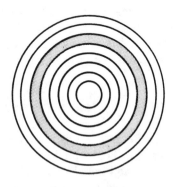

14.1 Introduction

The previous chapter described a stateless file server, showing how it accepted a request, performed the specified operation, and responded to the client. This chapter completes our study of remote file access by showing how a diskless station uses the server.

14.2 Remote File Pseudo-Devices

Our goal is to hide the details of whether a file is local or remote, and make access to all files uniform. The *principle of access transparency* will guide many of our design decisions:

> *Differences between remote and local file access should be invisible to processes using them.*

For now, we will consider only the remote file system, casting it into the Xinu device paradigm. The next chapter will add a uniform naming scheme to all the storage systems, completely hiding their differences.

Making the remote file system fit into the device mechanism consists of adding two new types of pseudo-devices. First, processes will use a single *remote file system* pseudo-device to establish remote access. Second, processes will use a specific *remote file pseudo-device* to access an individual file.

Processes access remote files analogous to the way they perform datagram communication. To establish access to a remote file, the process calls *open* on the remote file system pseudo-device, which returns the device id of an individual remote file pseudo-device. The process then calls *write* or *read* on the remote file pseudo-device to transfer data to or from the file. Once a process finishes using the remote file, it calls *close*, enabling the operating system to reallocate the pseudo-device id.

Choosing to make the remote file client a Xinu pseudo-device means that the code will be organized as a device driver. User processes will call upper-half driver routines that implement operations like *read* or *write*. These routines will formulate a request, send it to the server, and await a reply. Because the driver describes a pseudo-device, there will be no interrupts, and no need for lower-half routines to handle them. Instead, the upper-half routines that send requests and receive responses will block the calling process until a response packet arrives.

14.3 Maintaining State Information

Because the file server is stateless, the client must maintain all the state information. For example, the client is responsible for recording the access modes, file name, and initial position at the time the file is opened. Each time a user process attempts to read or write data, the client must verify that the access modes permit the requested operation, and update the file state information.

Maintaining the state information in a concurrent environment can be tricky because the delay between making a server request and receiving a response is large. If the client updates the file position when it sends a request to the server, lost requests will leave the position recorded incorrectly. If the client waits until it receives a reply before updating the position information, concurrent read requests may read from the same position. Our implementation avoids these problems two ways: it will prohibit concurrent access to a particular remote file pseudo-device, and it will always wait to receive a response from the server before updating state information.

14.4 Remote File Pseudo-Device Support Routines

Our examination of the remote file pseudo-device driver begins with the declarations of the pseudo-device control block and definition of symbolic constants used throughout the code. Recall from the previous chapter that the server includes file *fserver.h*. In addition to definitions in *fserver.h*, the client uses definitions found in *rfile.h*.

```
/* rfile.h */

#include <file.h>

/* Remote file device control block and defined constants */

/* Constants for server device control functions */

#define RFCLEAR          1                  /* Clear incoming messages       */

/* Constants for controlling retrys for server communication */

#define RTIMOUT          5                  /* Timeout for server response   */
#define RMAXTRY          2                  /* Number of retrys per op.      */

/* Constants for rf pseudo-device state variable */

#define RFREE           -1                  /* This pseudo-device is unused */
#define RUSED            1                  /* This pseudo-device is used    */

/* Declaration of rf pseudo-device I/O control block */

struct  rfblk   {                           /* Remote file control block     */
        int     rf_dnum;                    /* File's device num in devtab   */
        char    rf_name[RNAMLEN];           /* Name of remote file           */
        int     rf_state;                   /* State of this pseudo device   */
        int     rf_mode;                    /* FLREAD, FLWRITE or both        */
        int     rf_mutex;                   /* exclusion for this file       */
        long    rf_pos;                     /* current byte offset in file   */
};

#ifndef Nrf
#define Nrf      1
#endif
struct  rfinfo  {                           /* all remote server info.       */
        int     device;                     /* device descriptor for server */
        int     rmutex;                     /* mutual exclusion for server   */
        struct  rfblk   rftab[Nrf];         /* remote file control blocks    */
};

extern  struct  rfinfo  Rf;
```

With the declarations of data structures in place, we can explore the remote
file driver, starting with, *rfalloc*, a utility procedure that selects a free remote file
pseudo-device. The code for *rfalloc* appears in file *rfalloc.c*.

```
/* rfalloc.c - rfalloc */

#include <conf.h>
#include <kernel.h>
#include <fserver.h>
#include <rfile.h>


/*------------------------------------------------------------------------
 * rfalloc  --  allocate pseudo device for a remote file; return id
 *------------------------------------------------------------------------
 */
rfalloc()
{
        int     i;
        char    ps;

        disable(ps);
        for (i=0 ; i<Nrf ; i++)
                if (Rf.rftab[i].rf_state == RFREE) {
                        Rf.rftab[i].rf_state = RUSED;
                        restore(ps);
                        return(i);
                }
        restore(ps);
        return(SYSERR);
}
```

Rfalloc mentions several variables that are declared in *rfile.h*, especially the
external variable *Rf*. *Rf* is a structure of type *rfinfo* that contains all the external
variables used by the client, including *rftab*, the array of control blocks for remote
file pseudo devices.

Allocating a pseudo-device consists of searching through *rftab* until an available entry is found. An available entry has field *rf_state* marked free. Once an
available entry is found, *rfalloc* marks it used, and returns its index to the caller.

Procedure *rfsend* forms a second utility routine that underlies the remote file
driver. *Rfsend*, found below in file *rfsend.c*, is responsible for sending a message to
the server and awaiting a reply.

```
/* rfsend.c - rfsend */

#include <conf.h>
#include <kernel.h>
#include <network.h>

/*------------------------------------------------------------------------
 * rfsend  --  send message to remote server and await reply
 *------------------------------------------------------------------------
 */
rfsend(fptr, reqlen, rplylen)
struct  fphdr   *fptr;
int     reqlen;
int     rplylen;
{
        int     trys;
        int     ret;
        char    ps;

        /* Clear server queue, and send packet to it */

        if (Rf.device == RCLOSED) {
                Rf.device = open(INTERNET, RSERVER, ANYLPORT);
                if (Rf.device == SYSERR ||
                    control(Rf.device, DG_SETMODE, DG_DMODE|DG_TMODE)
                    == SYSERR)
                        return(SYSERR);
        }
        disable(ps);
        control(Rf.device, DG_CLEAR);
        for (trys=0 ; trys<RMAXTRY ; trys++) {
                if ( write(Rf.device, fptr, reqlen)
                        == SYSERR) {
                        restore(ps);
                        return(SYSERR);
                }
                if ( (ret=read(Rf.device, fptr, rplylen) )
                    !=SYSERR && ret != TIMEOUT) {
                        restore(ps);
                        return(ret);
                }
        }
        restore(ps);
        return(SYSERR);
}
```

Rfsend takes three arguments that specify the address of a request packet, the length of the request, the length of the expected reply. It writes replies back into the area from which it takes the request, and returns the length of the request as its function value.

The operation of *rfsend* is as expected. It assumes that the calling process has exclusive use of the server. Before sending a request, it checks to see if a datagram device has been opened to the server, and opens the datagram device if needed. It sets the datagram device mode to transfer data only, instructs the datagram device to time every read operation, and records the datagram device id in the device control block.

With a datagram device open to the server, *rfsend* enters a loop that iterates *RMAXTRY* times. Before iterating, *rfsend* clears any waiting datagrams. It sends the message using a *write* operation, and blocks on a read request waiting for a reply. If a response arrives, *rfsend* returns the response length to its caller. Otherwise, it returns *SYSERR* to inform the caller that a problem occurred.

14.5 Composing Request Packets

Because each of the upper-half routines will need to compose a request packet, the code for composing requests has been isolated in procedure *rfmkpac*, shown in file *rfmkpac.c*. When reading the code, remember that file *fserver.h* from Chapter 13 contains the declarations of the request packet format and contents.

```
/* rfmkpac.c - rfmkpac */

#include <conf.h>
#include <kernel.h>
#include <network.h>

static  struct  fpacket packet;

/*------------------------------------------------------------------------
 * rfmkpac -- make a remote file request packet and send it
 *------------------------------------------------------------------------
 */
rfmkpac(rop, rname, rpos, buff, len)
int     rop;
char    *rname;
long    *rpos;
char    *buff;
int     len;
{
```

```
struct  fphdr   *fptr;
int     reqlen, rplylen;

wait(Rf.rmutex);
fptr = (struct fphdr *) &packet;
fptr->f_op = hs2net(rop);
fptr->f_pos = hl2net(*rpos);
fptr->f_count = hs2net(len);
strncpy(fptr->f_name, rname, RNAMLEN);
reqlen = rplylen = FPHLEN + len;
switch (rop) {

    case FS_WRITE:
    case FS_RENAME:
        if (len > RDATLEN) {
                signal(Rf.rmutex);
                return(SYSERR);
        }
        blkcopy(packet.fpdata, buff, len);
        rplylen = FPHLEN;
        break;

    case FS_CLOSE:
    case FS_OPEN:
    case FS_UNLINK:
    case FS_MKDIR:
    case FS_RMDIR:
    case FS_ACCESS:
        rplylen = FPHLEN;
        /* fall through */

    case FS_READ:
        if (len > RDATLEN) {
                signal(Rf.rmutex);
                return(SYSERR);
        }
        reqlen = FPHLEN;
        break;

    default:
        ;
}
if (rfsend(fptr, reqlen, rplylen) == SYSERR ||
    net2hs(fptr->f_op) == FS_ERROR) {
        signal(Rf.rmutex);
```

```
                return(SYSERR);
        }
        switch (rop) {

            case FS_READ:
                blkcopy(buff, packet.fpdata, len);
                /* fall through */

            case FS_WRITE:
                *rpos = net2hl(fptr->f_pos);
                len = net2hs(fptr->f_count);
                break;

            default:
                len = OK;
        }
        signal(Rf.rmutex);
        return(len);
}
```

Composing a packet consists of converting the supplied arguments to network byte order and placing them in the header portion of the message. Once the request packet has been generated, *rfmkpac* computes the length of request packet, copies in the data, if any, and computes the request length and the response length.

The lengths of response and request packets can be computed from the operation code and the additional data (if any). Most requests contain only a header, but *write* requests must include the header plus the data being written. Similarly, although most responses require only a header, the response to a *read* request will need space for a header plus the data being read.

After calling *rfsend* to send the request packet and await a response, *rfmkpac* again uses the operation code to determine how to handle the response. For example, data received in response to a *read* command must be copied back into the user's buffer area.

Once *rfmkpac* receives a response, it examines the operation field *f_op* to determine how to handle it. For read operations, *rfmkpac* copies the data from the response packet into the caller's buffer. For any transfer operation, it must update the stored file position. Finally, *rfmkpac* returns the length of the data transferred, or *OK* if the operation did not involve data transfer.

14.6 A Universal Remote I/O Routine

With a procedure to make and send packets in place, we can build a universal I/O routine that makes a request based on information in the remote file control block. The universal remote I/O routine is named *rfio*, and can be found in file *rfio.c*, below. As we will see, most of the upper-half procedures use *rfio* to form packets, send them and accumulate the results.

```
/* rfio.c - rfio */

#include <conf.h>
#include <kernel.h>
#include <network.h>


/*------------------------------------------------------------------------
 *  rfio  --  perform input or output using remote file server
 *------------------------------------------------------------------------
 */
rfio(devptr, rop, buff, len)
struct  devsw   *devptr;
int     rop;
char    *buff;
int     len;
{
        struct  rfblk   *rfptr;
        int     retcode;

        rfptr = (struct rfblk *)devptr->dvioblk;
        wait(rfptr->rf_mutex);
        if (len < 0 || rfptr->rf_state == RFREE) {
                signal(rfptr->rf_mutex);
                return(SYSERR);
        }
        retcode = rfmkpac(rop, rfptr->rf_name, &rfptr->rf_pos, buff, len);
        signal(rfptr->rf_mutex);
        return(retcode);
}
```

Rfio works for a specified remote file pseudo-device, waiting for exclusive use of the device before calling *rfmkpac* to form and send the request. Once the transaction completes, *rfio* signals the exclusion semaphore and returns to its caller.

14.7 Opening A Remote File

To open a remote file, the user invokes system call *open* on the remote file system pseudo-device, producing the device id of one of the individual remote file pseudo-devices. *Read*, *write*, *seek* and *control* operations apply only to the individual file device; the system pseudo-device is used only to open remote files.

Our examination of upper-half driver routines begins with the remote file system *open* procedure, *rfopen*, shown in file *rfopen.c*.

```
/* rfopen.c - rfopen */

#include <conf.h>
#include <kernel.h>
#include <network.h>


/*------------------------------------------------------------------------
 * rfopen  --  open a remote file
 *------------------------------------------------------------------------
 */
rfopen(devptr, name, mode)
struct  devsw   *devptr;
char    *name;
char    *mode;
{
        struct  rfblk   *rfptr;
        int     i;
        int     mbits;
        int     devnum;
        char    ps;

        disable(ps);
        if (strlen(name) > RNAMLEN || (mbits=ckmode(mode)) == SYSERR
            || (i=rfalloc()) == SYSERR) {
                restore(ps);
                return(SYSERR);
        }
        rfptr = &Rf.rftab[i];
        devnum = rfptr->rf_dnum;
        strcpy(rfptr->rf_name, name);
        rfptr->rf_mode = mbits;
        rfptr->rf_pos = 0L;

        /* send remote file open request */
```

```
        if ( rfio(&devtab[devnum], FS_OPEN, NULLSTR, mbits) == SYSERR ) {
                rfptr->rf_state = RFREE;
                restore(ps);
                return(SYSERR);
        }
        restore(ps);
        return(devnum);
}
```

Rfopen performs three principle chores. It allocates a free remote file pseudo-device, initializes the control block for that device, and contacts the server to make sure the file can be opened. The code shows that *rfopen* calls procedure *ckmode* to check the mode and convert it from a string to an integer with bits set according to the constants defined in *file.h*. It then uses *rfalloc* to find and reserve a remote file pseudo-device. After initializing the remote file pseudo-device control block, *rfopen* uses *rfio* to send an *open* request to the remote server before it returns the new file's device id to its caller.

Because the server is stateless, it does not guarantee to keep a file open. In fact, we have seen that high activity at the server can force it to close an open file (when it becomes the least recently used entry in the cache). We have also seen that the client must always specify the full file name and file position in a request, so the server can automatically reopen files if needed. Thus, asking the server to open files is not necessary.

Why should *rfopen* bother to interact with the server? To answer the question, consider what it means to open a file. Most programmers depend on the result returned by *open* to tell them whether the file can be accessed; they think of the result returned by *read* or *write* as showing the success or failure of that particular operation. Thus, delaying contact with the server until the first data transfer produces confusing results. More important, making *open* behave differently for remote files than for local ones violates the principle of access transparency.

14.8 Closing A Remote File

We have seen how *rfopen* allocates a remote file pseudo-device. Procedure *rfclose* is the upper-half driver routine called when a user closes a remote file pseudo-device. It contacts the server to close the file, and then releases the remote file pseudo-device, making it available for future use. File *rfclose.c* contains the code.

```
/* rfclose.c - rfclose */

#include <conf.h>
#include <kernel.h>
#include <network.h>

/*------------------------------------------------------------------------
 * rfclose  --  close a remote file by deallocating pseudo device
 *------------------------------------------------------------------------
 */
rfclose(devptr)
struct  devsw   *devptr;
{
        struct  rfblk   *rfptr;
        long    junk;           /* argument to rfmkpac; not really used */

        rfptr = (struct rfblk *)devptr->dvioblk;
        if (rfptr->rf_state == RFREE)
                return(SYSERR);
        wait(rfptr->rf_mutex);
        junk = 0L; /* 0L is long zero constant */
        rfmkpac(FS_CLOSE,rfptr->rf_name,&junk,(char *)&junk,0);
        rfptr->rf_state = RFREE;
        signal(rfptr->rf_mutex);
        return(OK);
}
```

Should *rfclose* contact the server? Answering such design questions is not easy because the cost and benefits are often incomparable. On one hand, having a stateless server makes it possible to simply close the local pseudo-device and not bother informing the server. Everything would work correctly, and it would certainly take less time than sending a message to the server and waiting for its response. On the other hand, failing to close files may cause overhead at the server.

We chose to have *rfclose* inform the server for two reasons. First, programmers seldom mind the delay associated with file opening and closing. Second, the client should not depend on a particular server implementation, and leaving files open may make the server implementation inefficient.

14.9 Reading From A Remote File

We are now ready to consider the two basic transfer operations, *read* and *write*. With the utility procedures described earlier in this chapter, reading and writing to a remote file becomes trivial. Procedure *rfread*, shown in file *rfread.c*, transfers data from the remote file to the user.

```
/* rfread.c - rfread */

#include <conf.h>
#include <kernel.h>
#include <network.h>

/*------------------------------------------------------------------
 *  rfread  --  read one or more bytes from a remote file
 *------------------------------------------------------------------
 */
rfread(devptr, buff, len)
struct  devsw   *devptr;
char    *buff;
int     len;
{
        return( rfio(devptr, FS_READ, buff, min(len,RDATLEN) ) );
}
```

14.10 Writing To A Remote File

Procedure *rfwrite*, shown in file *rfwrite.c* forms the upper-half *write* routine, allowing a process to transfer data to a remote file. As the code shows, *rfwrite* consists of a call to *rfio* with appropriate arguments.

```
/* rfwrite.c - rfwrite */

#include <conf.h>
#include <kernel.h>
#include <network.h>

/*------------------------------------------------------------------------
 *  rfwrite  --  write one or more bytes to a remote file
 *------------------------------------------------------------------------
 */
rfwrite(devptr, buff, len)
struct  devsw   *devptr;
char    *buff;
int     len;
{
        int     i;

        if (len < 0)
                return(SYSERR);
        for (i=len ; i > 0 ; i-=RDATLEN, buff+=RDATLEN)
                if (rfio(devptr,FS_WRITE,buff,min(i,RDATLEN)) == SYSERR)
                        return(SYSERR);
        return(len);
}
```

14.11 Single Character Transfer Operations

With upper-half procedures in place that implement the *read* and *write* operations, single character transfers with *getc* and *putc* can be built easily. The upper-
half routines for single character transfers from or to a remote file follow:

```
/* rfgetc.c - rfgetc */

#include <conf.h>
#include <kernel.h>
#include <network.h>

/*------------------------------------------------------------------------
 *  rfgetc  --  get a character from a remote file
 *------------------------------------------------------------------------
 */
rfgetc(devptr)
struct  devsw   *devptr;
```

```
{
        char    ch;
        int     retcode;

        if ( (retcode=read(devptr->dvnum, &ch, 1)) == 1)
                return(ch);
        else if (retcode != EOF)
                retcode = SYSERR;
        return(retcode);
}
```

As the code shows, *rfgetc* simply calls *read*, requesting a transfer of one character. *Read* passes the call to *rfread*, and then returns the character read to its caller. Similarly, the code for *rfputc*, shown below, uses *write* to write a single character to the specified file.

```
/* rfputc.c - rfputc */

#include <conf.h>
#include <kernel.h>
#include <network.h>

/*------------------------------------------------------------------------
 * rfputc  --  put a single character into a remote file
 *------------------------------------------------------------------------
 */
rfputc(devptr, ch)
struct  devsw   *devptr;
char    ch;
{
        char    outch;

        outch = ch;
        if ( write(devptr->dvnum, &outch, 1) == 1)
                return(OK);
        else
                return(SYSERR);
}
```

14.12 Seeking In A Remote File

A process calls *seek* to change the position of an open file, so that the next transfer operation begins at the new position. Implementing *seek* for remote files is trivial because the client maintains the file position information locally. Thus, the driver routine only needs to change the local position as shown by procedure *rfseek*.

```
/* rfseek.c - rfseek */

#include <conf.h>
#include <kernel.h>
#include <fserver.h>
#include <rfile.h>

/*------------------------------------------------------------------------
 * rfseek  --  seek to a specified position of a remote file
 *------------------------------------------------------------------------
 */
rfseek(devptr, offset)
struct  devsw   *devptr;
long    offset;
{
        struct  rfblk   *rfptr;

        rfptr = (struct rfblk *)devptr->dvioblk;
        wait(rfptr->rf_mutex);
        rfptr->rf_pos = offset;
        signal(rfptr->rf_mutex);
        return(OK);
}
```

14.13 Operations On Remote Files

In addition to the basic operations like *read* and *write*, processes may need to manipulate files or test their status. For example, because most files persist once they have been created, a process may need to explicitly remove temporary files. Our remote file system accommodates operations like removal through the *control* primitive.

How should the designer choose a set of file manipulation operations? The principle of access transparency suggests that we should select a few basic operations that apply to all files whether local or remote. In Xinu, there are three of these *universal* file manipulation functions, as defined in file *file.h*. They are: *FLACCESS*, an operation to test file accessibility, *FLREMOVE*, an operation to remove (destroy) a file, and *FLRENAME* an operation that changes the name of a file.

The server built in Chapter 13 accommodates each of the three universal file operations, so we only need to incorporate these operations into our remote file pseudo-device driver. We will use the Xinu *control* operation, making it possible to use each of the universal file manipulation functions as an argument. Thus, the user could call *control*(*R*, *FLREMOVE*, "abc") to remove file *abc*, where *R* denotes the remote file system pseudo-device.

Procedure *rfcntl*, found in file *rfcntl.c*, implements the upper-half driver routine for the remote file system pseudo-device. It supports four possible control operations: the three universal file manipulation operations and an operation to clear the datagram port associated with the remote server. To clear server messages, *rfcntl* uses *control* on the datagram pseudo-device associated with the server. We have already seen that *rfsend* uses the same call to clear old messages from the datagram device before attempting to communicate with the server.

```
/* rfcntl.c - rfcntl */

#include <conf.h>
#include <kernel.h>
#include <network.h>

/*------------------------------------------------------------------
 * rfcntl  --  control the remote file server access system
 *------------------------------------------------------------------
 */
rfcntl(devptr, func, addr, addr2)
struct  devsw   *devptr;
int     func;
char    *addr;
char    *addr2;
{
        long    junk;
        int     len;

        junk = 0L;
        switch (func) {

        case RFCLEAR:
                /* clear port associated with rfserver */
                control(Rf.device, DG_CLEAR);
                return(OK);

        /* Universal file manipulation functions */

        case FLACCESS:
                return(rfmkpac(FS_ACCESS,addr,&junk,(char *)&junk,addr2));

        case FLREMOVE:
                return( rfmkpac(FS_UNLINK, addr, &junk, NULLSTR, 0) );

        case FLRENAME:
                len = strlen(addr2) + 1;
                return( rfmkpac(FS_RENAME, addr, &junk, addr2, len) );

        default:
                return(SYSERR);
        }
}
```

Implementing the universal file manipulation functions is trivial because the server directly supports operations that correspond to each of them. *Rfcntl* uses *rfmkpac* to create and send a server packet that contains the appropriate request. If the operation is successful, the server responds positively, *rfmkpac* returns *OK*, and *rfcntl* passes the same result to its caller. If the server returns an error message or the datagram port runs out of time before it receives a response, *rfmkpac* returns *SYSERR*, and so does *rfcntl*. Note that a *FLRENAME* operation causes *rfcntl* to place the new file name in the data area of the message it sends to the remote server, and includes the terminating null byte in the length it passes to *rfmkpac*.

14.14 Remote File Device Initialization

Initializing the remote file pseudo-devices is straightforward, as shown by procedure *rfinit* in file *rfinit.c*.

```
/* rfinit.c - rfinit */

#include <conf.h>
#include <kernel.h>
#include <fserver.h>
#include <rfile.h>


/*------------------------------------------------------------------------
 *  rfinit  --  initialize remote file pseudo devices
 *------------------------------------------------------------------------
 */
rfinit(devptr)
struct  devsw    *devptr;
{
        struct  rfblk    *rfptr;

        devptr->dvioblk = (char *) (rfptr = &Rf.rftab[devptr->dvminor]);
        rfptr->rf_dnum = devptr->dvnum;
        rfptr->rf_name[0] = NULLCH;
        rfptr->rf_state = RFREE;
        rfptr->rf_mutex = screate(1);
        rfptr->rf_pos = 0L;
        if (devptr->dvminor == 0) {       /* done just once */
                Rf.device = RCLOSED;
                Rf.rmutex = screate(1);
        }
}


struct  rfinfo  Rf;
```

The system calls *rfinit* at startup for each remote file pseudo-device, passing it a pointer to the device's entry in the device switch table. *Rfinit* uses the minor device number to locate the I/O control block for the device, and then initializes fields in the control block. It sets the state field to *RFREE*, showing that the pseudo-device is available for allocation, it clears the name and position fields, and copies the device id for the device into field *rf_dnum*. It also creates the device mutual exclusion semaphore, and places its id in field *rf_mutex*.

Once *rfinit* finishes initializing the control block, it checks the minor device number to see whether it has just initialized minor device 0. If so, it also creates the remote file system mutual exclusion semaphore, and marks the server device *RCLOSED* to show that no datagram device has been opened for the client to access the server. This code may seem strange, and it is a bit crude. It might be easier to understand if we built two initialization routines, one for the remote file pseudo-devices, and another for the remote file system pseudo-device. Marking the server device closed and allocating the server mutual exclusion semaphore belongs in the remote file system initialization routine (which would only be called once). Including it here is a short-cut, but requires us to check the minor device number to prevent executing the code once per remote file pseudo-device.

14.15 Remote File Pseudo-Device Configuration

We have seen a set of procedures that comprise the remote file pseudo-device driver. It may be easier to see how they fit together if we consider how a remote file device is configured into the system. The declarations, shown below in the format required by the *config* program, specify that the remote file procedures are partitioned into two device types: a *master* device used only by *open*, and the remote file pseudo-devices used for I/O. The device named *RFILSYS* is a master device, while devices named *RFILEi* are individual file devices.

```
/* Remote file system master device (open to get rf device) */
rfm:
        on DGM         -i ioerr        -o rfopen       -c ioerr
                       -r ioerr        -w ioerr        -s ioerr
                       -n rfcntl       -g ioerr        -p ioerr
                       -iint ioerr     -oint ioerr     -csr 0
                       -ivec 0         -ovec 0

/* A remote file (pseudo-device returned by rfm open) */
rf:
        on DGM         -i rfinit       -o ioerr        -c rfclose
                       -n rfcntl       -g rfgetc       -p rfputc
                       -iint ioerr     -oint ioerr     -csr 0
                       -ivec 0         -ovec 0
%
/* Remote file system master pseudo-device */

RFILSYS        is rfm  on DGM

/* Pseudo-device slots for remote files */

RFILE1         is rf   on DGM
RFILE2         is rf   on DGM
RFILE3         is rf   on DGM
RFILE4         is rf   on DGM
```

Note that a call to open on device *RFILSYS* returns the device id of one of the *RFILEi* devices.

14.16 Summary

The principle of access transparency suggests that designers should hide differences between remote and local files. Following this principle, we have built a remote file system that works similar to the way a Xinu local file system works. A user process opens the remote file system pseudo-device, passing a file name and access mode. The call to *open* allocates an individual remote file pseudo-device, records information including the file name and position, and corresponds with the server to verify that the file can be used.

Once a file has been established, user processes invoke *read* or *write* operations to transfer data, the *seek* operation to change the current file position, and the *close* operation to discontinue use. Other file manipulation, including the universal file operations *rename, remove,* and *access* are supplied through the *control* primitive.

We looked at a driver for the remote file pseudo-devices, and saw that a few utility procedures made the implementation of most upper-half routines trivial. Because the server was stateless, it was not always necessary to correspond with it when performing an operation. The *open* routine did inform the server when a process opened a file, as did the *close* routine. However, the *seek* routine updated the local position information without informing the server. In each case, the decision was made based primarily on the principle of access transparency, with cost considerations playing a secondary role.

FOR FURTHER STUDY

The use of I/O primitives *open*, *read*, *write*, and *close* for communication follows most remote file systems built on UNIX (e.g., Weinberger [1985]). Alternative approaches involve mapping files into virtual memory (see Fitzgerald and Rashid [1986]), or using a remote procedure call mechanism built into a special-purpose language (see Birrell and Nelson [1984]).

EXERCISES

14.1   Consider how two diskless machines can interfere with one another. Assume that only one process executes on each machine. Suppose the process on machine 1 writes file *A*, seeks to position 0, and then reads the file, while the process on machine 2 accesses the file server but *does not write to file A*. Explain how machine 1 can find that when it reads *A*, the last byte is correct but the first byte contains 0.

14.2   Modify the remote file system so that each remote file pseudo-device contains a local buffer of 512 bytes. Have *rfopen* obtain the first 512 bytes of the file, and perform all *read* and *write* operations locally, writing modified data back to the file and reading the next 512 bytes when the current file position moves beyond the data in the buffer. Remember that *rfclose* may have to transfer the data from the buffer back to the file.

14.3   What strange behavior does the modified system of the previous exercise display?

14.4   Under what network workloads is system throughput maximized if *rfclose* does not inform the server of file closing? If it does?

14.5   Might it be beneficial for the client to inform the server when a file position changes?

14.6   How often does the client retransmit requests at your site?

14.7   In some systems, reading *n* characters merely executes a loop that reads one character *n* times. Modify *read* to make it a loop that reads characters one-at-a-time, and measure the performance difference when reading a remote file.

14.8   Generalize the remote file client software to accommodate multiple servers. One generalization uses multiple remote file system pseudo-devices, one per server.

14.9   UNIX keeps a protection mode associated with each file. Discuss the advantages and disadvantages of adding a function to *rfcntl* that changes a file's protection modes.

14.10   Add *control* functions that permit a process to create or remove directories.

14.11   Modify the driver to have it check response packets to make sure they match requests.

14.12   Can the remote file client misbehave if the network delivers messages out of order or loses packets?

14.13   Why does *rfinit* delay opening a datagram pseudo-device for the server? (Hint: the answer involves Xinu device initialization.)

15

A Syntactic Namespace

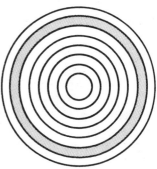

15.1 Introduction

Taken as a whole, the previous chapters describe levels of software that, when added to a basic operating system, provide a powerful computing environment by supplying general purpose communication among multiple computers, and special purpose communication to a large remote file system. While the augmented operating system permits access to local and remote files, the system, as it stands, violates the principle of access transparency announced in Chapter 13 because it requires the user to know whether files are local or remote. Opening a remote file requires the user to adopt the naming conventions used by the server's file system, while local files must be opened using the local file naming convention.

This chapter introduces a new, higher-level mechanism called a *syntactic namespace*, or just *namespace*, that knits together many apparently diverse file naming schemes into a single unified whole, allowing users to open files without knowing their location. What makes this particular implementation of the namespace especially fascinating is its combination of simplicity and power. By thinking of names syntactically, we can understand their similarity. By using the relationship between strings and trees, we can manipulate names without much effort. By following the principle of access transparency, we can improve the system dramatically. Thus, just a small layer of software added to existing mechanisms will allow us to completely unify naming.

Before looking at the namespace, we will review a few examples of file naming so we understand the problem at hand. Following the discussion of existing names, we will look at a general purpose syntactic naming scheme, and then examine a simpler, less general solution. Finally, we will examine an implementation of the simple scheme.

15.2 The Problem With File Names

The problem designers face when inventing a namespace is simple: they must glue together a myriad of unrelated naming schemes, each of which has evolved into a self-contained system. On some systems, file names specify the storage device on which the file resides. On others, the filename includes a suffix that tells the file type or version. Still others map all files into a single flat namespace in which each name is merely a string of alphanumeric characters. The following sections give examples of file names on several systems, and help the reader understand the types and formats of names our namespace must accommodate.

15.2.1 MS-DOS

Names in MS-DOS or PC-DOS consist of two parts: a device specification and a file name. Syntactically, an MS-DOS name has the form *L:file*, where *L* is a single letter that designates the disk device on which the file resides, and *file* is the name of the file. Typically, the letter *F* denotes the system hard disk, so a name like *F:abc* refers to file *abc* on the hard disk.

15.2.2 UNIX

UNIX organizes files into a hierarchical, tree structured directory system. A file name is either relative to the current directory or a full *path name* that specifies a path from the root of a directory tree to a file. Because we are interested in the file names supported by the remote file server of Chapter 13, we can restrict attention to UNIX full path names.

Syntactically, full path names consist of slash-separated components, where each component except the last specifies a directory. Thus, the UNIX name */usr/dec/x* refers to file *x* in subdirectory *dec*, which is found in subdirectory *usr*, which is contained in the root directory. The root directory itself is named by a single slash (*/*). Notice that the prefix */usr/dec/* refers to a directory, and that the names of all files in that directory share the prefix.

The importance of the *prefix property* will become apparent later. For now, it is sufficient to remember that tree structure relates to name prefix.

> *When components in a file name specify a path through a tree-structured directory, the names of all files that reside in the same directory share a common prefix that denotes the directory.*

15.2.3 V System

Full names in the V system specify a *context* in which names are resolved, as well as a file name. The syntax uses brackets to enclose the context. Thus, [*ctx*] *abc* refers to file *abc* in context *ctx*. Usually, one thinks of each context as the set of files on a particular file server.

15.2.4 Newcastle Connection

The *Newcastle Connection*, sometimes called *UNIX United*, provides software that allows multiple UNIX file systems to be interconnected. Files on a remote machine can be named with syntax of the form: */../machine/path*, where *machine* is the name of the remote machine, and *path* is a full UNIX path on that machine. The syntax is derived from conventional UNIX in which .. refers to the parent directory. Thus, */..* refers to the parent of the root of the entire tree, making it appear as if an imaginary global root has been added to connect all UNIX file systems.

15.2.5 IBIS

The IBIS system provides yet another syntax for multiple-machine connections. In IBIS, names have the form *machine:path*, where *machine* denotes a particular computer system, and *path* is the file name on that machine (e.g., a UNIX full path name).

15.2.6 TILDE

The TILDE system stores files in multiple directory hierarchies called *tilde trees*, where each tilde tree is known by its *tilde name*. Syntactically, file names have the form ~*T/path*, where *T* gives the tilde name and *path* is a UNIX-like path name within the specified tilde tree. Thus, a name like ~*xinu/bin/download* names file *download* in directory *bin* in the tilde tree *xinu*.

15.3 Naming System Design Alternatives

We seek a single naming system that provides the user a unified view of all possible file names, independent of the location of the file or the operating system under which it resides. It seems that a designer could choose between two basic approaches in solving this problem: define yet another file naming scheme, or adopt an existing naming system. Surprisingly, the Xinu namespace uses neither of these two approaches. Instead, it adds a syntactic naming mechanism that accommodates many underlying naming schemes while allowing the user to choose a uniform interface to the naming software. The namespace software maps names that the user supplies into names appropriate for the underlying system.

A naming mechanism that accommodates many underlying schemes has several advantages. First, it allows the designer to integrate existing file systems and devices into a single, uniform namespace, even when implemented by remote servers on a set of heterogeneous systems. Second, it permits designers to add new devices or file systems without requiring recompilation of user programs that use them. Third, it avoids two unattractive extremes. At one extreme choosing the simplest possible naming scheme ensures that all file systems can handle the names, but means that the user cannot take advantage of the complexity offered by some servers. At the other extreme, choosing a complex naming scheme may exclude file systems that handle only simple names.

15.4 A Syntactic Namespace

To understand how to handle names, think of them syntactically. Each name is merely a string of characters. The namespace itself provides neither files nor directories; it merely translates names by mapping strings from the uniform representation chosen by the user into strings appropriate for particular subsystems. For example, the namespace might translate the string *alf* into the string *F:alongfilename*.

What makes a syntactic namespace so powerful? Syntactic manipulation is both natural and flexible. Thus, it is easy to specify and understand as well as easy to adapt to many underlying naming schemes. The user can imagine a consistent set of names and use the namespace software to translate them into the forms required by underlying file systems. For example, suppose a system has access to a local file system that uses MS-DOS naming and a remote file system that uses UNIX full path names. The user might adopt UNIX full path name syntax for all names, making the local disk names start with */local*. In such a scheme, the name */local/abc* would refer to file *abc* on the local disk, while the name */etc/passwd* would refer to a remote file. The namespace must translate */local/abc* into *F:abc* so the local file system could understand it, but it would pass */etc/passwd* onto the remote file system without change.

15.5 Patterns And Replacements

Exactly how should the syntactic namespace operate? One convenient method uses a *pattern* string to specify name syntax and a *replacement* string to specify the mapping. For example, consider the pattern replacement pair ("/local", "F:") which might mean *translate all occurrences of the string /local into the string F:*. Under the pattern-replacement scheme, the user specifies all namespace mappings with a set of such pairs.

Patterns that consist of fixed strings cannot specify replacement unambiguously. In the previous example, the pattern works well on strings like /local/*x*, but it fails on strings like */usr/local/bin* because */local* is an internal substring that should not be changed. To be effective, more powerful patterns are needed. However, implementations that allow arbitrary patterns and replacements tend to be cumbersome and the patterns become difficult to read.

15.6 Prefix Patterns

The problem at hand is to find a useful pattern-replacement mechanism that allows the user to specify how names map onto a subsystem without introducing more complexity than is needed. Before thinking about complex patterns, consider what can be done with patterns that consist of fixed strings. The key is to imagine files organized into a hierarchy, and to use the prefix property to understand why patterns should specify prefixes.

In a hierarchy, name prefixes group files into subdirectories, making it easy to define the relationship between names and the underlying file systems or devices. For example, consider a set of prefix patterns and replacements, each of which is a fixed string. Restricting the patterns to prefixes makes it easy to specify that names beginning with the prefix */local* map to the local file system, while names beginning with the prefix */remote* map to the remote file system.

15.7 Implementation Of A Simple Syntactic Namespace

A concrete example will clarify the details of how a syntactic namespace uses the pattern-replacement paradigm, and show how the namespace hides subsystem details. In the example, patterns will consist of fixed strings, and only prefixes will be matched. Fixed string prefix patterns make the naming system powerful while keeping the implementation surprisingly compact and easy to understand. Later sections will discuss alternative implementations and generalizations.

15.7.1 The Pseudo-Device NAMESPACE

The example namespace implementation consists of a pseudo-device, *NAMESPACE*, that programs use when opening a file by name. The *NAMESPACE* pseudo-device maps the name using the prefix patterns, and then passes it to the appropriate underlying device. Thus, user programs specify only the *NAMESPACE* device when opening a file; prefix mappings determine the file system or device to which the name corresponds.

The next sections present the namespace software, beginning with declarations of the basic data structures, and culminating in device driver routines of the *NAMESPACE* pseudo-device. Following the declarations, two procedures are presented that map names according to the prefix patterns. These form the basis of the most important piece of namespace software, the upper-half routine for *open*.

15.7.2 Definitions Of Data Structures And Constants

File *name.h* contains declarations for the data structures and constants used in the example namespace.

```
/* name.h - fopen */

/* Constants that define the name mapping table sizes */

#define NAMPLEN          32              /* max size of a name prefix    */
#define NAMRLEN          32              /* max size of a replacement    */
#define NAMLEN           80              /* maximum size of a file name  */
#define NNAMES           14              /* number of prefix definitions */

/* Definition of the name prefix table that defines all name mappings */

struct  nament  {                       /* definition of prefix mapping */
        char    npre[NAMPLEN];          /* prefix of a name             */
        char    nrepl[NAMRLEN];         /* replacement for that prefix  */
        int     ndev;                   /* device for this prefix       */
};

struct  nam     {                       /* all name space variables     */
        int     nnames;                 /* number of entries in nametab */
        struct  nament  nametab[NNAMES];/* actual table of mappings     */
} Nam;
#ifndef NAMESPACE
#define NAMESPACE        SYSERR
#endif

#define fopen(n,m)       open(NAMESPACE, n, m)
```

The principle data structure is array *nametab*. It holds up to *NNAMES* entries, each of which contains a prefix pattern string, replacement string, and device id. External variable *Nam* holds all the variables related to naming, including the *nametab* array and a count of valid entries in it.

15.7.3 Adding Mappings To The Prefix Table

Processes call procedure *mount* to add mappings to the prefix table, passing arguments that specify a prefix, device id, and replacement. *Mount* searches the prefix table, *nametab*, replacing an existing table entry if the prefix is already in use, or adding a new entry if it is not. When adding a new entry to the table, *mount* updates *Nam.nnames*, which counts the currently valid entries. File *mount.c* contains the code.

```
/* mount.c - mount */

#include <conf.h>
#include <kernel.h>
#include <name.h>


/*------------------------------------------------------------------------
 *  mount  -  give meaning to a prefix in the abstract name space
 *------------------------------------------------------------------------
 */
SYSCALL mount(prefix, dev, replace)
char    *prefix;
char    *replace;
int     dev;
{
        struct  nament  *nptr;
        struct  nament  *last;
        int     i;
        char    ps;

        if (prefix == NULL)
                prefix == NULLSTR;
        if (replace == NULL)
                replace == NULLSTR;
        if (strlen(prefix) >= NAMPLEN || strlen(replace) >= NAMRLEN)
                return(SYSERR);
        disable(ps);
        for (i=0 ; i<Nam.nnames ; i++) {
                nptr = &Nam.nametab[i];
                if (strcmp(prefix,nptr->npre) == 0) {
                        strcpy(nptr->nrepl, replace);
                        nptr->ndev = dev;
                        restore(ps);
                        return(OK);
                }
```

```
        }
        if (Nam.nnames >= NNAMES) {
                restore(ps);
                return(SYSERR);
        }
        nptr = last = &Nam.nametab[Nam.nnames++];
        if (Nam.nnames > 1) {    /* preserve last name prefix */
                nptr = last - 1;
                *last = *nptr;
        }
        strcpy(nptr->npre, prefix);
        strcpy(nptr->nrepl, replace);
        nptr->ndev = dev;
        restore(ps);
        return(OK);
}
```

Mount inserts new entries in *nametab* just before the last valid entry. Choosing to insert before the last entry may seem strange, but as later routines show, it simplifies maintenance of the default mapping.

15.7.4 Removing A Name Mapping

Procedure *unmount* removes entries from the name mapping table. Given a prefix, *unmount* searches for the corresponding entry and then compresses the table to remove it. Once the table has been updated, *unmount* decrements the count of valid entries in *Nam.nnames*. File *unmount.c* contains the code.

```
/* unmount.c - unmount */

#include <conf.h>
#include <kernel.h>
#include <name.h>

/*------------------------------------------------------------------------
 * unmount - remove an entry from the name prefix mapping table
 *------------------------------------------------------------------------
 */
SYSCALL unmount(prefix)
char    *prefix;
{
        struct  nament  *nptr;
        char    ps;
        int     i;
```

```
        if (prefix == NULL)
                prefix = NULLSTR;
        else if (strlen(prefix) >= NAMPLEN)
                return(SYSERR);
        disable(ps);
        for (i=0 ; i<Nam.nnames ; i++) {
                nptr = &Nam.nametab[i];
                if (strcmp(prefix, nptr->npre) == 0) {
                        for(Nam.nnames-- ; i<Nam.nnames ; i++)
                                Nam.nametab[i] = Nam.nametab[i+1];
                        restore(ps);
                        return(OK);
                }
        }
        restore(ps);
        return(SYSERR);
}
```

15.7.5 Mapping Names With The Prefix Table

With the prefix table in place, name translation becomes easy. Mapping consists of finding a prefix match and substituting the corresponding replacement string. Procedure *namrepl* performs one step of the translation process. It can be found in file *namrepl.c*.

```
/* namrepl.c - namrepl */

#include <conf.h>
#include <kernel.h>
#include <name.h>

/*------------------------------------------------------------------------
 * namrepl - using namespace, replace name with (newname,device)
 *------------------------------------------------------------------------
 */
SYSCALL namrepl(name, newname)
char    *name;
char    *newname;
{
        register struct nament  *nptr;
        register struct nament  *nlast;
        int     plen, rlen;
        char    ps;

        disable(ps);
        nlast = &Nam.nametab[Nam.nnames];
        for (nptr= Nam.nametab ; nptr<nlast ; nptr++) {
                plen = strlen(nptr->npre);
                if (strncmp(nptr->npre, name, plen) == 0) {
                        rlen = strlen(nptr->nrepl);
                        if ((rlen+strlen(name)-plen) >= NAMLEN)
                                break;
                        strcpy(newname, nptr->nrepl);
                        strcat(newname, name + plen);
                        restore(ps);
                        return(nptr->ndev);
                }
        }
        strcpy(newname, "");
        restore(ps);
        return(SYSERR);
}
```

Namrepl searches the prefix table sequentially for the first entry such that the specified prefix matches the name being translated. In the code, variable *nptr* starts at the first element of array *nametab* and moves along one element at a time. Once it finds a match, *namrepl* forms a mapped name by appending the unmatched portion of the original name onto the replacement string. Finally, it returns the device id from the prefix table entry.

If intermediate string size exceeds the maximum allowed, or none of the prefix patterns in *nametab* match the original name, *namrepl* copies the null string into the mapped name, and returns *SYSERR*.

15.7.6 Iterative Resolution Of Recursive Mappings

Each entry in *nametab* contains a device id as well as a prefix pattern and replacement. If the device id refers to pseudo-device *NAMESPACE*, it means that the resulting file name will be resolved recursively by passing it to the *NAMESPACE* again. While recursive definition of names is easy to express, recursive resolution can be inefficient. To avoid unnecessary recursion, procedure *nammap*, shown below in file *nammap.c*, resolves names iteratively.

```
/* nammap.c - nammap */

#include <conf.h>
#include <kernel.h>
#include <name.h>

/*------------------------------------------------------------------------
 * nammap - using namespace, iteratively map name onto (newname,device)
 *------------------------------------------------------------------------
 */
SYSCALL nammap(name, newname)
char    *name;
char    *newname;
{
        char    ps;
        int     dev;
        char    tmpnam[NAMLEN];

        disable(ps);
        dev = namrepl(name, newname);
        while (dev == NAMESPACE) {
                strcpy(tmpnam, newname);
                dev = namrepl(tmpnam, newname);
        }
        restore(ps);
        return(dev);
}
```

Initially, *nammap* calls *namrepl* to translate the name passed as an argument. It then repeats the translation until the name maps onto a device other than *NAMESPACE*.

Nammap is potentially dangerous because it may iterate forever if substitution does not map onto a device other than *NAMESPACE*. To make matters worse, *mount* allows users to change the set of mappings dynamically, and does not check for mappings that could cause loops. The exercises suggest several ways to avoid infinite loops.

15.7.7 Opening A Named File

Now that *nammap* has been built, constructing the upper-half *open* routine becomes trivial. Remember that the basic goal is to define the name space pseudo-device, *NAMESPACE*, such that opening it causes the system to open the appropriate underlying device. Once the name has been mapped and a new device identified, *namopen* merely invokes *open*, shown in file *namopen.c*.

```
/* namopen.c - namopen */

#include <conf.h>
#include <kernel.h>
#include <name.h>

/*------------------------------------------------------------------------
 * namopen  -  open an object (e.g., remote file) based on the name
 *------------------------------------------------------------------------
 */
namopen(devptr, filenam, mode)
struct  devsw   *devptr;
char    *filenam;
char    *mode;
{
        int     dev;
        char    newname[NAMLEN];

        if ( (dev=nammap(filenam, newname)) == SYSERR)
                return(SYSERR);
        return( open(dev, newname, mode) );
}
```

15.7.8 Namespace Initialization

How should the prefix table be initialized? There are two answers: one that specifies an initialization mechanism, and one that specifies the initial contents of the prefix table. The mechanism answer is easy. Because the namespace has been designed as a pseudo-device, the system carries out initialization at startup when it calls *init*. Knowing how to initialize the prefix table is more difficult.

For now, consider only the initialization mechanism, as exemplified by procedure *naminit*, shown in file *naminit.c*:

```
/* naminit.c - naminit */

#include <conf.h>
#include <kernel.h>
#include <name.h>

#ifndef RFILSYS
#define RFILSYS SYSERR
#endif
#ifdef  Nnsys
struct  nam      Nam;
#endif

/*------------------------------------------------------------------------
 * naminit  -  initialize the syntactic namespace pseudo-device
 *------------------------------------------------------------------------
 */
naminit()
{
        Nam.nnames = 0;

        /* Xinu namespace definition */

        mount("",                NAMESPACE, "Xinu/storage/");
        mount("Xinu/",           RFILSYS,   "/usr/Xinu/");
        mount("h/",              NAMESPACE, "Xinu/src/sys/h/");
        mount("kernel/",         NAMESPACE, "Xinu/src/sys/sys/");
        mount("core11",          NAMESPACE, "kernel/core11");
        mount("a.out",           NAMESPACE, "kernel/a.out");
        mount("/dev/console",    CONSOLE,   NULLSTR);
        mount("/dev/null",       RFILSYS,   "/dev/null");
        mount("/dev/",           SYSERR,    NULLSTR);
        mount("/",               RFILSYS,   "/");
        mount("~/",              NAMESPACE, "Xinu/");
}
```

Ignore the specific prefix and replacement names and look only at how simple initialization is. After setting the number of valid entries to zero, *naminit* calls *mount* to add entries to the prefix table, where each entry contains a prefix pattern, replacement string, and device id.

15.8 Choosing Initial Prefix Mappings

The table of prefix mappings defines the set of names that the user sees, and determines the organization of file systems and devices. Choosing a set of mappings may be difficult because there are many possibilities. This section considers only a few possibilities, but emphasizes the correlation between file organization and naming.

It is tempting to think of the namespace as merely a shorthand for longer names, but focusing on abbreviations can be misleading. The key to choosing meaningful prefix names lies in thinking of a hierarchy into which files can be placed. Then the namespace defines the organization of the hierarchy.

> *All file names are organized into a hierarchy, and entries in the name mapping table specify how specific subsets of files relate to the rest of the hierarchy.*

Imagine, for a minute, a system that can access files on a local disk, as well as files on a remote server. Do not think about how to abbreviate specific file names; think instead of how you might like to organize the files. Three possible organizations come to mind as Figure 15.1 shows. Local and remote files could be placed at equal, but distinct positions in the hierarchy, the local system could form the main part of the hierarchy with remote files in a sub-hierarchy, or the remote files could form the main hierarchy with local files as a sub-hierarchy. Among these choices, the size of the two file systems and the frequency of access may help determine which organization is preferable. For example, if the remote file system has thousands of files while the local file system has only ten, it may be natural to think of the remote file system as the main hierarchy with the local files grafted onto a sub-hierarchy.

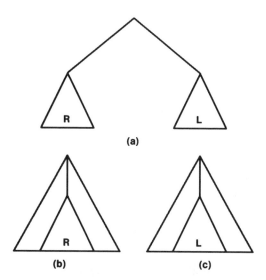

Figure 15.1 Three possible hierarchical organizations of local and remote
files: (a) both local and remote directories at the same level,
(b) remote files in a subdirectory of local files, and (c) local
files as a subdirectory of remote files.

15.8.1 Default Hierarchy And The Null Prefix

The namespace software was designed so it easily supports any of the hierarchies shown in Figure 15.1. In particular, *mount* permits the user to choose one
subsystem as the default, and organize the remaining files with respect to that
hierarchy.

How does one particular subsystem become the default? First, the prefix for
that subsystem must be such that it matches all names not matched by other table
entries. The null prefix provides guaranteed matching for our example namespace.
Second, the default entry, which carries the null prefix, must be examined only
after all other prefixes have been tested. Because *namrepl* searches the prefix table
sequentially, the default should be placed at the end of the table.

Our example namespace software helps maintain a default table entry because
it leaves the last table entry in place when adding new mappings or removing old
ones. Thus, the default mapping is mounted first. Later insertions precede the default in the table, and are, therefore, tested first during name mapping.

Look at *naminit* again to see how the remote file system becomes the default.
The first call to *mount* inserts the default mapping with the null prefix. It specifies
that unmatched file names should be placed in directory */usr/Xinu/v7/storage* on
the remote file system. The next call to *mount* defines the location of *Xinu* files
with respect to the remote file system. Later entries map the name */dev/console*

onto the *CONSOLE* device, and then remove all other *I dev* files by mapping them onto device *SYSERR*.

15.8.2 A Common Name Syntax

Once an organization has been selected, selection of a common naming syntax becomes easier. The idea is to choose a uniform syntax that is the most natural. Again, the relative size of the underlying file systems may influence the decision. However, a user might select a syntax that is familiar, even if none of the underlying systems use it. For example, a user familiar with UNIX might choose to organize names into a UNIX-like hierarchy, even if none of the underlying systems supported UNIX-like names.

15.9 Additional File Manipulation Commands

Although the namespace allows users to manipulate file names syntactically, it does not subsume all file manipulation operations. The principle can be summarized by the following rule:

> *The namespace should be used to organize the naming hierarchy*
> *by manipulating sets of names; underlying file systems manipu-*
> *late individual file names.*

For example, most file systems allow the user to change the name of a file. Our system needs primitives that specify such changes, and pass the request on to the appropriate underlying file system.

Besides the conventional *open*, *read*, *write*, and *close* operations, primitives are needed that change the name of a file, destroy a file, and determine the accessibility of a file. Defining file manipulation primitives can be tricky because the user relies on the namespace to translate names into forms appropriate for underlying file systems. Thus, it may be difficult or impossible to specify an arbitrary name in the underlying system without changing the namespace mapping. Consider the sample namespace defined above. A user cannot refer to file *I dev I abc* on the remote file system because the name mapping returns *SYSERR*.

15.9.1 Removing A File

The *remove* primitive allows a user to destroy an individual file, by removing it from the file system. Several implementations are possible. The designer could choose to build many versions of *remove*, one for each underlying file system, and force the user to choose among them. The designer might provide a single *remove* primitive, allowing the user to pass the device id of the underlying file system as an argument.

However, the namespace already provides a mechanism for identifying the underlying file system from a given file name. Using the namespace to map names onto underlying systems or devices hides the details of where files reside from the user, making it easier to specify file destruction. Furthermore, the namespace allows the user to think only of high-level names without knowing the details of underlying names.

Procedure *remove*, shown below in file *remove.c*, performs file destruction.

```
/* remove.c - remove */

#include <conf.h>
#include <kernel.h>
#include <file.h>
#include <name.h>


/*------------------------------------------------------------------------
 * remove  -  remove a file given its name (key is optional)
 *------------------------------------------------------------------------
 */
SYSCALL remove(name, key)
char    *name;
int     key;
{
        char    fullnam[NAMLEN];
        struct  devsw   *devptr;
        int     dev;

        if ( (dev=nammap(name, fullnam)) == SYSERR)
                return(SYSERR);
        devptr = &devtab[dev];
        return( (*devptr->dvcntl)(devptr, FLREMOVE, fullnam, key) );
}
```

Remove uses procedure *nammap* to map its argument into a new form, and then calls *control* on the appropriate underlying device to remove the file. Each underlying file system used in the namespace honors the function *FLREMOVE*. Because some file systems require a password or other key, *remove* takes an optional second argument that it passes to *control*. File systems that do not use the key ignore the second argument.

15.9.2 Renaming A File

The second universal file manipulation primitive, *rename*, allows the user to change
the name of a file. Unlike changes made at the namespace level, *rename* propagates the request to the underlying file system, making the change permanent.
The code can be found in file *rename.c*.

```
/* rename.c - rename */

#include <conf.h>
#include <kernel.h>
#include <file.h>
#include <name.h>


/*------------------------------------------------------------------
 *  rename  -  rename a file (key is optional)
 *------------------------------------------------------------------
 */
SYSCALL rename(old, new)
char    *old;
char    *new;
{
        char    fullold[NAMLEN];
        char    fullnew[NAMLEN];
        struct  devsw   *devptr;
        int     dev, dev2;

        /* map names through namespace and restrict to single device */

        if ( (dev = nammap(old, fullold)) == SYSERR ||
             (dev2= nammap(new, fullnew)) == SYSERR ||
            dev != dev2)
                        return(SYSERR);
        devptr = &devtab[dev];
        return( (*devptr->dvcntl)(devptr,FLRENAME,fullold,fullnew) );
}
```

Rename maps both its arguments through the namespace, and then checks to
be sure the resulting names lie on the same file system. If they do, *rename* passes
the request to the underlying file system with a *control* call. Thus, *rename* does not
provide for file movement across underlying file systems.

15.9.3 Testing File Accessibility

Sometimes a programmer needs to test whether a file can be accessed without opening it. The routine *access* provides for such tests. It takes a file name and an access mode as arguments. The code can be found in file *access.c*.

```
/* access.c - access */

#include <conf.h>
#include <kernel.h>
#include <file.h>
#include <name.h>


/*------------------------------------------------------------------------
 * access  -  determine accessability given file name and desired mode
 *------------------------------------------------------------------------
 */
SYSCALL access(name, mode)
char    *name;
int     mode;
{
        char    fullnam[NAMLEN];
        struct  devsw   *devptr;
        int     dev;

        if ( (dev=nammap(name, fullnam)) == SYSERR)
                return(SYSERR);
        devptr = &devtab[dev];
        return( (*devptr->dvcntl)(devptr, FLACCESS, fullnam, mode) );
}
```

Like the other file manipulation routines, *access* maps the file name through the namespace to determine the underlying system on which the file resides. It then calls *control* to pass the request to the file system.

15.10 Advantages Of The Namespace Approach

A syntactic namespace isolates programs from the underlying file systems, allowing one to reorganize the imagined hierarchy without changing programs. To appreciate the power of a namespace, consider a system that keeps temporary files on a local disk, using the prefix */tmp/* to distinguish them from other files. Moving them to the remote file system consists of changing the namespace entry that specified how to handle prefix */tmp/*. Because programs always refer to files using names as defined by the namespace, they continue to operate correctly without change. The key observation here is that reorganizing the conceptual hierarchy may not require recompilation of programs that use it.

Because users can access and understand the syntactic namespace, they can choose between transparent and non-transparent naming as desired. Naming systems are called *transparent* if they hide the details of underlying file systems from the user completely. The syntactic namespace is transparent in the sense that processes need not know the location of a file when opening it. However, procedures like *namrepl* and *nammap* provide information about file location when it is needed, allowing programs to find out the location of a file. Thus, a program that manipulates directories on the remote file system can check names to make sure they refer to the remote file system before manipulating them.

15.11 The Limits Of Fixed Prefix Patterns

Namespace software that uses only prefix patterns cannot handle all possible hierarchical organizations or file mappings. For example, in UNIX, the name */dev/tty* refers to a process' control terminal; the file server should never use it. The namespace on client machines can prevent accidental access use by mapping the prefix */dev/tty* onto device id *SYSERR*. Unfortunately, such a mapping prevents the client from accessing other entries in the */dev* directory that refer to terminals (e.g., */dev/ttyhf*).

Using fixed strings as prefix patterns also prevents the namespace from changing separator characters when they occur in the middle of names. For example, suppose a computer has two underlying file systems, one of which follows the UNIX convention of using the slash character to separate components along a path, while the other uses the dollar sign character to separate components. Because it deals only with prefix patterns our sample namespace cannot map dollar signs to slashes or vice versa, without restricting the possible names to a few directories. The next section describes a namespace generalization that overcomes these limitations.

15.12 Generalized Patterns

Many of the namespace limitations can be overcome by more general patterns. For example, if it is possible to specify a *full string match* instead of just a prefix match, the problem of distinguishing a name like */dev/tty* from the name */dev/ttyhf* can be solved. We could introduce an extra argument to *mount* that encodes whether full string or prefix matching is desired, but an additional argument complicates the namespace software without solving the problem of non-prefix substitution.

Generalizing patterns to allow more than fixed strings solves more problems and keeps all the matching information in the pattern itself. For example, suppose characters have special meanings in a pattern as shown below†:

Character	Meaning
↑	match beginning of string
$	match end of string
.	match any single character
*	repeat 0 or more of a pattern
\	take next character in pattern literally
other	self match as in a fixed string

Thus, a pattern like ↑*/dev/tty*$ specifies a full match of the string */dev/tty*, while a pattern like \$ matches a dollar sign that may be embedded in the string.

Two additional rules are necessary to make generalized pattern matching useful in the namespace. First, we assume the left-most possible match will be used. Second, we assume that among all left-most matches, the longest will be taken. The exercises suggest how to use these generalized patterns to map the names that fixed prefixes cannot handle.

15.13 Configuring The Namespace Pseudo-Device

The namespace procedures that we examined form the pseudo-device driver for device *NAMESPACE* as shown in the Xinu configuration below:

```
/* Name system (topmost level of name resolution mechanism) */
nam:
        on TOP          -i naminit      -o namopen      -c ioerr
                        -r ioerr        -w ioerr        -s ioerr
                        -n ioerr        -g ioerr        -p ioerr
                        -iint ioerr     -oint ioerr     -csr 0
                        -ivec 0         -ovec 0
%
/* Pseudo device for the abstract (file) name space */

NAMESPACE       is nam on TOP
```

The declarations specify that device *NAMESPACE* supports only two operations: *init* and *open*. Other namespace primitives operations (e.g., *mount*) are not part of the driver; they must be called explicitly.

---

†the pattern matching given here corresponds to that of the UNIX *sed* command.

15.14 Summary

Dealing with file names is difficult, especially if the operating system supports multiple underlying naming schemes. One way to solve the naming problem employs a layer of namespace software between users and the underlying file systems. The namespace does not implement files itself, but merely treats names as strings, mapping them into forms appropriate for underlying systems based on information in a mapping table.

We have examined the implementation of a syntactic namespace that uses a pattern-replacement scheme in which patterns are fixed strings representing name prefixes. The software includes procedures like *mount* and *unmount* that manipulate the mapping table, as well as procedures like *nammap* that map names into their target form. Our example namespace comprises a *NAMESPACE* pseudo-device that users specify when opening a file. The *NAMESPACE* maps the specified file name, and then opens the designated file.

The namespace software is both small and elegant. With only a few routines and the simplistic notion of prefix matching, it can accommodate many naming schemes. In particular, it accommodates the UNIX remote file system consisting of the server described in Chapter 13 and the client described in Chapter 14.. However, our simplistic version cannot handle all possible mappings. To provide for more complex naming systems, the notion of pattern must be generalized. One possible generalization assigns special meaning to some characters in the pattern.

FOR FURTHER STUDY

Naming is among the most interesting topics in distributed systems. Oppen and Dalal [1981] describe a method of resolving names by storing bindings on a remote server. Cheriton and Mann [1984] present a variation in which the name of the server is incorporated into the namespace. Lampson [1985] uses a novel approach in which the namespace can grow without old names becoming obsolete.

Welch and Osterhaut [1986] discovered name interpretation based on prefix matching independent of work on the Xinu namespace. Unlike the Xinu first-match scheme, their system uses a longest-match rule, and implements prefix matching at the server as well as at the client.

Of the example naming schemes described here, MS-DOS is the most widely used because it is part of the standard software for the popular personal computer manufactured by IBM. Tichy and Ruan [1984] describes names in IBIS, without giving much justification for the choice. Ritchie and Thompson [1974] covers UNIX naming and the directory structure to support it. Brownbridge, Marshall, and Randall [1982] discuss names in UNIX United, and point out that the scheme preserves local names while adding network file access to UNIX.

All objects in a distributed system must be named. Peterson [1985] presents a syntactic model for naming messages and message processors. Solomon, Landweber, and Neuhegen [1982] describes a server that resolves user's names. Saltzer [1978] presents a model for name binding, and Saltzer [1982] extends it to distributed systems.

EXERCISES

15.1 Why should users have access to both *namrepl* and *nammap*?

15.2 Can you modify *mount* so it refuses to mount prefix-replacement pairs that could cause *nammap* to enter an infinite loop?

15.3 Modify *nammap* so it returns *SYSERR* after iterating 100 times. Is it enough to limit iteration to *NNAMES* times?

15.4 Minimize the code in *namopen* by replacing the body with a single statement consisting of two procedure calls.

15.5 Implement an upper-half *control* routine for the *NAMESPACE* device, and make *nammap* a control function.

15.6 Which basic namespace routine cannot easily be transformed into a *control* function?

15.7 Can you add the *NETWORK* device to the namespace easily? Explain why or why not.

15.8 What is the advantage of separating the definition of *Xinu/* from the definition of *a.out*?

15.9 Implement generalized pattern matching. Refer to UNIX *sed* command for additional ways to define pattern match characters.

15.10 Build a namespace that has both prefix matches and full string matches.

15.11 Suppose the namespace used fixed string patterns, but allowed full string matching in addition to the current prefix matching. Are there instances when it makes sense to have a full string pattern identical to a prefix pattern?

15.12 What additional file manipulation primitives might you need beside *rename, remove,* and *access*? Hint: reread Chapter 14.

15.13 Assume generalized pattern matching has been added to the name space. Exactly what arguments would you pass to *mount* to map all the dollar signs in a name into slashes?

16

User Interface Design

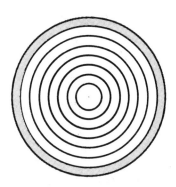

16.1 Introduction

Users do not think of an operating system as a set of system calls. Instead, they view it as a set of commands that can be executed from a terminal, and an environment for editing files, entering data, and controlling processing. Thus, the details of input devices, display formats, command invocation, and system response are critically important because they define the psychological "feel" of a system, the elusive characteristic that distinguishes one system from another, and the basis upon which most users compare systems.

It is impossible to design command interpreter software without understanding the interface hardware on one side, and the user's perception on the other. This chapter reviews interface hardware, and then discusses the design of user interfaces, pointing out issues and alternatives. It considers basic philosophies and contrasts approaches. The next chapter focuses on the details of a specific style of interface, showing the design and implementation of a UNIX-like command interpreter.

16.2 What Is A User Interface?

Technically, a *user interface* is the hardware and software with which users interact to specify computation and observe the results. Restricted to the operating system context, the term usually refers to the interactive software that accepts commands from the user and carries out the processing they specify. Thus, the user interface software lies between a human who specifies a computation and a system capable of carrying it out.

Designing user interfaces means much more than choosing efficient mechanisms to interpret commands. It means creatively blending the available interface hardware with the computational problem domain and the psychology of users to produce an attractive and effective computational tool. The test of a good environment is user satisfaction and productivity:

> *The goal of user interface design is to create an environment in which users can solve computational problems conveniently and productively.*

Note that the emphasis here is on the user and the computational problems to be solved, not on the system.

16.3 The Definition Of Goodness

If the goal of interface design is to make users productive and satisfied, measuring the "goodness" of designs will be difficult. First, because humans have individual preferences, we cannot expect universal agreement on convenience. Second, because humans have individual talents and dexterities, we cannot expect universal agreement on which features result in greatest productivity. Third, because users employ computing systems to solve a wide variety of computational problems, we cannot expect universal agreement about the best language of discourse. So, instead of trying to define a single measure of "goodness", we will consider design possibilities and tradeoffs, and try to understand the characteristics that each possible design induces.

16.4 What We Seek

Knowing that a problem-specific interface can make users more productive may seem to imply that designers need to build many problem-specific (or user-specific) interfaces. However, such efforts would be futile for two reasons. First, a user's computing activities change over time. Second, no computational subsystem survives in isolation. Users quickly realize that although they may use a few services heavily, the inconvenience of not having access to all computational services when they are needed makes using a general-purpose user interface worthwhile.

So, instead of looking for user interfaces that improve the efficiency of individuals, we will concentrate on general-purpose interfaces that provide access to all computing services. However, we also understand that user talents and preferences vary, so we should plan to allow each user some latitude in controlling the environment. To summarize:

We seek to understand fundamental human-machine interaction paradigms that support a wide community of users and uses; within a given paradigm, we wish to allow users to tailor the environment for individual preferences.

16.5 Interface Hardware

One cannot design user interface software without considering the technical details of the hardware and its effect on the user. The hardware at hand determines the physical presentation of information to the user, and gives the user a tactile sense of the system.

16.5.1 Keyboard Input Hardware

Most users interact with a computing system through a typewriter-like keyboard and a character display with 24 lines of 80 columns. Usually, the keyboard and display are packaged into a terminal device with a cable connecting the terminal to the computer.

The origin of the keyboard component is no mystery: it evolved directly from the keyboards on ordinary office typewriters. Users find that entering characters by pushing keys is both convenient and efficient. With practice, most achieve speeds of between 50 and 100 words per minute.

Alternative keyboards have been proposed and studied. Some differ only in physical appearance while others have increased functionality. For example, like typewriter keyboards, keyboards on computer terminals include a *SHIFT* key that may be pressed simultaneously with any other key to obtain the upper-case version of a letter. In essence, the *SHIFT* key doubles the number of characters a user can enter without doubling the number of keys. In addition to the *SHIFT* key, most computer keyboards include a *CONTROL* key that provides a third set of characters without adding keys. Some keyboards offer a *META SHIFT* key to expand the character set even further.

How far can the shift-key idea be extended? Only a few shift keys can be added before the user becomes overwhelmed. However, using shift keys simultaneously can add even more characters without adding more keys. Thus, holding both the *META* and *CONTROL* shift keys while typing the letter *a* produces a different character than either *META*-a or *CONTROL*-a. The idea generalizes to allow keyboards to accept *chords* consisting of multiple simultaneous keystrokes of arbitrary keys. For example, one might choose to honor chords consisting of two adjacent keys.

Besides the various shift keys, many computer keyboards have special keys that make interaction with a computer easy. For example, users who enter numeric values often prefer keyboards with separate numeric keypads (a collection of keys for the digits).

Many computer keyboards have special keys with labels like *ABORT*, *HELP*, or *EXIT*. Although these keys cause the terminal to send characters to the computer like other keys, the system software and terminal have been designed together, so the label on the key tells how software interprets that keystroke. For example, the system assumes that a *HELP* keystroke means that the user is confused; it responds by displaying status information or advising the user about possibilities.

Having special-purpose keys is a good idea, but choosing the specific set of functions that they perform limits the keyboard to one system or one application. To overcome such limitations, many terminals offer keyboards with general-purpose *function keys*. Like other keys, function keys cause the device to transmit a character or sequence of characters when pressed. However, no interpretation is assigned to the key: software is free to choose how they are used. It is possible, for example, to have a particular function key mean *HELP* when typed to the command line interpreter, but have it mean *next page* when typed to an editor.

A function key is *programmable* if the character(s) it transmits can be changed. The computer sends the terminal a message that identifies a function key and specifies a string for that key. When a programmable function key is pressed, the terminal emits the sequence of characters currently stored with the key. Thus, the user can change the meaning of function keys without rewriting existing software.

16.5.2 Display Hardware

Conventional terminal displays use cathode ray tube (*CRT*) technology, using an electron beam to paint a phosphor-coated glass screen. The beam scans across the screen repeatedly, drawing over 500 horizontal lines to cover the entire screen. The term *raster* refers to the screen, and the process of painting it with electrons is called a *raster scan*. At each instant of the raster scan, hardware controls whether electrons are emitted. Once bombarded with electrons, the phosphor glows, emitting light that is visible through the glass screen. Because the glow lasts only a small fraction of a second, the hardware must repaint the screen many times per second to make an illuminated image appear to be static.

Although the display hardware uses a raster scan technique, the operating system views CRT displays as character-oriented. The terminal divides the screen into roughly 24 lines of 80 characters each. The operating system sends the terminal characters to be displayed along with position information. The terminal, which has the image of each character stored in it, records one screenful of information in its local memory. During the raster scan, the display hardware consults the local memory to determine the character being painted, and controls the electron beam to paint the appropriate horizontal slice of the character.

Like the keyboard, a 24 by 80 character-oriented display has become the standard mechanism for presenting information to the user. Conventional character-oriented displays are popular because the compact presentation follows the familiar form of organizing characters on lines as in books, and because the technology is inexpensive. Thus, most interface software is designed around character-oriented displays. However, such displays have a major drawback: they cannot present graphics except in the simplest form.

Presenting graphics requires more complex display hardware than presenting text. Many alternatives exist. Some displays provide simple line drawings; others understand how to project a 3-dimensional image onto a 2-dimensional display, including the removal of hidden lines.

One particularly popular form of hardware, called a *bit-mapped display*, defines the screen to consist of a 2-dimensional array of *pixels*, where a pixel is the smallest illuminable area of phosphor. The display maps bits in memory into pixels, using *0* to mean that the pixel should be off and *1* to mean that it should be on. Because the bit-mapped display hardware examines bits during the raster scan, changing the bits in memory produces an immediate change on the screen.

Another recent innovation in display technology makes it possible to retain bit-mapped hardware but have color display. Because many colors are possible, the display hardware cannot afford to keep an absolute encoding of the hue for each pixel. So, the hardware requires a user to specify a few colors (usually between 8 and 256) that will be used simultaneously, and encodes pixel colors by using their index in the list.

16.5.3 Pointing Device

Graphics displays emphasize the need for another piece of interface hardware, the *pointing device*. Unlike conventional character-oriented display terminals that can use a *cursor* to mark a position on the screen, graphics displays need to mark positions with much finer granularity (e.g., at the level of a pixel). A pointing device allows the user to control positions precisely, without relying on row and column locations. Usually, the pointing device resides on a desk top near the terminal, and the system projects a small image (e.g., an arrow) on the screen. The image moves as the user moves the pointing device, making it appear that the two are physically connected.

Many pointing devices have been developed. The earliest were *light pens* that the user held to the screen to indicate position. Other pointing devices include finger pads (small rectangular boxes that are sensitive to a user's finger moving on them), tracking balls (similar to the spheres used to control video games), and touch sensitive screens.

The most popular pointing device is called a *mouse*. It consists of a small object that fits into the palm, and is connected to the computer by a single, flexible cable. The mouse, which may use a rubber ball or optical sensors to track movement, slides easily across a desktop, sending horizontal and vertical position information to the computer.

In addition to sensing movement, the mouse contains from 1 to 3 buttons that the user can push. Because the user can press or release buttons while positioning the mouse, the interface software often uses so-called *mouse clicks* to invoke functions related to position or movement.

16.6 The Two-Tier Interface Model

We have reviewed the major interface hardware, and set the stage for a discussion of the software that uses it. But before diving into design issues and details, we need to understand that there is a profound relationship between the underlying computing system and the details of the interface. This section discusses that relationship by partitioning the issues in a way that makes them easier to grasp.

Conceptually, user interface software can be divided into two tiers that stand between the user and the rest of the system. The first tier consists of lexical and syntactic conventions. It includes the details of keystroke handling, the position, size and style of the display, as well as the rules for parsing command line input, and the interpretation of names. The second tier consists of the semantic functionality provided by the system. It includes those operating system facilities visible through the interface, the set of possible commands, and access to the file system.

Intuitively, the semantic tier determines *what* computations are possible, and the syntactic tier determines *how* to invoke those computations. In essence, then, the semantic tier defines the power of the computing system, while the syntactic tier determines its appearance. Taken together, the two tiers encompass the computing environment and all its detail.

Of course, the boundary between syntax and semantics is blurry. Part of the confusion arises because syntax and semantics are usually designed simultaneously, making it difficult to separate an idea from the syntax used to express it. For example, no designer would incorporate a syntactic construct for concurrency if the underlying system does not support concurrent processing. Similarly, facilities like concurrent processing are meaningless in the underlying system if there is no way for a user to use them. Thus, the syntactic and semantic tiers tend to reflect one another.

16.7 Syntactic Flexibility

Why should designers distinguish between the syntactic and semantic tiers? The answer is simple: it helps the designer understand which pieces of the interface are easy to modify and which pieces are not. Because syntactic manipulation is well understood, and usually better defined, it is easy to change the syntactic aspects of an interface. Thus, the two-tier model helps designers understand the importance of choices:

> *Syntactic design decisions are among the least important because syntactic features of a user interface are the easiest to change.*

Recall that we seek to accommodate individual preferences and abilities. Understanding the distinction between semantic and syntactic aspects of the interface also helps designers know which parts of the interface can be parameterized or extended, and which cannot, because syntactic constructs are easy to parameterize.

The next sections explore the semantic and syntactic aspects of the user interface in more detail, presenting examples that will further clarify the two-tier model.

16.8 Semantic Features And Issues

Semantic aspects of the user interface include such things as the file storage system, interprocess communication facilities, and command set. We will consider some of these.

16.8.1 Command Set

The set of commands available to the user forms the most easily identifiable part of the semantic tier. Early systems supported only a few commands. The user could invoke an editor, compile a source program, or execute the resulting binary object deck. Later systems added commands to display system status information so users could locate their jobs in the processing mix. Most modern systems have users share a system-wide command set, but permit individual users to add their own commands.

How should command sets be chosen? There are two approaches: the orthogonal approach, and the integrated subsystem approach. In the orthogonal approach, the designer chooses a large set of small, simple commands that each perform a well-defined task, and requires the user to invoke several to perform a complex computation. The integrated subsystem approach offers users a few large, complex subsystems. Each subsystem covers one problem domain, offering all the tools necessary to solve problems in that domain.

Choosing the integrated subsystem approach offers some advantages, especially for users who tend to focus on one computing activity. It reduces the number of commands a user must remember, and avoids forcing the user to know whether complex commands invoke many small commands or operate independently. Because the subsystem can be designed for a particular class of problem, it can be tailored to the problem area. Thus, it is often more effective than a general-purpose mechanism.

The orthogonal approach also has advantages. Building orthogonal commands reduces duplication of code because each command does only one thing. It also means that efforts to improve a particular computational method can be focused on a single program. Finally, it means that the user only needs to learn and remember one set of details for each particular computing function.

16.8.2 Design Principles

Although no single user interface will be best for all users, we can establish a few principles that help guide our design decisions. Here are four such principles.

Principle of functionality:

> *The user should have access to all the facilities provided by the operating system.*

Principle of orthogonality:

> *There should be exactly one way to perform a computation.*

Principle of consistency:

> *The syntax and semantics of all parts of the user interface should be consistent.*

Principle of least astonishment:

> *The user should be able to predict the output and syntax of any command.*

16.8.3 Concurrent Processing

Because concurrency is fundamental in computing, we have assumed from the outset that the operating system supports it. However, having support for concurrent activities at the operating system level does not necessarily imply that users can specify multiple, concurrent computing activities.

The principle of functionality asserts that the user interface should support concurrent activities. We also know that concurrent activity makes users more productive in two ways. First, it allows them to execute long, complicated computations without waiting for them to complete. Second, it allows them to switch among several ongoing activities analogous to the way they switch among ongoing work in an office or laboratory.

The issue is not whether concurrent activity should be supported, but how. Notice that the two activities above may require two different facilities in a user interface. In one case, users decide when they start a computation that it should be performed concurrent with other activity; in the other, they decide dynamically to switch among activities. The important point is that the user interface *controls* concurrent processing.

> *The operating system provides basic computational services; the user interface provides mechanisms to invoke and control them.*

16.8.4 Interprocess Communication

Like concurrent processing, interprocess communication is a basic service provided by the operating system. The user interface does not deal with underlying mechanisms or low-level details. Instead, it is concerned with ways to establish and control interprocess communication, especially at the program level. Thus, the user interface may include conventions that allow it to inform processes about connections to other processes.

16.8.5 I/O And File Specification

Because file systems usually provide the only nonvolatile data storage, users learn to equate files with permanent storage. They are conscious of file names, locations, and contents.

The user interface has an important responsibility regarding files — it must provide the binding between files and an executing program. Of course, programs could be written to contain absolute file names, so little need be done by the user interface. However, delaying the binding to real files until load-time or run-time increases the flexibility and generality of programs.

So, the file binding issue is one of generality. The program-to-file bindings offered by the user interface determine whether the user can invoke an arbitrary program on an arbitrary file, or whether the programmer needs to know what files a program will use when building it.

16.8.6 Response To Requests

Our discussion of semantic issues has dealt with functionality. However, increasing functionality is not always the best approach. Response time is a crucial property of any human interface. Users seem to detest slow response time more than limited functionality, unreliable storage systems, or enigmatic command syntax. They take pride in conquering and memorizing the absurdly complex incantations required by some interfaces, but seem unwilling to wait more than a few seconds for response.

So, despite our discussion of desired functionality, successful human interfaces always follow a simple precept above all others:

When designing a user interface, there is no substitute for speed.

Looking at this another way reveals that trading off speed for added functionality is only worthwhile if the increased functionality improves the system in overwhelmingly significant ways.

16.9 Syntactic Features And Issues

Syntactic details are important because it is the small annoyances that can make otherwise well-designed systems unusable or unenjoyable. Moreover, users are more likely to complain about syntactic problems because they consider syntax easy to change. In a sense, they are right. Certainly it is easier to change user interface syntax than to change basic system functionality. However, the effort required to make even small changes is much greater after the interface has been built.

This section looks at some of the syntactic design issues and possibilities. We begin by focusing on issues related to textual input from keyboards.

16.9.1 Lexical Conventions And Quoting

Although the keyboard hardware determines how characters are entered, the software determines their interpretation. Unfortunately, the operating system usually interprets some characters specially, leaving only a subset of the characters available for the user interface to define. For example, the terminal device driver may use the *BACKSPACE* character to erase the previous character.

What lexical conventions does the user interface add to the terminal interface? It defines the meaning of each character, and the rules by which characters are grouped into lexical tokens. Finally, it defines the meaning of each token. For example, the user interface might choose to make the plus sign (**+**) a special character that separates tokens, but treat the minus sign like any alphabetic character. Under these rules, the input *abc+bcd-efg* contains three tokens, *abc*, **+**, and *bcd-efg*.

A quoting mechanism is usually included to allow users to override the lexical conventions. For example, many systems take the sequence of characters between two single quotes literally. Thus, the input *'abc+def'* might produce a single lexical token *abc+def*, independent of the usual meaning of the plus sign.

16.9.2 Command History And Editing

Most systems that use keyboard input expect the user to enter commands one after the other. In such systems, a few syntactic mechanisms can improve user productivity. One mechanism keeps a history of all commands typed, allowing the user to select a previous command and execute it again without retyping it. Recalling previous commands is especially useful in systems that require users to type long or complex commands.

Another useful mechanism permits a user to edit commands while typing them. The operating system may already supply primitive editing, allowing users to delete a partial line or erase characters. However, the user interface can provide more complex editing, allowing users to move forward or backward, insert characters, delete characters, or change characters until the desired input has been produced. Editing is especially helpful when combined with a command history mechanism because it allows a user to recall a previously typed command line, make a minor change, and then pass the result to the command interpreter.

16.9.3 Abbreviations And Command Aliases

Many systems allow users to define aliases or abbreviations. Aliases are particularly useful for commands with long names. After the system parses the command line input and determines the command name, it consults an alias table to map the user's input into a valid name that the system understands. Aliases help improve productivity by allowing users to abbreviate commonly used commands (and by allowing users to choose command names that they prefer).

Abbreviations differ from command aliases because they apply to all the input, regardless of whether it is a command name. Some interfaces use a general abbreviation mechanism that maintains an abbreviation table and maps each input token once the command line has been parsed. Separating command name abbreviations (i.e., aliases) from argument abbreviations makes more sense because the abbreviations used for command names and those used for general arguments differ.

The UNIX user interface employs a particularly useful form of argument abbreviation. It recognizes a set of special characters, interpreting them as file name pattern-matching operators. For example, the asterisk is a pattern that denotes zero or more characters, so the string '$x*$' is a pattern that matches all file names beginning with x. When such a string appears on the command line, the user interface replaces it with the set of all file names it matches before invoking the command. If no file name matches the pattern, the user interface declares that the input is incorrect.

16.9.4 Command Name Expansion

User interfaces that support *command name expansion* supply missing phrases on request. Typically, the user types a command prefix and presses a key that requests the interface to fill out the remainder of the command name. If the prefix uniquely specifies a command name, the interface inserts the missing characters. If not, the interface reminds the user of all possible commands that match the prefix.

Naturally, command name expansion works best in an environment that has long command names and few common prefixes. One of the tradeoffs here is that choosing short commands names can increase productivity for users who do not prefer command name expansion.

16.9.5 Typed Vs. Untyped Arguments

Should the user interface understand the purpose and type of command arguments? If it does, it can check arguments for correctness and prompt the user for missing or incorrect arguments. For example, suppose the user interface understands that a *copy* command takes two arguments: a source file and a destination

file. After dividing the input line into tokens, and finding that the command specifies a *copy*, it can check to see that the second token specifies a file that is readable, and that the third token specifies a writable file, before it invokes the *copy*
command. Notice that having the user interface understand and check command
arguments makes the system uniform because all commands must use the same argument syntax.

There are two disadvantages to strongly-typed command arguments. First, the
user interface and command set must be integrated. Whenever a new command is
added to the system, or whenever command arguments are modified, the user interface must be informed. Thus, commands cannot be treated as completely independent programs; they must be viewed as part of the user interface. Such a view
might make it difficult for users to define their own commands or to have their
commands treated exactly the same as system commands. Second, because each
argument of every command must have a particular type, it becomes difficult or
impossible to build commands that take varying numbers and types of arguments.
Thus, although strong typing may help the novice, its limitations make it unattractive for general-purpose systems that have an extensive command library.

16.9.6 Programming Language Constructs

Often, users need to invoke many commands to perform a computation. If the
system allows one to type keystrokes before a program is ready to consume them,
the user may choose to type a sequence of commands while waiting for the current
command to complete. However, it is sometimes much more convenient to think
about command interpretation in procedural terms, using conditional execution and
iteration to express a computation. For example, the conventional user interface in
UNIX allows a user to express iteration using a *for* statement:

```
for each i in aa bb cc  do  print $i
```

where *i* denotes a string variable that takes on the values *aa*, *bb*, and *cc*, and the
statement

```
print $i
```

prints a file with name given by the current contents of variable *i*. Presumably, *aa*,
bb, and so on, are the names of files that the user wishes to print.

Programming language constructs can increase the power of a user interface
because they allow the user to specify repetitive operations conveniently. It is especially important to have iteration if the underlying command set tends to be small
or the command syntax is cryptic. Consider how difficult it might be to invoke a
command on 100 different files without an iteration construct. Conditional execution also improves productivity because it allows the user to express conditions
under which commands should be carried out, or alternatives. For example, with
iteration and conditional execution, it might be possible to write a short sequence of

statements that checks every file in a long list, and removes those that have not been accessed in the last year.

16.9.7 Windows

The advent of bit-mapped display technology made possible large screen displays and better graphics. Many uses have been found for bit-mapped technology, but probably the most impressive interfaces are those that provide multiple windows. A *window* is a rectangular piece of the screen that acts like the display of a terminal. Interfaces that support windows often treat each window as a *virtual terminal*; software that uses the window treats it exactly like a real terminal. Window manager software allows the user to *create, destroy, shrink, expand*, or *move* windows, or invoke processes in windows.

In some systems, windows are *tiled*, meaning that they fill the screen like ceramic tiles in a roof or floor. In other systems, windows *overlap*, meaning that a window may obscure parts of other windows. A large window may totally obscure smaller ones. Usually all windows update their display when they receive output, with the user aware only of updates to portions of windows visible on the screen. At a given time, only one window is designated to receive input from the keyboard' or pointing devices.

In overlapping window environments, the user thinks of rectangular windows on the screen like pieces of paper on a desk. The user interface provides a way to push a window to the bottom of the pile or pull a window to the top of a pile.

Typically, users create a group of one or more windows for each computing activity in which they engage. For example, a user may create a pair of windows for reading electronic mail, then decide to create another window to edit a file, and later return to the mail windows, continuing at exactly the point where activity was suspended. Thus, an average user may have four or five windows on the screen at one time.

Another advantage of windows is that, with appropriate software support, they permit the user to interact with several machines simultaneously. Consider, for example, debugging the network software in this book. A user might choose to connect one window to a Xinu machine and another to a UNIX system running the file server. Thus, it would be possible to observe output from the file server (e.g., diagnostics), while typing input to the diskless Xinu system. Naturally, such an interface is more productive than switching a single terminal session back and forth between the file server and the Xinu system.

What are the design issues in window systems? Because window systems and bit-mapped displays are new, there is much room for experimentation. The designer has to decide whether the window manager or the user has control of window placement and shape. Should the user be forced to position each window, or can the window manager choose positions automatically? How can a pointing device like a mouse be combined with bit-mapped display output to make the user more productive?

Two techniques have already surfaced that blend the mouse with a window system. The first is a *pop-up menu*, which consists of a miniature window that appears at the current mouse position in response to pressing a mouse button. The menu, which lists a set of possible operations one per line, changes as the user moves the mouse across it, so that the item under the current mouse position is highlighted (e.g., in reverse video so it shows a black background with white lettering). Finally, when the user invokes an available operation, the system executes the specified command, and the menu disappears from the screen. In some systems, a second mouse button invokes the operation, while in others, invocation is associated with release of the initial button. Menu items might include such things as *create new window*, *destroy this window*, or *hide this window*, as well as conventional operations like *logout*.

The second technique uses graphics to display information, and allows the user to specify changes graphically (usually using the mouse). For example, a text editor may display part of a text file in a window. Because the file can be larger than a single window, only part of the file is visible on the screen at any time. Editors that use graphic interfaces sometimes display the relative position of the visible text graphically, using a long thin bar down the left hand side of the window to represent the file, and adding a mark to represent the visible text. When editing the beginning of the file, the mark appears at the top of the position bar. It appears at the bottom when the end of the file is on the screen, and half way down the bar when the text being displayed comes from the middle of the file.

To change position in a file, nongraphical editors require the user to specify changes textually. In a graphic interface, the user moves the mouse to the mark, presses a button, and "drags" the mark up or down. The editor responds by changing the current file position, making the visible text correspond to the region of the file indicated by the position of the mark.

It is possible to use windows, pop-up menus, and the graphical input with conventional terminals. However, the small screen size and course granularity of the display make using windows unpleasant. Because each window is smaller, less text is visible. Window borders take a character position. Graphic display is impossible. Thus, only primitive window managers are used.

16.10 Modifying The Syntactic Interface

We have described user interfaces with a two-tier model, separating syntactic and semantic issues. By keeping the distinction in mind, a designer can understand how easy or difficult it would be to make changes. The next two sections describe two ways that users modify the interface.

16.10.1 Parameterization Vs. Extensibility

A good designer anticipates individual preferences and abilities when designing a user interface, and tries to provide each user with the ability to tailor the interface for individual needs. The ability to adapt can be provided by *parameters*, where the user assigns values to a fixed set of variables, or by an *extension* mechanism, where the user specifies procedures or functions that implement some part of the interface.

Most interfaces are parameterized. Often, however, parameterization results from indecision, not because it is necessary. When a design decision cannot be settled easily, the designer builds several alternatives, and allows the user to set a variable specifying the desired alternative. Parameters invented to circumvent design decisions can easily get out of hand, leading to systems with too many options. The term *overfeatured* is sometimes used to describe such systems.

When are parameters needed? We can summarize their use with the following statement:

> *Parameters are useful to control the syntactic presentation of information, or to describe default actions; they should never be used to provide multiple methods of operation when the methods conflict with the basic system or with other parameters.*

Thus, a good test of a proposed parameter is, "do the possible values for this parameter conflict with the meaning of values for any other parameter?" Under this test, parameters are orthogonal. Each controls one aspect of the interface. Furthermore, setting one parameter does not change others.

A parameterized user interface is more flexible than one without parameters, but it is still limited by the original designer, who determines exactly which parameters the user can change, and exactly what values the user can assign to each parameter. An *extensible* interface provides even more flexibility in accommodating changes. Extensible interfaces permit the user to build functions or procedures that control the way the interface interprets input, presents output, or controls processing. The advantage of a procedural approach is that users can specify exactly how the interface should carry out operations.

16.10.2 Multiple Syntactic Interfaces

Another reason for distinguishing between the syntactic and semantic aspects of the user interface emerges when designing systems that support a wide variety of users. Some users may have bit-mapped display hardware while others have only a conventional terminal. Thus, it may be necessary to have several different user interfaces. If the designer is careful, it may be possible to define a single semantic tier and have multiple syntactic front-ends share it.

Of course, the user interface software may not be divided into two easily identifiable pieces; the boundary between syntax and semantics is certainly not as clear
as the boundary between process management and device management. However,
restricting the differences between any two interfaces to syntactic differences does
have two advantages. First, it means that the designer has a goal to work toward,
namely, keeping the differences among interfaces syntactic. Second, it means that
the underlying semantic tier must be powerful enough to support the most sophisticated of all the interfaces. Thus, it will be easy to enhance the simplest interface
because only syntactic changes are needed to allow it to express more complex computations.

16.11 Summary

The user interface consists of hardware and software that stands between a
user and the services an operating system provides. Care must be exercised when
designing an interface because users judge systems primarily by the interface, and
small flaws can ruin an otherwise good design.

Conceptually, the interface software can be divided into two tiers, a syntactic
tier that includes the tactile, lexical, and presentation details, and a semantic tier
that contains the command set, operating system access, and computational services. The semantic tier defines *what* computation a user can invoke, while the
syntactic tier defines *how* the user invokes it. Although syntactic features are easiest to change, we saw that the two tiers tend to be designed simultaneously, resulting in interface software that is more tightly integrated than other parts of the
operating system. Nevertheless, we learned that the designer should think of the
two tiers separately to help understand how difficult it will be to change design decisions.

FOR FURTHER STUDY

Researchers at Xerox Palo Alto Research Center conducted many early studies
of programming environments, including some of the first workstations with bit-
mapped display output and mouse input. Teitelman [1984] summarizes the work
at Xerox on a programming language and environment called Cedar. Goldberg
[1983] discusses work on Smalltalk, another system that makes extensive use of
bit-mapped display technology. Deutsch and Taft [1980] report a survey of
researchers at Xerox that defines what they thought were the most desirable properties of a personal workstation and its user interface.

The July 1986 issue of the *Communications of the ACM* covers another aspect
of user interface studies, reporting on research that measures human satisfaction
and productivity. The research, known as *human factors research*, provides a
scientific evaluation of hardware and software features.

While properties like extensibility and adaptability are difficult to quantize, good examples can be found in existing systems. Stallman [1984] describes how the text editor EMACS allows users to rebind keys and build new editing primitives. Gosling [1983] presents an extensible window system that runs under UNIX.

EXERCISES

16.1 How do interface designers take advantage of a 1-button, 2-button and 3-button mouse?

16.2 Report on at least three input or output devices not discussed in this chapter.

16.3 Read about a commercial bit-mapped display that uses color. How many colors are available simultaneously? How much memory is needed for the display?

16.4 Read about the V operating system in Cheriton [1983]. Describe its user interface philosophy.

16.5 Contrast a system that permitted a single process to control up to three windows with a system that permitted exactly one process per window. When is one better than the other?

16.6 Would you find a voice recognition unit easier or more difficult to use than a keyboard.

16.7 Study the three kinds of quotes used by the UNIX user interface. When are they needed?

16.8 Observe that all I/O has been cast into a single, device-independent abstraction that uses primitives like *open*, *close*, *read*, *write*, and so on. Can you imagine a set of hardware-independent operations sufficient to describe the interaction between a user and the system?

16.9 Try to specify the boundary between syntactic and semantic portions of the user interface by specifying a set of primitive operations that the semantic tier provides and the syntactic tier uses.

17

An Example User Interface:
The Xinu Shell

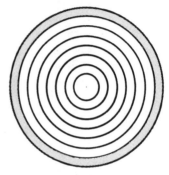

17.1 Introduction

The previous chapter discussed user interface design in general. This chapter presents the details of a simple user interface called a *shell*.† Following the pattern established by other parts of the system, our design emphasizes simplicity and elegance, not features. We concentrate on a few fundamental ideas that make the shell powerful without requiring large amounts of code.

17.2 The Assumed Interface Hardware

Although color graphic display hardware and a pointing device present exciting possibilities for user interaction, we chose to design an interface that uses conventional hardware. The sample shell accepts input from a keyboard and delivers output to a character-oriented screen. The chief advantage of character-oriented interaction is that the hardware is universally available. Thus, no special-purpose hardware will be needed to use our shell.

An important point underlies our choice of hardware and interface features: the most powerful mechanisms are not always the result of advanced hardware. Instead of trying to take advantage of the latest technology, our sample shell will be built around a handful of powerful mechanisms that make it a small, convenient, and powerful base to which additional features can be added easily.

---

†The term *shell* and many of the ideas used here come from UNIX.

17.3 A Basic Design Decision

Should our interface allow the terminal device driver to handle the details of backspacing, character echoing, and line erasing, or should it handle those details itself? This is an important decision because it determines the extent to which the shell can control input. On one hand, choosing to control every detail means that the shell can interpret special characters differently than the system usually does. It might choose, for example, to use *CONTROL-Q* for something other than flow control. On the other hand, taking responsibility for all such details makes the shell large and difficult to modify.

We will choose to use the system terminal driver, and allow it to interpret line kill, flow control, and backspace as usual. There are three principle reasons. First, switching between two interpretations of input characters can be confusing for users. The principle of consistency suggests that keeping a uniform interpretation of characters will make the user more productive. Second, having two pieces of software that handle character processing makes it difficult for programmers who want to use a terminal device without knowing whether input is being interpreted by the shell or the usual device driver. In particular, it becomes impossible to write a single input procedure that can be called both from within the shell and from outside the shell. Third, our goal is to concentrate on the design of the shell itself; introducing low-level character handling details confuses the issue and obscures the design.

17.4 Overview Of Shell Organization And Operation

How should the shell operate? A few basic design choices are crucial because they determine the interface architecture and decide which extensions are possible. The next sections review these basic design choices, and give an overview of the structure of our sample interface.

17.4.1 Input Form

What general form should input take? Our sample interface will be line-oriented, where each line represents a complete unit of input to be recognized by the interface.

17.5 Imperative Vs. Interrogative Interaction Form

How should users phrase their input? Our shell will be procedural, expecting users to provide imperatives to be carried out by the system. Thus, a user might think of directing the interface to "tell me about processes", but would not ask questions like "what are the processes doing?"

17.5.1 Processes Vs. Procedures

Should the shell call a procedure to carry out each imperative, or should the shell invoke a process? Using a procedure is more efficient, but it implies that there can only be one concurrent activity. Because we want to allow for the possibility of many concurrent activities, our shell must be able to use a process to execute each command.

Like most command interpreters, our sample shell will also need to execute some commands without invoking a separate process. Thus, we need a mechanism that allows commands to execute either as separate processes or as procedures called directly from the shell.

17.5.2 File Name Independence

Building file names into commands makes them less general than if they can be compiled without knowing the names of particular files. To keep commands independent of files, the shell must provide a mechanism that attaches commands to particular files when they are invoked.

17.6 Command Syntax

Command-line interpretation is a syntactic recognition problem, so our shell needs to parse the input just like a compiler parses a C program. Thinking of the compiler analogy helps us to understand exactly how to specify the command syntax precisely, making it clear to the user how the shell parses input and to the shell designer exactly how to build a parser. It is tempting to think that the command syntax is so simple no precise definition will be needed. However, failure to produce a precise specification usually leads to ambiguous interpretation rules, a syntax that users cannot understand.

Following standard practice, we will break the syntax description into two parts: a lexical specification that describes how the shell collects characters into *tokens*, and a context specification that describes the ways tokens can be ordered to form valid command-lines.

The division between lexical and context pieces may seem unnecessary for the simple syntax of our sample shell. More to the point, it may seem that dividing the software into two pieces introduces inefficiency. However, we want to start with a good organization that permits future expansion. Even if we decide eventually to optimize the software and blend the two parts into one procedure, it will be important to document the original design to make later changes possible.

17.6.1 The Definition Of Lexical Tokens

At the lexical level, our shell collects input characters into tokens. It recognizes eight possible token types, and records each token type as well as the characters that comprise the token. The following table defines the eight token types:

Token Name	Input Symbol	Description
LESS	<	less-than symbol
GREATER	>	greater-than symbol
AMPERSAND	&	ampersand
QUOTE	'...'	quoted string
DOUBLEQ	"..."	quoted string using double quotes
ENDLINE	\n	end-of-line
ENDSTRING	\0	end-of-string
OTHER	other	sequence of non-blanks

Figure 17.1 The definition of tokens in the Xinu shell.

The chart omits two important details in the definition. First, blanks are significant within quoted strings, and at least one blank must separate adjacent occurrences of type OTHER tokens; otherwise blanks are insignificant. Second, double quotes may appear inside a singly quoted string and vice-versa, but there is no way to place a single quote inside a singly quoted string, or a double quote inside a doubly quoted string.

17.6.2 The Definition Of Command-Line Syntax

Once the lexical tokens have been defined, a BNF-style grammar can be used to give a precise definition of the command-line syntax.

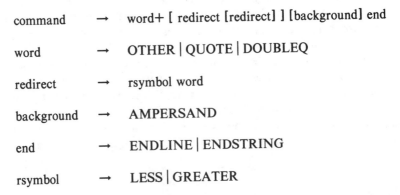

command → word+ [redirect [redirect]] [background] end

word → OTHER | QUOTE | DOUBLEQ

redirect → rsymbol word

background → AMPERSAND

end → ENDLINE | ENDSTRING

rsymbol → LESS | GREATER

Figure 17.2 BNF definition of the command-line syntax

The bracket notation [ ] denotes an optional occurrence; + denotes one or more occurrences of a token. Thus, a command line is a sequence of words followed by zero, one, or two redirection specifications, followed by an optional background specification.

We interpret the BNF definition as a replacement system in which names on the left-hand side can be replaced by the sequence of tokens on the right-hand side. Thus, replacing the symbol *command* with its right-hand side produces a new sequence of tokens (one must choose whether to include an optional part of a right-hand side when a replacement is made). On the right-hand side, the notation $A \mid B$ means that either A or B can be used as replacements. Continuing the replacement process eventually produces a sequence of lexical tokens that cannot themselves be replaced. The set of all possible sequences of lexical tokens that can be derived by such a replacement process is exactly the set of valid commands.

As usual, the BNF grammar does not specify everything we have in mind. For example, we will see that the syntax for redirection is intended to allow at most one input redirection and at most one output redirection. Thus, we must add the restriction that if two redirections appear, one must use *LESS* and the other must use *GREATER*.

The BNF definition of a valid command line makes the syntax clear, and provides the answers to many questions. For example, it shows that no valid command-line can begin with a less-than symbol. Furthermore, we know from the lexical definition that blanks are insignificant, so no valid command line can begin with blanks followed by a less-than symbol.

17.7 Shell Semantics

Syntax cannot be specified or appreciated without an understanding of the underlying computing system. The syntactic definition results from careful consideration of the computational facilities to be provided, and of a convenient form for expressing them. Our syntax draws from ideas and experience with user interfaces in UNIX and other systems. To complete the specification of the sample interface, we need to define the meaning of each token.

The sample command interpreter divides the input into words and takes the first word on each line to be a *command name*. Words following the command name are passed to the command as arguments when it is invoked. We have in mind that the run-time system will not interpret or check command arguments, but merely pass each argument as a string. Thus, if the user types:

```
command arg1 arg2
```

the command interpreter will pass *command* two arguments, which are pointers to the character strings *arg1* and *arg2*†.

---

†In practice, the shell passes an array of pointers to strings.

The syntax has been designed to allow the user to specify concurrent command execution. If the input line ends with an ampersand, the command will be executed in *background*. That is, the shell will not wait for execution of the command to complete before it continues the cycle of issuing a prompt and interpreting the next command. In terms of the underlying system, a process will execute the command asynchronously while the process executing the shell continues.

The redirection syntax is intended to allow a user to bind specific files to a command when invoking it. By convention, each command has a standard input device and a standard output device. A less-than sign preceding a file name means that the command's standard input should come from that file; a greater-than sign means that the command's output should be directed to the named file.

17.8 Implementation Of The Xinu Shell

Having written a precise definition of the shell syntax and given an intuitive definition of the intent of each operator, we are ready to examine a detailed implementation. The implementation begins with a file that contains declarations for shell variables and constants, and then examines procedures for command interpretation and user login.

17.8.1 Shell Definitions

File *shell.h* contains declarations for most shell variables, and definitions of important constants:

```
/* shell.h */

#include <mark.h>

/* Declarations for the Xinu shell */

#define SHEXIT          -5          /* shell exit return           */
#define SHNAMLEN        9           /* length of user name + 1      */
#define SHBUFLEN        80          /* length of general buffer     */
#define SHARGLEN        82          /* length of area for arguments */
#define SHMAXTOK        16          /* maximum tokens per line      */
#define SHMLEN          12          /* maximum length of mach. name */
#define SHCMDSTK        450         /* size of command proc. stack  */
#define SHCMDPRI        20          /* command process priority     */

struct   shvars  {                  /* shell variables             */
         long    shlast;            /* time shell last touched     */
         long    shlogon;           /* time user logged on         */
```

```
    int      shncmds;          /* number of commands available */
    MARKER   shmark;           /* marked if shused valid       */
    Bool     shused;           /* TRUE => user using shell      */
    char     shuser[SHNAMLEN]; /* current user name             */
    char     shmach[SHMLEN];   /* name of this machine          */
    char     shbuf[SHBUFLEN];  /* general purpose buffer        */
    char     *shtok[SHMAXTOK]; /* pointers to input tokens      */
    char     shtktyp[SHMAXTOK];/* type of token in shtok[i]     */
    char     shargst[SHARGLEN];/* actual strings of arguments   */
};

extern  struct  shvars  Shl;
```

External variable *Shl* contains most of the shell variables in a structure of type *shvars*. Much of the information in *Shl* records information about the user who logged in, the time of login, and the time of the last command completion.

Three fields in struct *shvars* should be pointed out. When the command line is divided into tokens, each is added to field *shargst*, terminated by a null character. Thus, *shargst* contains a set of null-terminated strings, one after the other. Field *shtok* is an array of pointers to the strings in *shargst*. The array in field *shtktyp* contains a one-character type for each token. Finally, field *shbuf* is a general purpose buffer used for reading input and other temporary purposes.

17.8.2 Declaration Of Commands

File *cmd.h*, shown below, completes the shell declarations by defining data structure *cmds* to contain information about possible commands. Only the general organization of the *cmds* array is pertinent to the shell; the next chapter describes the details of particular commands and the procedures that implement them.

```
/* cmd.h */

/* Declarations for all commands known by the shell */

struct  cmdent  {                        /* entry in command table     */
        char    *cmdnam;                 /* name of command            */
        Bool    cbuiltin;                /* Is this a builtin command? */
        int     (*cproc)();              /* procedure that implements cmd*/
};

extern  int
        x_bpool(),      x_cat(),      x_close(),    x_cp(),
        x_creat(),      x_date(),     x_devs(),     x_dg(),
        x_echo(),       x_exit(),     x_help(),     x_kill(),
        x_mem(),        x_mount(),    x_mv(),       x_net(),
        x_ps(),         x_reboot(),   x_rf(),       x_rls(),
        x_rm(),         x_routes(),   x_sleep(),    x_snap(),
        x_unmou(),      x_uptime(),   x_who();

/* Commands:      name            Builtin?        procedure       */

#define CMDS       "bpool",       FALSE,          x_bpool,        \
                   "cat",         FALSE,          x_cat,          \
                   "close",       FALSE,          x_close,        \
                   "cp",          FALSE,          x_cp,           \
                   "create",      FALSE,          x_creat,        \
                   "date",        FALSE,          x_date,         \
                   "devs",        FALSE,          x_devs,         \
                   "dg",          FALSE,          x_dg,           \
                   "echo",        FALSE,          x_echo,         \
                   "exit",        TRUE,           x_exit,         \
                   "help",        FALSE,          x_help,         \
                   "kill",        TRUE,           x_kill,         \
                   "logout",      TRUE,           x_exit,         \
                   "mem",         FALSE,          x_mem,          \
                   "mount",       FALSE,          x_mount,        \
                   "mv",          FALSE,          x_mv,           \
                   "netstat",     FALSE,          x_net,          \
                   "ps",          FALSE,          x_ps,           \
                   "reboot",      TRUE,           x_reboot,       \
                   "rf",          FALSE,          x_rf,           \
                   "rls",         FALSE,          x_rls,          \
                   "rm",          FALSE,          x_rm,           \
                   "routes",      FALSE,          x_routes,       \
                   "ruptime",     FALSE,          x_uptime,       \
```

```
        "sleep",        FALSE,        x_sleep,        \
        "snap",         FALSE,        x_snap,         \
        "time",         FALSE,        x_date,         \
        "unmount",      FALSE,        x_unmou,        \
        "uptime",       FALSE,        x_uptime,       \
        "who",          FALSE,        x_who,          \
        "?",            FALSE,        x_help

extern  struct  cmdent  cmds[];
```

The command declarations have been separated from the declaration of other shell variables so it is possible to reconfigure the set of commands easily.

17.8.3 Dividing The Command Line Into Tokens

After reading an input line, the shell breaks it into tokens, and then checks the sequence of tokens to be sure the line is syntactically correct. In compiler terminology, dividing input into tokens is called *lexical analysis*, and the software that collects tokens is called the *lexical analyzer*.

There are well-known formal language and automata-theoretic methods used to build conventional lexical analyzers. However, because the lexical conventions for our shell are extremely simple, we have decided to save space by building an ad hoc lexical analyzer. The code is contained in file *lexan.c*:

```
/* lexan.c - lexan */

#include <conf.h>
#include <kernel.h>
#include <shell.h>

/*------------------------------------------------------------------
 * lexan  -  ad hoc lexical analyzer to divide command line into tokens
 *------------------------------------------------------------------
 */
lexan(line)
char    *line;
{
        char    **tokptr;
        int     ntok;
        char    *p;
        char    ch;
        char    *to;
        char    quote;

        to = Shl.shargst;               /* area to place token strings */
        tokptr = &Shl.shtok[ntok = 0];  /* array of ptrs to tokens */
        for  (p = line ; *p!='\0' && *p!='\n' && ntok < SHMAXTOK ;) {
                while ( (ch = *p) == ' ')        /* skip leading blanks  */
                        p++;
                if (ch == '\0' || ch == '\n')   /* end of line or string*/
                        return(ntok);
                *tokptr++ = to;                  /* save start of token  */
                Shl.shtktyp[ntok++] = ch;
                if (ch == '"' || ch == '\'') {  /* check for quoted str.*/
                        quote = ch;
                        for (p++ ; (ch = *p++) != quote && ch != '\n'
                                && ch != '\0' ; )
                                *to++ = ch;
                        if (ch != quote)
                                return(SYSERR);
                } else {                          /* other possible tokens      */
                        *to++ = *p++;
                        if (ch!='>' && ch!='<' && ch!='&')
                                while ((ch = *p)!='\n' && ch !='\0' &&
                                        ch!='<' && ch!='>' && ch!=' ' &&
                                        ch!='"' && ch!='\'' && ch !='&')
                                        *to++= *p++; /* copy alphamerics*/
                }
                *to++ = NULLCH;                  /* terminate token string     */
```

```
    }
    return(ntok);
}
```

Lexan accepts as an argument the address of an input line to be scanned, and deposits its output in fields *shtok* and *shargst* of variable *Shl*. It begins by initializing pointers to the beginning of the string area (field *shargst*) and the list of argument pointers (field *shtok*). It then enters a *for* loop, using character pointer *p* to move across the input. *Lexan* skips leading blanks, and then examines the next character to determine how it should be processed. There are several possibilities. The character could begin a quoted string, be a single-character token (e.g., a less-than symbol), or start a "word" consisting of a sequence of non-blank characters. Quoted strings end at the first occurrence of a matching quote.

Token processing is simple. A quoted string that does not end before the end of the string is incorrect. *Lexan* copies string characters (excluding the quotes) to the string area. Other tokens are also copied to the string area. The single-character tokens less-than, greater-than, and ampersand are easiest to process because they can be copied in one statement. The remaining tokens are "words" consisting of contiguous nonblank characters; *lexan* uses a *while* loop to copy them. Once the copy has been completed, *lexan* appends a null character to define the end of the string.

In addition to copying tokens to the string area, *lexan* records the starting address of each token in the entries of array *Shl.shtok*. It assigns the corresponding entry of array *Shl.shtktyp* a value that records the token type.

When *lexan* reaches the end of the input line, it returns a count of the number of tokens found. If it detects an error, *lexan* returns *SYSERR* to its caller, making no attempt to recover or repair the problem. Notice that the action to be taken when an error occurs has been coded into *lexan*, a low-level procedure. The exercises discuss the choice of error handling and suggest alternatives.

17.8.4 The Heart Of The Command Interpreter

Procedure *shell*, shown below in file *shell.c*, implements most of the command interpretation. Although the procedure is long, it is not difficult to understand.

```
/* shell.c - shell */

#include <conf.h>
#include <kernel.h>
#include <proc.h>
#include <shell.h>
#include <cmd.h>
#include <tty.h>

struct  shvars  Shl;                    /* globals used by Xinu shell  */
struct  cmdent  cmds[] = {CMDS};        /* shell commands              */
LOCAL   char    errhd[] = "Syntax error\n";/* global error messages    */
LOCAL   char    fmt[]   = "Cannot open %s\n";
LOCAL   char    fmt2[]  = "[%d]\n";


/*------------------------------------------------------------------------
 * shell  -  Xinu shell with file redirection and background processing
 *------------------------------------------------------------------------
 */
shell(dev)
int     dev;
{
        int     ntokens;
        int     i, j, len;
        int     com;
        char    *outnam, *innam;
        int     stdin, stdout, stderr;
        Bool    backgnd;
        char    ch, mach[SHMLEN];
        int     child;

        Shl.shncmds = sizeof(cmds)/sizeof(struct cmdent);
        for (getname(mach) ; TRUE ; ) {
                fprintf(dev, "%s %% ", mach);
                getutim(&Shl.shlast);
                if ( (len = read(dev, Shl.shbuf, SHBUFLEN)) == 0)
                        len = read(dev, Shl.shbuf, SHBUFLEN);
                if (len == EOF)
                        break;
                Shl.shbuf[len-1] = NULLCH;
                if ( (ntokens=lexan(Shl.shbuf)) == SYSERR) {
                        fprintf(dev, errhd);
                        continue;
                } else if (ntokens == 0)
                        continue;
```

```
        outnam = innam = NULL;
        backgnd = FALSE;

        /* handle '&' */

        if (Shl.shtktyp[ntokens-1] == '&') {
                ntokens-- ;
                backgnd = TRUE;
        }

        /* scan tokens, accumulating length;  handling redirect */

        for (len=0,i=0 ; i<ntokens ; ) {
                if ((ch = Shl.shtktyp[i]) == '&') {
                        ntokens = -1;
                        break;
                } else if (ch == '>') {
                        if (outnam != NULL || i >= --ntokens) {
                                ntokens = -1;
                                break;
                        }
                        outnam = Shl.shtok[i+1];
                        for (ntokens--,j=i ; j<ntokens ; j++) {
                                Shl.shtktyp[j] = Shl.shtktyp[j+2];
                                Shl.shtok  [j] = Shl.shtok  [j+2];
                        }
                        continue;
                } else if (ch == '<') {
                        if (innam != NULL || i >= --ntokens) {
                                ntokens = -1;
                                break;
                        }
                        innam = Shl.shtok[i+1];
                        for (ntokens--,j=i ; j < ntokens ; j++) {
                                Shl.shtktyp[j] = Shl.shtktyp[j+2];
                                Shl.shtok  [j] = Shl.shtok  [j+2];
                        }
                        continue;
                } else {
                         len += strlen(Shl.shtok[i++]);
                }
        }
        if (ntokens <= 0) {
                fprintf(dev, errhd);
                continue;
```

```
        }
        stdin = stdout = stderr = dev;

        /* Look up command in table */

        for (com=0 ; com<Shl.shncmds ; com++) {
                if (strcmp(cmds[com].cmdnam,Shl.shtok[0]) == 0)
                        break;
        }
        if (com >= Shl.shncmds) {
                fprintf(dev, "%s: not found\n", Shl.shtok[0]);
                continue;
        }

        /* handle built-in commands with procedure call */

        if (cmds[com].cbuiltin) {
                if (innam != NULL || outnam != NULL || backgnd)
                        fprintf(dev, errhd);
                else if ( (*cmds[com].cproc)(stdin, stdout,
                        stderr, ntokens, Shl.shtok) == SHEXIT)
                        break;
                continue;
        }

        /* Open files and redirect I/O if specified */

        if (innam != NULL && (stdin=open(NAMESPACE,innam,"ro"))
                == SYSERR) {
                fprintf(dev, fmt, innam);
                continue;
        }
        if (outnam != NULL && (stdout=open(NAMESPACE,outnam,"w"))
                == SYSERR) {
                fprintf(dev, fmt, outnam);
                continue;
        }

        /* compute space needed for string args. (in bytes) */

        len += (ntokens+2) * (sizeof(char *) + sizeof(char));
        if (isodd(len))
                len--;
        control(dev, TCINT, getpid());
```

```
                    /* create process to execute conventional command */

            if ( (child = create(cmds[com].cproc, SHCMDSTK, SHCMDPRI,
                              Shl.shtok[0],(len/sizeof(int)) + 4,
                              stdin, stdout, stderr, ntokens))
                              == SYSERR) {
                    fprintf(dev, "Cannot create\n");
                    close(stdout);
                    close(stdin);
                    continue;
            }
            addarg(child, ntokens, len);
            setdev(child, stdin, stdout);
            if (backgnd) {
                    fprintf(dev, fmt2, child);
                    resume(child);
            } else {
                    setnok(getpid(), child);
                    recvclr();
                    resume(child);
                    if (receive() == INTRMSG) {
                            setnok(BADPID, child);
                            fprintf(dev, fmt2, child);
                    }
            }
    }
    return(OK);
}
```

After computing the number of commands, procedure *shell* begins a cycle of issuing a prompt, reading a single command line, and interpreting the command. During each iteration, the shell records the current time in *Shl.shlast*, making it possible to tell how long the shell has been idle.

The shell calls *lexan* to divide the input line into tokens, and begins checking the command line syntax. First it checks the last token for an ampersand, and assigns Boolean variable *backgnd TRUE* if one occurs. It then enters a *for* loop, indexing through the remaining tokens one at a time.

While scanning tokens, the shell records and removes I/O redirection combinations like the *LESS* token followed by an arbitrary file name. To ensure correct syntax, the shell must be sure that symbols like *LESS* are not the last symbol on the input line. When removing a token, the shell must remember to move token types in array *Shl.shtktyp* whenever moving token pointers in *Shl.shtok*.

Once the scan of tokens completes, the shell needs to be sure that at least one token remains. The first remaining token is taken to be the command name, and other tokens are assumed to be arguments for the command.

17.8.5 Command Lookup And Invocation Of Builtins

After parsing the sequence of tokens, the shell searches array *cmds* for the named command, and prepares to invoke it. Our shell requires an exact match between the command name typed as input and the name in the table, so lookup is simple.

Once a command name match has been found, the shell examines field *cbuiltin* in the *cmds* table entry. If the specified command is marked as *builtin*, the shell invokes it with a procedure call. It is necessary to distinguish builtin commands from other commands because the builtin mechanism provides the only way for a command to control the shell itself. In particular, commands like *logout* that cause the shell to exit cannot be executed by a separate process.

17.8.6 I/O Redirection

For non-builtin commands, the shell redirects input and output before invoking the command. Initially, it assigns the three variables *stdin*, *stdout*, and *stderr* the device id of the terminal device it uses for input and output. To redirect input, the shell opens the input file and assigns *stdin* the new device id. Similarly, it redirects output by opening an output file and assigning *stdout* the device id.

We know that some commands will execute concurrently, so the shell will not always wait for command completion. However, the shell cannot leave devices open or it would quickly exhaust the available device entries. To summarize:

> *The shell opens standard I/O devices before a command begins; it must arrange to have them closed when the command exits.*

Because Xinu does not keep a per-process device or file table, it does not know the standard input and standard output device descriptors that the shell provided. How can the shell arrange to close devices at process exit? There are three alternatives: force all commands to close the standard input and output before they exit, design the shell to monitor command processes and close devices whenever a process exits, or modify the Xinu process manager so it closes devices automatically.

Forcing all commands to close their standard I/O devices before exiting makes command procedures difficult to understand and difficult to program correctly. It means that commands must close devices without opening them. Having the user interface monitor command processes and close standard I/O devices is difficult because all processes are independent and any process can exit or be killed at any time. Thus, we have chosen to modify the process manager.

Recall that the process executing the shell is independent of the process executing a command. In addition, the command may be terminated by a third process. Thus, information needed at process exit must be stored in the process table where it can be accessed by whatever process terminates the command. Our implementation adds a two-element array, *pdevs* to the process table entry.† When a process is created, procedure *create* initializes the *pdevs* array to *BADDEV*, a constant that cannot be a valid device id. Then, after the shell creates a process to execute a command, it fills the two entries in *pdevs* with the device ids of the command's standard input and standard output devices. Finally, procedure *kill* checks the two entries at process exit and closes specified devices.

To set device entries in the process table, the shell uses procedure *setdev*, shown below in file *setdev.c*:

```
/* setdev.c - setdev */

#include <conf.h>
#include <kernel.h>
#include <proc.h>

/*------------------------------------------------------------------------
 *  setdev  -  set the two device entries in the process table entry
 *------------------------------------------------------------------------
 */
SYSCALL setdev(pid, dev1, dev2)
int     pid;                            /* process to change          */
int     dev1, dev2;                     /* device descriptors to set  */
{
        int     *nxtdev;

        if (isbadpid(pid))
                return(SYSERR);
        nxtdev = (int *) proctab[pid].pdevs;
        *nxtdev++ = dev1;
        *nxtdev = dev2;
        return(OK);
}
```

17.8.7 Passing Arguments To The Command Process

Once files have been opened for redirected I/O, little work remains to be done before the command can be invoked. The most difficult task involves preparing arguments for the command.

---

†Interested readers can find listings of modified files in Appendix 2.

What arguments should a command receive? Certainly, it needs to receive the arguments that appear on the command line. In addition, the designer must choose how to pass it information about I/O redirection. We have chosen to have the shell pass each command five explicit arguments: three integer device descriptors corresponding to *stdin*, *stdout*, and *stderr*, an integer count of string arguments, and the address of an array of string argument pointers. The latter two arguments correspond to the UNIX *argc* and *argv* described in Chapter 13.

Passing the strings from the command line is not easy because we expect that commands may execute concurrently. As a result, the shell cannot pass pointers to the tokens in structure *Shl* because it is global to all commands and will be changed each time the shell parses a new command. Furthermore, because commands can execute in background, and because Xinu does not automatically release heap storage when a process completes, the shell cannot use heap storage for command line arguments. Finally, although the system releases stack space when a process completes, the process creation primitive *create* does not provide for string arguments.

There are two possible solutions to the argument passing problem. We could modify *create* (or invent a slightly different version) so it allocates space on the process stack for string arguments, or we could reserve stack space and have the shell copy string arguments into it. The first solution is more elegant, and preserves the separation between process management software and user interface. However, we view the current shell as a sample for experimentation, and have chosen to use the second approach so that all the details of argument passing are contained here, making it possible to change the conventions without changing *create* (some of the exercises suggest alternative arrangements).

Procedure *addarg* implements string argument passing. It takes a process id, and copies string arguments from the global structure *Shl* onto the specified process stack. File *addarg.c* contains the code.

```
/* addarg.c - addarg */

#include <conf.h>
#include <kernel.h>
#include <proc.h>
#include <shell.h>


/*------------------------------------------------------------------
 * addarg  -  copy arguments to area reserved on process stack
 *------------------------------------------------------------------
 */
addarg(pid, nargs, len)
int     pid;                    /* process to receive arguments */
int     nargs;                  /* number of arguments to copy  */
int     len;                    /* size of arg. area (in bytes) */
```

```
{
        struct   pentry  *pptr;
        char     **fromarg;
        int      *toarg;
        char     *to;

        if (isbadpid(pid) || (pptr= &proctab[pid])->pstate != PRSUSP)
                return(SYSERR);
        toarg = (int *) ( ((unsigned)pptr->pbase) - (unsigned)len );
        to = (char *) (toarg + (nargs + 2));
        *toarg++ = (int) (toarg + 1);
        for (fromarg=Shl.shtok ; nargs > 0 ; nargs--) {
                *toarg++ = to;
                strcpy(to, *fromarg++);
                to += strlen(to) + 1;
        }
        *toarg = 0;
        return(OK);
}
```

Addarg checks to see that the process has been suspended before modifying its stack. It assumes that the process has been created with enough dummy arguments so that space remains above the pseudo-call for both the string arguments and an array of pointers to each argument. It computes the address on the process stack just beyond the arguments left by *create*, and assigns that address to variable *toarg*.

Starting at the address in *toarg*, procedure *addarg* stores a pointer to an array of string pointers, the array of string pointers, a zero to mark the end of the array, and the set of null-terminated strings. Figure 17.3 shows the memory layout in detail.

address	contents	description
process stack base →	0	
s_3	$string_3$	
	0	
s_2	$string_2$	string area
	0	
to starts here → s_1	$string_1$	
	0	
	s_3	array of
	s_2	string pointers
s_a	s_1	
toarg starts here →	s_a	string array arg.
	nargs	
	stderr	arguments set
	stdout	up by create
	stdin	
process initial SP →	ret. addr	return address
	↓	process stack area

Figure 17.3 The details of a command process stack with arguments *stdin*, *sdtout*, *stderr*, *nargs*, and *args*, a pointer to the array of string argument pointers.

Addarg can determine where the strings will start relative to the initial value of *toarg* because it knows there will be *nargs* pointers in the array of pointers plus two additional locations for the initial pointer and zero word. Thus, it initializes pointer *to* to the first location of the string area.

The main loop of *addarg* copies arguments from structure *Shl* onto the stack, updating the position in the string area as given by *to*, and updating the array of pointers so each successive element points to a new string.

After having looked at the code in *addarg* that initializes string arguments, it will be easy to understand why procedure *shell* specifies a large argument count when it creates a process. It must specify enough arguments to force *create* to leave space for the strings themselves plus the array of pointers. Computing the size needed is tedious, but not difficult. One byte is needed for each character in the string arguments. In addition, a word is needed for a pointer to the string, and two words are needed for the pointer to the array, and zero word. The shell computes the space needed in bytes, and then converts the result to words because *create* expects word-sized arguments.

17.8.8 Starting A Command In Background

After creating a process to execute the command, setting up string arguments, and redirecting I/O, the shell merely needs to call *resume* to start the process executing. It also prints the process id of the background process so the user can uniquely identify the command. The process executing the command will execute concurrently with the shell.

Of course, the user must decide whether it makes sense to execute a command in background. If a background command writes messages to the user's terminal it may be confusing, but a background command that reads input can be much worse. Consider what happens when both the shell and a background command attempt to interact with the user. They both issue a prompt and then read input. Unfortunately, the user has no control over which process receives the input line. Thus, commands typed to the shell may be received by the background process, and vice versa. The interface designer can help avoid the problem of having two processes contend for input by carefully choosing commands that do little interaction. The next chapter shows how such a set of commands can be designed.

17.8.9 Foreground Processing And Command Expansion

Executing a command in the foreground differs from executing it in background only because the shell process itself must wait for the command to complete. Again, because the basic Xinu system relies on processes to coordinate activities with semaphores or messages, there is no easy way for the shell to await the completion of an arbitrary process. Two alternative designs are possible: have commands inform the user interface when they complete, or modify the process manager.

For the same reasons we chose to have the system automatically close standard input and output descriptors, we will choose to have it notify the user interface of command expansion. The method consists of an additional field in the process table entry, *pnok* (next of kin), and a change to procedure *kill*†. When *kill* is about to terminate a process, it examines the next-of-kin field, and sends a termination message to whatever process id it finds there.

The shell uses the termination message mechanism as follows. After creating a process, *P*, to execute the command, the shell calls procedure *setnok*, shown below in file *setnok.c*, to set *P*'s *next of kin* field to the shell's process id. The shell then clears any waiting messages, starts the command process executing, and calls *receive* to wait for a message to arrive. When the command completes (or is terminated for any reason), *kill* sends a termination message to the shell, allowing it to continue execution. The code for *setnok* is straightforward:

---

†Code for the *kill* procedure can be found in Appendix 2.

```
/* setnok.c - setnok */

#include <conf.h>
#include <kernel.h>
#include <proc.h>

/*------------------------------------------------------------------------
 * setnok - set next-of-kin (notified at death) for a given process
 *------------------------------------------------------------------------
 */
SYSCALL setnok(nok, pid)
int     nok;
int     pid;
{
        char    ps;
        struct  pentry  *pptr;

        disable(ps);
        if (isbadpid(pid)) {
                restore(ps);
                return(SYSERR);
        }
        pptr = &proctab[pid];
        pptr->pnxtkin = nok;
        restore(ps);
        return(OK);
}
```

Looking at the code in *shell.c* shows how it uses *setnok*. Variable *backgnd* determines whether the user requested that the command execute in background or foreground. In the foreground case, the shell does not check for a termination message explicitly. It only checks for message value *INTRMSG*, and assumes that any other message must be a termination message.

17.8.10 Moving A Command To Background

A user seldom knows exactly how long a command will take to execute, especially when execution time depends on the size of input files and the current machine load. In an interactive system, users usually execute commands in foreground. So, it is common for a user to become impatient for a command to complete, and wish that the command could finish executing in background.

Once a command starts executing in foreground, it becomes difficult to move it to background because the shell does not execute. Therefore, adding the ability to move an executing command to background means choosing a mechanism that allows the user to interrupt an executing process or a mechanism that allows the user to communicate with the shell.

We have chosen to build a mechanism that allows the user to inform the shell that the current command should be continued in background, and allow the shell to control the command process explicitly. The mechanism adds a reserved character to the set of characters processed specially by the terminal device driver. We think of the new special character, *CONTROL-B*, as meaning "send this process into background". Pressing the background key does not enter a character on the input line. It only causes the terminal device driver to send message *INTRMSG* to a specified process.

To receive the interrupt message, a process must register with the terminal device driver. The driver keeps only one process id, so when a process registers to receive interrupt messages, the previously registered process loses control. Modified terminal device driver routines can be found in files *ttyiin.c* and *ttycntl.c* in Appendix 3.

As the code in *shell.c* shows, the shell process calls *control* to register its process id with the terminal device from which it receives input. Thereafter, whenever the user types the background key, the shell receives message *INTRMSG*.

Recall that the shell uses message passing to tell when a command completes. In reality, the shell can receive either an interrupt message (indicating that the user typed the background key), or a termination message (indicating that the command completed). When an interrupt message arrives, the shell uses *setnok* to prevent receipt of the termination message. Before continuing its main loop, the shell also prints the process id of the process, which will now be considered to be executing in background. Nothing needs to be done to the command process itself because processes execute identically in foreground and background.

17.8.11 User Login

We have seen how the shell read commands, parses them, redirects input or output, creates processes to execute commands, and controls both foreground and background processing. The only other significant part of the user interface handles user authentication. The term *user login* refers to authentication where the users identify themselves to the system; the *login processor* software handles user login, checking that the user has a valid account on the system and can supply a secret password.

Usually, login processors require users to type an *account number* or *user id* by which they are known, and a secret *password* to ensure that no one impersonates the specified user.

Typically, the system repeats the same action for every possible terminal device from which users can log in. First, it calls the login processor to prompt for a login id and password. Once it receives a valid login, the login processor returns, and the system invokes a shell on the device, allowing users to execute commands. When the shell returns, the system repeats the login sequence.

Our sample login processor does little to authenticate users. It merely prints a prompt, accepts a non-null user name, saves the name and login time in global structure *Shl*, and returns. Adding password authentication is left as an exercise. File *login.c* contains the code.

```
/* login.c - login */

#include <conf.h>
#include <kernel.h>
#include <shell.h>

/*------------------------------------------------------------------------
 *  login  -  log user onto system
 *------------------------------------------------------------------------
 */
login(dev)
int     dev;
{
        int     len;

        Shl.shused = FALSE;
        Shl.shuser[0] = NULLCH;
        for (getname(Shl.shmach) ; TRUE ; ) {
                fprintf(dev,"\n\n%s - The magic of Xinu\n\nlogin: ",
                        Shl.shmach);
                while ( (len=read(dev,Shl.shbuf,SHBUFLEN))==0 ¦¦ len==1)
                        fprintf(dev, "login: ");
                if (len == EOF) {
                        read(dev, Shl.shbuf, 0);
                        Shl.shused = FALSE;
                        continue;
                }
                Shl.shbuf[len-1] = NULLCH;
                strncpy(Shl.shuser, Shl.shbuf, SHNAMLEN-1);
                Shl.shused = TRUE;
                getutim(&Shl.shlogon);
                mark(Shl.shmark);
                fprintf(dev,"\n%s\n\n",
                "    Welcome to Xinu (type ? for help)" );
                getutim(&Shl.shlast);
                return(OK);
        }
}
```

17.9 Summary

We have examined a user interface built around conventional keyboard input and character-oriented display. The interface, called a *shell*, is powerful because it supports concurrent command execution, redirection of input and output, and arbitrary string argument passing.

Our design began with a precise definition of the command line syntax. At the lowest level, the lexical definition described how the shell collected input characters into tokens, and specified the possible tokens. At a higher level, we used a BNF grammar to describe the sequences of tokens that produce valid commands. Although the sample shell had a simple syntax, we chose to build an ad hoc parser. Having the precise specification helped simplify the software design, and makes it easy to modify later.

Although the shell used facilities like concurrent execution that the underlying system provides, implementation required making minor changes to system routines as well as building a command line parser. We found, for example, that the shell needed to wait for completion of foreground command processes. In addition, the shell needed the system to close devices at process exit that it had opened for redirected input or output, and to inform it when the user wished to move a foreground process to the background. Thus, in terms of the two-tier user interface model, adding a syntactic tier required minor modifications in the semantic tier.

The sample shell clearly demonstrates the relationship between the user interface and the facilities provided by the underlying system. Concurrent processing is an excellent example. We saw that the system provided support for concurrent processes, but it was the shell that controlled concurrency and made it available to the user. When adding mechanisms like the one that permits a user to move foreground processing into the background, we were building ways to control existing facilities, not adding new ones.

Login processing forms the final piece of the user interface. It is responsible for authenticating users and recording information about them. We examined a sample login processor that merely recorded information without requiring users to specify a password.

FOR FURTHER STUDY

Few operating system texts discuss user interface issues or command language interpreters. Calingaert [1982] describes command language procedures, and the collection of articles edited by Unger [1975] covers several aspects of command interpreters.

Most of the syntax and semantics of the shell presented here are derived from the original UNIX shell by Bourne [1978]. Korn [1983] describes an extended shell with the same general semantics, but which supports an editor-like interface.

EXERCISES

17.1 Add command aliases to the Xinu shell. Include a builtin command that reports the current aliases set as well as commands to add or delete aliases.

17.2 Implement a cache of the ten most recently typed commands, and allow users to recall a previous command by typing !X, where X is the unique prefix of some previous command.

17.3 Why does the shell pass standard input and output device ids to the command as arguments? What are the advantages and disadvantages of having the command obtain them from the process table instead?

17.4 Modify the shell and *printf* to keep standard input and standard output device ids in the process table without passing them explicitly.

17.5 Rewrite the BNF grammar for command line syntax to remove the optional notation [ ] and repetition notation **+**, replacing them with additional rules. Consult a text on compiler construction if you need more information on BNF.

17.6 Discuss the advantages and disadvantages of having low-level routines like *lexan* print error messages as opposed to merely returning a value that shows an error occurred.

17.7 Change *lexan* to keep pointer p and an error value global so its caller can report detailed information about the cause and location of errors.

17.8 The parser in our shell does not implement the shell syntax exactly as it was specified. Find and repair the subtle problem(s). Do you prefer to use the syntax as specified or as implemented?

17.9 Modify the shell to allow I/O redirection on builtin commands. Be careful: shell exit is not the same as system termination.

17.10 Should the shell allow users to specify at the time of command invocation whether to invoke the command as a builtin?

17.11 Find out about the builtin commands offered by a UNIX shell. Could any of them be executed as conventional commands?

17.12 Devise a modified version of *create* that handles string arguments for the shell, automatically performing the same function as *addarg* when creating the process.

17.13 Revise *login* to keep a file of secret passwords and look up a user's password.

17.14 As written, the shell cannot execute on multiple terminals simultaneously. Rewrite it to keep a separate copy of *Shl* for each login.

17.15 Modify the shell so it can be used as a command. That is, allow the user to invoke command *shell* and start with a new shell process. Have control return to the original shell when the subshell exits. Be careful.

17.16 Modify the shell so it can accept input from a text file (i.e., allow the user to build a file of commands and then start a shell interpreting them).

17.17 Modify the shell to allow a user to redirect standard error as well as standard output.

17.18 Modify the shell and all commands so it passes standard input, standard output, and standard error device ids in the process table entry and not as explicit parameters.

17.19 Modify the shell to allow a user to detach processing from the CONSOLE device and reattach it to another terminal without causing the shell to exit.

17.20 What is the UNIX *environment*, and how does the UNIX shell use it to pass information to command processes?

17.21 Read about shell variables in a UNIX shell, and implement a similar mechanism in the Xinu shell.

17.22 Find out how the UNIX shell passes environment variables to command processes, and implement a similar mechanism in the Xinu shell.

17.23 Implement in-line input redirection, allowing the user to type

```
command << stop
```

followed by lines of input terminated by a line that begins with the sequence of characters *stop*. Have the shell save the input in a temporary file and execute the command with the temporary file as standard input.

17.24 Why does the UNIX shell have three types of quotes?

17.25 It would be possible to extend the command table to include information on the number and types of arguments each command needed, and to have the shell check arguments before passing them to the command. List two advantages and two disadvantages of having the shell check arguments.

17.26 Suppose the designer decided to add a *for* statement to the shell so a user could execute a command repeatedly as in

```
foreach (1 2 3 4 5 6 7 8 9) command-line
```

where *foreach* is a keyword, and *command-line* is a command line exactly like commands the shell now accepts. Should the designer modify the shell syntax and parser or try to make *foreach* a builtin command? Why?

17.27 Add an iterative facility to the shell as described in the previous exercise.

17.28 Modify the shell to accept an alternative output redirection with syntax ">>", and have it mean *append this output to the end of the file* instead of having it write the output to the beginning of the file. (Note: you may find it easiest to define a standard way to *seek* to the end of a file, and add the new facility to all file systems.)

17.29 Add command expansion to the shell by having the user type a unique prefix of a command followed by carriage return; have the shell type out the complete command and wait for arguments or a second carriage return to show that there are none. Should the shell execute the command immediately if the user types a complete command name the first time, or should it wait for a second carriage return?

17.30 Suppose you had a bit-mapped display and a pointing device. How could you improve the shell? Assume multiple windows.

17.31 UNIX allows command lines of the form:

```
command1 | command2 | command3
```

where the symbol |, called a *pipe*, specifies that the standard output of one command is connected to the standard input of the next command. Implement a *pipe* device for Xinu, and modify the shell to allow a pipeline of commands. Hint: Start with two commands.

17.32   Modify the *tty* device driver and shell so that pressing CONTROL-k kills the currently executing processing analogous to the way pressing CONTROL-b places it in background.

18

An Example Set Of Shell Commands

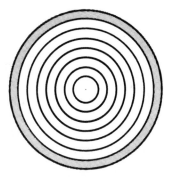

18.1 Introduction

The previous chapter described the design of a simple shell, showing how the shell invoked commands and passed string arguments to them. This chapter considers a sample set of commands, and illustrates how they use string arguments.

Two fundamental ideas will become apparent from the sample commands. First, the command interface differs from the system call interface because commands provide information to the user as well as perform computational chores. Second, the string argument mechanism, which supplies variable numbers and types of arguments, allows commands to be parameterized so a single command can provide several, related functions.

18.2 Command And Procedure Names

18.2.1 Choosing Command Names

Before looking at specific commands, it is important to decide how they should be named. Novice users often prefer long, explanatory names like *renamefile*. Experienced users prefer short names that require less typing. Thus, the best names are short and mnemonic.

Users also carry subtle prejudices from past experience. For example, some of the sample command names in this chapter were taken from similar commands in the UNIX operating system. Users with UNIX experience will find them easy to remember, while users without UNIX experience may find them puzzling.

Many command names have been taken from the names of underlying Xinu system calls. For example, the *close* command closes devices by invoking the Xinu *close* system call. Using the same name for a command and a system call establishes consistency throughout the system. Programmers who understand the *close* system call are not surprised by the *close* command. Similarly, users familiar with the *close* command find closing a device from within a program natural.

18.2.2 Choosing Procedure Names

Once command names have been chosen, procedures must be built that implement each command. How should these procedures be named? The designer must be careful to avoid conflicts with existing system call procedures, especially if command names and system call names overlap. There are two approaches to solving the problem: avoid duplicate names, or reuse names and bind command procedures separately from system call procedures. The latter is extremely difficult because a command like *close* invokes the underlying system call of the same name.

Choosing to avoid duplicate names does not solve the problem completely because it still leaves the question of exactly what names to use. The choice becomes more difficult because multiple command names can map to the same command procedure (e.g., *help* and *?* both invoke the help command). Rather than invent slight misspellings of existing names, we will add a unique prefix to the most common name for each command. For example, the help command procedure is named *x_help*.

18.3 Types Of Commands

The sample set of commands can be divided into three broad categories: *system status*, *general information*, and *computational service*. Each type is important; no single type can replace the others. Taken together, the three types of commands provide a useful and productive environment that satisfies the user's need for information and processing, as well as allowing the user to examine the system.

System status commands inform the user how the operating system has allocated resources, and how it is performing. They display the contents of internal system tables and lists in a readable form. In a sense, such commands shape the user's view of the system by providing the only concrete presentation of abstract concepts like processes and process states. Perhaps more important, system status commands permit the system designer to examine and debug the system from a new perspective. The designer can use the command interface to interrogate system data structures and display information dynamically and asynchronously without deciding *a priori* the conditions under which a snapshot should be taken.

Using interactive commands to monitor a system helps the designer more clearly understand system operation because it shows the cases that arise in practice, and reveals unanticipated anomalies.

General information commands supply the user with data that is useful in problem solving. For example, a command that prints the time or date falls into the information category. The primary characteristic of information commands is that they require little computation, and do not alter the system state.

Most commands fall into the third category: they are imperative commands that invoke computational services and permanently alter the system state. For example, a command like "copy file *x* to file *y*" permanently changes the system by creating or rewriting file *y*. A single computational imperative may imply seconds, minutes or hours of processing, and small, medium, or large volumes of input or output traffic.

18.4 Command Implementation

The next sections consider each sample command in detail, describing its purpose, use, implementation, and design features that distinguish the command from others. Although the descriptions focus on particular commands, the reader should observe a pattern in the general approach, as well as patterns in the general program schema. In particular, most commands parse arguments incrementally, and attempt to preserve system state by closing files they open explicitly and releasing any storage they allocate. In addition, the style of interaction we have chosen is terse: commands say little to report errors to the user. They assume that users are experienced, and that most errors result from simple typographical mistakes, not from basic misunderstandings about the command (some of the exercises discuss changes to the error messages).

18.5 General Information Commands

The first type of command we will consider are those that provide general information for the user.

18.5.1 Time And Date Command

The *date* command causes the system to print the current date accurate to seconds, in a form like:

```
Jan 12 1986 10:46:27
```

Before looking at the code for the date command itself, we need to examine a general-purpose utility routine it uses to format the date, *ascdate*. The code can be found in file *ascdate.c*.

```
/* ascdate.c - ascdate */

#include <conf.h>
#include <kernel.h>
#include <date.h>

/*------------------------------------------------------------------------
 *  ascdate  -  print a given date in ascii including hours:mins:secs
 *------------------------------------------------------------------------
 */
ascdate(time, str)
long    time;
char    *str;
{
        long    tmp;
        int     year, month, day, hour, minute, second;
        long    days;

        /* set year (1970-1999) */
        for (year=1970 ; TRUE ; year++) {
                days = isleap(year) ? 366 : 365;
                tmp = days * SECPERDY;
                if (tmp > time)
                        break;
                time -= tmp;
        }
        /* set month (0-11) */
        for (month=0 ; month<12 ; month++) {
                tmp = Dat.dt_msize[month] * SECPERDY;
                if (tmp > time)
                        break;
                time -= tmp;
        }
        /* set day of month (1-31) */
        day = (int)( time/SECPERDY ) + 1;
        time %= SECPERDY;
        /* set hour (0-23) */
        hour = (int) ( time/SECPERHR );
        time %= SECPERHR;
        /* set minute (0-59) */
        minute = time / SECPERMN;
        time %= SECPERMN;
        /* set second (0-59) */
        second = (int) time;
```

```
        sprintf(str, "%3s %2d %4d %2d:%02d:%02d", Dat.dt_mnam[month],
            day, year, hour, minute, second);
        return(OK);
}


struct  datinfo Dat = {31, 28, 31, 30, 31, 30, 31, 31, 30, 31, 30, 31,
                "Jan", "Feb", "Mar", "Apr", "May", "Jun",
                "Jul", "Aug", "Sep", "Oct", "Nov", "Dec"};
```

Ascdate takes as an argument a long integer that contains the time in seconds since January 1, 1970, and forms, in its second argument, a readable version of the date. The computation performed by *ascdate* is straightforward. It iteratively counts years, subtracting from the time the number of seconds in each year, stopping when less than a year remains. It then iterates through the months, subtracting from the time the number of seconds in each month. *Ascdate* then computes the day of the month by dividing the remaining time by the number of seconds per day. Finally, it computes the remaining hours, minutes, and seconds. When all information has been computed, *ascdate* calls procedure *sprintf* to write the date into a string in the proper format.

Before implementing any command, the designer must decide on the arguments. For the *date* command, we have chosen only one, optional argument ($-s$). When the argument is present, *date* causes the system to reset the local time and date by contacting a time server using the network. Whether it resets the system clock or leaves it alone, *date* prints the date and time.

Ascdate makes building a *date* command trivial. The command procedure *x_date*, shown below in file *x_date.c* provides the necessary implementation.

```
/* x_date.c - x_date */

#include <conf.h>
#include <kernel.h>
#include <sleep.h>
#include <date.h>

/*------------------------------------------------------------------------
 * x_date  -  (command date) print the date and time
 *------------------------------------------------------------------------
 */
COMMAND x_date(stdin, stdout, stderr, nargs, args)
int     stdin, stdout, stderr, nargs;
char    *args[];
{
        long    now;
        char    str[80];

        if (nargs == 2)
                clktime = 0L;
        gettime(&now);
        ascdate(now, str);
        strcat(str, "\n");
        write(stdout, str, strlen(str));
        return(OK);
}
```

Several features of *x_date* are worth noting. Primarily, it provides an example
of how to declare command arguments, and shows how they are used. Each command has exactly five arguments that correspond to the standard input device, the
standard output device, the standard error device, the number of string arguments,
and the address of an array of string argument pointers. Remember that the string
arguments include the command name itself as *args*[0]. The count of arguments in
nargs specifies the total number of string arguments, including the command name.
Thus, *nargs* is *1* if the user typed a command name with no additional arguments,
2 if the user typed a command name followed by one additional argument.

The actions taken by *x_date* depend on the string arguments passed to it from
the command line, but a shortcut is taken when processing string arguments. The
definition of *date* specifies that it only accepts one optional argument, −*s*, which
means that the date should be reset using a server on the network. In this implementation, *x_date* does not examine the contents of the string argument at all. It
uses the argument count in *nargs* to decide whether to reset the date. If the user
supplies *any* single string argument following the command name, *x_date* resets the
date.

Forcing the system to reset the date from the network server is easy because *gettime* does it automatically if it finds the time close to zero. In the code, *x_date* checks the number of arguments, and sets external system variable *clktime* to zero if it finds that the user has typed a second argument. In any case, it calls *gettime* to obtain the current time in binary, and *ascdate* to convert the time to a string with the month, day, year, hours, minutes, and seconds all spelled out in readable form. Finally, *x_date* concatenates an end-of-line character onto the formatted date.

Note that *x_date* first formats its output, uses *strlen* to count the length of the formatted string, and then calls *write* to write the string on its standard output. Although *x_date* could be written easier if it used *fprintf*, the use of *write* is important. To understand why, think of redirecting output to the remote file system. *Fprintf* calls *putc* for each character it produces. Because the remote file system driver sends each character over the network to the remote server, the overhead is high. Using *write* instead of *putc* reduces the overhead by sending only one request to the remote server (the entire date string fits into one request packet).

Should command procedures understand the details of the underlying system? The goal is to hide low-level details, allowing the programmer to choose primitives like *fprintf* or *write* without understanding the underlying implementation. As a simple experiment shows (the exercises suggest performing such an experiment), the penalty for sending individual characters to a remote file is high enough to warrant optimizing the command procedures. One alternative, also suggested in the exercises, uses local buffering to avoid high overhead.

18.5.2 Help Command

The *help* command provides information for a user who is confused or unsure about what to do. The version we will examine is simplistic — it merely lists the possible commands that are available without any explanation or hints on how to use them. It has been included here merely to illustrate how multiple command names can be mapped into the same procedure (the exercises suggest improvements to the help command itself).

Code for the simplistic version of help is shown in file *x_help.c*.

```
/* x_help.c - x_help */

#include <conf.h>
#include <kernel.h>
#include <shell.h>
#include <cmd.h>

#define COLUMNS 4                          /* number of columns to print  */

/*------------------------------------------------------------------------
 *  x_help  -  (command help) print possible command names for user
 *------------------------------------------------------------------------
 */
COMMAND x_help(stdin, stdout, stderr, nargs, args)
int     stdin, stdout, stderr, nargs;
char    *args[];
{
        int     inc;                    /* command names per column    */
        int     i;                      /* move through printed rows    */
        int     j;                      /* move across printed columns  */


        if ( (inc=(Shl.shncmds+COLUMNS-1)/COLUMNS) <= 0)
                inc = 1;
        fprintf(stdout, "Commands are:\n");
        for(i=0 ; i<inc && i<Shl.shncmds ; i++) {
                fprintf(stdout, "  ");
                for (j=i ; j<Shl.shncmds ; j+=inc)
                        fprintf(stdout, "%-16s", cmds[j].cmdnam);
                fprintf(stdout, "\n");
        }
        return(OK);
}
```

X_help formats the command names and prints them in a two-dimensional array, with names arranged alphabetically in columns. Names are arranged so the alphabetical progression runs from top to bottom of the left-most column, then from top to bottom of the next column, and so on. However, because output must be generated by row, *x_help* uses two index variables, *i* and *j*, to compute the rows. Before beginning output, *x_help* computes the number of rows needed. It then enters the outermost *for* loop, using variable *i* as the row index. For each row, the inner loop runs across the row, jumping through the array of command names one "column" at a time until it runs off the end of the command list.

X_help illustrates that a single procedure can implement more than one command. Recall from the command declarations in Chapter 17 that the array *cmds* maps command names onto procedures. A look at the entries for commands named *help* and *?* reveals that both commands invoke procedure *x_help*.

18.5.3 Uptime And Ruptime Commands

The two commands *uptime* and *ruptime* provide information about the local computer system and other computers on the network. *Uptime* tells how long the local system has been running; *ruptime* tells about all systems. You may be surprised to learn that both commands invoke the same underlying command procedure, *x_uptime*.

We have already seen two commands that invoke the same command procedure to give the same results. That is, we have seen two names that were aliases for the same command. The names *uptime* and *ruptime* are not aliases, however, because the output from the two commands differs.

How can a single procedure decide how it was invoked? Recall that the shell removed only I/O redirection and background tokens from the command line, and passed *all* other tokens to the command procedure as string arguments. In particular, the first string argument contains the command name. Thus, the command procedure only needs examine *args*[0] to find out what the user typed to invoke it. As shown in file *x_uptime.c*, procedure *x_uptime* uses this method to determine how it was invoked.

```
/* x_uptime.c - x_uptime */

#include <conf.h>
#include <kernel.h>
#include <network.h>
#include <rwho.h>


/*------------------------------------------------------------------------
 *  x_uptime  -  (command uptime or ruptime) print remote machine status
 *------------------------------------------------------------------------
 */
COMMAND x_uptime(stdin, stdout, stderr, nargs, args)
int     stdin, stdout, stderr, nargs;
char    *args[];
{
        int     i, j;
        struct  rwent   *rwptr;
        long    tottim;
        int     hours, days, mins;
        Bool    up;
        Bool    found, all;
        long    now;
        char    mach[32];
        char    str[80];

        switch (nargs) {

        case 1:
                if (strcmp(args[0],"ruptime") == 0) {
                        all = TRUE;
                        break;
                }
                getname(mach); /* called as "uptime" */
                args[1] = mach;
                /* fall through */
        case 2:
                all = FALSE;
                break;
        default:
                fprintf(stderr, "use: %s [host]\n", args[0]);
                return(SYSERR);
        }
        gettime(&now);
        found = FALSE;
        for (i=0 ; i<Rwho.rwnent ; i++) {
```

```
            rwptr = &Rwho.rwcache[i];
            if (!all && strcmp(rwptr->rwmach,args[1])!=0)
                    continue;
            found = TRUE;
            sprintf(str,"%-14s", rwptr->rwmach);
            tottim = now - rwptr->rwlast;
            if (up = (tottim < RWCDOWN))
                    tottim = rwptr->rwslast - rwptr->rwboot + 59;
            days = tottim / (24L * 60L * 60L);
             tottim %= (24L * 60L * 60L);
            hours = tottim / (60L * 60L);
             tottim %= (60L * 60L);
            mins = tottim / 60L;
            sprintf(&str[strlen(str)], "%s", up?"up  " : "down");
            if (days > 0)
                    sprintf(&str[strlen(str)], " %2d +", days);
            else
                    strcat(str, "      ");
            sprintf(&str[strlen(str)], " %2d:%02d", hours, mins);
            if (!up) {
                    strcat(str, "\n");
                    write(stdout, str, strlen(str));
                    continue;
            }
            sprintf(&str[strlen(str)],
                    "  %2d users,    load ", (int)rwptr->rwusers);
            for (j=0 ; j<RWNLOAD ; j++) {
                    if (j >0)
                            strcat(str, ", ");
                    sprintf(&str[strlen(str)], "%2d.%02d",
                            rwptr->rwload[j] / 100,
                            rwptr->rwload[j] % 100);
            }
            strcat(str, "\n");
            write(stdout, str, strlen(str));
    }
    if (!found && !all)
            fprintf(stderr, "%s ???\n", args[1]);
    return(OK);
}
```

As the code shows, either *uptime* or *ruptime* can be given a specific system's name as an argument to restrict output to just that system. If no argument is present, *uptime* prints information about the local system; *ruptime* prints information about all known systems.

For each system that is to be printed, procedure *x_uptime* computes the time the system has been active by subtracting the current time from the time the system reports as its boot time (being careful to make all times relative to the local clock). Next, *x_uptime* converts the system uptime into days, hours, minutes, and seconds by successively dividing by the number of seconds in a day, hour, and minute. Finally, *x_uptime* formats the result in readable form, and writes it on the standard output device before going on to the next entry.

18.6 System Information Commands

Although the *uptime* command prints information about the local computer system, it also provides information about other systems. In this section we consider commands that provide a window into an executing operating system. Their primary use is system inspection. While casual users may find them interesting, they are essential to systems programmers who want to examine and control internal data structures in a running system. Indeed, such commands often help system designers and implementors understand the behavior of their systems in ways that would be impossible otherwise.

18.6.1 Bpool Command

Command *bpool* is a good example of a command that the system designer finds more useful than an average programmer. It allows a user to see, at any time, how many buffer pools have been allocated, and how many free buffers each contains. The designer might, for example, watch how many buffers the network subsystem used during a file transfer.

When invoked, command *bpool* writes on its standard output device, producing one line of output for each allocated buffer pool. The output includes the buffer pool id, buffer size, the id of the pool's semaphore, and a count of buffers available (or processes waiting for buffers). Its implementation, shown in file *x_bpool.c*, is straightforward:

```
/* x_bpool.c - x_bpool */

#include <conf.h>
#include <kernel.h>
#include <mark.h>
#include <bufpool.h>


/*------------------------------------------------------------------------
 * x_bpool - (command bpool) format and print buffer pool information
 *------------------------------------------------------------------------
 */
```

```
COMMAND x_bpool(stdin, stdout, stderr, nargs, args)
int     stdin, stdout, stderr, nargs;
char    *args[];
{
        struct  bpool   *bpptr;
        char    str[80];
        int     i;

        for (i=0 ; i<nbpools ; i++) {
                bpptr = &bptab[i];
                sprintf(str,
                    "pool=%2d. bsize=%4d, sem=%2d, count=%d\n",
                        i, bpptr->bpsize, bpptr->bpsem,
                        scount(bpptr->bpsem));
                write(stdout, str, strlen(str));
        }
        return(OK);
}
```

As the code shows, writing information about an internal system table is easy in Xinu. Procedure *x_bpool* merely indexes through each buffer pool, formatting and writing information about that entry on a single line.

18.6.2 Devs Command

The *devs* command also prints information about an internal system table, the device switch table. Procedure *x_devs* implements the command by formatting and writing a single line for each device. Because a device switch table entry contains too much information to fit on a single line, a few key fields have been selected. The addresses of device driver routines that implement upper and lower half functions do not change, so they have been omitted. File *x_devs.c*, shown below, contains the code.

```
/* x_devs.c - x_devs */

#include <conf.h>
#include <kernel.h>

LOCAL    char hd1[] =
         "Num Device    minor   CSR   i-vect. o-vect. cntrl blk\n";
LOCAL    char hd2[] =
         "--- --------   -----  ------- ------- ------- ---------\n";


/*-----------------------------------------------------------------------
 * x_devs - (command devs) print main fields of device switch table
 *-----------------------------------------------------------------------
 */
COMMAND x_devs(stdin, stdout, stderr, nargs, args)
int      stdin, stdout, stderr, nargs;
char     *args[];
{
        struct devsw    *devptr;
        char    str[60];
        int     i;

        write (stdout, hd1, strlen(hd1) );
        write (stdout, hd2, strlen(hd2) );
        for (i=0 ; i<NDEVS ; i++) {
                devptr = &devtab[i];
                sprintf(str, "%2d. %-9s %3d   %07o %07o %07o  %07o\n",
                        i, devptr->dvname, devptr->dvminor,
                        devptr->dvcsr, devptr->dvivec, devptr->dvovec,
                        devptr->dvioblk);
                write(stdout, str, strlen(str));
        }
}
```

18.6.3 Dg Command

As we have seen, the *devs* command prints some information for each device. However, knowing more about the device types permits us to print more information. For example, the *dg* command prints information about all the open datagram pseudo-devices. Procedure *x_dg*, found in file *x_dg.c*, shows the implementation.

```
/* x_dg.c - x_dg */

#include <conf.h>
#include <kernel.h>
#include <network.h>

/*------------------------------------------------------------------------
 *  x_dg  -  (command dg) print info for currently open datagram devices
 *------------------------------------------------------------------------
 */
COMMAND x_dg(stdin, stdout, stderr, nargs, args)
int     stdin, stdout, stderr, nargs;
char    *args[];
{
        struct  dgblk   *dgptr;
        char    str[80];
        int     i;

        for (i=0 ; i<Ndg ; i++) {
                dgptr = &dgtab[i];
                if (dgptr->dg_state == DG_FREE)
                        continue;
                sprintf(str, "Dev=%2d: lport=%4d, fport=%4d, ",
                        dgptr->dg_dnum, dgptr->dg_lport, dgptr->dg_fport);

                sprintf(&str[strlen(str)],
                        "mode=%03o, xport=%2d addr=%d.%d.%d.%d\n",
                                dgptr->dg_mode, dgptr->dg_xport,
                                dgptr->dg_faddr[0] &0377,
                                dgptr->dg_faddr[1] &0377,
                                dgptr->dg_faddr[2] &0377,
                                dgptr->dg_faddr[3] &0377);
                write(stdout, str, strlen(str));
        }
        return(OK);
}
```

18.6.4 Mem Command

Knowing about free and available memory is especially important in Xinu because processes that fail to free memory before they exit can cause the system to run out of memory. The *mem* command does not prevent errors, but it may help the identify them by making it easy to monitor the free list at run time. Procedure *x_mem*, contained in file *x_mem.c*, implements the *mem* command.

```
/* x_mem.c - x_mem */

#include <conf.h>
#include <kernel.h>
#include <proc.h>
#include <mem.h>

/*------------------------------------------------------------------------
 *  x_mem  -  (command mem) print memory use and free list information
 *------------------------------------------------------------------------
 */
COMMAND x_mem(stdin, stdout, stderr, nargs, args)
int     stdin, stdout, stderr, nargs;
char    *args[];
{
        int     i;
        struct  mblock  *mptr;
        char    str[80];
        unsigned free;
        unsigned avail;
        unsigned stkmem;

        /* calculate current size of free memory and stack memory */

        for( free=0,mptr=memlist.mnext ; mptr!=(struct mblock *)NULL ;
            mptr=mptr->mnext)
                free += mptr->mlen;
        for (stkmem=0,i=0 ; i<NPROC ; i++) {
                if (proctab[i].pstate != PRFREE)
                        stkmem += (unsigned)proctab[i].pstklen;
        }
        sprintf(str,
                "Memory: %u bytes real memory, %u text, %u data, %u bss\n",
                1 + (unsigned)maxaddr, (unsigned) &etext,
                (unsigned) &edata - (unsigned) &etext,
                (unsigned) &end - (unsigned) &edata);
        write(stdout, str, strlen(str));
        avail = (unsigned)maxaddr - (unsigned) &end + 1;
        sprintf(str," initially: %5u avail\n", avail);
        write(stdout, str, strlen(str));
        sprintf(str," presently: %5u avail, %5u stack, %5u heap\n",
                free, stkmem, avail - stkmem - free);
        write(stdout, str, strlen(str));
        sprintf(str," free list:\n");
```

```
        write(stdout, str, strlen(str));
        for( mptr=memlist.mnext ; mptr!=(struct mblock *)NULL ;
            mptr=mptr->mnext) {
                sprintf(str,"    block at %6o, length %5u (0%o)\n",
                        mptr, mptr->mlen, mptr->mlen);
                write(stdout, str, strlen(str));
        }
        return(OK);
}
```

As the code shows, *x_mem* does three things. First, it computes the current allocation by examining the amount of memory initially devoted to program text and data, the amount currently allocated for process stacks, and the amount on the free list. Second, it writes on the standard output device a description of memory allocation at system boot as well as a description of the current allocations. Third, it traces the free list, writing a single line of output for each free block. Note that memory addresses are cast as *unsigned* to avoid having the compiler treat them as signed integer values.

18.6.5 Netstat Command

The command *netstat* provides information about the internal queues that hold incoming internet datagrams. In a heading, it gives the network buffer pool identifier and shows the mutual exclusion semaphore id and count. Following the heading, *netstat* displays information about datagram queues, one queue per line. A line identifies the datagram port id, the corresponding Xinu port on which datagrams are queued, and the current queue size. The code for *x_net* is found in file *x_net.c* (abbreviated versions of command names are used to avoid procedure names longer than eight characters).

```
/* x_net.c - x_net */

#include <conf.h>
#include <kernel.h>
#include <network.h>


/*------------------------------------------------------------------------
 *  x_net  -  (command netstat) print network status information
 *------------------------------------------------------------------------
 */
COMMAND x_net(stdin, stdout, stderr, nargs, args)
int     stdin, stdout, stderr, nargs;
char    *args[];
{
        struct  netq    *nqptr;
        char    str[80];
        int     i;

        sprintf(str,
                "bpool=%d, mutex/cnt=%d/%d, nxt prt=%d, addr %svalid\n",
                Net.netpool, Net.nmutex, scount(Net.nmutex), Net.nxtprt,
                Net.mavalid ? "" : "in");
        write(stdout, str, strlen(str));
        sprintf(str,"Packets: recvd=%d, tossed=%d (%d for overrun)\n",
                Net.npacket, Net.ndrop, Net.nover);
        write(stdout, str, strlen(str));
        for (i=0; i<NETQS; i++) {
                nqptr = &Net.netqs[i];
                if ( !nqptr->valid)
                        continue;
                sprintf(str,
                        "%2d. uport=%4d, pid=%3d, xprt=%2d, size=%2d\n",
                        i, nqptr->uport, nqptr->pid, nqptr->xport,
                        pcount(nqptr->xport) );
                write(stdout, str, strlen(str));
        }
        return(OK);
}
```

Netstat is particularly helpful in showing whether datagrams are being processed. Consider a scenario in which a process opens a local datagram port, and then fails to read from the port. *Netstat* will show that the size of the queue is nonzero. It also shows the count of datagrams that had to be discarded because the queues were filled when the datagram arrived.

18.6.6 Ps Command

Command *ps* is among the most useful of all system information commands because it provides a way for users and systems programmers to look at concurrent process execution.   Procedure *x_ps* implements the *ps* command by iterating through the process table and printing one line for each active process.

Of course, information about the currently executing process cannot be obtained from the process table.   To provide more accurate information about the current process, *x_ps* invokes an assembler language instruction that stores the current stack pointer in the process table entry for the currently executing process. It then formats and prints the current process entry just like any other.   The code can be found in file *x_ps.c.*

```
/* x_ps.c - x_ps */

#include <conf.h>
#include <kernel.h>
#include <proc.h>

LOCAL   char   hd1[] =
        "pid    name    state prio  stack range  stack length sem message\n";
LOCAL   char   hd2[] =
        "--- -------- ----- ---- ------------- ------------ --- -------\n";
LOCAL   char   *pstnams[] = {"curr ","free ","ready","recv ",
                             "sleep","susp ","wait ","rtim "};
LOCAL   int    psavsp;


/*------------------------------------------------------------------------
 * x_ps  -  (command ps) format and print process table information
 *------------------------------------------------------------------------
 */
COMMAND x_ps(stdin, stdout, stderr, nargs, args)
int     stdin, stdout, stderr, nargs;
char    *args[];
{
        int    i;
        char   str[80];
        struct pentry *pptr;
        unsigned currstk;

        asm("mov sp,_psavsp");  /* capture current stack pointer */
        proctab[currpid].pregs[SP] = psavsp;
        write(stdout, hd1, strlen(hd1));
        write(stdout, hd2, strlen(hd2));
        for (i=0 ; i<NPROC ; i++) {
                if ((pptr = &proctab[i])->pstate == PRFREE)
                        continue;
                sprintf(str, "%3d %8s %s ", i, pptr->pname,
                        pstnams[pptr->pstate-1]);
                write(stdout, str, strlen(str));
                sprintf(str, "%4d %6o-%6o ", pptr->pprio,  pptr->plimit,
                        (unsigned)pptr->pbase + 1);
                write(stdout, str, strlen(str));
                currstk = pptr->pregs[SP];
                if (currstk < pptr->plimit || currstk > pptr->pbase)
                        sprintf(str, " OVERFLOWED)");
                else
                        sprintf(str, "%4d /%4d    ", pptr->pbase - currstk,
```

```
                              pptr->pbase - pptr->plimit + sizeof(int));
        write(stdout, str, strlen(str));
        if (pptr->pstate == PRWAIT)
                sprintf(str, "%2d", pptr->psem);
        else
                sprintf(str, "- ");
        write(stdout, str, strlen(str));
        if (pptr->phasmsg)
                sprintf(str, "0%6o\n", pptr->pmsg);
        else
                sprintf(str, "   -\n");
        write(stdout, str, strlen(str));
    }
}
```

18.6.7 Rf Command

Another useful command, *rf*, allows the user to find out about remote files. It prints one line for each remote file that is open, giving the file name and current file position. The information is obtained from the remote file device control block.

Procedure *x_rf* implements command *rf* using the code shown in file *x_rf.c*.

```
/* x_rf.c - x_rf */

#include <conf.h>
#include <kernel.h>
#include <fserver.h>
#include <rfile.h>


/*------------------------------------------------------------------------
 * x_rf  -  (command rf) format and print remote file status
 *------------------------------------------------------------------------
 */
COMMAND x_rf(stdin, stdout, stderr, nargs, args)
int     stdin, stdout, stderr, nargs;
char    *args[];
{
        struct  rfblk   *rfptr;
        char    str[80];
        int     i;

        sprintf(str, "Remote files: server on dev=%d, server mutex=%d\n",
                        Rf.device, Rf.rmutex);
        write(stdout, str, strlen(str));
        for (i=0 ; i<Nrf; i++) {
                if ((rfptr = &Rf.rftab[i])->rf_state == RFREE)
                        continue;
                sprintf(str,
                        " %2d. name=%-20s, pos=%6D, mode=%03o, sem=%d\n",
                                rfptr->rf_dnum, rfptr->rf_name,
                                rfptr->rf_pos,  rfptr->rf_mode,
                                rfptr->rf_mutex);
                write(stdout, str, strlen(str));
        }
        return(OK);
}
```

18.6.8 Routes Command

The command *routes* prints information from the system's routing cache, using procedure *x_routes*. The code merely indexes through the ARP cache and prints current routes. It can be found in file *x_routes.c*.

```
/* x_routes.c - x_routes */

#include <conf.h>
#include <kernel.h>
#include <proc.h>
#include <network.h>


LOCAL    char    st[] = "F?GD";

/*------------------------------------------------------------------------
 *  x_routes  -  (command routes) format and print routing cache entries
 *------------------------------------------------------------------------
 */
COMMAND x_routes(stdin, stdout, stderr, nargs, args)
int     stdin, stdout, stderr, nargs;
char    *args[];
{
        int     arindex;
        char    str[80];
        struct  arpent  *atabptr;

        if (nargs > 1) {
                Arp.atabsiz = Arp.atabnxt = 0;
                return(OK);
        }
        sprintf(str, "Routing cache: size=%d, next=%d\n",
                Arp.atabsiz, Arp.atabnxt);
        write(stdout, str, strlen(str));
        for (arindex=0; arindex<Arp.atabsiz; arindex++) {
                atabptr = &Arp.arptab[arindex];
                if (atabptr->arp_state == AR_FREE)
                        continue;
                sprintf(str, " %2d. Route=%c, Dev=%2d",
                        arindex,st[atabptr->arp_state],atabptr->arp_dev);
                sprintf(&str[strlen(str)],
                        " IPaddr=%03d.%03d.%03d.%03d, ",
                                atabptr->arp_Iad[0] & 0377,
                                atabptr->arp_Iad[1] & 0377,
                                atabptr->arp_Iad[2] & 0377,
                                atabptr->arp_Iad[3] & 0377);
                sprintf(&str[strlen(str)],
                        "Ether addr=%02x%02x.%02x%02x.%02x%02x\n",
                                atabptr->arp_Ead[0]&0377,
                                atabptr->arp_Ead[1]&0377,
                                atabptr->arp_Ead[2]&0377,
```

```
                              atabptr->arp_Ead[3]&0377,
                              atabptr->arp_Ead[4]&0377,
                              atabptr->arp_Ead[5]&0377 );
                write(stdout, str, strlen(str));
        }
        return(OK);
}
```

18.6.9 Who Command

On UNIX, the *who* command prints information about each user logged into
the system. The shell of Chapter 17 provides for only one user, recording the user
id in field *shuser* of global variable *Shl*. The *who* command shown here merely
prints the system name and name of the user who is logged in. It is most useful to
identify a user who forgets to log out.

Procedure *x_who*, shown in file x_who.c, implements the *who* command.

```
/* x_who.c - x_who */

#include <conf.h>
#include <kernel.h>
#include <date.h>
#include <shell.h>

/*------------------------------------------------------------------------
 *  x_who  -  (command who) print name user is logged in under
 *------------------------------------------------------------------------
 */
COMMAND x_who(stdin, stdout, stderr)
int     stdin, stdout, stderr;
{
        char    machine[32];
        char    str[80];

        if (marked(Shl.shmark) && Shl.shused) {
                getname(machine);
                sprintf(str, "%10s!%-10s Console : ", machine, Shl.shuser);
                write(stdout, str, strlen(str));
                ascdate(ut2ltim(Shl.shlogon), str);
                strcat(str, "\n");
                write(stdout, str, strlen(str));
        }
        return(OK);
}
```

18.7 Computational Commands

This section describes a set of commands that perform computation. The sample set is not intended to provide a complete computing environment; it serves only to show how useful commands can be built. The exercises suggest extending and enhancing the sample set.

18.7.1 Cat Command

Command *cat* concatenates a set of named files and writes them to the standard output device. The command line arguments specify the files to be concatenated, but if no arguments are specified, *cat* reads from the standard input device. So, despite its name and intended purpose, *cat* is a generally useful command. For example, typing

```
cat  file1 > file2
```

copies *file1* to *file2*. So does

```
cat < file1 > file2
```

If the user does not redirect standard output, it remains attached to the terminal, so the command

```
cat file
```

will display *file* on the terminal screen.

Procedure *x_cat* implements the *cat* command. It can be found in file *x_cat.c*.

```
/* x_cat.c - x_cat */

#include <conf.h>
#include <kernel.h>

/*-------------------------------------------------------------------------
 *  x_cat  -  (command cat) concatenate files and write on stdout
 *-------------------------------------------------------------------------
 */
COMMAND x_cat(stdin, stdout, stderr, nargs, args)
int     stdin, stdout, stderr, nargs;
char    *args[];
{
        int     device;
        char    *buf;
        int     ret;
        int     len;
        int     i;

        if ( (buf = (char *)getmem(512)) == SYSERR) {
                fprintf(stderr, "no memory\n");
                return(SYSERR);
        }
        ret = OK;
        if (nargs == 1) {
                while ( (len=read(stdin, buf, 512)) > 0)
                        write(stdout, buf, len);
        }
        for (i=1 ; i<nargs ; i++) {
                if ( (device = open(NAMESPACE,args[i],"ro")) == SYSERR) {
                        fprintf(stderr, "Cannot open %s\n", args[i]);
                        ret = SYSERR;
                        break;
                }
                while ( (len=read(device, buf, 512)) > 0)
                        write (stdout, buf, len);
                close(device);
        }
        freemem(buf, 512);
        return(ret);
}
```

As the code shows, *x_cat* allocates a buffer and then enters a loop. At each iteration of the loop, *cat* moves to the next command-line argument, opens a file using the argument as the file name, and copies the file to standard output by reading and writing one buffer full at a time. Once it reaches the end of an input file, *cat* closes the input and continues with the next command-line argument.

18.7.2 Close Command

Sometimes, it is useful to be able to invoke system operations from the shell. For example, if a process is killed, it might not close all open file descriptors. The *close* command handles such circumstances by allowing the user to close a specified file descriptor. It takes as an argument the number of a device to be closed, and calls the system's *close* operation for that device.

Close provides a good example of the naming conflict that occurs between system calls and command procedures. Remember that we elected to name command procedure *x_something* to avoid such conflicts. Thus, the procedure that implements the *close* command is named *x_close*. It is shown in file *x_close.c*.

```
/* x_close.c - x_close */

#include <conf.h>
#include <kernel.h>


/*------------------------------------------------------------------------
 * x_close  -  (command close) close a device given its id
 *------------------------------------------------------------------------
 */
COMMAND x_close(stdin, stdout, stderr, nargs, args)
int     stdin, stdout, stderr, nargs;
char    *args[];
{
        if (nargs != 2) {
                fprintf(stderr, "use: close device-number\n");
                return(SYSERR);
        }
        return(close(atoi(args[1])));
}
```

Arguments passed to *x_close* consist of character strings, not integers. *X_close* calls the library routine *atoi* to convert its string argument to an integer so it can be passed to the *close* system call.

18.7.3 Cp Command

We have seen that the *cat* command is capable of copying data from one file to another (copying one file is a special case of concatenating several files). However, because copying data from one file to another is an activity that users do frequently, we have invented a separate file copying command, *cp*. *Cp* takes two arguments that give the names of files, and copies data from the first named file to the second, creating the second file if it does not exist.

Procedure *x_cp* implements command *cp*, as shown in file *x_cp.c*.

```
/* x_cp.c - x_cp */

#include <conf.h>
#include <kernel.h>

LOCAL   char    errfmt[] = "Cannot open %s\n";

/*------------------------------------------------------------------------
 * x_cp  -  (copy command) copy one file to another
 *------------------------------------------------------------------------
 */
COMMAND x_cp(stdin, stdout, stderr, nargs, args)
int     stdin, stdout, stderr, nargs;
char    *args[];
{
        char    *buf;
        int     from, to;
        int     ret;
        int     len;

        if (nargs != 3) {
                fprintf(stderr, "usage: cp file1 file2\n");
                return(SYSERR);
        }
        if ( (from=open(NAMESPACE, args[1], "ro")) == SYSERR) {
                fprintf(stderr, errfmt, args[1]);
                return(SYSERR);
        }
        if ( (to=open(NAMESPACE, args[2], "w")) == SYSERR) {
                close(from);
                fprintf(stderr, errfmt, args[2]);
                return(SYSERR);
        }
        if ( ((int) (buf = (char *)getmem(512)) ) == SYSERR) {
```

```
                    fprintf(stderr, "no memory\n");
                    ret = SYSERR;
        } else {
                    while ( (len = read(from, buf, 512)) > 0 )
                            write(to, buf, len);
                    freemem(buf, 512);
                    ret = OK;
        }
        close(from);
        close(to);
        return(ret);
}
```

18.7.4 Create Command

The *create* command allows a user to explicitly create a process, by invoking the *create* system call. Command arguments consist of the procedure at which the process should start executing, the stack size, process priority, and, optionally, a process name. For example, the user might type:

```
create udpecho 400 20
```

to create a process executing procedure *udpecho* with stack size 400, and priority 20. To name the process something other than *udpecho*, an additional argument is supplied.

Create is among the most interesting (and convoluted) of the sample commands, but it clearly demonstrates the power of the mechanisms we have built. Consider its implementation. The *create* system call provides exactly the service needed to implement the *create* command. However, the arguments are not in the correct form. We can sum up the differences:

> *Arguments passed to command procedures are character strings; arguments passed to system calls usually consist of objects like integers, and addresses.*

We have already seen that character strings that represent integers can be converted to internal binary integers with the library routine *atoi*, so that is not a problem. The chief difficulty centers on the argument that specifies the procedure at which execution begins. The *create* system call requires the *address* of the procedure, while the command is passed a procedure *name*. How can the name be bound to the address?

The problem of mapping object names to locations within the kernel is not unique to Xinu. It occurs in most compiled systems. When the operating system begins to execute, it must be loaded in memory. But only the text and data are

loaded — the symbol table that was prepared by the compiler and loader is not
loaded. Thus, a running program cannot map arbitrary procedure names into locations.

The *create* command takes an ingenious approach to symbol mapping. It assumes that it can locate and read the a.out file from which it was booted! *Create*
does not even know whether the file is local or remote. All it assumes is that the
namespace maps the name *a.out* to the boot file, and that the boot file is in PDP11
format. It opens a.out, seeks to the symbol table portion, and then searches for the
name that the user supplies. When it finds the name in the symbol table, the
create command retrieves the corresponding address that it passes to the *create* system call. Looking at the code in procedure *x_creat* will clarify the sequence of
events. It is contained in file *x_create.c*.

```
/* x_create.c - x_creat */

#include <conf.h>
#include <kernel.h>
#include <a.out.h>

LOCAL   char    symfile[] = "a.out";    /* name of object file to search*/

/*------------------------------------------------------------------------
 * x_creat  -  (command create) create a process given a starting address
 *------------------------------------------------------------------------
 */
COMMAND x_creat(stdin, stdout, stderr, nargs, args)
int     stdin, stdout, stderr, nargs;
char    *args[];
{
        int     ssize, prio;
        struct  exec    *aoutptr;
        int     dev, len;
        int     pid;
        char    *loc;
        char    *buf;
        Bool    found;
        long    offset;
        struct  nlist   *symptr;
        struct  nlist   *last;
        char    tmp[30];


        if (nargs <4 || nargs > 5) {
            fprintf(stderr,
```

```
                    "usage: create procedure stack-size prio [name]\n");
            return(SYSERR);
    }
    ssize = atoi(args[2]);
    prio = atoi(args[3]);
    if ( (dev=open(NAMESPACE, symfile, "ro")) == SYSERR) {
            fprintf(stderr, "Cannot open %s\n", symfile);
            return(SYSERR);
    }
    if ( ((int) (buf=(char *)getmem(512)) ) == SYSERR) {
            fprintf(stderr, "no memory\n");
            return(SYSERR);
    }
    strcpy(tmp, "_");
    strcat(tmp, args[1]);
    printf("Looking up %s\n", tmp);
    read(dev, buf, 16);
    aoutptr = (struct exec *)buf;
    offset = (long) (aoutptr->a_text + aoutptr->a_data
                            + (unsigned) sizeof(struct exec));
    seek(dev, offset);
    for (found=FALSE ; !found ;) {
            len = read(dev, buf, 42*sizeof(struct nlist));
            if (len <= 0 ) {
                    fprintf(stderr, "not found\n");
                    close(dev);
                    freemem(buf, 512);
                    return(SYSERR);
            }
            last = (struct nlist *)&buf[len];
            for (symptr=(struct nlist *)buf ; symptr<last ;symptr++) {
                    if (symptr->n_type == (N_TEXT|N_EXT) &&
                            strncmp(symptr->n_name,tmp,8)==0) {
                            loc = (char *)symptr->n_value;
                            found = TRUE;
                            break;
                    }
            }
    }
    close(dev);
    freemem(buf, 512);
    pid = create(loc, ssize, prio, nargs==5?args[4]:tmp, 0);
    fprintf(stderr, "[%d]\n", pid );
    return(resume(pid));
}
```

As the code shows, *x_creat* prefixes an underscore to the name that the user supplies before looking it up. It does so because the C compiler prefixes an underscore to all external symbols during compilation. Thus, a symbol like *x* appears in the symbol table as *_x*.

The format of *a.out* files is needed to understand other details in *x_creat*. It can be found in file *a.out.h*, shown below:

```
/* a.out.h */

struct  exec {  /* a.out header */
        short           a_magic;        /* magic number                 */
        unsigned short  a_text;         /* size of text segment         */
        unsigned short  a_data;         /* size of initialized data     */
        unsigned short  a_bss;          /* size of uninitialized data   */
        unsigned short  a_syms;         /* size of symbol table         */
        unsigned short  a_entry;        /* entry point                  */
        unsigned short  a_unused;       /* not used                     */
        char            a_flag;         /* relocation info stripped     */
        char            a_v6;           /* UNIX V6 compatibility  mode  */
};

#define A_MAGIC1        0407            /* normal                       */
#define A_MAGIC2        0410            /* read-only text               */
#define A_MAGIC3        0411            /* separated I&D                */
#define A_MAGIC4        0405            /* overlay                      */

struct  nlist {                         /* symbol table entry           */
        char            n_name[8];      /* symbol name                  */
        short           n_type;         /* type flag                    */
        unsigned short  n_value;        /* value                        */
};

/* values for type flag */

#define N_UNDF          0               /* undefined                    */
#define N_ABS           01              /* absolute                     */
#define N_TEXT          02              /* text symbol                  */
#define N_DATA          03              /* data symbol                  */
#define N_BSS           04              /* bss symbol                   */
#define N_TYPE          037
#define N_REG           024             /* register name                */
#define N_FN            037             /* file name symbol             */
#define N_EXT           040             /* external bit, or'ed in       */
#define FORMAT          "%06o"          /* to print a value             */
```

As the declarations show, the first 16 bytes of the file contain a header that describes, among other things, the size of the text and data sections. *X_creat* uses *seek* to move past the text and data to the beginning of the symbol table. Once positioned at the beginning of the symbol table, *x_creat* reads one block of entries (42) at a time, and searches the block for the symbol in question.

Once the symbol address has been found, *x_creat* closes open files, releases the storage it allocated, and invokes the system call *create* to create the necessary process. Finally, it prints the process id so the user can identify the process if needed.

18.7.5 Echo Command

The *echo* command provides one small function that seems almost useless. It writes a copy of its arguments to the standard output device. Commands like *echo* are invaluable to programmers who build or modify shells because they help debug argument passing and I/O redirection.

Procedure *x_echo* implements the *echo* command. It can be found in file *x_echo.c*.

```
/* x_echo.c - x_echo */

#include <conf.h>
#include <kernel.h>

/*------------------------------------------------------------------------
 *  x_echo  -  (command echo) echo arguments separated by blanks
 *------------------------------------------------------------------------
 */
COMMAND x_echo(stdin, stdout, stderr, nargs, args)
int     stdin, stdout, stderr, nargs;
char    *args[];
{
        char    str[80];
        int     i;

        if (nargs == 1)
                str[0] = NULLCH;
        else {
                for (strcpy(str, args[1]),i=2 ; i<nargs ; i++) {
                        strcat(str, " ");
                        strcat(str, args[i]);
                }
        }
        strcat(str, "\n");
        write(stdout, str, strlen(str));
        return(OK);
}
```

18.7.6 Exit And Logout Commands

Procedure *x_exit.c* implements the *exit* or *logout* commands that allow a user to terminate an interactive session and leave the shell. *X_exit* must execute as a builtin, because the shell uses its return value to decide whether to exit or continue interpreting commands. The implementation, shown in file *x_exit.c*, is trivial. *X_exit* simply returns the value *SHEXIT* whenever called.

```
/* x_exit.c - x_exit */

#include <conf.h>
#include <kernel.h>
#include <shell.h>

/*------------------------------------------------------------------------
```

```
 *   x_exit  -  (builtin command exit) exit from the shell
 *------------------------------------------------------------------------
 */
BUILTIN x_exit(stdin, stdout, stderr, nargs, args)
int     stdin, stdout, stderr, nargs;
char    *args[];
{
        return(SHEXIT);
}
```

18.7.7 Kill Command

The *kill* command permits a user to terminate a process by specifying its numeric process id as an argument. *X_kill* converts the argument to integer form and then invokes the system call *kill*. The code can be found in file *x_kill.c*.

```
/* x_kill.c - x_kill */

#include <conf.h>
#include <kernel.h>
#include <shell.h>


/*------------------------------------------------------------------------
 *   x_kill  -  (command kill) terminate a process
 *------------------------------------------------------------------------
 */
BUILTIN x_kill(stdin, stdout, stderr, nargs, args)
int     stdin, stdout, stderr, nargs;
char    *args[];
{
        int     pid;

        if (nargs != 2) {
                fprintf(stderr, "use: kill process-id\n");
                return(SYSERR);
        }
        if ( (pid=atoi(args[1])) == getpid() )
                fprintf(stderr, "Shell killed\n");
        return( kill(pid) );
}
```

18.7.8 Mount Command

The *mount* command illustrates the flexibility that arguments offer. When invoked with no arguments, *mount* prints a formatted version of the current namespace prefix mapping table on its standard output device. When three arguments are supplied, *mount* takes them to be a new triple of prefix, device, and replacement, and adds them to the namespace mapping table. Thus, *mount* either displays or modifies the table, depending on its parameters.

Procedure *x_mount* implements the *mount* command, as shown in file *x_mount.c*.

```
/* x_mount.c - x_mount, mprint */


#include <conf.h>
#include <kernel.h>
#include <io.h>
#include <name.h>


#define PADTO   24


/*------------------------------------------------------------------------
 *  x_mount  -  (command mount) change or display namespace table
 *------------------------------------------------------------------------
 */
COMMAND x_mount(stdin, stdout, stderr, nargs, args)
int     stdin, stdout, stderr, nargs;
char    *args[];
{
        int     dev;

        if (nargs == 1)
                return(mprint(stdin, stdout, stderr));
        if (nargs != 4) {
                fprintf(stderr,"use: mount [prefix device new_prefix]\n");
                return(SYSERR);
        }
        for (dev=0 ; dev<NDEVS ; dev++)
                if (strcmp(args[2], devtab[dev].dvname) == 0)
                        break;
        if (dev >=  NDEVS)
                if (strcmp(args[2],"SYSERR") == 0)
                        dev = SYSERR;
                else {
                        fprintf(stderr, "Device %s not found\n", args[2]);
```

```
                              return(SYSERR);
                    }
          if (mount(args[1], dev, args[3]) == SYSERR) {
                    fprintf(stderr, "Mount failed\n");
                    return(SYSERR);
          }
          return(OK);
}



/*-------------------------------------------------------------------------------
 * mprint  -  print the current contents of the namespace prefix table
 *-------------------------------------------------------------------------------
 */
LOCAL   mprint(stdin, stdout, stderr)
int     stdin, stdout, stderr;
{
          struct nament  *nptr;
          int    i, len, dev;
          char   str[80];
          char   *p;

          for (i=0 ; i<Nam.nnames ; i++) {
                    nptr = & Nam.nametab[i];
                    sprintf(str, "\"%-s\"", nptr->npre);
                    for (len=strlen(str) ; len < PADTO ; len++)
                              str[len] = ' ';
                    write(stdout, str, PADTO);
                    dev = nptr->ndev;
                    p = isbaddev(dev) ? "SYSERR" : devtab[dev].dvname;
                    sprintf(str, " -> (%-9s) \"%s\"\n", p, nptr->nrepl);
                    write(stdout, str, strlen(str));
          }
          return(OK);
}
```

As the code shows, procedure *mprint* formats the name table and writes it to standard output. It has been declared local, to prevent access from other procedures.

Most of the work of adding a new entry to the table is carried out by the *mount* system call, which expects the device argument to be given as an integer. To translate the device name into a numeric id, *x_mount* searches the device table for a match. If no match is found, *x_mount* declares that an error has occurred, and returns immediately. Otherwise, it invokes the *mount* system call, and reports an error if it fails.

18.7.9 Mv Command

The *mv* command invokes the *rename* system call, which "moves" a file by changing its name. Procedure *x_mv* implements the *mv* command with the code shown in file *x_mv.c*.

```
/* x_mv.c - x_mv */

#include <conf.h>
#include <kernel.h>
#include <file.h>

/*------------------------------------------------------------------------
 *  x_mv  -  (command mv) move (rename) a file
 *------------------------------------------------------------------------
 */
COMMAND x_mv(stdin, stdout, stderr, nargs, args)
int     stdin, stdout, stderr, nargs;
char    *args[];
{
        if (nargs != 3) {
                fprintf(stderr, "usage: mv file tofile\n");
                return(SYSERR);
        }
        if (rename(args[1], args[2]) == SYSERR ) {
                fprintf(stderr, "Cannot move %s\n", args[1]);
                return(SYSERR);
        }
        return(OK);
}
```

18.7.10 Reboot Command

If the system data structures become corrupt, or the system runs out of some resource (e.g., memory), it may be necessary to reinitialize the entire system and start over. The *reboot* command allows the user to reinitialize the system for just such emergencies. Procedure *x_reboot*, shown below in file *x_reboot.c*, implements the *reboot* command by passing control to the *restart* entry point. *Restart* is not an ordinary procedure, but merely an address just before the system startup code. *Reboot* is a deadly command because it aborts everything. Devices, the network, processes, semaphores, and ports will all be reinitialized.

```
/* x_reboot.c - x_reboot */

#include <conf.h>
#include <kernel.h>


/*------------------------------------------------------------------------
 * x_reboot  -  (builtin command reboot) restart the system from scratch
 *------------------------------------------------------------------------
 */
BUILTIN x_reboot(stdin, stdout, stderr, nargs, args)
int     stdin, stdout, stderr, nargs;
char    *args[];
{
        restart();        /* warning! This terminates everything. */
}
```

18.7.11 Rm Command

Users invoke the *rm* command to remove (destroy) a file. *Rm* takes a file name as an argument, and invokes the *remove* system call on that file. Procedure *x_rm* implements the *rm* command as shown in file *x_rm.c*.

```
/* x_rm.c - x_rm */

#include <conf.h>
#include <kernel.h>
#include <file.h>


/*------------------------------------------------------------------------
 *  x_rm  -  (command rm) remove a file given its name
 *------------------------------------------------------------------------
 */
COMMAND x_rm(stdin, stdout, stderr, nargs, args)
int     stdin, stdout, stderr, nargs;
char    *args[];
{
        if (nargs != 2) {
                fprintf(stderr, "usage: rm file\n");
                return(SYSERR);
        }
        if ( remove(args[1]) == SYSERR ) {
                fprintf(stderr, "Cannot remove %s\n", args[1]);
                return(SYSERR);
        }
        return(OK);
}
```

18.7.12 Rls Command

Command *rls* provides another example of the power of the mechanisms we have constructed. *Rls* takes as an argument the name of a UNIX directory, and lists the files in that directory. It uses the remote file server to open the directory (in UNIX, a directory can be read like any other file). It then reads the directory and prints the names of files it finds. In keeping with UNIX convention, *rls* does not list file names beginning with a period unless it is invoked with argument *-a*.

Procedure *x_rls* implements command *rls*. To understand how it works, some explanation of UNIX directory format is needed. Directories are written as a sequence of 512-byte blocks. Each block has one or more entries as specified by structure *dirent*. The entry is of variable length, with total length given by field *d_rlen*. The file name itself starts at field *d_nam*, and has length given by field *d_nlen*.

To print files, *x_rls* repeatedly reads a block from the directory, and then scans through the entries in the block using pointer *p*. At each entry, *x_rls* prints the file name it finds, and then increments *p* by the record size to move to the next entry. While examining an entry, *x_rls* uses a second pointer, *d*. Both pointers have the same value, but different types, making it easy to dereference the entry

using *d* and easy to move through the block using *p*. The code, found in file *x_rls.c*
will help clarify the details.

```
/* x_rls.c - x_rls */

#include <conf.h>
#include <kernel.h>
#include <shell.h>


/*------------------------------------------------------------------------
 * x_rls  -  (command rls) list contents of remote file system directory
 *------------------------------------------------------------------------
 */
COMMAND x_rls(stdin, stdout, stderr, nargs, args)
int     stdin, stdout, stderr, nargs;
char    *args[];
{
        char    *p, *buf;
        int     dev, len;
        char    str[32];
        struct  dirent  {               /* UNIX directory entry         */
                long    d_inum;         /* file's inode number          */
                short   d_rlen;         /* length of this record        */
                short   d_nlen;         /* length of this file's name   */
                char    d_nam[1];       /* start of file name           */
        };
        struct  dirent  *d;
        Bool    aflag;


        aflag = FALSE;
        if (nargs > 1 && strcmp(p=args[1],"-a") == 0) {
                nargs--;
                aflag = TRUE;
                p = args[2];
        }
        if (nargs == 1)
                p = ".";
        else if (nargs != 2) {
                printf("use: rls [-a] directory\n");
                return(SYSERR);
        }
        if ( ((int)(buf=(char *)getmem(512))) == SYSERR) {
                fprintf(stderr, "rls: no memory\n");
```

```
                    return(SYSERR);
      }
      if (nammap(p, buf) != RFILSYS ||
         (dev=open(NAMESPACE, p, "ro")) == SYSERR) {
              fprintf(stderr, "cannot open %s\n", p);
              freemem(buf, 512);
              return(SYSERR);
      }
      len = read(dev, buf, 512);
      for( ; len > 0 ; len=read(dev, buf, 512)) {
              for (p=buf ; p< &buf[512] ;) {
                      d = (struct dirent *)p;
                      if (d->d_nlen != strlen(d->d_nam) ||
                          d->d_nlen > 32 || d->d_rlen < 0 ||
                          d->d_rlen > 512) {
                              fprintf(stderr, "Not a directory\n");
                              close(dev);
                              freemem(buf, 512);
                              return(SYSERR);
                      }
                      if (aflag || d->d_nam[0] != '.') {
                              strcpy(str, d->d_nam);
                              strcat(str, "\n");
                              write(stdout, str, strlen(str));
                      }
                      if (d->d_rlen == 0)
                              break;
                      p += d->d_rlen;
              }
      }
      freemem(buf, 512);
      close(dev);
      return(OK);
}
```

18.7.13 Sleep Command

The sleep command gives users access to the *sleep* system call, allowing them to stop the command process for a specified number of seconds. Procedure *x_sleep* implements the *sleep* command by converting the argument to an integer and then passing it to system call *sleep*. The code is shown below in file *x_sleep.c*.

```
/* x_sleep.c - x_sleep */

#include <conf.h>
#include <kernel.h>

/*------------------------------------------------------------------------
 *  x_sleep  -  (command sleep) delay for a given number of seconds
 *------------------------------------------------------------------------
 */
COMMAND x_sleep(stdin, stdout, stderr, nargs, args)
int     stdin, stdout, stderr, nargs;
char    *args[];
{
        if (nargs != 2) {
                fprintf(stderr, "usage: sleep delay\n");
                return(SYSERR);
        }
        return( sleep( atoi(args[1]) ) );
}
```

18.7.14 Snap Command

The *snap* command provides another demonstration of how flexible and power-ful the remote file system can be. *Snap* writes a memory image into a file in the same format as the Xinu *upload* utility. As a result, it is possible to invoke snap, and then use the conventional post mortem debugger on the host machine to inter-pret the results. Of course, *snap* is not useful for debugging a crash, because Xinu must be executing to use it. However, the result of *snap* can be useful in helping to track down problems while the system is still executing.

Procedure *x_snap* implements the *snap* command as shown in file *x_snap.c*.

```
/* x_snap.c - x_snap */

#include <conf.h>
#include <kernel.h>
#include <core11.h>
#include <mem.h>

LOCAL    int      snapreg;
#define SNAPSIZ 512

/*------------------------------------------------------------------------
 * x_snap  -  (command snap) write snapshot of memory to a core file
 *------------------------------------------------------------------------
 */
COMMAND x_snap(stdin, stdout, stderr, nargs, args)
int     stdin, stdout, stderr, nargs;
char    *args[];
{
        int     dev;
        struct  core11  hdr;
        char    *p, *limit;
        unsigned len;

        if (nargs > 2) {
                fprintf(stderr, "use: snap [core-file]\n");
                return(SYSERR);
        }
        p = nargs==1 ? "core11" : args[1];
        if ((dev=open(NAMESPACE, p, "w")) == SYSERR) {
                fprintf(stderr, "snap: cannot write %s\n", p);
                return(SYSERR);
        }

        /* make up a core image using core11 structure heading format */

        hdr.c_magic = COREMAGIC;
        hdr.c_size = hdr.c_zero1 = hdr.c_zero2 = hdr.c_zero3 =
                hdr.c_zero4 = hdr.c_zero5 = 0;

        /* Capture machine registers */

        asm("mov r0,_snapreg"); hdr.c_regs[0] = snapreg;
        asm("mov r1,_snapreg"); hdr.c_regs[1] = snapreg;
        asm("mov r2,_snapreg"); hdr.c_regs[2] = snapreg;
        asm("mov r3,_snapreg"); hdr.c_regs[3] = snapreg;
```

```
    asm("mov r4,_snapreg"); hdr.c_regs[4] = snapreg;
    asm("mov r5,_snapreg"); hdr.c_regs[5] = snapreg;
    asm("mov sp,_snapreg"); hdr.c_regs[6] = snapreg;
    asm("mov pc,_snapreg"); hdr.c_regs[7] = snapreg;
    asm("clr _snapreg;mfps _snapreg"); hdr.c_psw = snapreg;
    fprintf(stderr, "Writing core image");
    write(dev, &hdr, sizeof(struct core11));

    /* Add contents of real memory to core image */

    limit = (char *) ( 1 + (unsigned)maxaddr );
    for (p=NULL ; p <= limit ; p += SNAPSIZ) {
            putc(stderr, '.');
            len = 1 + ( (unsigned)limit - (unsigned)p );
            if ( len > (unsigned) SNAPSIZ )
                    len = SNAPSIZ;
            write(dev, p, len);
    }
    putc(stderr, '\n');
    close(dev);
    return(OK);
}
```

The format of the memory image produced by *x_snap* is described by structure *core11* in file *core11.h*. It contains a 32-byte header that includes information like the contents of machine registers, followed by the bytes of the memory image.

```
/* core11.h */

/* Definitions and constants for LSI 11 core dump files */

#define REGISTERS      8               /* number of g.p. registers    */
#define NREGS          REGISTERS+1     /* total regs including PS      */
#define COREMAGIC      0477            /* unix "magic number" for core */
struct  core11 {                       /* header of 11 core dump file  */
        short c_magic;                 /* UNIX convention              */
        short c_size;                  /* size of valid info (0=>entire*/
                                       /*  file contains core dump     */
        short c_zero1;                 /* padding to follow UNIX style */
        short c_zero2;                 /*    "       "    "     "     " */
        short c_regs[REGISTERS];       /* dump of machine registers    */
        short c_psw;                   /* dump of program status reg   */
        short c_zero3;                 /* more padding (as in UNIX)    */
        short c_zero4;                 /*    "       "    "   "     "   */
        short c_zero5;                 /*    "       "    "   "     "   */
                                       /* Core image follows header    */
};

/* Names used for registers */

#define R0      0
#define R1      1
#define R2      2
#define R3      3
#define R4      4
#define R5      5
#define R6      6
#define R7      7
```

Procedure *x_snap* must invoke assembler language instructions to capture machine register values for the currently executing process. However, once the header has been written, the contents of memory can be written to the file easily.

An optional argument to the *snap* command specifies a file into which the memory image should be written. If no file is given, *x_snap* opens file *core11*. A look at the definition of our sample namespace shows that *core11* maps to *core11* in the Xinu source directory on the remote file system. Thus, if no explicit argument is given, *x_snap* places the output in the directory in which the currently executing system was compiled, making it easy to run the post mortem debugger.

18.7.15 Unmount Command

Command *unmount* takes as an argument, a string that is a prefix from the name mapping table, and removes the entry with that prefix. As the code in procedure *x_unmou* shows, system call *unmount* does most of the work:

```
/* x_unmou.c -  x_unmou */

#include <conf.h>
#include <kernel.h>
#include <io.h>
#include <name.h>

/*------------------------------------------------------------------------
 * x_unmou  -  (command unmount) remove a prefix from the namespace table
 *------------------------------------------------------------------------
 */
COMMAND x_unmou(stdin, stdout, stderr, nargs, args)
int     stdin, stdout, stderr, nargs;
char    *args[];
{
        if (nargs != 2) {
                fprintf(stderr, "use: unmount prefix\n");
                return(SYSERR);
        }
        if (unmount(args[1]) == SYSERR) {
                fprintf(stderr, "unmount fails.\n");
                return(SYSERR);
        }
        return(OK);
}
```

18.8 Summary

We have examined a sample set of commands that show how command procedures are implemented, and how they receive command-line arguments. The commands were divided into three broad categories: general information, system information, and computation.

FOR FURTHER STUDY

Choosing a set of commands is not easy because no single set satisfies everyone's needs. Bourne [1978] suggests fixing only a few commands and control structures, while allowing the user to add (or modify) the rest. Brunt and Tuffs [1976] describe a command language with richer functionality. Fraser and Hanson [1985] consider an entirely different approach in which the user can depend on stable storage of objects like command language variables.

EXERCISES

18.1   Design a builtin command *fg* that takes a process id as an argument, and brings the specified process into the foreground.

18.2   Add a builtin command, *source*, that takes a file name as an argument and temporarily inserts the contents of the file in the shell's input stream. (Note: this requires modifying the shell itself.)

18.3   List the advantages and disadvantages of making *echo* a builtin command.

18.4   Modify   *x_date*   to   correctly   check   its   argument.   What   are   the advantages/disadvantages of each approach?

18.5   Modify the system so it keeps a count of seconds since the date was last set from the network server, and have *getutim* automatically reset the date if it finds that more than 2 hours have elapsed since it was last set. Does this mechanism eliminate the need for an argument to the *date* command?

18.6   Pick a command, rewrite it to use *fprintf* instead of *write*, and measure the performance with output redirected to a remote file.

18.7   Rewrite the remote file system interface to buffer output locally. Measure the improvement in performance by modifying a command to use *fprintf* instead of *write*. What is the disadvantage of local buffering?

18.8   Improve procedure *x_help* so it places an asterisk by all names that are aliases for other commands (e.g., place an asterisk by both *help* and *?*).

18.9   Modify the help command to keep information in files in a help directory. Have it accept an optional argument, so typing

```
help xxx
```

provides information on topic *xxx*, as found in file *xxx* located in the help directory.

18.10   Modify the process manager to record machine load averages, where the load is defined to be the average number of processes in the CPU ready list. Arrange for the *rwho* system to broadcast, and procedure *x_uptime* to print the load average information.

18.11 Add commands that format the semaphore table, and allow a user to *signal*, *reset*, or *delete* a semaphore.

18.12 Revise the *devs* command to print more information about each device.

18.13 Can *cat* know whether its standard input and standard output are directed to the same file? What happens if they are?

18.14 Modify *cat* to treat an argument that consists of a single minus sign as meaning "read from standard input". Thus, the command

```
cat a - b < c > f
```

would concatenate files *a*, *c*, and *b* in that order.

18.15 Modify *x_close* to accept a list of device ids as arguments, and arrange to have it close *all* the devices listed.

18.16 Modify *x_close* to allow the user to specify either integer device ids or the symbolic name of a device.

18.17 Add a file mode, *a*, that denotes *append*, and arrange for files opened with mode *a* to be positioned at the end of the current data.

18.18 Why might the command *create* be useful even though the shell supports background processing?

18.19 Build commands that allow the user to *suspend* or *resume* a process.

18.20 Modify *x_kill.c* so it acts on one or more processes, where the command-line arguments specify the processes either by numeric process id or by process names.

18.21 Should the *mount* command allow users to specify devices by numeric id? Why or why not?

18.22 Consider modifying the *mount* system call to accept a string as the second argument, where the string specified the name of a device instead of its device id. What is the chief disadvantage?

18.23 Add a UDP echo command that takes an internet address as an argument, reads a line of input from the standard input device, sends the line to the UDP echo port at the specified internet address, and waits up to 10 seconds for a reply. Hint: you do not need to modify the datagram pseudo-device interface.

18.24 Should commands like *reboot* warn the user about the consequences, and then ask for verification? Should commands with less serious consequences (e.g., *rm*)? Why or why not?

18.25 Is there a good reason for making *reboot* a builtin command?

18.26 Identify the problem caused by invoking *x_creat* repeatedly when no free memory exists, and repair it.

18.27 It is possible to implement command *rm* without using the system call *remove*. What are the advantages and disadvantages of each implementation?

18.28 Should commands describe errors in syntactic terms (e.g., "greater than sign cannot appear at end of line"), or in semantic terms (e.g., "output redirection requires a file name")? Why?

18.29 Modify the shell and commands so they try to spot errors and give detailed error messages.

18.30 Why is *kill* a builtin command?

19

Resolving High-Level Machine Names

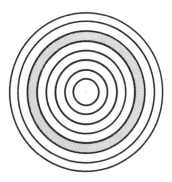

19.1 Introduction

So far we have used 32-bit integers called Internet Protocol Addresses (IP addresses) to identify machines. Although such addresses provide a convenient, compact representation for specifying the source and destination in packets sent across the internet, users prefer to assign machines pronounceable, easily remembered names. We have already seen, for example, that the *ruptime* command from Chapter 18 reports machine status using high-level machine names taken from incoming status messages.

This chapter considers how meaningful high-level names can be assigned to a large set of machines, and discusses a mechanism that maps between high-level machine names and IP addresses. It considers both the translation from high-level names to IP addresses and the translation from IP addresses to high-level machine names.

19.2 Naming Machines

The earliest computer systems forced users to understand machine addresses for objects like system tables and peripheral devices. Timesharing systems advanced computing by allowing users to invent meaningful symbolic names for both physical objects (e.g., peripheral devices) and abstract objects (e.g., files). A similar pattern has emerged in computer networking. Early systems supported point-to-point connections between computers, and used low-level hardware addresses to specify machines. Internetworking introduced universal addresses, as well as protocol software to map universal addresses into low-level hardware addresses. When users became aware of multiple machines in their computing environment, they wanted to use meaningful, symbolic names to identify them.

Early machine names reflected the small environment in which they were chosen. It was quite common for a site with a handful of machines to choose names based on the machines' purpose. For example, machines often had names like *research*, *production*, *accounting*, and *development*. Users find such names appealing, and prefer to use them instead of the more cumbersome hardware address.

Although the distinction between *address* and *name* is intuitively appealing, it is artificial. Any *name* is merely an identifier that consists of a sequence of characters chosen from a finite alphabet. Names are only useful if the system can map them to the object they denote. Thus, an Internet addresses is a low-level name, and it would be correct to say that users prefer high-level names for machines.

The form of high-level names is important because it determines how names are translated to lower-level names or bound to objects, as well as how name assignments are authorized. When only a few machines interconnect, choosing names is easy, and any form will suffice. On an internet where thousands of machines interconnect, however, choosing symbolic names becomes difficult. For example, when the Computer Science Department at Purdue University connected to the DARPA Internet in 1980, it chose the name *purdue* to identify the connected machine. The list of potential conflicts contained only a few dozen names. By 1986, the official list of hosts on the DARPA Internet contained 3100 officially registered names and 6500 official aliases. Although the list was growing rapidly, most sites had many additional machines (e.g., personal computers) that were not registered.

19.3 Flat Namespace

The DARPA Internet names described above formed a *flat namespace* in which each name consists of a sequence of characters. A central site, the Network Information Center, administered the namespace and determined whether a new name was appropriate. (The central authority prohibited sites from choosing illegal or obscene names).

The chief advantage of a flat namespace is that names are convenient and short; the chief disadvantage of a flat namespace is that it cannot generalize to large sets of machines for both technical and administrative reasons. First, because names are drawn from a single set of identifiers, the potential for conflict increases as the number of sites increases. Second, because authority for adding new names must rest at a single site, the administrative workload at that site increases as the number of sites increases. To understand the severity of the problem, imagine an internet with thousands of sites, each of which has hundreds of individual personal computers and workstations. Every time someone acquires and connects a new personal computer, its name must be approved by the central authority. Third, because the name-to-address bindings change frequently, the cost of maintaining correct copies at each site is high, and increases as the number of sites increase. Alternatively, if the name database resides at a single site, traffic to that site increases as the number of sites increases.

19.4 Hierarchical Names

How can a naming system accommodate a large, rapidly expanding set of names without requiring a central site to administer them? The answer lies in decentralizing the naming mechanism by delegating authority for parts of the namespace, and distributing responsibility for mapping between names and addresses.

The division of the namespace must be made in such a way that it supports efficient name mapping and guarantees autonomous control of name assignment. Optimizing only for efficient mapping can lead to solutions that retain a flat namespace and reduce traffic by dividing the names among multiple mapping machines. Optimizing only around administrative authority can lead to solutions that make delegation of authority easy but name mapping expensive or complex.

To understand how the namespace should be divided, think of the internal structure of large organizations. At the top, the chief executive has overall responsibility. Because the chief executive cannot oversee everything, the organization may be partitioned into divisions, with an executive in charge of each division. The chief executive grants each division autonomy within specified limits. More to the point, the executive in charge of a particular division can hire or fire employees, assign offices, and delegate authority, without obtaining direct permission from the chief executive.

Besides making it easy to delegate authority, the hierarchy of a large organization introduces autonomous operation. For example, when average office workers need information like telephone numbers of new employees, they begin by asking local clerical workers (who may have to contact clerical workers in other divisions). The point is that although authority always passes down the corporate hierarchy, information can flow across the hierarchy from one office to another.

19.5 Distributed Hierarchical Namespace

A distributed hierarchical naming scheme works like the management of a large organization. The namespace is partitioned at the top level, and authority for names in the subdivisions is passed to a designated agent. For example, we might choose to partition the namespace based on *site name*, and to delegate to each site responsibility for maintaining names within its partition. The topmost level of the hierarchy partitions the namespace and delegates authority for the partitions; it need not be bothered by changes within one partition.

The name syntax often reflects the hierarchical distribution of authority. As an example, consider a namespace with names of the form

site / other

where *site* is the name of a site authorized by the central authority, *other* is the part of a name controlled by the site, and the slash character is a delimiter used to separate them. When the topmost authority approves adding a new site, X, it adds X to the list of valid sites, and delegates to site X authority for all names beginning $X/$.

19.6 Subset Authority

In a hierarchical namespace, authority may be further subdivided at each level. In our example of partition by sites, the site itself may consist of several administrative groups, and the site authority may choose to subdivide its namespace among the groups. The idea is to keep subdividing the namespace until each subdivision is small enough to be manageable.

Syntactically, subdividing the namespace introduces another level of hierarchical name. For example, adding a *group* subdivision to names already partitioned by site produces the following name syntax:

site / group / other

Because the topmost level delegates authority, group names do not have to agree between sites. A university site might choose group names like *engineering*, *science*, and *arts*, while a corporate site might choose group names like *production*, *accounting*, and *personnel*.

The U.S. Telephone system provides another example of hierarchical naming syntax. The 10 digits of a phone number have been partitioned into a 3-digit *area code*, 3-digit *exchange*, and 4-digit *subscriber number* within the exchange. Each exchange has authority for assigning subscriber numbers within its piece of the namespace.

19.7 Nameservers

A *nameserver* is a server process that supplies name-to-address translation. Often, server software executes on a dedicated processor, and the machine itself is called the nameserver. The client software, called the *name resolver*, uses one or more nameservers when translating a name.

In distributed systems, nameservers may be replicated to achieve high reliability or the namespace may be divided among several nameservers to improve performance. Some systems strive for both efficiency and reliability by partitioning the namespace and replicating servers. One popular method partitions the namespace onto multiple machines and then achieves high reliability by replicating information among existing machines. To keep traffic evenly distributed among all servers, client software first tries to resolve a name using the primary server for that name. If it cannot contact the primary server, the client sends the request to a backup server.

In a distributed hierarchical naming system, the organization of nameservers may or may not follow the authority hierarchy. It is possible, for example, to store all names on all servers, or to have each server store mappings only for the subset of names for which it is an authority. The nameserver architecture determines the cost of searching for a name as well as the cost of updating the information.

19.8 Efficient Distributed Name Resolution

Using a hierarchical namespace solves the problem of managing frequent changes because it spreads the administrative work to subsets of the community. Authority for subparts of the namespace passes down the hierarchy. If a nameserver at each point of the hierarchy implements mappings for which the site has authority, changes to the name mapping are efficient because they are controlled locally. However, a good distributed naming scheme must also support efficient name translation.

Recall that the process of translating names is known as *name resolution*, and consists of mapping a high-level name to a low-level name that can be used to access the object. For example, resolving a machine name produces its internet address. In a distributed system, name resolver software must contact one or more nameserver processes to translate a name.

Forcing the name resolution process to pass down the hierarchy of nameservers would be incorrect for three reasons. First, most name resolution refers to local names, those found within the same subdivision of the namespace as the machine from which the request originates. Tracing a path through the hierarchy to contact the local authority would be inefficient. Second, if each name resolution always started by contacting the topmost level of the hierarchy, the machine at that point would become saturated. Third, failure of machines at the topmost levels of the hierarchy would prevent name resolution, even if the local authority could resolve the name.

The telephone example helps explain why resolution need not follow the authority hierarchy. Although telephone numbers are assigned hierarchically, they are resolved bottom-up. As with most name resolution, the majority of telephone calls are local, so they can be resolved by the local exchange without searching the hierarchy. Furthermore, calls within a given area code can be resolved without contacting sites outside the area code.

19.9 Name Abbreviation

The telephone example illustrates *name abbreviation*, a method of shortening names when the resolving process can supply part of the name automatically. Normally, a subscriber omits the area code when dialing a local telephone number. The resulting digits form an abbreviated name assumed to lie within the same area code as the subscriber's phone.

Abbreviation also works well for machine names. Given a name like *abc* the resolving process can assume it lies in the same local authority as the machine on which it is being resolved. Thus, the resolver can supply missing parts of the name automatically.

19.10 The DARPA Domain Name System

The DARPA Internet uses a distributed, hierarchical naming scheme known as *domain names*. Like our previous examples, a domain name consists of a sequence of subnames separated by a delimiter character. However, there are two differences between our examples and the DARPA domain scheme. First, domain names are written with the most local subname first and the topmost subname last. Second, DARPA domain names use a period to delimit subnames.

DARPA, which has ultimate authority for the namespace, has chosen a top level partition of

COM	Commercial organizations
EDU	Educational institutions
GOV	Government institutions
MIL	Military groups
NET	Major networks
ORG	Organizations other than those above
ARPA	Temporary ARPANET domain
country	Countries other than USA

Figure 19.1 The top-level DARPA domains and their meaning.

When a foreign country wants to participate in the domain naming system, the central authority assigns it a new top-level domain consisting of its international standard 2-letter country identifier. When an organization in the United States wants to participate in the domain naming system, the central authority at DARPA assigns it a subdomain under one of the existing top-level domains.

An example domain name will help clarify the authority structure. The machine named *xinu* in the Computer Science Department at Purdue University has the official domain name *xinu.cs.purdue.edu*

The name was approved and registered by the system staff in the Computer Science Department, who had previously obtained authority to manage the subdomain *cs.purdue.edu* from the university administrator, who had obtained permission from DARPA to manage the subdomain *purdue.edu*. DARPA retains authority for the *edu* domain, so new universities can only be added with DARPA's permission.

19.11 Domain Nameservers

DARPA requires that before an organization can be granted authority for a second-level domain, the organization must agree to operate a domain nameserver that meets DARPA's standards. Domain nameservers partition the namespace along boundaries of authority, with a given nameserver taking responsibility for all names in a particular subdomain. Each domain name server must know the address of all nameservers that handle subdomains. In addition, to insure that a domain nameserver can pass requests that it cannot resolve up the hierarchy, all domain nameservers know the address of the next name server up the hierarchy (called the *parent*).

A given domain nameserver may handle more than one level of the naming hierarchy as long as the levels all lie under a common point in the naming hierarchy. For example, a single nameserver at Purdue University handles both the second-level domain *purdue.edu* as well as the third-level domain *cs.purdue.edu*. The set of names managed by a given nameserver forms a *zone of authority*.

DARPA requires that the information in every domain nameserver be replicated in at least one additional domain nameserver that shares no single common point of failure with the original. Avoiding common points of failure means that the two nameservers cannot even obtain electrical power from the same source. To meet the requirements, a site must find another site that agrees to operate a backup nameserver. Of course, the parent nameserver knows how to locate both the primary and backup nameservers for a given name, and can direct queries to the backup nameserver if the primary nameserver is unavailable.

19.12 DARPA Domain Name Resolution

Domain name resolution proceeds bottom-up, starting with the local nameserver and proceeding to remote ones only when a name cannot be resolved locally. There are two ways to use the domain name system: by contacting nameservers one at a time or asking the nameserver to perform the complete translation. In either case, the client software forms a domain name query that contains the name to be resolved, a declaration of the type of the name, the type of mapping desired, and a code that specifies whether the nameserver should translate the name completely. The client sends the query to its local nameserver which attempts to resolve it.

When a domain nameserver receives a query, it checks to see if the name lies in the subdomain for which it is an authority. If so, it performs the translation and appends an answer to the query before sending it back to the client. If the nameserver cannot resolve the name, it checks to see what type of interaction the client specified. If the client requested complete translation (*recursive resolution* in domain name terminology), the server contacts a domain nameserver that can resolve the name, and returns the answer to the client. If the client requested non-recursive resolution, the nameserver cannot supply an answer. It generates a reply that specifies the nameserver the client should contact to resolve the name.

19.13 Pointer Queries And Inverse Mappings

The domain name system supports an unusual form of mapping using *pointer queries*. In a pointer query, the question presented to a domain nameserver specifies a fictitious domain name made up of an Internet address encoded as a printable string. Pointer queries request the domain nameserver to return the correct high-level domain name for the machine with the specified Internet address. Pointer queries are especially useful for diskless machines because they allow the system to obtain a high-level name given only an Internet address (We have already seen in Chapter 5 how a diskless machine obtains its Internet address at system startup).

Pointer queries are not difficult to generate. If we think of the Internet address written in dotted-decimal form, it would look like the following:

$$xxx.yyy.zzz.www$$

To form a pointer query, the nameserver client rewrites the string in the following form:

$$www.zzz.yyy.xxx.in\text{-}addr.arpa$$

The local nameserver is not likely to be an authority for either the *arpa* domain or the *in-addr.arpa* domain, so it needs to contact other nameservers to complete the resolution.

19.14 Example Domain Name Resolution Software

Looking at a simple example of how client software uses the domain name system will clarify many of the ideas presented above. We begin by examining the format of messages exchanged between the domain name client and nameserver. File *domain.h* contains both message formats and pertinent constants.

```
/* domain.h - dn_cat */

#ifndef DSERVER
#define DSERVER        "128.10.2.5:53" /* Server IP address & UDP port */
#endif

/* Definitions of bits in the operation and parameter field */

#define DN_QR          0100000         /* Query (0) or request (1) bit */
#define DN_OPCDE       0074000         /* operation  code for query:   */
                                       /*  0 => standard query         */
                                       /*  1 => inverse query,         */
                                       /*  2 => completion query,      */
                                       /*  3 => completion (1 answer), */
                                       /*  4-15 => reserved.           */
#define DN_AA          0002000         /* 1 if authoritative answer    */
#define DN_TR          0001000         /* 1 if message truncated       */
#define DN_RD          0000400         /* 1 if recursion desired       */
#define DN_RA          0000200         /* 1 if recursion available     */
#define DN_RESVD       0000160         /* reserved                     */
#define DN_RESP        0000017         /* response code:               */
                                       /*  0 => no errors in query     */
                                       /*  1 => format error in query  */
                                       /*  2 => server failure         */
                                       /*  3 => name does not exist    */

struct  dn_mesg {                      /* domain system message format */
        short   dn_id;                 /* message id                   */
        short   dn_opparm;             /* operation and parmameter bits*/
        short   dn_qcount;             /* # entries in question seciton*/
        short   dn_acount;             /* # RRs in answer section      */
        short   dn_ncount;             /* # RRs in nameserver section  */
        short   dn_dcount;             /* # RRs in additional section  */
        char    dn_qaaa[1];            /* start of rest of the message */
        /* remaining fields of the domain name message are of variable */
        /* length, and consist of (1) a question section, (2) an answer */
        /* section, (3) an authority section (which says where to find  */
        /* answers when they cannot be supplied), and (4) an addition   */
        /* information section.  Entries in these are Resource Records. */
};

struct  dn_qsuf {                      /* question section name suffix */
        short   dn_type;               /* type of this name            */
        short   dn_clas;               /* class of this name           */
```

```
};
```

```
#define DN_MLEN          128                /* message length (small query) */
#define dn_cat(t,f)      {*t++ =(char)strlen(f);strcpy(t,f);t+=strlen(f);}
```

```
/* Query type codes */
```

```
#define DN_QTHA          1          /* Host address                  */
#define DN_QTNS          2          /* Authoratative name server     */
#define DN_QTMD          3          /* Mail destination (obsolete)   */
#define DN_QTMF          4          /* Mail forwarder (obsolete)     */
#define DN_QTCN          5          /* Canonical name for an alias   */
#define DN_QTSZ          6          /* Start of zone of authority    */
#define DN_QTMB          7          /* Mailbox domain name           */
#define DN_QTMG          8          /* Mail group member             */
#define DN_QTMR          9          /* Mail rename domain name        */
#define DN_QTNL          10         /* Null resource record          */
#define DN_QTWK          11         /* Well-known service descriptor*/
#define DN_QTPR          12         /* Domain name pointer           */
#define DN_QTHI          13         /* Host information              */
#define DN_QTMI          14         /* Mailbox or mail list info.    */
#define DN_QTMX          15         /* Mail, replaces MD & MF        */
```

```
/* Query class codes */
```

```
#define DN_QCIN          1          /* The DARPA Internet            */
#define DN_QCCS          2          /* CSNET (now obsolete)          */
#define DN_QCHA          3          /* Chaos network                 */
```

```
#define DN_CMPRS         0300       /* Compressed format is pointer */
#define DN_CPTR          037777     /* Compressed format bits of ptr*/
#define DN_RLEN          10         /* resource record heading len. */
```

Structure *dn_mesg* defines the format of a message sent between the client and nameserver. The first 12 bytes of the message form a header that contains an identifying sequence number, an operation and parameter specification, and counts that specify the size of the remaining fields in the message.

All domain names are encoded as variable length strings, with each segment of the name coded separately. A segment consists of a 1-byte count, C, followed by C characters. A count byte of zero terminates the name. In the question section, the name must be followed by a 32-bit suffix that specifies the *type* and *class*. Structure *dn_qsuf* gives the format for query suffixes. Constants for type and class are also given in *domain.h*.

19.15 Compressed Name Format

Domain nameservers often return multiple answers to a query. To conserve
space in the reply packet, the nameservers compress names by storing only one copy
of the higher levels of the domain name. When following a domain name, the
client software must check each segment to see whether it consists of a pointer or
has been encoded in the standard format of a 1-byte count followed by the string.
When it encounters a pointer, the client must follow the pointer to a new place in
the message to find the remainder of the name.

Pointers always occur at the beginning of segments. If the top 2 bits of the 8-
bit segment count field are 1s, the client must take the next 14 bits as an integer
pointer. If the top two bits are zero, the next 6 bits represent a count of characters
that follow as usual. Constants *DN_CMPRS* and *DN_CPTR* are used to mask the
pointer code bits and the pointer offset field, respectively.

19.16 Mapping An Internet Address To A Domain Name

Procedure *ip2name* takes an Internet address as an argument and translates it
to a domain name using a domain nameserver. The code can be found in file
ip2name.c.

```
/* ip2name.c - ip2name */

#include <conf.h>
#include <kernel.h>
#include <network.h>

/*------------------------------------------------------------------------
 *  ip2name  -  return DARPA Domain name for a host given its IP address
 *------------------------------------------------------------------------
 */
SYSCALL ip2name(ip, nam)
IPaddr  ip;
char    *nam;
{
        char    tmpstr[20];               /* temporary string buffer    */
        char    *buf;                     /* buffer to hold domain query */
        int     dg, i;
        register char    *p;
        register struct dn_mesg *dnptr;

        dnptr = (struct dn_mesg *) (buf = (char *) getmem(DN_MLEN));
        *nam = NULLCH;
        dnptr->dn_id = 0;
        dnptr->dn_opparm = hs2net(DN_RD);
        dnptr->dn_qcount = hs2net(1);
        dnptr->dn_acount = dnptr->dn_ncount = dnptr->dn_dcount = 0;
        p = dnptr->dn_qaaa;

        /* Fill in question with  ip[3].ip[2].ip[1].ip[0].in-addr.arpa  */

        for (i=3 ; i >= 0 ; i--) {
                sprintf(tmpstr, "%d", ip[i] & LOWBYTE);
                dn_cat(p, tmpstr);
        }
        dn_cat(p, "in-addr");
        dn_cat(p, "arpa");
        *p++ = NULLCH;  /* terminate name */

        /* Add query type and query class fields to name */

        ( (struct dn_qsuf *)p )->dn_type = hs2net(DN_QTPR);
        ( (struct dn_qsuf *)p )->dn_clas = hs2net(DN_QCIN);
        p += sizeof(struct dn_qsuf);

        /* Broadcast query */
```

```
dg = open(INTERNET, DSERVER, ANYLPORT);
control(dg, DG_SETMODE, DG_DMODE | DG_TMODE);
write (dg, buf, p - buf);
if ( (i = read(dg, buf, DN_MLEN)) == SYSERR || i == TIMEOUT)
        panic("No response from name server");
close(dg);
if (net2hs(dnptr->dn_opparm) & DN_RESP ||
    net2hs(dnptr->dn_acount) <= 0) {
        freemem(buf, DN_MLEN);
        return(SYSERR);
}

/* In answer, skip name and remainder of resource record header */

while (*p != NULLCH)
        if (*p & DN_CMPRS)          /* compressed section of name   */
                *++p = NULLCH;
        else
                p += *p + 1;
p += DN_RLEN + 1;

/* Copy name to user */

*nam = NULLCH;

while (*p != NULLCH) {
        if (*p & DN_CMPRS)
                p = buf + (net2hs(*(int *)p) & DN_CPTR);
        else {
                strncat(nam, p+1, *p);
                strcat(nam, ".");
                p += *p + 1;
        }
}
if (strlen(nam))            /* remove trailing dot */
        nam[strlen(nam) - 1] = NULLCH;
freemem(buf, DN_MLEN);
return(OK);
}
```

As the code shows, *ip2name* allocates a buffer to hold the query and reply. After filling in the message header, it forms a pointer query from the IP address.

To perform the translation, *ip2name* opens a datagram connection to the nameserver and sends the query. Bit *DN_RD* requests the server to resolve the name recursively. The nameserver returns the query with answers appended and fields in the header modified to show the status. When the answer arrives, *ip2name* checks the response field in the header to make sure the server did not report an error, and checks the count of answers to make sure the server returns at least one answer.

If the nameserver was able to answer the query, *ip2name* extracts the response from the answer field of the message, just beyond the end of the query. To extract an answer, *ip2name* must skip by both the first name in the answer field (which is a duplicate of the question), as well as the 10-byte record header. It then copies the answer into the address specified by the caller.

19.17 Obtaining A Machine Name

With *ip2name* in place, it is easy for the diskless machine to obtain its own name. Procedure *getname* shows one method. File *getname.c* contains the code.

```
/* getname.c - getname */

#include <conf.h>
#include <kernel.h>
#include <network.h>

/*------------------------------------------------------------------------
 * getname  -  get name of this host and place it where specified
 *------------------------------------------------------------------------
 */
SYSCALL getname(nam)
char    *nam;
{
        IPaddr  myaddr[4];
        char    *p;

        *nam = NULLCH;
        if (!Net.mnvalid) {
                getaddr(myaddr);
                if (ip2name(myaddr, Net.myname) == SYSERR)
                        return(SYSERR);
                Net.mnvalid = TRUE;
        }
        for (p=Net.myname ; *p != NULLCH && *p != '.' ; )
                *nam++ = *p++;
```

```
        *nam = NULLCH;
        return(OK);
}
```

Getname uses field *myname* in the global structure *Net* to hold the machine's name. Initially, field *mnvalid* is *FALSE*. The first process to execute *getname* uses *getaddr* to obtain the machine's IP address, and then uses *ip2name* to translate the address into a name. Once the name has been obtained, *getname* sets field *mnvalid* to *TRUE* so subsequent calls will not go to the server.

19.18 Summary

Hierarchical naming systems allow delegation of authority for names, making it possible to accommodate an arbitrarily large set of names without overwhelming a central site with administrative duties. Although name resolution is separate from delegation of authority, it is possible to create hierarchical naming systems in which resolution is an efficient, bottom-up process even though delegation of authority flows from the top of the hierarchy downward.

We briefly examined the DARPA domain name system, an example of a distributed, hierarchical naming scheme. Domain nameservers map high-level domain names to Internet addresses, and Internet addresses to domain names. We saw how clients contact the nameserver, and how a diskless machine can use the domain name system to obtain its symbolic name given only an Internet address.

FOR FURTHER STUDY

Mockapetris [1983] discusses DARPA domain naming in general, giving the overall philosophy, while Mockapetris [1983a] provides a protocol standard for domain naming, which is updated by Mockapetris [1986]. Postel and Reynolds [1984] state the requirements that a DARPA domain nameserver must meet. Finally, Partridge [1986] relates domain naming to electronic mail addressing.

EXERCISES

19.1   Machine names should not be bound into the operating system at compile time. Explain why.

19.2   Would you prefer to use a machine that obtained its name from a remote file or from a nameserver? Which method produces the cleanest operating system design?

19.3   Build a procedure, *name2ip*, that takes a domain name as an argument and returns the Internet address for that name.

19.4   Why should each nameserver know the Internet address of its parent?

19.5   Devise a naming scheme that tolerates changes to the naming hierarchy. As an example, consider that two large companies each have an independent hierarchy and they merge. Can you arrange to have all previous names still work correctly?

19.6   The DARPA domain naming system can also accommodate mailbox names. Find out how.

19.7   Can you modify the *NETWORK* pseudo-device *open* routine to accept symbolic (domain) names as well as Internet addresses?

19.8   How would you accommodate abbreviations in the DARPA domain naming scheme? Sketch nameservers for two departments at each of two universities as well as a top level nameserver, and explain how each server would treat each type of abbreviation.

19.9   Obtain the official description of the DARPA domain name system and build a nameserver.

19.10   How could you use the syntactic namespace of Chapter 15 to build a distributed hierarchical name system.

20

Higher-Level Protocols

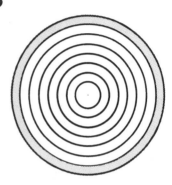

20.1 Introduction

Higher levels of network protocol software provide increased communication functionality and also support special-purpose communication. This chapter summarizes important high-level protocols, discussing each briefly. It points out how the high-level protocols depend on one another and on the low-level protocols seen in previous chapters. While a short summary cannot cover details of any particular protocol, it does introduce important terminology, and identify key concepts needed to understand other network protocols. Perhaps most important, it describes the network services users are likely to have encountered, and relates them to the protocols we have studied.

20.2 Reliable End-To-End Communication

The Internet and User Datagram Protocols presented so far offer only an unreliable, "best effort" form of data delivery. Gateways or packet switches may choose to discard packets due to congestion, delays, or hardware failures. Thus, there is no guarantee an Internet datagram will ever arrive at its destination.

Unreliable datagram delivery mechanisms map well on hardware like the Ethernet (which offers unreliable, best-effort delivery), but they do not suit most application programs. When programmers write software, they want to imagine reliable, guaranteed communication service that does not depend on network traffic. To accommodate users, most protocol families provide protocols that provide reliable delivery using only the unreliable datagram service provided by low-level protocols.

We have already seen an example of protocol software that provides reliable delivery in the remote file system of Chapters 13 and 14. The technique, known as *positive acknowledgement with retransmission*, requires the client to send a request, and time the reply. The server always acknowledges messages, even if the message requires no data to be sent back. Because the server acknowledges all messages (positive acknowledgement), the client knows when a message has been delivered successfully. However, if the client fails to receive an acknowledgement before its timeout expires, it assumes the message has been lost and retransmits the request.

Timeout and retransmission form the basis for all reliable packet-switched network communication protocols. Several refinements are needed, however, to make reliable delivery systems. First, because machine failure on a multiple-network path can lead to delivery failure even if each machine pair along the path delivers packets reliably, acknowledgements and retransmission must be negotiated between the original source and the final destination. Protocols that acknowledge from original source to final destination are called *end-to-end protocols*. Second, to make end-to-end protocols general enough to operate on an internet they must accommodate high-speed local networks with short delays as well as long-haul networks with high delays. Thus, the protocol must monitor the end-to-end delay and adjust the timeout accordingly. Timeout mechanisms that adjust to network delay are called *adaptive*. Third, because acknowledgements take time and add to network congestion, they should be combined with normal traffic flowing in the opposite direction. Protocols that permit data to flow in two directions at once are called *full duplex*; in such protocols, acknowledgements flowing in one direction can be *piggybacked* by encoding them in the header of packets flowing in the opposite direction. Fourth, protocols need to handle miscellaneous errors such as failure of the network hardware. Even when the hardware is operating correctly, it may truncate or duplicate packets, or deliver them out of order (e.g., because there are multiple routes between the source and destination).

To make reliable, end-to-end protocols match the user's model of communication, designers often choose to provide *stream connections*. A stream can be thought of as a sequence of bytes with the property that the sequence of bytes received at the destination is exactly the sequence of bytes sent by the source. Furthermore, the stream abstraction implies that protocol software continuously monitors the stream connection, and informs the user's process of communication failure. Thus, a process sending bytes to a stream cannot go on if the protocol software cannot deliver the data being sent.

20.3 The DARPA Transmission Control Protocol (TCP)

A key part of the DARPA protocol suite, the Transmission Control Protocol (TCP), is a reliably delivered full-duplex stream-oriented protocol that uses an adaptive retransmission algorithm. It forms the foundation on which most of the higher-level protocols depend. Like the UDP protocol described in Chapter 9, TCP supports demultiplexing based on a port number, making it possible for individual processes to establish stream connections without interfering with each other.

20.4 Remote Interactive Computing

We have already seen how the client—server model can provide specific computational services like file access across multiple machines. Reliable stream protocols like TCP make it possible to imagine interactive use of remote machines as well. For example, a remote editor server could be constructed that allows a user to edit files at the remote site. To invoke the remote editor, a user would establish a full duplex (TCP) connection from their local machine to the server, passing keystrokes on one direction and screen updates back.

How can remote interactive computing be generalized? The problem with using one server for each computational service is that machines quickly become clogged with server processes. We can eliminate most specialized servers and provide more generality by allowing the user to establish a login session on the remote machine and then execute commands. With a *remote login* facility, users have access to all the commands available on the remote system, and system designers need not provide specialized servers.

Of course, providing remote login may not be simple. Most extant timesharing systems were designed before networks became popular, so they expect login sessions only from directly connected terminals. On some systems, building interactive client software may be difficult. Consider, for example, systems that assign special meaning to some keystrokes. If the local system interprets Control—C to mean "abort the currently executing command process," it may be impossible to pass Control—C to the remote machine. But if the client chooses to pass Control-C to the remote site, it may be impossible to abort the local client process.

Despite the technical difficulties, system programmers have managed to build remote login client and server software for most operating systems. Often, the client software overrides the local interpretation of all keys except one, allowing the user to interact with the remote machine exactly as one would from a locally connected terminal. In addition, some remote login protocols recognize a set of *trusted hosts*, permitting remote login from such hosts without verifying passwords.

20.5 DARPA TELNET Protocol

The Internet protocol suite includes a simple remote login protocol called *TELNET*. TELNET allows a user at one site to establish a TCP connection to a login server at another, and then passes keystrokes from the local machine directly to the remote machine. TELNET is not sophisticated, but is widely available on the Internet. One significant advantage of TELNET is that it allows the user to specify a remote machine by name or by Internet address. Because it accepts Internet addresses, TELNET can be used with hosts even if the name-to-address binding cannot be established (e.g., when domain naming software is being debugged).

20.6 4.2 UNIX Rlogin

The 4.3BSD UNIX system includes a remote login service, *rlogin*, that understands trusted hosts. It allows system administrators to choose a set of machines over which login names and file access protections are globally shared, and to establish equivalences among user logins. Users can control access to their account by authorizing remote login based on remote host and remote user name. Thus, it is possible for a user to have login name X on one machine and Y on another, and be able to remotely login across the machine without typing a password each time.

Having automatic authorization makes remote login facilities useful for general purpose programs as well as human interaction. One variant of the 4.3BSD *rlogin* command, *rsh*, invokes a shell on the remote UNIX machine and passes the command line arguments to the shell. Thus, typing

```
rsh merlin ps
```

executes the *ps* command on machine merlin (with standard input and standard output connected across the network to the local terminal). The user sees the output as if logged into machine *merlin.* Because the user can arrange to have *rsh* to invoke remote commands without prompting for a login password, it can be used in programs as well as from the keyboard.

Because protocols like *rlogin* understand the local and remote computing environments, they communicate between them better than general purpose remote login protocols like TELNET. For example, *rlogin* understands the UNIX notions of *standard input*, *standard output*, and *standard error* file descriptors, and establishes three separate TCP connections to the remote machine for them. Thus, it is possible to type

```
rsh merlin ps > xxx
```

and have output from the remote command directed into file *xxx*. *Rlogin* also understands terminal control functions like flow control characters (typically Control—S and Control—Q), and arranges to stop output immediately without waiting for the delay required to send them across the network to the remote host. As a result, remote login sessions appear to behave almost exactly like local login sessions.

20.7 File Transport

File transport means copying a file from one machine to another. It is among the most frequently used network operations, and because files can be large objects, an operation that can generate much network traffic. Given a reliable end-to-end transport protocol like TCP, file transfer might seem trivial. However, the transfer of bytes from one machine to another can only be accomplished after files have been identified and transfer authorized.

Even though a process at one machine must initiate the transfer, many file transport protocols permit transfer in either direction. The client may send a file to the server or request a file from the server. To do so, the client must identify itself and obtain access permissions. Local permission is handled by the local operating system (e.g., by having users identify themselves at login using a password). Users accessing remote files must also identify themselves to the server machine's file system.

We have already seen an example remote file server and client in Chapters 13 and 14. It avoided the problem of access permission completely by executing the server as a user level process, and allowing the server to pass any file over the network that it could read. As a result, files on the server's machine that were marked *readable* became *world readable* without other users knowing it. Good file transport protocols provide better protection by restricting file access to only authorized users.

Remote authorization can be difficult, however, especially in an insecure network. File transport protocols that have clients send unencrypted passwords over a network are susceptible to eavesdroppers who, once they have discovered the password, will have access to all the files it protects. One way to simplify a family of protocols is to solve the authorization problem once and build other protocols on top of it.

20.8 DARPA File Transport Protocol (FTP)

The DARPA Internet protocol suite includes a file transport protocol, *FTP*. FTP allows authorized users to log into a remote system, identify themselves, list remote directories, copy files to or from the remote machine, and execute a few simple commands remotely (e.g., to obtain help with the remote machine file name syntax). In addition many implementations provide statistics on transfer rates and diagnostic aids like packet tracing.

A second DARPA protocol provides a Trivial File Transport Protocol, *TFTP*, intended for applications where the complex interactive environment is not needed. For example, manufacturers of diskless workstations can encode TFTP in read-only memory (ROM) chips, and use it to obtain an initial memory image when the machine is powered on. The program in ROM is called the system *bootstrap*. The advantage of using TFTP is that it allows bootstrapping code to use the same underlying internet protocols that the running system uses.

20.9 Mail Transport Protocols

Most users first encounter computer networks when they send or receive electronic mail to or from a remote site. Indeed, many users never use a network except for electronic mail. Mail is popular because it offers a fast, convenient method of transferring information. It can accommodate small notes or large voluminous memos, with a single mechanism. It should not surprise you to learn that more users send files with electronic mail than with file transfer protocols.

Mail delivery is a new concept because it differs fundamentally from other uses of networks that we have discussed. In all our examples, network protocols send packets directly to destinations, using short timeouts and immediate retransmission if no acknowledgement returns. When sending network mail, however, we must provide for cases where the remote machine or the network connections have failed. The user does not want to wait for the remote machine before continuing work, nor does the user want to have the transfer abort if the remote machine is not available.

To handle delayed delivery, mail systems use a technique known as *spooling*. When the user "sends" a mail message, the system places a copy in its private storage (spool) area along with identification of the recipient, and initiates transfer in background. The background process attempts to deliver the message by contacting the mail server on the destination machine. If it succeeds, the background process copies the message to the destination system's spool area and removes the local copy. If it fails, the background process records the time it tried, and terminates. Later, when some other user deposits mail or when the system mail daemon finds the message during its periodic sweep through the spool area, delivery will be attempted again. Finally, if the software finds that a mail message cannot be delivered after an extended time (e.g., 3 days), it returns the mail message to the sender.

20.10 DARPA Simplified Mail Transport Protocol (SMTP)

The DARPA mail transport protocol is known as *SMTP*, the Simplified Mail Transport Protocol. As you might guess, SMTP represents a simplification of an earlier Mail Transport Protocol (MTP). SMTP specifies how connections are made and how mail is transferred from one machine to another, but not how the user interface accepts mail from the user or presents the user with incoming mail.

20.11 Protocol Dependencies

The chart in Figure 20.1 shows dependencies among the example protocols we have discussed. Each enclosed polygon corresponds to one protocol, and resides directly above the polygons representing protocols that it uses. For example, the mail protocol, SMTP, depends on TCP, which depends on IP. On most systems, user processes can only access protocols at the level of TCP/UDP and higher. Both ARP and RARP appear in the diagram, even though not all machines or network technologies use them. In particular, RARP is seldom used except for diskless machines.

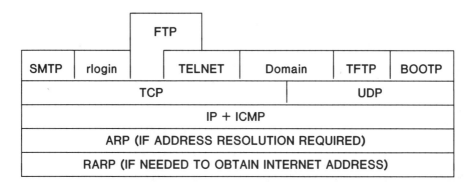

Figure 20.1 Dependencies among example higher-level protocols

20.12 Summary

Higher level protocols build on the concept of reliable delivery, using a positive acknowledgement with timeout and retransmission to achieve reliable delivery on an unreliable network. To make reliable protocols useful on an internetwork, they must adapt to varying delay, and must use end-to-end acknowledgements.

The highest levels of protocols provide user services like file and mail transfer, and remote login. To keep protocols orthogonal, such services usually allow lower levels of protocols for reliable delivery and authentication.

FOR FURTHER STUDY

Many high-level protocols have been proposed, but only a few are in common use. Tanenbaum [1981] discusses the International Standards Organization (ISO) protocol model, and the CCITT reliable end-to-end protocol, X.25. Falk [1983] contrasts the ARPANET with IBM's SNA network architecture.

Edge [1979] compares end-to-end protocols with the hop-by-hop approach. Saltzer, Reed, and Clark [1984] argue for having the highest level protocols perform end-to-end acknowledgement and error detection.

Details on the DARPA protocols discussed throughout this chapter can be found in Feinler *et. al.* [1985].

EXERCISES

20.1   What is a three-way handshake, and why is it needed?

20.2   How does a *sliding window* work in a reliable stream protocol?

20.3   Why should a stream protocol begin sending additional data before the acknowledgement for the first packet arrives?

20.4   Build a reliable stream protocol like TCP.

20.5   Use both TELNET and rlogin. What are the noticeable differences?

20.6   Why should file transport protocols compute a checksum on the file data they receive even when using a reliable end-to-end stream transfer protocol like TCP.

20.7   Find out whether FTP computes a checksum for files it transfers.

20.8   Outline a method that uses TFTP to bootstrap a diskless machine. Be careful. Exactly what Internet addresses do you use?

20.9   Implement TFTP for Xinu.

20.10 Some mail systems force the user to specify a sequence of machines through which the message should travel to reach its destination. The mail protocol in each machine merely passes the message on to the next machine. List three disadvantages of such a scheme.

20.11 Experiment with FTP or an equivalent protocol to see how fast you can transfer a file between two reasonably large systems across an Ethernet. Try the experiment when the network is busy and when it is idle. Explain the result.

20.12 What is a remote procedure call?

20.13 Folk lore says that operating systems come and go while protocols last forever. Survey your local computing site to see whether the operating systems or protocols have changed most recently.

20.14 Build TELNET client software for Xinu.

20.15 Create bootstrap ROMs for Xinu that load an initial memory image from a remote file server using TFTP.

20.16 Find out if your computing systems allows you to invoke SMTP directly.

Appendix 1

Differences Between Xinu Versions 6 and 7

Versions of the code

Xinu has evolved over six years, and has enjoyed many experiments and variations. Researchers and students at Bell Labs, Purdue, and elsewhere have used Xinu as a convenient utility, transported it to many new machines, and made substantial extensions. Throughout the evolution, versions have been frozen and stabilized, primarily to provide a base for further experiments. The stabilized versions are numbered as follows:

Versions 1−5. Early versions, numbered 1 through 5, were developed pell-mell. Within 6 weeks from the start of the project, Version 5 was running. It contained most of the Xinu process management code, including the context switch, scheduler, and semaphore implementation, as well as enough I/O routines to support I/O to the console device. However, version 5 suffered two major problems. It lacked consistency among subsystems, and the code still contained vestiges of early designs and mechanisms that had been abandoned.

Version 6. Over several months following the completion of version 5, the author refined the multilevel structure of Xinu, producing a new version in which the old mechanisms were completely restructured. During that time, messages, ports, the device switch table, and the Xinu ring software was added. When the new version became stable enough for others to use, it was released as version 6.

Version 6b. Version 6 became the basis for the code in volume I of the *Operating System Design* text. To accommodate printing in the text, the code from version 6 was reformatted in minor ways (e.g., long comment lines were wrapped onto two lines to make them fit the page). The resulting software, which became known as version 6b, was distributed widely, and is often referred to as version 6.

Version 7. In the two years following publication of volume I, Xinu evolved further, with emphasis being placed on new components that would support a diskless workstation. The internetwork software was incorporated to form version 7, the code shown throughout this book. The additions to version 6b are substantial, both in size and scope. However, the amount of code that was modified to support the new additions is relatively small.

The remainder of this appendix is broken into three sections. The next section summarizes the additions to version 6b code found in version 7. Following the list of additions comes a short section that summarizes changes to version 6b routines made to accommodte version 7. Finally, the bulk of the appendix consists of listings of the modified routines. They have been included here merely for reference.

Version 7 Additions

The following components comprise the primary additions made between version 6b and version 7 Xinu.

- Ethernet Device Driver.
- ARP protocol software to place ARP queries to other systems and to reply to incoming queries.
- RARP protocol software to broadcast RARP requests and interpret responses.
- IP protocol software to send and receive Internet datagrams.
- ICMP protocol software to handle ICMP echo request messages.
- UDP protocol software to send and receive UDP datagrams through a pseudo-device interface.
- Remote file system using a pseudo-device interface that allows a process to open, read, write, and close remote files, as well as a stateless file server that executes under UNIX.
- Generic file commands *access*, *remove*, and *rename*.
- Syntactic namespace that provides an abstract naming environment using prefix patterns to map names to underlying devices.
- User interface patterned after the UNIX shell.
- Procedures for setting and interpreting a time-of-day-clock.
- Small set of shell commands.
- Mechanism for timing message reception.

Modifications to Version 6

In adding the new communications and user interface components, the following minor modifications were made to existing Xinu software:

- Changes to the process table (*proctab*) and process management routines (*kill, resched, send,* and *receive*) to accommodate a new process state for receiving a message with timeout.
- Changes to the scheduler (*resched*) to perform stack range checking at each context switch.
- Changes to the clock initialization and clock interrupt handler (*clkinit,* and *clkint*) to keep a time-of-day clock.
- Changes to routines that handle real-time clock management to allow removing a sleeping process from the clock queue (*wakeup* and *kill*).
- Changes to the tty driver to honor an interrupt character (*tty.h* and *ttyinit*), and a modification that permits users to open tty devices (*ttyopen*).
- Changes to the process table, process creation, and process termination routines (*proctab, create, kill*) to handle automatic closing of standard input and output files.
- Changes to the process termination routine (*kill*) to send a message to the next-of-kin process.
- Changes to the tty driver to make it line oriented (*ttyread, ttygetc, ttyiin*).

The following pages contain listings of modified files in alphabetical order, beginning with the clock interrupt dispatcher.

```
/* clkinit.c - clkinit */

#include <conf.h>
#include <kernel.h>
#include <sleep.h>

/* real-time clock variables and sleeping process queue pointers        */

#ifdef  RTCLOCK
int     count6;                 /* counts in 60ths of a second 6-0       */
int     count10;                /* counts in 10ths of a second 10-0      */
int     clmutex;                /* mutual exclusion for time-of-day      */
long    clktime;                /* current time in seconds since 1/1/70 */
int     defclk;                 /* non-zero, then deferring clock count */
int     clkdiff;                /* deferred clock ticks                  */
int     slnempty;               /* FALSE if the sleep queue is empty     */
int     *sltop;                 /* address of key part of top entry in   */
                                /* the sleep queue if slnempty==TRUE     */
int     clockq;                 /* head of queue of sleeping processes   */
int     preempt;                /* preemption counter.  Current process  */
                                /* is preempted when it reaches zero;    */
                                /* set in resched; counts in ticks       */
int     clkruns;                /* set TRUE iff clock exists by setclkr   */
#else
int     clkruns = FALSE;        /* no clock configured; be sure sleep    */
#endif                          /*   doesn't wait forever                */

/*
 *------------------------------------------------------------------------
 * clkinit - initialize the clock and sleep queue (called at startup)
 *------------------------------------------------------------------------
 */
clkinit()
{
        int *vector;

        vector = (int *) CVECTOR;       /* set up interrupt vector       */
        *vector++ = clkint;
        *vector = DISABLE;
        setclkr();
        preempt = QUANTUM;              /* initial time quantum          */
        count6 = 6;                     /* 60ths of a sec. counter       */
        count10 = 10;                   /* 10ths of a sec. counter       */
        clmutex = screate(1);           /* semaphore for tod clock       */
```

```
        clktime = 0L;            /* initially a low number       */
        slnempty = FALSE;        /* initially, no process asleep */
        clkdiff = 0;             /* zero deferred ticks          */
        defclk = 0;              /* clock is not deferred        */
        clockq = newqueue();     /* allocate clock queue in q    */
}
```

```
/* clkint.s -  clkint */


/*------------------------------------------------------------------------
/* clkint  --  real-time clock interrupt service routine
/*------------------------------------------------------------------------
        .globl  _clkint
_clkint:
        dec     _count6          / Is this the 6th interrupt?
        bgt     clret            / no => return
        mov     $6,_count6       / yes=> reset counter&continue
        dec     _count10         / Is this 10th tick?
        bgt     clckdef          / no => process tick
        mov     $10.,_count10    / yes=> reset counter&continue
        add     $1,2+_clktime    / increment time-of-day clock
        adc     _clktime
clckdef:
        tst     _defclk          / Are clock ticks deferred?
        beq     notdef           / no => go process this tick
        inc     _clkdiff         / yes=> count in clkdiff and
        rtt                      /        return quickly
notdef:
        tst     _slnempty        / Is sleep queue nonempty?
        beq     clpreem          / no => go process preemption
        dec     *_sltop          / yes=> decrement delta key
        bgt     clpreem          /        on first process,
        mov     r0,-(sp)         /        calling wakeup if
        mov     r1,-(sp)         /        it reaches zero
        jsr     pc,_wakeup       /        (interrupt routine
        mov     (sp)+,r1         /         saves & restores r0
        mov     (sp)+,r0         /         and r1; C doesn't)
clpreem:
        dec     _preempt         / Decrement preemption counter
        bgt     clret            /   and call resched if it
        mov     r0,-(sp)         /   reaches zero
        mov     r1,-(sp)         /      (As before, interrupt
        jsr     pc,_resched      /       routine must save &
        mov     (sp)+,r1         /       restore r0 and r1
        mov     (sp)+,r0         /       because C doesn't)
clret:
        rtt                      / Return from interrupt
```

```
/* create.c - create, newpid */

#include <conf.h>
#include <kernel.h>
#include <proc.h>
#include <mem.h>
#include <io.h>

/*------------------------------------------------------------------------
 *  create  -  create a process to start running a procedure
 *------------------------------------------------------------------------
 */
SYSCALL create(procaddr,ssize,priority,name,nargs,args)
        int     *procaddr;              /* procedure address          */
        int     ssize;                  /* stack size in words        */
        int     priority;               /* process priority > 0       */
        char    *name;                  /* name (for debugging)       */
        int     nargs;                  /* number of args that follow */
        int     args;                   /* arguments (treated like an */
                                        /* array in the code)         */
{
        int     pid;                    /* stores new process id      */
        struct  pentry *pptr;           /* pointer to proc. table entry */
        int     i;
        int     *a;                     /* points to list of args     */
        int     *saddr;                 /* stack address              */
        char    ps;                     /* saved processor status     */
        int     INITRET();
        disable(ps);
        ssize = roundew(ssize);
        if ( ssize < MINSTK || ((saddr=getstk(ssize)) == SYSERR ) ||
                (pid=newpid()) == SYSERR || isodd(procaddr) ||
                priority < 1 ) {
                restore(ps);
                return(SYSERR);
        }
        numproc++;
        pptr = &proctab[pid];
        pptr->pstate = PRSUSP;
        for (i=0 ; i<PNMLEN && (pptr->pname[i]=name[i])!=0 ; i++)
                ;
        pptr->pprio = priority;
        pptr->pbase = (short)saddr;
        pptr->pstklen = ssize;
```

```
        pptr->psem = 0;
        pptr->phasmsg = FALSE;
        pptr->plimit = (short)((unsigned)saddr - ssize + sizeof(int));
        *saddr-- = MAGIC;
        pptr->pargs = nargs;
        for (i=0 ; i<PNREGS ; i++)
                pptr->pregs[i]=INITREG;
        pptr->pregs[PC] = pptr->paddr = (short)procaddr;
        pptr->pregs[PS] = INITPS;
        pptr->pnxtkin = BADPID;
        pptr->pdevs[0] = pptr->pdevs[1] = BADDEV;
        a = (&args) + (nargs-1);        /* point to last argument       */
        for ( ; nargs > 0 ; nargs--)    /* machine dependent; copy args */
                *saddr-- = *a--;        /* onto created process' stack  */
        *saddr = (int)INITRET;          /* push on return address       */
        pptr->pregs[SP] = (int)saddr;
        restore(ps);
        return(pid);
}


/*------------------------------------------------------------------------
 * newpid  --  obtain a new (free) process id
 *------------------------------------------------------------------------
 */
LOCAL   newpid()
{
        int     pid;                    /* process id to return         */
        int     i;

        for (i=0 ; i<NPROC ; i++) {     /* check all NPROC slots        */
                if ( (pid=nextproc--) <= 0)
                        nextproc = NPROC-1;
                if (proctab[pid].pstate == PRFREE)
                        return(pid);
        }
        return(SYSERR);
}
```

```
/* kill.c - kill */

#include <conf.h>
#include <kernel.h>
#include <proc.h>
#include <sem.h>
#include <mem.h>
#include <io.h>

/*------------------------------------------------------------------------
 * kill  --  kill a process and remove it from the system
 *------------------------------------------------------------------------
 */
SYSCALL kill(pid)
        int     pid;                    /* process to kill              */
{
        struct  pentry *pptr;           /* points to proc. table for pid*/
        int     dev;
        char    ps;

        disable(ps);
        if (isbadpid(pid) || (pptr= &proctab[pid])->pstate==PRFREE) {
                restore(ps);
                return(SYSERR);
        }
        if (--numproc == 0)
                xdone();
        dev = pptr->pdevs[0];
        if (! isbaddev(dev) )
                close(dev);
        dev = pptr->pdevs[1];
        if (! isbaddev(dev) )
                close(dev);
        send(pptr->pnxtkin, pid);
        freestk(pptr->pbase, pptr->pstklen);
        switch (pptr->pstate) {

          case PRCURR:  pptr->pstate = PRFREE;  /* suicide */
                        resched();

          case PRWAIT:  semaph[pptr->psem].semcnt++;
                                                /* fall through */
          case PRREADY: dequeue(pid);
                        pptr->pstate = PRFREE;
```

```
                    break;

        case PRSLEEP:
        case PRTRECV: unsleep(pid);

                                                /* fall through */
        default:      pptr->pstate = PRFREE;
        }
        restore(ps);
        return(OK);
}
```

```
/* proc.h - isbadpid */

/* process table declarations and defined constants                       */

#ifndef NPROC                          /* set the number of processes  */
#define NPROC          10              /*  allowed if not already done */
#endif


/* process state constants */

#define PRCURR         '\001'          /* process is currently running */
#define PRFREE         '\002'          /* process slot is free         */
#define PRREADY        '\003'          /* process is on ready queue    */
#define PRRECV         '\004'          /* process waiting for message  */
#define PRSLEEP        '\005'          /* process is sleeping          */
#define PRSUSP         '\006'          /* process is suspended         */
#define PRWAIT         '\007'          /* process is on semaphore queue*/
#define PRTRECV        '\010'          /* process is timing a receive  */


/* miscellaneous process definitions */

#define PNREGS         9               /* size of saved register area  */
#define PNMLEN         8               /* length of process "name"     */
#define NULLPROC       0               /* id of the null process; it   */
                                       /*  is always eligible to run   */
#define BADPID         -1              /* used when invalid pid needed */

#define isbadpid(x)    (x<=0 || x>=NPROC)


/* process table entry */

struct  pentry  {
        char    pstate;                /* process state: PRCURR, etc.  */
        short   pprio;                 /* process priority             */
        short   pregs[PNREGS];         /* saved regs. R0-R5,SP,PC,PS   */
        short   psem;                  /* semaphore if process waiting */
        short   pmsg;                  /* message sent to this process */
        Bool    phasmsg;               /* True iff pmsg is valid       */
        short   pbase;                 /* base of run time stack       */
        short   pstklen;               /* stack length                 */
        short   plimit;                /* lowest extent of stack       */
        char    pname[PNMLEN];         /* process name                 */
        short   pargs;                 /* initial number of arguments  */
        short   paddr;                 /* initial code address         */
```

```
        short    pnxtkin;                /* next-of-kin notified of death*/
        short    pdevs[2];               /* devices to close upon exit   */
};

extern  struct   pentry proctab[];
extern  int      numproc;                /* currently active processes   */
extern  int      nextproc;               /* search point for free slot   */
extern  int      currpid;                /* currently executing process  */
```

```
/* send.c - send */

#include <conf.h>
#include <kernel.h>
#include <proc.h>

/*------------------------------------------------------------------------
 *  send  --  send a message to another process
 *------------------------------------------------------------------------
 */
SYSCALL send(pid, msg)
int     pid;
int     msg;
{
        struct  pentry *pptr;           /* receiver's proc. table addr. */
        char    ps;

        disable(ps);
        if (isbadpid(pid) || ( (pptr= &proctab[pid])->pstate == PRFREE)
           || pptr->phasmsg) {
                restore(ps);
                return(SYSERR);
        }
        pptr->pmsg = msg;               /* deposit message               */
        pptr->phasmsg = TRUE;
        if (pptr->pstate == PRRECV)     /* if receiver waits, start it   */
                ready(pid, RESCHYES);
        else if (pptr->pstate == PRTRECV) {
                unsleep(pid);
                ready(pid, RESCHYES);
        }
        restore(ps);
        return(OK);
}
```

```
/* sendf.c - sendf */

#include <conf.h>
#include <kernel.h>
#include <proc.h>


/*------------------------------------------------------------------------
 *  sendf  --  sendf a message to another process, forcing delivery
 *------------------------------------------------------------------------
 */
SYSCALL sendf(pid, msg)
int     pid;
int     msg;
{
        struct  pentry  *pptr;
        char    ps;

        disable(ps);
        if (isbadpid(pid)||((pptr= &proctab[pid])->pstate == PRFREE)) {
                restore(ps);
                return(SYSERR);
        }
        pptr->pmsg = msg;
        pptr->phasmsg = TRUE;
        if (pptr->pstate == PRRECV)
                ready(pid, RESCHYES);
        else if (pptr->pstate == PRTRECV) {
                unsleep(pid);
                ready(pid, RESCHYES);
        }
        restore(ps);
        return(OK);
}
```

```
/* resched.c  -  resched */

#include <conf.h>
#include <kernel.h>
#include <proc.h>
#include <q.h>


/*------------------------------------------------------------------------
 * resched  --  reschedule processor to highest priority ready process
 *
 * Notes:        Upon entry, currpid gives current process id.
 *               Proctab[currpid].pstate gives correct NEXT state for
 *                      current process if other than PRCURR.
 *------------------------------------------------------------------------
 */
int     resched()
{
        register struct pentry  *optr;  /* pointer to old process entry */
        register struct pentry  *nptr;  /* pointer to new process entry */

        /* no switch needed if current process priority higher than next*/

        if ( ( (optr= &proctab[currpid])->pstate == PRCURR) &&
            (lastkey(rdytail)<optr->pprio))
                return(OK);

        /* force context switch */

        if (optr->pstate == PRCURR) {
                optr->pstate = PRREADY;
                insert(currpid,rdyhead,optr->pprio);
        }

        /* remove highest priority process at end of ready list */

        nptr = &proctab[ (currpid = getlast(rdytail)) ];
        nptr->pstate = PRCURR;                  /* mark it currently running     */
#ifdef  STKCHK
        if ( *( (int *)nptr->pbase  ) != MAGIC ) {
                kprintf("Bad magic pid=%d, value=%o, at %o\n",
                        currpid, *( (int *)nptr->pbase ), nptr->pbase);
                panic("stack corrupted");
        }
        if ( ((unsigned)nptr->pregs[SP]) < ((unsigned)nptr->plimit) ) {
```

```
              kprintf("Bad SP pid=%d (%s), lim=%o will be %o\n",
                      currpid, nptr->pname, nptr->plimit,
                      nptr->pregs[SP]);
              panic("stack overflow");
      }
#endif
#ifdef  RTCLOCK
      preempt = QUANTUM;                      /* reset preemption counter   */
#endif
      ctxsw(optr->pregs,nptr->pregs);

      /* The OLD process returns here when resumed. */
      return(OK);
}
```

```
/* receive.c - receive */

#include <conf.h>
#include <kernel.h>
#include <proc.h>


/*------------------------------------------------------------------------
 *  receive  -  wait for a message and return it
 *------------------------------------------------------------------------
 */
SYSCALL receive()
{
        struct  pentry  *pptr;
        int     msg;
        char    ps;

        disable(ps);
        pptr = &proctab[currpid];
        if ( !pptr->phasmsg ) {          /* if no message, wait for one  */
                pptr->pstate = PRRECV;
                resched();
        }
        msg = pptr->pmsg;                /* retrieve message             */
        pptr->phasmsg = FALSE;
        restore(ps);
        return(msg);
}
```

```
/* recvclr.c - recvclr */

#include <conf.h>
#include <kernel.h>
#include <proc.h>


/*------------------------------------------------------------------------
 *  recvclr  --  clear messages, returning waiting message (if any)
 *------------------------------------------------------------------------
 */
SYSCALL recvclr()
{
        char    ps;
        int     msg;

        disable(ps);
        if ( proctab[currpid].phasmsg ) {         /* existing message?    */
                proctab[currpid].phasmsg = FALSE;
                msg = proctab[currpid].pmsg;
        } else
                msg = OK;
        restore(ps);
        return(msg);
}
```

```
/* ttyopen.c - ttyopen */

#include <conf.h>
#include <kernel.h>

/*------------------------------------------------------------------------
 *  ttyopen - open tty device and return descriptor (for namespace)
 *------------------------------------------------------------------------
 */
ttyopen(devptr, nam, mode)
struct  devsw   *devptr;
char    *nam;
char    *mode;
{

        /* This routine is not usually used to open tty devices,   */
        /* but is provided so that automatic calls to open do not  */
        /* fail.  It returns SYSERR unless called with a null name */

        if (*nam == '\0')
                return( devptr->dvnum );
        else
                return(SYSERR);

}
```

```
/* ttyread.c - ttyread, readcopy */

#include <conf.h>
#include <kernel.h>
#include <tty.h>
#include <io.h>

/*------------------------------------------------------------------------
 *  ttyread - read one or more characters from a tty device
 *------------------------------------------------------------------------
 */
ttyread(devptr, buff, count)
struct  devsw   *devptr;
int count;
char *buff;
{
        char ps;
        register struct tty *iptr;
        int avail, nread;
        char ch, eofch;
        int     donow, dolater;

        if (count < 0)
                return(SYSERR);
        disable(ps);
        if ( (avail=scount((iptr= &tty[devptr->dvminor])->isem)) < 0)
                avail = 0;
        if (count == 0) {         /* read whatever is available */
                if (avail == 0) {
                        restore(ps);
                        return(0);
                }
                count = avail;
        }
        if (count < avail) {
                donow = count;
                dolater = 0;
        } else {
                donow = avail;
                dolater = count - avail;
        }
        nread = 0;
        if (donow > 0) {
                ch = iptr->ibuff[iptr->itail++];
```

```
                    if (iptr->itail >= IBUFLEN)
                            iptr->itail = 0;
                    if ( ((eofch=iptr->ieofc) == ch) && iptr->ieof) {
                                    sreset(iptr->isem, avail-1);
                                    restore(ps);
                                    return(EOF);
                    }
                    *buff++ = ch;
                    for (nread=1 ; nread < donow ; ) {
                            ch = iptr->ibuff[iptr->itail];
                            if ( (ch==eofch) && iptr->ieof) {
                                    sreset(iptr->isem, avail - nread);
                                    restore(ps);
                                    return(nread);
                            }
                            *buff++ = ch;
                            if (++iptr->itail >= IBUFLEN)
                                    iptr->itail = 0;
                            nread++;
                            if (ch == NEWLINE || ch == RETURN) {
                                    sreset(iptr->isem, avail - nread);
                                    restore(ps);
                                    return(nread);
                            }
                    }
                    sreset(iptr->isem, avail - nread);
            }
            donow = nread;
            for (nread=0 ; nread < dolater ; ) {
                    wait(iptr->isem);
                    ch = iptr->ibuff[iptr->itail];
                    if (ch == iptr->ieofc && iptr->ieof) {
                            if (nread == 0 && donow == 0) {
                                    if (++iptr->itail >= IBUFLEN)
                                    iptr->itail = 0;
                                    restore(ps);
                                    return(EOF);
                            }
                            signal(iptr->isem);
                            break;
                    }
                    *buff++ = ch;
                    nread++;
                    if (++iptr->itail >= IBUFLEN)
                            iptr->itail = 0;
```

```
                if (ch == NEWLINE || ch == RETURN)
                        break;
        }
        restore(ps);
        return(donow + nread);
}
```

```
/* ttygetc.c - ttygetc */

#include <conf.h>
#include <kernel.h>
#include <tty.h>
#include <io.h>

/*------------------------------------------------------------------------
 *   ttygetc - read one character from a tty device
 *------------------------------------------------------------------------
 */
ttygetc(devptr)
struct  devsw   *devptr;
{
        char    ps;
        int     ch;
        struct  tty     *iptr;

        disable(ps);
        iptr = &tty[devptr->dvminor];
        wait(iptr->isem);                       /* wait for a character in buff */
        ch = LOWBYTE & iptr->ibuff[iptr->itail++];
        if (iptr->itail >= IBUFLEN)
                iptr->itail = 0;
        if (iptr->ieof && (iptr->ieofc == ch) )
                ch = EOF;
        restore(ps);
        return(ch);
}
```

```
/* ttyiin.c ttyiin, erase1, eputc, echoch */

#include <conf.h>
#include <kernel.h>
#include <tty.h>
#include <io.h>
#include <slu.h>


/*------------------------------------------------------------------------
 *  ttyiin  --  lower-half tty device driver for input interrupts
 *------------------------------------------------------------------------
 */
INTPROC ttyiin(iptr)
        register struct tty     *iptr;  /* pointer to tty block        */
{
        register struct csr *cptr;
        register int    ch;
        int     ct;

        cptr = iptr->ioaddr;
        if ( (ch=cptr->crbuf) & SLUERMASK)        /* read char from device*/
                return;                           /* discard if error     */
        if (iptr->imode == IMRAW) {
                if (scount(iptr->isem) >= IBUFLEN) {
                        return;                   /* discard if no space  */
                }
                iptr->ibuff[iptr->ihead++] = ch & SLUCHMASK;
                if (iptr->ihead >= IBUFLEN)       /* wrap buffer pointer  */
                        iptr->ihead = 0;
                signal(iptr->isem);
        } else {                                  /* cbreak | cooked mode */
                ch &= SLUCHMASK;
                if ( ch == RETURN && iptr->icrlf )
                        ch = NEWLINE;
                if (iptr->iintr && ch == iptr->iintrc) {
                        send(iptr->iintpid, INTRMSG);
                        eputc(ch, iptr, cptr);
                        return;
                }
                if (iptr->oflow) {
                        if (ch == iptr->ostart) {
                                iptr->oheld = FALSE;
                                cptr->ctstat = SLUENABLE;
                                return;
```

```
                        }
                        if (ch == iptr->ostop) {
                                iptr->oheld = TRUE;
                                return;
                        }
                }
                iptr->oheld = FALSE;
                if (iptr->imode == IMCBREAK) {              /* cbreak mode  */
                        if (scount(iptr->isem) >= IBUFLEN) {
                                eputc(iptr->ifullc,iptr,cptr);
                                return;
                        }
                        iptr->ibuff[iptr->ihead++] = ch;
                        if (iptr->ihead >= IBUFLEN)
                                iptr->ihead = 0;
                        if (iptr->iecho)
                                echoch(ch,iptr,cptr);
                        if (scount(iptr->isem) < IBUFLEN)
                                signal(iptr->isem);
                } else {                                    /* cooked mode  */
                        if (ch == iptr->ikillc && iptr->ikill) {
                                iptr->ihead -= iptr->icursor;
                                if (iptr->ihead < 0)
                                        iptr->ihead += IBUFLEN;
                                iptr->icursor = 0;
                                eputc(RETURN,iptr,cptr);
                                eputc(NEWLINE,iptr,cptr);
                                return;
                        }
                        if (ch == iptr->ierasec && iptr->ierase) {
                                if (iptr->icursor > 0) {
                                        iptr->icursor--;
                                        erase1(iptr,cptr);
                                }
                                return;
                        }
                        if (ch == NEWLINE || ch == RETURN ||
                            (iptr->ieof && ch == iptr->ieofc)) {
                                if (iptr->iecho) {
                                        echoch(ch,iptr,cptr);
                                        if (ch == iptr->ieofc)
                                                echoch(NEWLINE,iptr,cptr);
                                }
                                iptr->ibuff[iptr->ihead++] = ch;
                                if (iptr->ihead >= IBUFLEN)
```

```
                                          iptr->ihead = 0;
                                  ct = iptr->icursor+1; /* +1 for \n or \r*/
                                  iptr->icursor = 0;
                                  signaln(iptr->isem,ct);
                                  return;
                          }
                          ct = scount(iptr->isem);
                          ct = ct < 0 ? 0 : ct;
                          if ((ct + iptr->icursor) >= IBUFLEN-1) {
                                  eputc(iptr->ifullc,iptr,cptr);
                                  return;
                          }
                          if (iptr->iecho)
                                  echoch(ch,iptr,cptr);
                          iptr->icursor++;
                          iptr->ibuff[iptr->ihead++] = ch;
                          if (iptr->ihead >= IBUFLEN)
                                  iptr->ihead = 0;
                  }
          }
}


/*-------------------------------------------------------------------------
 * erase1 -- erase one character honoring erasing backspace
 *-------------------------------------------------------------------------
 */
LOCAL erase1(iptr,cptr)
        struct  tty     *iptr;
        struct  csr     *cptr;
{
        char    ch;

        if (--(iptr->ihead) < 0)
                iptr->ihead += IBUFLEN;
        ch = iptr->ibuff[iptr->ihead];
        if (iptr->iecho) {
                if (ch < BLANK || ch == 0177) {
                        if (iptr->evis) {
                                eputc(BACKSP,iptr,cptr);
                                if (iptr->ieback) {
                                        eputc(BLANK,iptr,cptr);
                                        eputc(BACKSP,iptr,cptr);
                                }
                        }
                        eputc(BACKSP,iptr,cptr);
```

```
                              if (iptr->ieback) {
                                      eputc(BLANK,iptr,cptr);
                                      eputc(BACKSP,iptr,cptr);
                              }
                      } else {
                              eputc(BACKSP,iptr,cptr);
                              if (iptr->ieback) {
                                      eputc(BLANK,iptr,cptr);
                                      eputc(BACKSP,iptr,cptr);
                              }
                      }
              } else
                      cptr->ctstat = SLUENABLE;
      }


      /*-------------------------------------------------------------------
       * echoch  --  echo a character with visual and ocrlf options
       *-------------------------------------------------------------------
       */
      LOCAL echoch(ch, iptr, cptr)
              char    ch;             /* character to echo                */
              struct  tty   *iptr;    /* pointer to I/O block for this devptr */
              struct  csr   *cptr;    /* csr address for this devptr      */
      {
              if ((ch==NEWLINE||ch==RETURN)&&iptr->ecrlf) {
                      eputc(RETURN,iptr,cptr);
                      eputc(NEWLINE,iptr,cptr);
              } else if ((ch<BLANK||ch==0177) && iptr->evis) {
                      eputc(UPARROW,iptr,cptr);
                      eputc(ch+0100,iptr,cptr);            /* make it printable  */
              } else {
                      eputc(ch,iptr,cptr);
              }
      }


      /*-------------------------------------------------------------------
       * eputc - put one character in the echo queue
       *-------------------------------------------------------------------
       */
      LOCAL eputc(ch,iptr,cptr)
              char    ch;
              struct  tty   *iptr;
              struct  csr   *cptr;
      {
              iptr->ebuff[iptr->ehead++] = ch;
```

```
        if (iptr->ehead >= EBUFLEN)
                iptr->ehead = 0;
cptr->ctstat = SLUENABLE;
}
```

```
/* wakeup.c - wakeup */

#include <conf.h>
#include <kernel.h>
#include <proc.h>
#include <q.h>
#include <sleep.h>

/*------------------------------------------------------------------------
 * wakeup  --  called by clock interrupt dispatcher to awaken processes
 *------------------------------------------------------------------------
 */
INTPROC wakeup()
{
        while (nonempty(clockq) && firstkey(clockq) <= 0)
                ready(getfirst(clockq),RESCHNO);
        if ( slnempty = nonempty(clockq) )
                sltop = (int *) & q[q[clockq].qnext].qkey;
        resched();
}
```

Appendix 2

Xinu Programmer's Manual

Version 7

(XINU IS NOT UNIX)

The Xinu Programmer's Manual contains a description of the Xinu software. It has been divided into three sections, following the style of the *UNIX Programmer's Manual*. This introduction explains how to use the Xinu software to compile, download, execute, and debug a C program. It also contains a set of informal implementation notes that give the character of Xinu.

The body of the manual gives a terse description of Xinu procedures and the details of their arguments — it is intended as a quick reference for programmers, not as a way to learn Xinu. Section 1 describes cross-development commands that run on the host computer. These cross-compile, cross-assemble, cross-load, download, upload, and analyze programs. Section 2 describes Xinu system procedures that programs call to invoke operating system services. Section 3 describes procedures available from the standard libraries. (From the programmer's point of view, there is little distinction between library routines and system calls.)

As in the UNIX manual, each page describes one command, system call, or library routine; section numbers appear in the page footer as "(digit)" following the name of the program. Within a section all pages are arranged in alphabetical order. References have the same form as headers (e.g., "getc(2)" refers to the page for "getc" in section 2). Related commands are sometimes mentioned on one page (which may make it difficult for beginners to find them).

413

A Short Introduction To Xinu
and the Cross-Development Software

How to Use Xinu

Architecture. Xinu comes in two parts: a cross-development environment that runs on the host machine (usually a Digital Equipment Corp. VAX), and an independent system that runs on the microcomputer (usually a Digital Equipment Corporation LSI 11/2). The microcomputer is connected to the host over an asynchronous serial line like those used to connect terminals. From the point of view of the host, the microcomputer is simply another device that transmits and receives characters; from the point of view of the micro, the host is merely a console terminal that transmits and receives characters.

Overview. To run a program under Xinu, you create the source file on the host machine, and invoke cross-development software to compile and load the program along with the Xinu system. Once a complete memory image has been produced, it can be downloaded onto the microcomputer where it executes independent of the host. During execution, you invoke a program on the host that captures characters emitted by the micro and displays them on the terminal screen, and sends characters typed at the keyboard to the micro. Thus, your terminal on the host appears to be connected directly to the micro. If the micro crashes, it can be restarted without downloading (provided the crash did not destroy the program in memory). To help debug severe crashes, the contents of memory on the micro can be uploaded to a file on the host where a post-mortem program can analyze the state and report problems.

Cross-Development commands. The cross-development system contains a C compiler, linking loader, downloader, uploader, and post-mortem debugger as well as a few miscellaneous commands. The details can be found in section 1 of this manual. These commands probably reside in the Xinu "bin" directory on your system; the directory name must be part of your PATH for you to execute them. If they are not in directory /usr/Xinu/bin, consult whoever installed Xinu to find out the bin directory name and add it to your path.

Compiling programs. The command *cc11* works like the UNIX *cc* command. It invokes the C cross-compiler, cross-assembler, and cross-loader to translate C programs into a memory image. Like *cc*, the actions of *cc11* depend on the file names passed to it as arguments — names ending in ".c" are assumed to be C programs, those ending in ".s" are assumed to be assembler programs, and those ending in ".o" are assumed to be previously compiled object programs. Unless you specify otherwise, *cc11* compiles C programs, assembles assembler programs, and loads object programs to produce a memory image in file *a.out*. Normally, the memory image contains the Xinu operating system along with your program (you can ask *cc11* to leave out the operating system and just prepare a "stand-alone" program).

Downloading. Command *download* reads file *a.out*, and loads the memory image into the microcomputer (it will look for the memory image in a different file if you instruct it to do so). Usually, *download* is invoked with an argument "-a5" that causes the microcomputer to delay for five seconds before starting execution of the downloaded program.

Interacting with the Micro. The microcomputer on which Xinu runs is attached to the host like a peripheral device. The program *odt* "connects" your terminal to the microcomputer by relaying characters between the terminal and the device. Characters that arrive from the micro are sent to your terminal, while characters typed on your keyboard are sent to the micro. *Odt* can be invoked at any time, but it is most often used just after a *download* so you can see the output of the program as it runs. *Odt* will halt the microcomputer for you by "breaking" the console line if you type the 2-character sequence backslash (\) followed by null (CONTROL-@). To proceed again, type uppercase-P (see the LSI 11 manual for more information on the "odt" mode).

Debugging a crash. If the program running on the micro crashes, the cause of the trouble may not be easy to spot. Help is available from a post-mortem debugger, *pm*. You must first execute command *upload* to copy the complete memory image from the micro into a file on the host. By default, the image file is named *core11*. After the *core11* file has been created, run command *pm* to cull through it and print out the system status. *Pm* uses both *core11* and *a.out* to diagnose the problem (as usual, the actual file names can be changed if you don't happen to like them).

An Example

Create a C program. For example, here is a C program that prints the string "Hello world." on the console terminal and exits. (*Printf* is a system (library) procedure that prints formatted strings on the console; other system commands are described in sections 2 and 3 of this manual):

```
/* example C program in file example.c */
main( )
{
    printf("Hello world.\n");
}
```

Compile and Download. Cross-compile the program, download it onto the micro, and connect your terminal to the micro with the following commands:

```
cc11 example.c
download -a5
odt
```

The cross-compiler will compile the C program, and load it along with the Xinu system, leaving file *a.out* in your current directory. The downloader will copy the image from *a.out* into the micro and start it executing (after a delay of five seconds). During downloading, you will see a count of the bytes remaining as blocks are transferred. Finally, *odt* will connect your terminal to the micro (the 5-second delay leaves time for the VAX to start *odt*). When the micro begins execution you will see a few Xinu system startup messages followed by the program output. When all of your processes complete (in this case, when the single program terminates), you will see a system termination message. The output is:

```
Xinu Version 7.2 5/10/86
57346 real mem
21268 avail mem
clock enabled


Hello world.


All user processes have completed.
```

Re-run the program. To re-run the program without downloading the micro again, type:

```
\ CNTL-@
1000G
```

The 2-character sequence backslash (\) null (CNTL-@) causes *odt* to halt the LSI 11 and place it in "ODT" mode. The LSI 11 responds with an at-sign prompt. The sequence "1000G" starts the machine executing at location 1000 (octal). To get out of *odt*, kill the process by typing the "DELETE" key (or Control-C if you use 4.2 bsd UNIX). Note that killing *odt* does not stop the micro — it merely disconnects your terminal.

Upload the memory. You may want to see what processes are (were) running. To retrieve the memory image and analyze it, run the commands:

```
upload
pm
```

Warning: *upload* destroys the contents of memory on the micro as it executes, so the micro cannot be restarted again after uploading. Also note that if you interrupt (i.e. kill) the uploader and then restart it, the image it retrieves will be incorrect.

Interpreting pm. *Pm* reports whether the program text has been changed and the status of each process. If the output from *pm* seems unreasonable, check for the following common errors. If significant portions of the program have been changed, it may mean a stack overflow occurred; totally meaningless process information often indicates that the overflow extended into the process table. Having only one or two bad process states in an otherwise meaningful set may indicate that the context switch ended up with no ready or current processes; this only happens if you modify the system code or add your own device driver. When experimenting with device drivers, look carefully at the status of the null process after a crash — if you find it sleeping, waiting, receiving, or suspended then you probably have a lower-half driver routine that removes the null process from the current/ready lists.

System Termination. Xinu may not always print the system termination message even if all your processes exit, because it interprets the term "user process" to mean "all processes except the null process." This can be confusing because the network software starts processes that never terminate (they continue forwarding frames even if the CPU is otherwise idle). Also remember that the tty driver will continue to echo characters even if there are no processes running to consume them.

Hints on restarting. The LSI 11 ODT command 1000G sets the program counter to 1000 and starts execution with interrupts *enabled.* Xinu disables interrupts immediately after it starts executing to avoid being interrupted before the system is ready. If an interrupt occurs before the LSI 11 can execute the first instruction, it may cause the system to crash (ungracefully). If your processor gives you trouble with the "G" command, then type the following three lines to restart Xinu:

```
RS/xxxxxx 340
R7/xxxxxx 1000
P
```

The LSI 11 will print octal values in place of xxxxxx. Note: no carriage return is used after the "P" command (consult the LSI 11 manual for more information).

Xinu Directory Organization

The Xinu software distribution tape, available from the publisher, contains all Xinu software from the book as well as the VAX cross-development and library software described in this manual. Source files and manual pages are included. To run the software on the distribution tape, you will need a Digital Equipment Corp. VAX computer running Berkeley 4.2BSD or 4.3BSD UNIX operating system, and at least one Digital Equipment Corporation LSI 11/2, LSI 11/03, or LSI 11/23 microcomputer.

Directories on the tape form a UNIX tree as described below. Usually, the Xinu software is rooted in the UNIX directory */usr/Xinu*, although this is not necessary. In the directory listing, a number in front of a name gives its level of nesting. The Xinu directory (denoted ".") resides at level 1. Directories immediately below it lie at level 2. Thus, manual pages for library commands are found at level 3 in directory *./man/man3*.

Within source directories, C programs are found in *file.c*, while complex subsystems have a directory of their own. For example, the C compiler resides in subdirectory *./src/cmd/cc11*, while the file *./src/cmd/size11.c* contains the entire source for the command *size11*. Each source directory contains a *Makefile* that gives the UNIX utility *make* instructions for compiling and loading the programs in that directory.

    Included files can be found in directory *./include*, which contains links to the Xinu system include files (which reside in directory *./src/sys/h*), as well as include files for the cross-development software.

    As the directory chart shows, source files for Xinu itself are located in directory *./src/sys/sys* (a convention used by early UNIX systems). That directory also contains the *Configuration* file and the object version of *config*.

    The tape comes with further instructions needed to install the software and connect an LSI 11 to the VAX.

```
1 .                        Xinu-directory (usually /usr/Xinu)

   2 /bin                  All cross-development object programs

   2 /include              All include files

   2 /install             Installation shell script

   2 /man                  All manual pages:
      3 /man1                 for cross-development commands
      3 /man2                 for Xinu system calls
      3 /man3                 for library procedures
      3 /man4                 for device descriptions

   2 /src                  All source files subdivided:
      3 /cmd                  cross-development software
      3 /lib                  libraries
      3 /sys                  Xinu and configuration:
         4 /con                 configuration program
         4 /h                   Xinu include files
         4 /sys                 Xinu and Makefile
            5 shell                Xinu shell and commands
```

Section 1: Cross-Development Commands

This section of the manual describes the program development commands that run on the host computer. They are used to prepare programs for execution under Xinu, transfer the memory image into the micro, and monitor execution. None of these programs (e.g., the C compiler) executes on the micro itself.

NAME

as11 — PDP-11 cross-assembler

SYNOPSIS

as11 [**−u**] [**−o** outfile] [file ...]

DESCRIPTION

As11 assembles the specified files, using standard input if no file name is specified. If the optional **−u** argument is specified, the assembler makes all undefined symbols in the current assembly "undefined external"; otherwise the
assembler complains about undefined symbols (**.globl** can be used to declare
undefined externals when not using *−u*).

If the **−o** option is given, *as11* writes its output to *outfile*. If the **−o** option is
not included, *as11* writes output to file *a.out* in the current directory. Following convention, the mode of the output file is made executable if there were no
unresolved external references (even though the output file is not directly executable on the cross development machine).

FILES

/tmp/as*   temporary files
a.out   default object file

DIAGNOSTICS

As11 is built to accept assembler language output from compilers, not for
humans. Diagnostics, which consist of single-letter messages, are cryptic at
best. See Ritchie, "UNIX Assembler Reference Manual" for details.

SEE ALSO

cc11(1), ld(1), nm(1), size11(1)

NAME

cc11 − cross compiler for the LSI−11

SYNOPSIS

cc11 [option] ... file ...

DESCRIPTION

Cc11 is a general-purpose script that invokes the C preprocessor, C cross-compiler, cross-assembler, and cross-loader to produce code for an LSI 11. *Cc11* is easier to use than invoking the processors individually because it passes the necessary arguments like library directories and keeps track of intermediate files automatically. By default, *cc11* leaves the result in a file named 'a.out' that is ready for downloading into the LSI 11 memory. **N.B.:** *cc11* produces object code in the PDP−11 UNIX format; as expected, it is incompatible with the VAX UNIX object code format.

By default, *cc11* preprocesses, cross-compiles, cross-assembles, and cross-loads a program; arguments can limit which steps it performs and change such things as the order in which libraries are searched.

Arguments whose names end with '.c' are taken to be C source programs; they are compiled, and each object program is left on the file whose name is that of the source with '.o' substituted for '.c'.

In the same way, arguments whose names end with '.s' are taken to be assembly source language and are assembled, producing a '.o' file.

Arguments whose names end with '.o' are combined with '.o' files produced from '.c' and '.s' arguments by the loader to produce an 'a.out' file.

Arguments whose names end with '.a' are taken to be libraries of '.o' programs, and are searched by the loader in the order specified.

Other arguments to *cc11* control the process as follows:

−c   Suppress the loading phase of the compilation, and force *cc11* to stop after producing '.o' files.

−o *output*

Name the final output file *output*.

−v   Verbose output narrating each step of the compile. This is useful if you want to see what's going on.

−D*name*=*def*
−D*name*

Define the *name* to the preprocessor, as if by '#define'. If no definition is given, the name is defined as "1".

−E   Run only the macro preprocessor on the named C programs, and send the result to the standard output.

−I*dir*   '#include' files whose names do not begin with '/' are always sought first in the directory of the *file* argument, then in directories named in −**I** options, then in directories on a standard list.

−**L**   If loading, include the standalone startup routine in preparation for downloading without Xinu. The default load sequence includes Xinu startup routines.

−**O**   Invoke an object-code improver as part of the C cross-compilation.

−**P**   Run only the macro preprocessor on the named C programs, and send the result to corresponding files suffixed '.i'.

−**S**   Compile the named C programs into assembly language, and leave the assembler-language output on corresponding files suffixed '.s', without assembling or loading the result.

−**U***name*
           Remove any initial definition of *name*.

Other arguments are taken to be either loader option arguments, or C-compatible object programs, typically produced by an earlier *cc11* run, or perhaps libraries of C-compatible routines. These programs, together with the results of any compilations specified, are loaded (in the order given) to produce a file that may be downloaded to the LSI−11 for execution. Unless changed with the −*o* option, *cc11* leaves the result of the load in file 'a.out'.

EXAMPLES

To compile a C program and load it with the Xinu libraries, producing an image in 'a.out' that is ready for downloading:

            cc11 program.c

To compile C code in file f1.c and leave the object code in file f1.o:

            cc11 −c f1.c

To assemble code in file f2.s and leave the object code in file f2.o:

            cc11 −c f2.s

To compile C code in file f3.c and combine it with previously compiled code in file f1.o:

            cc11 f3.c f1.o

To load three previously compiled files f1.o, f2.o, and f3.o:

            cc11 f1.o f2.o f3.o

To compile and load the C code in file f4.c leaving the output in 'outfile' instead of 'a.out':

ccll —o outfile f4.c

FILES

file.c	input C file
file.s	input or output assembler language file
file.o	input or output object file
a.out	loaded output
/tmp/ctm?	temporary compiler files
Xinu-directory/lib/cpp11	preprocessor
Xinu-directory/lib/c0.11	first pass
Xinu-directory/lib/c1.11	second pass
Xinu-directory/lib/c2.11	optional optimizer
Xinu-directory/include	'#include' files

DIAGNOSTICS

The diagnostics produced by C itself are intended to be self-explanatory. Occasional messages may be produced by the assembler or loader.

BUGS

Ccll does not support arguments *-g*, *-w*, *-p*, *-R*, *-C*, *-B*, or *-t* that the VAX C compiler handles.

SEE ALSO

as11(1), ld11(1), ranlib11(1), download(1), ar(1)

NAME

cvt — Convert disable/restore assembler macros to standard assembler

SYNOPSIS

cvt *infile*

DESCRIPTION

Cvt is a special-purpose filter used to convert nonstandard assembler language code to standard form. The nonstandard code arises from the *disable* and *restore* macro definitions, which insert literal text into the assembler language output of *ccl1* without resolving symbolic references. When invoked, *cvt* reads the assembler language contained in *infile*, remembering the offset of the local variable *ps*. It replaces symbolic references to *ps* with the correct offset.

Cvt detects possible misuse of *disable* and *restore* by returning a nonzero exit code if it finds references to local variable *ps* without finding a definition.

BUGS

When multiple procedures have been compiled into one assembler file, *cvt* may fail to detect missing declarations of *ps* in later procedures because it treats the entire input file as a single text file.

NAME

dd58 — copy a file to or from a TU58 connected to an asynchronous VAX line

SYNOPSIS

dd58 [option[=value]] ...

DESCRIPTION

The TU58 tape drive is a block-addressable, random access cartridge tape storage unit often used with LSI 11 microcomputers. The program *dd58* provides a way to write TU58 tapes from the VAX (e.g., to create a bootable system tape). It copies standard input to the TU58, or a given number of blocks from the TU58 to its standard output. Because the TU58 controller is a block-oriented interface that relies on the driver to supply data quickly, one should **never** use a terminal as standard input. Options are:

option	values
option	*values*
sam	set special addressing mode
-sam	disable special addressing mode (default)
verify	check data after reading or writing (default)
-verify	do not check data after reading or writing
maint	set maintenance mode
-maint	disable maintenance mode (default)
drive=n	use drive number n (default 0)
posit=n	reading or writing begins with tape block n (default 0)
count=n	read or write n bytes (default for *writing* is to end of file; this must be specified for reading)
read	read from the TU58 and write to the standard output
write	read from the standard input and write to the TU58
seek	position the TU58 drive at the given block number

For example, to put the file *x* on a tape cartridge at block 31, using special address mode, use

dd58 sam posit=31 write < x

To read its first 512 bytes into the file *y*, use

dd58 sam posit=31 count=512 read > y

DIAGNOSTICS

Error messages are printed on the terminal; they are self-explanatory.

NAME
  download − load program into LSI−11

SYNOPSIS
  download [file] ... [option] ...

DESCRIPTION
  Download loads an absolute binary program image (PDP−11 a.out format) into the memory of an LSI-11/2 computer over an asynchronous line. After halting the LSI-11 with a break, *download* places a bootstrap in memory, and uses it to load the remainder of memory.

  Loading the object program takes time proportional to the size of the program itself. It takes about two seconds to load 1000 bytes.

  Download will normally leave the LSI 11 in **ODT**. The *-a* option requests *download* to auto-start the micro. The optional number N following *-a*, forces a delay of approximately N seconds before execution, allowing the user to reconnect the console port before output begins.

  The bootstrap program is loaded 100 words beyond the end of the user's object program. If there is insufficient memory for the bootstrap and stack, this program will fail. When using the $-n$ option, the user must assure that the bootstrap loadpoint has not changed since the last reload.

  Download loads the user's program as specified in the command line. If no program name is given, *a.out* is used.

  Options are:

  −n   Do not preload the bootstrap program, assume it is already loaded.

  −v   Verbose. Print details of the communications with the LSI-11/2.

  −s   Silent. Print no information messages (default is to print some messages).

  −a[N]   Autostart. After loading, start the user's program running in the LSI-11. Optionally delay N seconds.

  −lx   Use LSI number x as the LSI 11 for downloading. If this option is not specified, download selects the LSI-11 that the user has on reserve, or a free one if none is reserved. E.g., −19.

  −b f Use file f as the bootstrap program.

FILES
  /dev/LSI.i   LSI 11 device connections
  /tmp/LSI-*   Lock files for auto-select
  Xinu-directory/lib/dl   default bootstrap loader

NAME

fs — invoke server side of Xinu remote file system

SYNOPSIS

fs [**−p**port]

DESCRIPTION

Fs invokes the Xinu remote file system server on a UNIX host. The server executes with permissions set to that of the invoking user, or user "xinu" if it is able to change user id. Typically, the host machine invokes *fs* at system startup, making it available always.

Option **−p** allows the user to specify a *UDP* port number to which the server will respond. If **−p** is omitted, *fs* uses a default port number. Thus, it is possible to have several versions of the server in use simultaneously, with each version using a unique UDP port.

When started, *fs* forks a child in background to become the file server. The background process executes forever, but the foreground process exits. Thus, the *fs* command appears to complete instantly even though the server is still executing.

NAME

ld11 — LSI 11 cross-loader for the VAX

SYNOPSIS

ld11 [option] file ...

DESCRIPTION

Ld11 combines several object programs into one, resolves external references, and searches libraries. In the simplest case several object *files* are given, and *ld11* combines them, producing an object module which can be either executed or become the input for a further *ld11* run. (In the latter case, the −r option must be given to preserve the relocation bits.) By default, *ld11* leaves its output on file **a.out**.

The argument routines are concatenated in the order specified. The entry point of the output is the beginning of the first routine unless altered by the −e option.

If any argument is a library, it is searched exactly once at the point it is encountered in the argument list. Only those routines defining an unresolved external reference are loaded. If a routine from a library references another routine in the library, and the library has not been processed by *ranlib11* (1), the referenced routine must appear after the referencing routine in the library. Thus the order of programs within libraries may be important. If the first member of a library is named '__.SYMDEF', then it is understood to be a dictionary for the library such as produced by *ranlib11*; the dictionary is searched iteratively to satisfy as many references as possible.

The symbols '_etext', '_edata' and '_end' ('etext', 'edata' and 'end' in C) are reserved, and if referred to, are set to the first location above the program, the first location above initialized data, and the first location above all data respectively. It is erroneous to define these symbols.

Ld11 understands several options. Except for −l, they should appear before the file names.

−s   'Strip' the output, that is, remove the symbol table and relocation bits to save space (but impair the usefulness of the debugger). This information can also be removed by *strip11(1).*

−u   Take the following argument as a symbol and enter it as undefined in the symbol table. This is useful for loading wholly from a library, since initially the symbol table is empty and an unresolved reference is needed to force the loading of the first routine.

−l*x*   This option is an abbreviation for the library name 'Xinu-directory/lib/lib*x*.a', where *x* is a string. If that does not exist, *ld11* tries '/usr/lib/lib*x*.a'. A library is searched when its name is encountered, so the placement of a −l option is significant.

−x   Do not preserve local symbols (i.e., symbols not declared .globl) in the output symbol table; only enter external symbols. This option saves some space in the output file.

−X   Save local symbols except for those whose names begin with 'L'. This option is used by *cc11(1)* to discard internally generated labels while retaining symbols local to routines.

−r   Generate relocation bits in the output file so that it can be the subject of another *ld11* run. This flag also prevents final definitions from being given to common symbols, and suppresses the 'undefined symbol' diagnostics. The idea is that several object files may be combined into one large one using −r without losing information.

−d   Force definition of common storage even if the −r flag is present.

−n   Move the data areas up to the first possible 4K word boundary following the end of the text. Designed for systems that share text, this option only wastes space when used with Xinu -- it should not be specified except for debugging.

−i   Important that it not be used on an LSI 11/02. It causes the text and data areas to be allocated from separate address spaces (i.e. the data area relocation begins at location 0).

−o   The *name* argument after −o is used as the name of the output file, instead of **a.out**.

−e   The following argument is taken to be the name of the entry point of the loaded program; location 0 is the default.

−O   Not to be used on an LSI1/02. It makes the file an overlay.

−D   The next argument is a decimal number that sets the size of the data segment.

FILES
Xinu-directory/lib/lib*.a libraries
a.out   output file

SEE ALSO
as11(1), ar(1), cc11(1), ranlib11(1)

NAME

    lorder11 — find ordering relation for an LSI 11 object library

SYNOPSIS

    lorder11 file ...

DESCRIPTION

    Argument *file* is the input consisting of one or more object files or library
    archives (see *ar*(1)). The standard output is a list of pairs of object file names,
    meaning that the first file of the pair refers to external identifiers defined in
    the second. The output may be processed by UNIX *tsort* to find an ordering of
    a library suitable for one-pass access by *ld11*(1).

    This brash one-liner intends to build a new library from existing '.o' files.

        ar cr library `lorder11 *.o | tsort`

    The need for lorder11 is eliminated by *ranlib11*(1), which converts an ordered
    archive into a randomly accessed library.

FILES

    *symref, *symdef
    nm11(1), sed(1), sort(1), join(1)

SEE ALSO

    tsort(1), ld11(1), ar(1), ranlib11(1)

BUGS

    The names of object files, in and out of libraries, must end with '.o'; nonsense
    results otherwise.

NAME
lusers — list users holding odt lock reservations

SYNOPSIS
lusers

DESCRIPTION
Lusers lists the users who hold reservations on tty lines. Each line of output contains the machine name and number, the user who holds it, and the idle time, rounded to the nearest minute. Reservations are made by *odt*(1), *download*(1), and *upload*(1).

FILES
/tmp/LSI-∗ Lock files.

SEE ALSO
odtunlock(1), odt(1)

BUGS
Lusers lists reservations and idle time based on lock file times which may not be quite accurate. Machines with more than 10 minutes of idle time are listed even though the reservation software considers the reservation to have expired.

NAME

    nm11 — print name list for object file produced by cc11

SYNOPSIS

    nm11 [**−agnopru**] [file ...]

DESCRIPTION

    Nm11 prints the name list (symbol table) of each object *file* in the argument list. If no *file* is given, the symbols in 'a.out' are listed.

    Each symbol name is preceded by its value (blanks if undefined) and one of the letters **U** (undefined), **A** (absolute), **T** (text segment symbol), **D** (data segment symbol), **B** (bss segment symbol), **C** (common symbol), or **f** file name. If the symbol is local (non-external) the type letter is in lower case. The output is sorted alphabetically.

    Options are:

    −a   Include all symbols in candidates for printing; normally symbols destined for UNIX's *sdb*(1) are excluded.

    −g   Print only global (external) symbols.

    −n   Sort numerically rather than alphabetically.

    −o   Prepend file or archive element name to each output line rather than only once.

    −p   Don't sort; print in symbol-table order.

    −r   Sort in reverse order.

    −u   Print only undefined symbols.

NAME

odt − connect user's terminal to a micro console (odt) line

SYNOPSIS

odt [-lx]

DESCRIPTION

Odt connects a terminal on the VAX to a microcomputer tty line so the output of the micro appears on the terminal screen and characters typed at the keyboard are sent to the micro. *Odt* sets the micro tty line to raw mode, and the VAX terminal to cbreak mode. The connection can be broken by killing the odt process (e.g., by typing the interrupt character (e.g., CONTROL-C).

When *odt* receives a backslash from the terminal, it switches to raw mode to read one character, after which it switches back to cbreak mode. The backslash escape allows the user to send characters like CONTROL-C to the micro even though they are normally interpreted as signals. As a special case, an escaped null character (octal 0) causes *odt* to force the micro line into a break condition for 1 second. This is useful for trapping an LSI 11 into ODT mode.

FILES

/dev/LSI.i	default LSI 11 connection
/tmp/LSI-*	Lock files

NAME

odtunlock — release lock on a tty line

SYNOPSIS

odtunlock [−c*class*] [−l*x*]

DESCRIPTION

Odtunlock releases the caller's currently reserved microcomputer, making it available for others to use. Mutual exclusion locks are created automatically by *odt* and *download*, and are reported by *lusers*. Reservations expire after 10 minutes of idle time even if *odtunlock* is not used.

Without arguments, *odtunlock* removes the reservation on the tty line most recently accessed by the caller. Argument −c can be used to specify a *class*, in which case *odtunlock* removes the user's most recently held reservation in that class. Argument −l*x* forces *odtunlock* to cancel the reservation on line number *x* within the selected class.

Xinu's tty reservation system is a friendly, cooperative mutual-exclusion mechanism. All software that accesses tty lines for communicating with back-end microcomputers is expected to adhere to the reservation system to prevent multiple users from trying to access the same machine simultaneously. *Odtunlock* releases a tty line no matter who holds the reservation. Thus, care must be taken when using *odtunlock* to avoid removing a reservation when another user is actively using the tty line or downloading software will not work correctly.

FILES

/dev/CLASS.i	tty lines for a particular class.
/tmp/odtlock.*user*	records current line allocated by *user*
/tmp/*cname.i*	Lock file for line *i* in class *cname*.

SEE ALSO

lusers(1), odt(1), download(1), upload(1)

NAME
pm — Xinu post mortem debugger

SYNOPSIS
pm [**-p**] [**-s**] [**-t**] [*txtfil* [*corfil*]]

DESCRIPTION
Pm performs a post mortem given a core image from an LSI 11 running Xinu. It takes as input the memory image (in LSI 11 a.out format) that was *down-load*ed, and the core image (in LSI 11 core format) that was *upload*ed, and prints the following information:

Differences between the text portions (program instruction areas) of the file before downloading and after uploading. Except for interrupt vectors which are initialized at run-time, differences indicate that instructions were accidentally overwritten. Interrupt vectors lie below location 1000 (octal).

C traceback of the executing process, based on Xinu's *currpid*.

C traceback of all other processes.

The status of all semaphores. If a semaphore is in use and the count indicates that there are processes waiting, the list of waiting processes is printed along with an actual count. Backward links are checked for consistency.

The status of tty devices, including the buffer head and tail pointers along with buffer contents.

By default, *pm* takes the downloaded image from file *a.out,* the uploaded image from file *core11,* and produces all of the above output. *Pm* always prints information about the current process. If the following flags are present, *pm* prints only the information requested.

-p   dump the process table.

-s   dump the semaphore table.

-t   dump the tty tables.

Optional arguments *txtfil* and *corfil* can be specified to change the files used as the downloaded and uploaded image.

# SEE ALSO
download(1), upload(1)

BUGS
Pm may fault when given garbage files (e.g., a badly damaged core file) because it references symbols in the core image based on values obtained from the a.out file without checking their validity.

NAME

ranlib11 — convert LSI 11 cross-archives to random cross-libraries

SYNOPSIS

ranlib11 archive ...

DESCRIPTION

Ranlib11 converts each *archive* to a form which can be loaded more rapidly by the LSI 11 cross-loader, by adding a table of contents named __.**SYMDEF** to the beginning of the archive. It uses *ar*(1) to reconstruct the archive, so that sufficient temporary file space must be available in the file system containing the current directory.

SEE ALSO

ld11(1), ar(1)

BUGS

Because generation of a library by *ar* and randomization by *ranlib11* are separate, phase errors are possible. The cross-loader *ld11* warns when the modification date of a library is more recent than the creation of its dictionary; but this means you get the warning even if you only copy the library.

NAME

size11 — size of an 11 object file

SYNOPSIS

size11 [objectfile ...]

DESCRIPTION

Size11 prints the (decimal) number of bytes required by the text, data, and bss portions, and their sum in hex and decimal, of each object-file argument. If no file is specified, **a.out** is used.

SEE ALSO

ld11(1)

NAME

strip11 — remove symbols and relocation bits from 11 object file

SYNOPSIS

strip11 name ...

DESCRIPTION

Strip11 removes the symbol table and relocation bits ordinarily attached to the output of the assembler and loader. This is useful to save space after a program has been debugged.

The effect of *strip11* is the same as use of the −s option of *ld11*.

FILES

/tmp/stm?   temporary file

SEE ALSO

ld11(1)

NAME

subEIS — substitute code for LSI 11 extended instructions

SYNOPSIS

subASH
subASHC
subMUL
subDIV

DESCRIPTION

These programs read an LSI 11 assembly language program from the standard input, replace opcodes from the Extended Instruction Set (EIS) with a call to a library subroutine that simulates them, and write the new listing on the standard output. They are used mainly as filters for compiling LSI 11/02 programs for machines without the EIS chip.

Each program checks for a different instruction; *subMUL* checks for (and replaces) *mul* instructions, *subDIV* checks for (and replaces) *div* instructions, *subASH* checks for (and replaces) *ash* instructions, and *subASHC* checks for (and replaces) *ashc* instructions. The resulting assembly language program must be loaded with the library *libeis.a* , which contains the routines called.

SEE ALSO

cc11(1), EIS(2)

DIAGNOSTICS

The condition codes are correctly set by the above calling sequence.

BUGS

Setting the condition codes accounts for most of the work these routines perform. Unfortunately, they are so slow that most programs, including Xinu are unusable on an 11/2 without the EIS hardware.

NAME
tu58 — routines to access TU58 tape drives attached to the VAX

SYNOPSIS
topen(drive, mode, name)
char *drive;
int mode;
char *name;

tclose(dn)
int dn;

tseek(dn, offset, whence)
int dn;
int offset;
int whence;

tread(dn, buf, nbytes)
int dn;
char *buf;
int nbytes;

twrite(dn, buf, nbytes)
int dn;
char *buf;
int nbytes;

#include <tu58io.h>
tioctl(dn, request, arg)
int dn;
int request;
union tio *arg

#include <tu58errno.h> extern int terrno; tperror(str) char *str;

DESCRIPTION
These routines manipulate a TU58 tape drive unit that is attached directly to the VAX. They are obtained by loading the library *lib58.a*. These routines do all the tape controlling including mutual exclusion of users (but *not* that of a user's processes).

The TU58 has two drives on one controller. These routines treat each drive as a separate file; that is, each must be opened individually, operations may be intermixed, and they can be closed in any order.

Topen opens drive *drive* for reading (if *mode* is 0), writing (if *mode* is 1) or for both reading and writing (if *mode* is 2). *Drive* is the address of a string of ASCII characters representing the drive number; only the first character is used. Legal drive names are "0" and "1". *File* is the name of the port to which the TU58 is attached; if given as NULL, the port *ldev/LSIfast* is used.

The opened drive is positioned at the beginning (block 0), and is opened with the verification bit set and the special addressing and maintenance modes cleared. (To change these, see *tioctl*, below.) The returned drive descriptor must be used for subsequent calls for other input-output functions on the drive. On error, -1 is returned.

Given a drive descriptor *dn* returned from a *topen* call, *tclose* closes the associated drive. If all drives on the TU58 are closed, it also releases the unit. Note that this routine is *not* invoked automatically; it must be called explicitly.

Given a drive descriptor *dn* returned from a *topen* call, and the address *buf* which is the location of *nbytes* contiguous bytes into which the input will be placed, *tread* will read *nbytes* bytes into the buffer. The number of characters read, or -1 (on error), is returned. Note that reading begins at a block boundary, and that there is no concept of "end of file".

Given a drive descriptor *dn* returned from a *topen* call, and the address *buf* which is the location of *nbytes* contiguous bytes which are to be written to the drive, *twrite* will write *nbytes* bytes from the buffer to the drive. The number of characters written, or -1 (on error), is returned. Note that writing begins at a block boundary,

Given a drive descriptor *dn* returned from a *topen* call and a request *request*, *tioctl* will either alter a characteristic of the drive, or return information about the drive. Legal requests are:

request	*effect*
TU58SSAM	set special addressing mode
TU58CSAM	clear special addressing mode
TU58SVFY	set verification mode
TU58CVFY	clear verification mode
TU58SMTM	.set maintenance mode
TU58CMTM	clear maintenance mode
TU58SPOS	set new position; unlike *tseek*, this does not move the tape, but the next operation will take place at the current position. *Arg* is a pointer to an integer, which is the new block number.
TU58GDCB	return the drive control block. This copies the drive control block into the locations pointed to by *arg*; the structure is defined in *Xinu-directory/include/tu58io.h*.

On error, *tioctl* returns -1; on success, 0. The requests are defined in the include file *Xinu-directory/include/tu58io.h*.

ERROR HANDLING

Errors are handled uniformly; if the operation failed, the attempted command is aborted and an error flag is returned. This flag is always -1. To obtain more detailed error messages, there is a routine *tperror* which prints its argument string, followed by a brief message describing the last error that occurred. There is an external variable, *terrno*, that contains a code number indicating the last error. Its values are in *Xinu-directory/include/tu58errno.h*.

There is one error that will not return an error code, even though *terrno* is set (and so *tperror* will report it); namely, if the operation succeeded but retries were necessary. This is a TU58 error code; the only routine that ever sends something more than once is the routine that initializes communications between the VAX and the TU58.

AUTHOR

Matt Bishop (*mab*)

BUGS

Sometimes the TU58 does not respond to an initialization command. When this happens, check the connections and try again.

NAME

upload — copy LSI 11 memory to VAX

SYNOPSIS

upload [options] ... [[min addr] max addr]

DESCRIPTION

Upload copies the contents of an LSI 11 memory onto a file on the VAX. By default the image is placed in file core11.

Arguments *min addr* and *max addr* limit the image to specific addresses.

Options include the following:

- **−o**   Output file. Take the next argument as an output file name in place of *core11*.

- **−v**   Verbose. Print the details of communications between the LSI 11 and the host.

- **−s**   Silent. Print no information messages.

- **−n**   Noload. Assume the uploader code is already resident in the LSI 11.

- **−lx**   LSI number. Use LSI number *x* for uploading. If this option is not specified, *upload* selects the LSI 11 that the user has reserved.

- **−a**   a.out file. Take the next argument as the name of the object file in place of a.out.

FILES

/dev/LSI.i	LSI 11 device connections
/tmp/LSI-*	Lock files for auto-select
{Xinu-directory}/lib/ul	default bootstrap loader

BUGS

Upload reads the contents of some memory locations with ODT and then overwrites them with a bootstrap program; if aborted, it cannot be restarted because data has been lost.

Section 2: System Calls

The Xinu operating system kernel consists of a set of run-time procedures to implement operating system services on an LSI 11/2 microcomputer. The system supports multiple processes, I/O, synchronization based on counting semaphores, preemptive scheduling, and communication with other machines. Each page in this section describes a system routine that can be called by a user process.

Each page describes one system call, giving the number and types of arguments that must be passed to the procedure under the heading "SYNOPSIS" (by giving their declaration in C syntax). The heading "SEE ALSO" suggests the names of other system calls that may be related to the described function. For example, the "SEE ALSO" entry for system call *wait* suggests that the programmer may want to look at the page for *signal* because both routines operate on semaphores.

In general, Xinu blocks processes when requested services are not available. Unless the manual page suggests otherwise, the programmer should assume that the process requesting system services may be delayed until the request can be satisfied. For example, calling *read* may cause an arbitrary delay until data can be obtained from the device.

NAME
access — determine whether a file is accessible

SYNOPSIS
int access(filename, mode)
char   *filename;
char   *mode;

DESCRIPTION
Access examines file with name *filename* to determine if it is accessible according to the modes specified in the mode string *mode*. Valid characters in the mode string are **r** (check for read access) **w** (check for write access), **n** (check to see if a new file can be created), and **o** (check to see if file exists). If neither **r** nor **w** is specified, both are assumed.

# SEE ALSO
open(2), ckmode(3)

NAME

chprio — change the priority of a process

SYNOPSIS

int chprio(pid,newprio)
int pid;
int newprio;

DESCRIPTION

Chprio changes the scheduling priority of process *pid* to *newprio*. Priorities are positive integers. At any instant, the highest priority process that is ready will be running. A set of processes with equal priority is scheduled round-robin.

If the new priority is invalid, or the process id is invalid *chprio* returns SYSERR. Otherwise, it returns the old process priority. It is forbidden to change the priority of the null process, which always remains zero.

SEE ALSO

create(2), getprio(2), resume(2)

BUGS

Because *chprio* changes priorities without rearranging processes on the ready list, it should only be used on waiting, sleeping, suspended, or current processes.

NAME

close — device independent close routine

SYNOPSIS

int close(dev)
int dev;

DESCRIPTION

Close will disconnect I/O from the device given by *dev*. It returns SYSERR if *dev* is incorrect, or is not opened for I/O. Otherwise, *close* returns OK.

Normally tty devices like the console do not have to be opened and closed.

SEE ALSO

control(2), getc(2), open(2), putc(2), read(2), seek(2), write(2)

NAME
control — device independent control routine

SYNOPSIS
int control(dev, function, arg1, arg2)
int dev;
int function;
int arg1, arg2;

DESCRIPTION
Control is the mechanism used to send control information to devices and device drivers, or to interrogate their status. (Data normally flows through GETC(2), PUTC(2), READ(2), and WRITE(2).)

Control returns SYSERR if *dev* is incorrect or if the function cannot be performed. The values returned otherwise are device dependent. For example, there is a control function for "tty" devices that returns the number of characters waiting in the input queue.

SEE ALSO
close(2), getc(2), open(2), putc(2), read(2), seek(2), write(2)

NAME

create — create a new process

SYNOPSIS

int create(caddr,ssize,prio,name,nargs[,argument]•)
char •caddr;
int ssize;
int prio;
char •name;
int nargs;
int argument;   /• actually, type machine word •/

DESCRIPTION

Create creates a new process that will begin execution at location *caddr*, with a stack of *ssize* words, initial priority *prio*, and identifying name *name*. *Caddr* should be the address of a procedure or main program, If the creation is successful, the (nonnegative) process id of the new process is returned to the caller. The created process is left in the suspended state; it will not begin execution until started by a resume command. If the arguments are incorrect, or if there are no free process slots, the value SYSERR is returned. The new process has its own stack, but shares global data with other processes according to the scope rules of C. If the procedure attempts to return, its process will be terminated (see KILL(2)).

The caller can pass a variable number of arguments to the created process which are accessed through formal parameters. The integer *nargs* specifies how many argument values follow. *Nargs* values from the *arguments* list will be passed to the created process. The type and number of such arguments is not checked; each is treated as a single machine word. The user is cautioned against passing the address of any dynamically allocated datum to a process because such objects may be deallocated from the creator's run-time stack even though the created process retains a pointer.

SEE ALSO

kill(2)

NAME
    freebuf — free a buffer by returning it to its buffer pool

SYNOPSIS
    int freebuf(buf)
    char *buf;

DESCRIPTION
    Freebuf returns a previously allocated buffer to its buffer pool, making it avail-
    able for other processes to use. *Freebuf* returns SYSERR if the buffer address
    is invalid or if the pool id has been corrupted (this version stores pool ids in the
    integer preceding the buffer address).

SEE ALSO
    getbuf(2), mkpool(2), getmem(2), freemem(2)

NAME

freemem — deallocate a block of heap memory

SYNOPSIS

int freemem(addr, len)
char *addr;
int len;

DESCRIPTION

Freemem deallocates a contiguous block of memory previously obtained with GETMEM(2), and returns it to the free list. Argument *addr* specifies the lowest address of the block being deallocated, and argument *len* specifies the length of the block in bytes. In this version, memory is allocated in multiples of four bytes to guarantee that sufficient space is available in each block to link it onto the free list. However, the length passed to both *getmem* and *freemem* is rounded automatically, so the user need not be aware of any extra space in the allocated block.

SEE ALSO

getbuf(2), getmem(2), getstk(2), freebuf(2), freestk(2)

NAME

freestk — deallocate a block of stack memory

SYNOPSIS

int freestk(addr, len)
char *addr;
int len;

DESCRIPTION

Freestk deallocates a contiguous block of memory previously obtained with GETSTK(2), and returns it to the free list. Argument *addr* specifies the highest integer address in the block being deallocated, and argument *len* specifies the length of the block in bytes. In this version, memory is allocated in multiples of four bytes to guarantee that sufficient space is available in each block to link it onto the free list. However, both *getstk* and *freestk* rounds the specified length automatically, so the user need not be aware of any extra space in the allocated blocks.

SEE ALSO

getbuf(2), getmem(2), getstk(2), freebuf(2), freemem(2)

NAME

getaddr — obtain the local machine's Internet (IP) address

SYNOPSIS

int getaddr(ip)
IPaddr ip;

DESCRIPTION

Getaddr obtains the local machine's primary Internet (IP) address and places it in the 4-byte array specified by argument *ip*. Calling *getaddr* may trigger a Reverse Address Resolution Protocol (RARP) broadcast to find the address. If RARP succeeds, the address is kept locally for successive lookup requests. If RARP fails, *getaddr* calls *panic* to halt processing.

SEE ALSO

getname(2), getnet(2)

BUGS

There is no provision to obtain multiple addresses for machines that connect to multiple networks.

NAME

getbuf — obtain a buffer from a buffer pool

SYNOPSIS

char *getbuf(poolid)
int poolid;

DESCRIPTION

Getbuf obtains a free buffer from the pool given by argument *poolid,* and returns a pointer to the first word of the buffer. If all buffers in the specified pool are in use, the calling process will be blocked until a buffer becomes available. If the argument *poolid* does not specify a valid pool, getbuf returns SYSERR.

SEE ALSO

freebuf(2), getmem(2), getstk(2), freemem(2), freestk(2)

NAME

getc — device independent character input routine

SYNOPSIS

int getc(dev)
int dev;

DESCRIPTION

Getc will read the next character from the I/O device given by *dev*. It returns SYSERR if *dev* is incorrect. A successful call may return a character (widened to an integer) or the value EOF to denote end of file, depending on the device driver.

SEE ALSO

close(2), control(2), open(2), putc(2), read(2), seek(2), write(2)

BUGS

Not all devices report the end-of-file condition.

NAME
getmem, getstk — get a block of main memory

SYNOPSIS
char *getmem(nbytes)
int nbytes;

char *getstk(nbytes)
int nbytes;

DESCRIPTION
In either form, *getmem* rounds the number of bytes, *nbytes,* to an even-word multiple, and allocates a block of *nbytes* bytes of memory for the caller. *Getmem* returns the lowest word address in the allocated block; *getstk* returns the highest word address in the allocated block. If less than *nbytes* bytes remain, the call returns SYSERR.

Getmem allocates memory starting with the end of the loaded program. *Getstk* allocates memory from the stack area downward. The routines cooperate so they never allocate overlapping regions.

SEE ALSO
freemem(2) getbuf(2), freebuf(2)

BUGS
There is no way to protect memory, so the active stack may write into regions returned by either call; allocations returned by *getstk* are more prone to disaster because they lie closest to the dynamic stack areas of other processes.

NAME

getname — return the official Internet domain name of the local host

SYNOPSIS

int *getname(name)
char *name;

DESCRIPTION

Getname returns the least—significant component of the official Internet domain name of the local host using GETADDR(2) to obtain the host's IP address, and IP2NAME(2) to translate the IP address into a domain name. For example, when executed on host *merlin.cs.purdue.edu*, *getname* returns the string *merlin*.

Argument *name* gives the starting address of an area in which the name should be placed. *Getname* writes the name as a contiguous, null—terminated byte string.

SEE ALSO

ip2name(2), getaddr(2)

BUGS

There is no way to force *getname* to return the full domain name.

NAME

getnet — obtain the Internet (IP) address of local machine's network

SYNOPSIS

int getnet(ip)
IPaddr ip;

DESCRIPTION

Getnet obtains the Internet (IP) address of the local machine's primary network, and stores it in the 4-byte array specified by argument *ip*. Calling *getnet* may trigger a Reverse Address Resolution Protocol (RARP) broadcast to find the address. If RARP succeeds, the address is kept locally for successive lookup requests. If RARP fails, *getnet* calls *panic* to halt processing.

SEE ALSO

getaddr(2), getname(2), getnet(2)

BUGS

There is no provision to obtain multiple addresses for machines that connect to multiple networks.

NAME

getpid — return the process id of the currently running process

SYNOPSIS

int getpid()

DESCRIPTION

Getpid returns the process id of the currently executing process. It is necessary to be able to identify one's self in order to perform some operations (e.g., change one's scheduling priority).

NAME

getprio — return the scheduling priority of a given process

SYNOPSIS

int getprio(pid)
int pid;

DESCRIPTION

Getprio returns the scheduling priority of process *pid*. If pid is invalid, *getprio* returns SYSERR.

NAME

gettime — obtain the current local time in seconds past the epoch date

SYNOPSIS

int gettime(timvar)
long *timvar;

DESCRIPTION

Gettime obtains the local time measured in seconds past the epoch date, and places it in the longword pointed to by argument *timvar*. The epoch is taken to be zero seconds past Jan 1, 1970.

The correct time is usually kept by the real-time clock, but *gettime* may contact a time server on the network if the local time has not been initialized.

If *gettime* cannot obtain the current time, it returns SYSERR to the caller. Otherwise, *gettime* returns OK.

SEE ALSO

getutim(2)

BUGS

Local time computation does not take daylight savings into account. The local clock may drift, especially under heavy CPU activity or activities that require the operating system to mask interrupts for extended periods.

NAME

getutim — obtain current universal time in seconds past the epoch

SYNOPSIS

int getutim(timvar)
long *timvar;

DESCRIPTION

Getutim obtains the current time measured in seconds past the epoch date, and places it in the longword pointed to by argument *timvar*. The correct time is usually kept by the real-time clock, but *gettime* may contact a time server on the network if the local time has not been initialized.

The epoch is taken to be zero seconds past Jan 1, 1970. Universal time, formerly called Greenwich Mean Time, is the mean solar time of the meridian in Greenwich, England, and is used throughout the world as a standard for measuring time.

If *getutim* cannot obtain the current time, it returns SYSERR to the caller. Otherwise, *getutim* returns OK.

SEE ALSO

gettime(2)

BUGS

The local clock may drift, especially under heavy CPU activity or activities that require the operating system to mask interrupts for extended periods.

NAME

ip2name — translate an Internet address to a host Domain Name

SYNOPSIS

int *ip2name(ip, name)
IPaddr ip;

char *name;

DESCRIPTION

Ip2name accepts a 4-byte Internet (IP) address and returns the Domain Name for that host by consulting a DARPA Domain nameserver to perform the translation. Argument *ip* gives the address of a 4-byte host Internet address to be translated into a name. Argument *name* points to an area of memory in which the domain name will be written. The name is written as a null—terminated byte string with periods separating domain name components.

Ip2name returns *SYSERR* if the Internet address is invalid, if the nameserver does not respond, or if the translation fails. It returns *OK* otherwise.

SEE ALSO

getname(2), getaddr(2)

BUGS

There is no way to specify a long time delay, so name lookup that consults a distant nameserver may timeout due to network delays. Also, there is no way to specify a maximum name size.

NAME
kill — terminate a process

SYNOPSIS
int kill(pid)
int pid;

DESCRIPTION

Kill will stop process *pid* and remove it from the system, returning SYSERR if the process id is invalid, OK otherwise. *Kill* terminates a process immediately. If the process has been queued on a semaphore, it is removed from the queue and the semaphore count is incremented as if the process had never been there. Processes waiting to send a message to a full port disappear without affecting the port. If the process is waiting for I/O, the I/O is stopped (if possible).

One can kill a process in any state, including a suspended one. Once killed, a process cannot recover.

BUGS

At present there is no way to recover space allocated dynamically when a process terminates. However, *kill* does recover the stack space allocated to a process when it is created.

NAME

mark, unmarked — set and check initialization marks efficiently

SYNOPSIS

#include <mark.h>

int mark(mk)
MARKER mk;

int unmarked(mk)
MARKER mk;

DESCRIPTION

Mark sets *mk* to "initialized", and records its location in the system. It returns 0 if the location is already marked, OK if the marking was successful, and SYSERR if there are too many marked locations.

Unmarked checks the contents and location of *mk* to see if it has been previously marked with the *mark* procedure. It returns OK if and only if *mk* has not been marked, 0 otherwise. The key is that they work correctly after a reboot, no matter what was left in the marked locations when the system stopped.

Both *mark* and *unmarked* operate efficiently (in a few instructions) to correctly determine whether a location has been marked. They are most useful for creating self-initializing procedures when the system will be restarted. Both the value in *mk* as well as its location are used to tell if it has been marked.

Memory marking can be eliminated from Xinu by removing the definition of the symbol MEMMARK from the Configuration file. Self-initializing library routines may require manual initialization if MEMMARK is disabled (e.g., see BUFFER(3)).

BUGS

Mark does not verify that the location given lies in the static data area before marking it; to avoid having the system retain marks for locations on the stack after procedure exit, do not mark automatic variables.

NAME

mkpool — create a buffer pool

SYNOPSIS

int mkpool(bufsiz, numbufs)
int bufsiz;
int numbufs;

DESCRIPTION

Mkpool creates a pool of *numbufs* buffers, each of size *bufsiz,* and returns an integer identifying the pool. If no more pools can be created, or if the arguments are incorrect, *mkpool* returns SYSERR.

SEE ALSO

getbuf(2), freebuf(2), poolinit(2)

BUGS

At present there is no way to reclaim space from buffer pools once they are no longer needed.

NAME

mount — add a prefix mapping to the namespace

SYNOPSIS

int mount(prefix, dev, replace)
char *prefix;
int dev;
char *replace;

DESCRIPTION

Mount adds a prefix mapping to the syntactic namespace, inserting it just prior to the last entry. Argument *prefix* points to a string that contains a null-terminated prefix string, argument *dev* gives the device id of the device to which the prefix maps, and argument *replace* points to a null-terminated replacement string. As a special case, *dev* can specify the value SYSERR to indicate that names matching the prefix cannot be mapped or accessed.

If the namespace table is full, or if the specified prefix or replacement strings exceed the allowed size, *mount* returns SYSERR. Otherwise it returns OK.

SEE ALSO

open(2), nammap(2), namrepl(2), unmount(2), namespace(4)

NAME

nammap — map a name through the syntactic namespace

SYNOPSIS

int nammap(name, newname)
char *name;
char *newname;

DESCRIPTION

Nammap uses the syntactic namespace to translate a name into a new name and returns the id of a device to which the name maps. Names are mapped iteratively until they map to a device other than the *NAMESPACE*.

Argument *name* points to a null-terminated string containing the name to be mapped. Argument *newname* points to a string area large enough to hold the mapped version of the name. If successful, *nammap* returns the device id of the device to which the mapping corresponds. Otherwise, it returns SYSERR.

SEE ALSO

namrepl(2), open(2), mount(2), unmount(2), namespace(4)

BUGS

Nammap writes the mapped name into *newname* without checking to make sure it fits. There is no way to distinguish errors such as string overflow from names that map to device SYSERR.

NAME

namrepl — replace a name once using the syntactic namespace

SYNOPSIS

int namrepl(name, newname)
char *name;
char *newname;

DESCRIPTION

Namrepl uses the syntactic namespace to translate a name into a new name and returns the id of a device to which the name maps. The name is translated exactly once, independent of the device to which it maps. In particular, *namrepl* will return the device id *NAMESPACE* without further mapping for those names that map recursively through the syntactic namespace.

Argument *name* points to a null-terminated string containing the name to be mapped, and argument *newname* points to a string area large enough to hold the mapped version of the name. If successful, *namrepl* returns the device id of the device to which the name maps. Otherwise, it returns SYSERR.

SEE ALSO

nammap(2), open(2), mount(2), unmount(2), namespace(4)

BUGS

Namrepl writes the mapped name into *newname* without checking to make sure it fits. There is no way to distinguish errors such as string overflow from names that map to device SYSERR.

NAME

open − device independent open routine

SYNOPSIS

int open(dev, name, mode)
int dev;
char ∗name;
char ∗modes;

DESCRIPTION

Open will establish connection with the device given by *dev* using the null-terminated string *name* to name an object on that device, and null-terminated string *mode* to specify the access mode for that object. Valid access mode characters include **r** (read), **w** (write), **o** (old), and **n** (new) as specified in ACCESS(2).

Open returns SYSERR if *dev* is incorrect or cannot be opened. If successful, the value returned by *open* depends on the device. Most calls to open return a device descriptor that can be used in subsequent calls to *readfl or write*. For example, calling *open* on a disk device with a file name as an argument produces a descriptor by which that file can be accessed.

SEE ALSO

access(2), close(2), ckmode(3), namespace(4)

BUGS

Not all devices produce meaningful return values for *open*.

NAME

panic — abort processing due to severe error

SYNOPSIS

int panic(message)
char *message;

DESCRIPTION

Panic will print the character string *message* on the console, dump the machine registers and top few stack locations, and halt the processor. It uses *kprintf* rather than *printf,* so it may be called anywhere in the kernel (e.g., from an interrupt routine that may be executed by the null process). Typing **P** after the processor halts will cause panic to restore the machine state and continue, so it is possible to examine locations with **ODT** after the processor halts, and still restart processing.

There are alternate entry points to *panic* that are invoked by branch to location zero, illegal interrupts, or processor exceptions (traps).

SEE ALSO

kprintf(3), printf(3)

NAME

pcount — return the number of messages currently waiting at a port

SYNOPSIS

int pcount(portid)
int portid;

DESCRIPTION

Pcount returns the message count associated with port *portid*.

A positive count p means that there are p messages available for processing. This count includes the count of messages explicitly in the port and the count of the number of processes which attempted to send messages to the queue but are blocked (because the queue is full). A negative count p means that there are p processes awaiting messages from the port. A zero count means that there are neither messages waiting nor processes waiting to consume messages.

SEE ALSO

pcreate(2), pdelete(2), preceive(2), preset(2), psend(2)

BUGS

In this version there is no way to distinguish SYSERR (which has value −1) from a legal port count.

NAME

pcreate — create a new port

SYNOPSIS

int pcreate(count)
int count;

DESCRIPTION

Pcreate creates a port with *count* locations for storing message pointers.

Pcreate returns an integer identifying the port if successful. If no more ports can be allocated, or if *count* is nonpositive, *pcreate* returns SYSERR.

Ports are manipulated with PSEND(2) and PRECEIVE(2). Receiving from a port returns a pointer to a message that was previously sent to the port.

SEE ALSO

pcount(2), pdelete(2), preceive(2), preset(2), psend(2)

NAME
    pdelete — delete a port

SYNOPSIS
    int pdelete(portid, dispose)
    int portid;
    int (*dispose)();

DESCRIPTION
    Pdelete deallocates port *portid*. The call returns SYSERR if *portid* is illegal or
    is not currently allocated.

    The command has several effects, depending on the state of the port at the
    time the call is issued. If processes are waiting for messages from portid, they
    are made ready and return SYSERR to their caller. If messages exist in the
    port, they are disposed of by procedure *dispose*. If processes are waiting to
    place messages in the port, they are made ready and given SYSERR indica-
    tions (just as if the port never existed). *Pdelete* performs the same function of
    clearing messages and processes from a port as PRESET(2) except that *pdelete*
    also deallocates the port.

SEE ALSO
    pcount(2), pcreate(2), preceive(2), preset(2), psend(2)

NAME

pinit — initialize the ports table at system startup

SYNOPSIS

int pinit(maxmsgs)
int maxmsgs;

DESCRIPTION

Pinit initializes the ports mechanism by clearing the ports table and allocating memory for messages. It should be called only once (usually at system startup). Argument *maxmsgs* specifies an upper bound on the number of simultaneously outstanding messages at all ports.

SEE ALSO

pcreate(2), pdelete(2), psend(2), preceive(2)

NAME

preceive — get a message from a port

SYNOPSIS

char *preceive(portid)
int portid;

DESCRIPTION

Preceive retrieves the next message from the port *portid,* returning a pointer to the message if successful, or SYSERR if *portid* is invalid. (The sender and receiver must agree on a convention for passing the message length.)

The calling process is blocked if there are no messages available (and reawakened as soon as a message arrives). The only ways to be released from a port queue are for some other process to send a message to the port with PSEND(2) or for some other process to delete or reset the port with PDELETE(2) or PRESET(2).

SEE ALSO

pcount(2), pcreate(2), pdelete(2), preset(2), psend(2)

NAME

preset — reset a port

SYNOPSIS

int preset(portid, dispose)
int portid;
int (*dispose)();

DESCRIPTION

Preset flushes all messages from a port and releases all processes waiting to send or receive messages. *Preset* returns SYSERR if *portid* is not a valid port id.

Preset has several effects, depending on the state of the port at the time the call is issued. If processes are blocked waiting to receive messages from port *portid,* they are all made ready; each returns SYSERR to caller. If messages are in the port they are disposed of by passing them to function *dispose.* If process are blocked waiting to send messages they are made ready; each returns SYSERR to its caller (as though the port never existed).

The effects of *preset* are the same as PDELETE(2) followed by PCREATE(2), except that the port is not deallocated. The maximum message count remains the same as it was.

BUGS

There is no way to change the maximum message count when the port is reset.

SEE ALSO

pcount(2), pcreate(2), pdelete(2), preceive(2), psend(2)

NAME

psend — send a message to a port

SYNOPSIS

int psend(portid, message)
int portid;
char *message;

DESCRIPTION

Psend adds the pointer *message* to the port *portid*. If successful, *psend* returns OK; it returns SYSERR if *portid* is invalid. Note that only a pointer, not the entire message, is enqueued, and that psend may return to the caller before the receiver has consumed the message.

If the port is full at the time of the call, the sending process will be blocked until space is available in the port for the message.

SEE ALSO

pcount(2), pcreate(2), pdelete(2), preceive(2), preset(2)

NAME

putc — device independent character output routine

SYNOPSIS

int putc(dev, ch)
int dev;
char   ch;

DESCRIPTION

Putc will write the character *ch* on the I/O device given by *dev*. It returns SYSERR if *dev* is incorrect, OK otherwise.

By convention, *printf* calls *putc* on device CONSOLE to write formatted output. Usually CONSOLE is device zero.

SEE ALSO

close(2), control(2), getc(2), open(2), read(2), seek(2), write(2)

NAME

read — device independent input routine

SYNOPSIS

    int read(dev, buffer, numchars)
    int dev;
    char *buffer;
    int numchars;

DESCRIPTION

Read will read up to *numchars* bytes from the I/O device given by *dev*. It returns SYSERR if *dev* is incorrect. It returns the number of characters read if successful. The number of bytes actually returned depends on the device. For example, when reading from a device of type "tty", each read normally returns one line. For a disk, however, each read returns one block and the argument *numchars* is taken to be the index of the disk block desired.

SEE ALSO

close(2), control(2), getc(2), open(2), putc(2), seek(2), write(2)

NAME

receive — receive a (one-word) message

SYNOPSIS

int receive()

DESCRIPTION

Receive returns the one-word message sent to a process using SEND(2). If no messages are waiting, *receive* blocks until one appears.

SEE ALSO

preceive(2), psend(2), receive(2)

NAME

recvclr — clear incoming message buffer asynchronously

SYNOPSIS

int recvclr ()

DESCRIPTION

A process executes *recvclr* to clear its message buffer of any waiting message in preparation for receiving messages. If a message is waiting, *recvclr* returns it to the caller. If no messages are waiting, *recvclr* returns OK.

SEE ALSO

receive (2), send (2), preceive (2), psend (2)

NAME

recvtim — receive a message with timeout

SYNOPSIS

int recvtim(maxwait)
int maxwait;

DESCRIPTION

Recvtim allows a process to specify a maximum time limit it is willing to wait for a message to arrive. Like RECEIVE(2), *recvtim* blocks the calling process until a message arrives from SEND(2). Argument *maxwait* gives the maximum time to wait for a message, specified in tenths of seconds.

Recvtim returns integer SYSERR if the argument is incorrect or if no clock is present. It returns integer TIMEOUT if the time limit expires before a message arrives. Otherwise, it returns the message.

SEE ALSO

receive(2), recvclr(2), send(2), sleep10(2), sleep(2)

BUGS

There is no way to distinguish between messages that contain TIMEOUT or SYSERR and errors reported by *recvtim*.

NAME

remove — remove a file from the file system

SYNOPSIS

int remove(filename, key)
char *filename;
int key;

DESCRIPTION

Remove takes a file name as an argument and destroys the named file (i.e., removes it from the file system). Argument *filename* specifies the name of a file to remove, and the optional argument *key* gives a one-word protection key.

Remove uses the namespace to map the given file name to a new name, and invokes CONTROL(2) on the underlying device to destroy the file. It returns SYSERR if the name is illegal or cannot be mapped to an underlying device. It returns whatever CONTROL(2) returns otherwise.

SEE ALSO

control(2), nammap(2), namespace(4)

NAME

resume — resume a suspended process

SYNOPSIS

int resume(pid)
int pid;

DESCRIPTION

Resume takes process *pid* out of hibernation and allows it to resume execution. If *pid* is invalid or process *pid* is not suspended, *resume* returns SYSERR; otherwise it returns the priority at which the process resumed execution. Only suspended processes may be resumed.

SEE ALSO

sleep(2), suspend(2), send(2), receive(2)

NAME

scount — return the count associated with a semaphore

SYNOPSIS

int scount(sem)

int sem;

DESCRIPTION

Scount returns the current count associated with semaphore *sem*. A count of negative p means that there are p processes waiting on the semaphore; a count of positive p means that at most p more calls to WAIT(2) can occur before a process will be blocked (assuming no intervening sends occur).

SEE ALSO

screate(2), sdelete(2), signal(2), sreset(2), wait(2)

BUGS

In this version, there is no way to distinguish SYSERR from a legal semaphore count of −1.

NAME

screate — create a new semaphore

SYNOPSIS

int screate(count)
int count;

DESCRIPTION

Screate creates a counting semaphore and initializes it to *count*. If successful, *screate* returns the integer identifier of the new semaphore. It returns SYSERR if no more semaphores can be allocated or if *count* is less than zero.

Semaphores are manipulated with WAIT(2) and SIGNAL(2) to synchronize processes. Waiting causes the semaphore count to be decremented; decrementing a semaphore count past zero causes a process to be blocked. Signaling a semaphore increases its count, freeing a blocked process if one is waiting.

SEE ALSO

scount(2), sdelete(2), signal(2), sreset(2), wait(2)

NAME

    sdelete — delete a semaphore

SYNOPSIS

    int sdelete(sem)
    int sem;

DESCRIPTION

    Sdelete removes semaphore *sem* from the system and returns processes that were waiting for it to the ready state. The call returns SYSERR if *sem* is not a legal semaphore; it returns OK if the deletion was successful.

SEE ALSO

    scount(2), screate(2), signal(2), sreset(2), wait(2)

NAME

seek — device independent position seeking routine

SYNOPSIS

int seek(dev, position)
int dev;
char •buffer;
long position;

DESCRIPTION

Seek will position the device given by *dev* after the *position* byte. It returns SYSERR if *dev* is incorrect, or if it is not possible to position *dev* as specified.

Seek cannot be used with devices connected to terminals.

Note that the position argument is declared *long* rather than *int*.

SEE ALSO

close(2), control(2), getc(2), open(2), putc(2), read(2), write(2)

NAME

send — send a (one-word) message to a process

SYNOPSIS

int send(pid, msg)
int pid;
int msg;

DESCRIPTION

Send sends the one-word message *msg* to the process with id *pid*. A process may have at most one outstanding message that has not been received.

Send returns SYSERR if *pid* is invalid or if the process already has a message waiting that has not been received. Otherwise, it sends the message and returns OK.

SEE ALSO

receive(2), sendf(2), preceive(2), psend(2)

NAME

sendf − send a (one-word) message to a process, forcing delivery

SYNOPSIS

int sendf(pid, msg)
int pid;
int msg;

DESCRIPTION

Sendf sends the one-word message *msg* to the process with id *pid*. A process may have at most one outstanding message that has not been received. *Sendf* returns SYSERR if process id *pid* is invalid. Otherwise, it returns OK.

SEE ALSO

receive(2), recvtim(2), recvclr(2), preceive(2), psend(2)

NAME

setdev — set the standard input and output device ids for a process

SYNOPSIS

int setdev(pid, dev1, dev2)
int pid;
int dev1;
int dev2;

DESCRIPTION

Setdev records the device ids *dev1* and *dev2* in the process table entry for process *pid* so the system will automatically close the devices when the process exits. It is used primarily by the shell to record the process' standard input and standard output device ids.

SEE ALSO

close(2), kill(2)

BUGS

The limit of two device ids per process is fixed, and both must be set in a single call.

NAME

setnok — set next-of-kin for a specified process

SYNOPSIS

int setnok(nok, pid)
int nok;
int pid;

DESCRIPTION

Setnok sets *nok* to be the next-of-kin for process *pid* by recording *nok* in the process table entry for process *pid*. A call to *setnok* overwrites any previous information in the process table entry.

The next-of-kin for a process, *P*, is another process, *Q*, that the system notifies when *P* dies (i.e., exits). Notification consists of a message sent to *Q* containing only the process id, *P*.

Both arguments to *setnok* must be valid process ids. *Setnok* returns SYSERR to report errors in its arguments, and OK otherwise.

SEE ALSO

kill(2)

BUGS

There is no check to ensure that the next-of-kin remains in existence between the call to *setnok* and the termination of a process.

NAME
signal, signaln — signal a semaphore

SYNOPSIS
int signal(sem)
int signaln(sem, count)
int sem;
int count;

DESCRIPTION
In either form, *signal* signals semaphore *sem* and returns SYSERR if the semaphore does not exist, OK otherwise. The form *signal* increments the count of *sem* by 1 and frees the next process if any are waiting. The form *signaln* increments the semaphore by *count* and frees up to *count* processes if that many are waiting. Note that *signaln*(sem, x) is equivalent to executing *signal*(sem) x times.

SEE ALSO
scount(2), screate(2), sdelete(2), sreset(2), wait(2)

NAME

sleep, sleep10 — go to sleep for a specified time

SYNOPSIS

int sleep(secs)
int sleep10(tenths)
int secs;
int tenths;

DESCRIPTION

In either form, *sleep* causes the current process to delay for a specified time and then resume. The form *sleep* expects the delay to be given in an integral number of seconds; it is most useful for longer delays. The form *sleep10* expects the delay to be given in an integral number of tenths of seconds; it is most useful for short delays.

Both forms return SYSERR if the argument is negative or if the line time clock is not enabled on the processor. Otherwise they delay for the specified time and return OK.

SEE ALSO

suspend(2), unsleep(2)

BUGS

The maximum sleep is 32767 seconds (about 546 minutes, or 9.1 hours). Sleep guarantees a lower bound on delay, but since the system may delay processing of interrupts at times, sleep cannot guarantee an upper bound.

NAME
sreset — reset semaphore count

SYNOPSIS
int sreset(sem,count)
int sem;
int count;

DESCRIPTION
Sreset frees processes in the queue for semaphore *sem,* and resets its count to
count. This corresponds to the operations of sdelete(sem) and
sem=screate(count), except that it guarantees that the semaphore id *sem* does
not change. *Sreset* returns SYSERR if *sem* is not a valid semaphore id. The
current count in a semaphore does not affect resetting it.

SEE ALSO
scount(2), screate(2), sdelete(2), signal(2), wait(2)

NAME

suspend — suspend a process to keep it from executing

SYNOPSIS

int suspend(pid)
int pid;

DESCRIPTION

Suspend places process *pid* in a state of hibernation. If *pid* is illegal, or the process is not currently running or on the ready list, *suspend* returns SYSERR. Otherwise it returns the priority of the suspended process. A process may suspend itself, in which case the call returns the priority at which the process is resumed.

Note that hibernation differs from sleeping because a hibernating process can remain on I/O or semaphore queues. A process can put another into hibernation; a process can only put itself to sleep.

SEE ALSO

resume(2), sleep(2), send(2), receive(2)

NAME
unmount — remove an entry from the syntactic namespace mapping table

SYNOPSIS
int unmount(prefix)
char *prefix;

DESCRIPTION
Unmount searches the syntactic namespace mapping table and removes the mapping which has a prefix equal to the null-terminated string *prefix*. If no such entry exists, *unmount* returns SYSERR. Otherwise, it returns OK.

SEE ALSO
mount(2), namespace(4)

NAME

unsleep — remove a sleeping process from the clock queue prematurely

SYNOPSIS

int unsleep(pid)
int pid;

DESCRIPTION

Unsleep allow one process to take another out of the sleeping state before the time limit has expired. usually, only system routines like RECVTIM(2) and KILL(2) call *unsleep*. User-level processes can avoid using *unsleep* by arranging processes to cooperate using message passing primitives.

SEE ALSO

sleep(2), kill(2), recvtim(2)

NAME

wait — block and wait until semaphore signalled

SYNOPSIS

int wait(sem)
int sem;

DESCRIPTION

Wait decrements the count of semaphore *sem,* blocking the calling process if the count goes negative by enqueuing it in the queue for *sem.* The only ways to get free from a semaphore queue are for some other process to signal the semaphore, or for some other process to delete or reset the semaphore. *Wait* and SIGNAL(2) are the two basic synchronization primitives in the system.

Wait returns SYSERR if *sem* is invalid. Otherwise, it returns OK once freed from the queue.

SEE ALSO

scount(2), screate(2), sdelete(2), signal(2), sreset(2)

NAME

write — write a sequence of characters from a buffer

SYNOPSIS

int write(dev, buff, count)
int dev;
char *buff;
int count;

DESCRIPTION

Write writes *count* characters to the I/O device given by *dev,* from sequential
locations of the buffer, *buff. Write* returns SYSERR if *dev* or *count* is invalid,
OK for a successful write. Write normally returns when it is safe for the user
to change the contents of the buffer. For some devices this means write will
wait for I/O to complete before returning. On other devices, the data is copied
into a kernel buffer and the write returns while it is being transferred.

SEE ALSO

close(2), control(2), getc(2), open(2), putc(2), read(2), seek(2)

BUGS

Write may not have exclusive use of the I/O device, so output from other
processes may be mixed in.

Section 3: Library Procedures

This section of the manual describes the procedure (functions) available to programs from the standard libraries. C programmers will recognize some of the C-library functions (esp., those that manipulate strings). Be careful: not all procedure arguments are like those in UNIX.

NAME

blkcopy — copy a contiguous block of bytes

SYNOPSIS

int blkcopy(to, from, nbytes)
char *to;
char *from;
int nbytes;

DESCRIPTION

Blkcopy copies a block of *nbytes* contiguous bytes starting at location *from* into the area starting at location *to*. *Blkcopy* returns *OK* to the caller. *Blkcopy* will copy any byte value including the null character (zero).

SEE ALSO

blkequ(3), string(3)

BUGS

Blkcopy does not check for valid memory addresses.

NAME
blkequ — compare two contiguous blocks of memory for equality

SYNOPSIS
Bool blkequ(first, second, nbytes)
char *first;
char *second;
int nbytes;

DESCRIPTION
Blkequ compares two blocks of memory for equality. Each block contains exactly *nbytes* bytes. *Blkequ* returns FALSE if the two blocks differ, and TRUE if the blocks are equal. *Blkequ* compares all byte values including null (zero).

SEE ALSO
blkcopy(3), string(3)

BUGS
Blkequ does not check for valid memory addresses.

NAME

ckmode — check a file mode string and convert to integer representation

SYNOPSIS

#include <file.h>

int chmode(mode)
char *mode;

DESCRIPTION

Ckmode parses a null-terminated string, *mode*, containing characters that represent file modes, and produces an integer with mode bits set. The possible mode characters are:

r   The file is to be opened for reading (i.e., input).

w   The file is to be opened for writing (i.e., output).

n   The file must be new. That is, it must not already exist.

o   The file must be old. That is, it must already exist.

The file mode string, *mode*, can specify that the file is to be accessed for both reading and writing, but it cannot specify the mode to be both old and new. If neither reading nor writing is specified, *ckmode* assumes the file will be used for both. Similarly, if neither old or new files are specified, *ckmode* assumes either is allowed.

Given a legal mode string, *ckmode* returns an integer with bits *FLREAD*, FLWRITE, FLOLD, and FLNEW set according to the argument, *mode*. *Ckmode* returns SYSERR if it finds illegal or duplicated characters in the argument string, or if the mode string specifies that the file must be both old and new.

NAME

ctype — character type predicates and manipulation routines

SYNOPSIS

#include <ctype.h>

isalpha(c)

...

toascii(c)
tolower(c)
toupper(c)
char c;

DESCRIPTION

Routines beginning with *is* are predicates that classify the type of a character. Routines beginning with *to* convert characters. Each predicate returns *TRUE* if the condition is satisfied, and *FALSE* otherwise. In the current implementation, predicates are macros that use table lookup for efficiency.

isalnum	*c* is an alphanumeric character (i.e., a letter or digit)
isalpha	*c* is a lower- or upper-case letter
isascii	*c* is an ASCII character, code less than 0200
iscntrl	*c* has a value less than octal 040 or is a DEL (octal value 0177).
isdigit	*c* is a digit.
islower	*c* is a lower case letter.
isprint	*c* is a printable character with octal value 040 (blank) through 0176 (tilde).
isprshort	*c* is a printable short.
ispunct	*c* is a punctuation character (neither control nor alphanumeric).
isspace	*c* is a space, tab, carriage return, newline, or formfeed.
isupper	*c* is an upper case letter.
isxdigit	*c* is a hexadecimal digit (i.e., is 0—9 or a-f).
toascii	Converts *c* to an ascii by turning off high-order bits.
tolower	Converts argument *c* from upper to lower case.
toupper	Converts argument *c* from lower to upper case.

NAME

disable, enable, restore — change and restore processor interrupt status

SYNOPSIS

disable(ps);
enable(ps);
restore(ps);

char   ps;

DESCRIPTION

These routines change the processor interrupt status mode. Normally, procedures use *disable* and *restore* to save the interrupt status, mask interrupts off, and then restore the saved status. *Enable* explicitly enables interrupts; it is used only at system startup.

SEE ALSO

cvt(1)

BUGS

In this implementation, *disable* and *restore* are macros that must have local variable *ps* as an argument, and must use CVT(1) to convert the assembler code they produce to legal assembler.

NAME

dot2ip — convert dotted decimal notation to an IP address

SYNOPSIS

int dot2ip(ip, b1, b2, b3, b4)
IPaddr ip;
int   b1;
int   b2;
int   b3;
int   b4;

DESCRIPTION

Procedure *dot2ip* converts an Internet (IP) address from dotted decimal notation to its 32-bit integer form and stores it in argument *ip*. Each of the arguments *b1*, *b2*, *b3*, and *b4*, gives the value of one byte of the internet address.

NAME

EIS − extended instruction set for the LSI-11/2

SYNOPSIS

jsr pc,times2
jsr pc,over2
jsr pc,shift2
jsr pc,cshft2

DESCRIPTION

Library *eis.a* contains assembly language routines to simulate LSI-11 multiply, divide, arithmetic shift, and arithmetic shift combined instructions. Normally, an assembly language listing should be filtered through the programs *subMUL*, *subDIV*, *subASH*, and *subASHC* to replace any of the extended instructions with the proper calling sequence. The resulting assembly language program must be loaded with this library, which contains the routines called.

These routines do *not* use the C calling conventions. The multiply routine is called by:

mfps	-(sp)	/ push psw
mov	A,-(sp)	/ push multiplier
mov	R,-(sp)	/ push multiplicand
jsr	pc,times2	/ call mul simulation routine
mov	(sp)+,R	/ save low word of product
mov	(sp)+,R+1	/ save high word of product
mtps	(sp)+	/ put in new psw

where the instruction being mimicked is "mul A,R" and R is an even-numbered register (if R is odd, change the "mov (sp)+,R" to "tst (sp)+" and the "mov (sp)+,R+1" to "mov (sp)+,R").

The division routine is called by:

mfps	-(sp)	/ push psw
mov	A,-(sp)	/ push divisor
mov	R,-(sp)	/ push high word of dividend
mov	R+1,-(sp)	/ push low word of dividend
jsr	pc,over2	/ call div simulation routine
mov	(sp)+,R+1	/ save remainder
mov	(sp)+,R	/ save quotient
tst	(sp)+	/ reset stack pointer
mtps	(sp)+	/ put in new psw

where the instruction being mimicked is "div A,R".

The arithmetic shift routine is called by:

mfps	-(sp)	/ get psw
mov	A,-(sp)	/ push shift count onto the stack
mov	r0,-(sp)	/ push number to be shifted onto the stack
jsr	pc,shift2	/ call the simulation routine

mov	(sp)+,r0	/ save the result
tst	(sp)+	/ reset stack pointer
mtps	(sp)+	/ put in new psw

where the instruction being mimicked is "ash A,R". The arithmetic shift combined routine is called by:

mfps	-(sp)	/ get psw
mov	A,-(sp)	/ push shift count onto the stack
mov	r0,-(sp)	/ push high word onto the stack
mov	r1,-(sp)	/ push low word onto the stack
jsr	pc,shift2	/ call the simulation routine
mov	(sp)+,r1	/ save the low word
mov	(sp)+,r0	/ save the high word
tst	(sp)+	/ reset stack pointer
mtps	(sp)+	/ put in the new psw

where the instruction being mimicked is "ashc A,R".

FILES
    {Xinu-directory}/lib/libeis.a
    {Xinu-directory}/bin/subMUL
    {Xinu-directory}/bin/subDIV
    {Xinu-directory}/bin/subASH
    {Xinu-directory}/bin/subASHC

SEE ALSO
    cc11(1), subEIS(1)

DIAGNOSTICS
    The condition codes are correctly set by the above calling sequence.

NAME

fgetc, getchar — get character from a device

SYNOPSIS

#include <io.h>

int fgetc(dev)
int dev;

int getchar()

DESCRIPTION

These procedures are included for compatibility with UNIX. *Fgetc* returns the next character from the named input *device*.

Getchar() is identical to *getc(CONSOLE)*.

Note that *fgetc* is exactly equivalent to *getc*.

SEE ALSO

getc(2), putc(2), gets(3), scanf(3),

DIAGNOSTICS

These functions return SYSERR to indicate an illegal device or read error.

NAME

fputc, putchar — put character to a device

SYNOPSIS

#include <io.h>

int fputc(device, c)
int device;
char c;
putchar(c)

DESCRIPTION

These procedures are included for compatibility with UNIX. *Fputc* appends the character *c* to the named output *device*, and returns SYSERR if device is invalid; it is defined to be *putc(device, c)*.

Putchar(c) is also defined to be *putc(CONSOLE, c)*.

SEE ALSO

putc(2), puts(3), printf(3)

NAME

gets, fgets — get a string from a device

SYNOPSIS

#include <io.h>

char *gets(s)
char *s;

char *fgets(dev, s, n)
int   dev;
char *s;
int   n;

DESCRIPTION

Gets reads a string into *s* from the standard input device, CONSOLE. The string is terminated by a newline character, which is replaced in *s* by a null character. *Gets* returns its argument.

Fgets reads *n*−1 characters, or up to a newline character, whichever comes first, from device *dev* into the string *s*. The last character read into *s* is followed by a null character. *Fgets* returns its second argument.

SEE ALSO

getc(2), puts(2), scanf(3), fread(3),

DIAGNOSTICS

Gets and *fgets* return SYSERR if an error results.

BUGS

Gets deletes a newline, *fgets* keeps it, all in the name of backward compatibility.

NAME

    halt, pause — pause or halt the processor

SYNOPSIS

    #include <kernel.h>

    halt();
    pause();

DESCRIPTION

    Halt stops the processor immediately without affecting devices or direct-memory-access (DMA) operations on the bus. Once halted, the processor will not respond to interrupts. *Halt* is useful for debugging the operating system.

    Pause stops the processor until an interrupt occurs, allowing it to continue at the instruction following the *pause* when the interrupt returns. *Pause* is used in the null process instead of an infinite loop to avoid taking bus bandwidth needlessly.

    In the current implementation, both *halt* and *pause* are macros that expand to the assembler language *halt* and *pause* instructions. Thus, they can only be executed in kernel mode.

SEE ALSO

    disable(3), wait(2)

NAME

netnum — compute the network portion of a given Internet (IP) address

SYNOPSIS

#include <network.h>

int netnum(netpart, address)
IPaddr netpart;
IPaddr address;

DESCRIPTION

Netnum extracts the network portion of the Internet address specified by argument *address*, and places the result in argument *netpart*. It operates by using the IP class of argument *address* to determine whether the network part of the address occupies 1, 2, or 3 bytes, and it zeros the remaining bytes. *Netnum* always returns OK.

SEE ALSO

getaddr(2), getnet(2)

BUGS

Netnum does not understand subnets or subnet masks.

NAME

netutil — Network utilities hs2net, net2hs, hl2net, net2hl, vax2hl, hl2vax

SYNOPSIS

short net2hs(s)
short hs2net(s)
long net2hl(l)
long hl2net(l)
long vax2hl(l)
long hl2vax(l)

short s;
long l;

DESCRIPTION

These routines map binary integer data between network standard byte order and local host byte order. In the description, the term *short* refers to a 2-octet (16-bit) binary value, whether two's complement signed or unsigned, and the term *long refers to a 4-octet (32-bit) value. The individual routines are:*

net2hs

Converts a short item from network byte order to host byte order.

hs2net

Converts a short item from host byte order to network byte order.

net2hl

Converts a long item from network byte order to host byte order.

hl2net

Converts a long item from host byte order to network byte order.

vax2hl

Converts a long item from VAX byte order to host byte order (used in communication with a file server running on a VAX).

hl2vax

Converts a long from host byte order to VAX byte order (used in communication with a file server running on a VAX).

No conversion is needed for character strings because the local host order on most machines agrees with network standard byte order (i.e., the string extends upward in the memory address space).

NAME

printf, fprintf, sprintf − formatted output conversion

SYNOPSIS

printf(format [, arg] ...)
char *format;

fprintf(dev, format [, arg] ...)
int dev;
char *format;

sprintf(s, format [, arg] ...)
char *s, format;

DESCRIPTION

Printf writes formatted output on device *CONSOLE*. *Fprintf* writes formatted output on the named output *device*. *Sprintf* places formatted 'output' in the string *s*, followed by the character '\0'.

Each of these functions converts, formats, and prints its arguments after the format under control of the format argument. The format argument is a character string which contains two types of objects: plain characters, which are simply copied to the output stream, and conversion specifications, each of which causes conversion and printing of the next successive *arg*.

Each conversion specification is introduced by the character %. Following the %, there may be, in the following order,

- an optional minus sign '−' which specifies *left adjustment* of the converted value in the indicated field;

- an optional digit string specifying a *field width;* if the converted value has fewer characters than the field width it will be blank-padded on the left (or right, if the left-adjustment indicator has been given) to make up the field width; if the field width begins with a zero, zero-padding will be done instead of blank-padding;

- an optional period '.' which serves to separate the field width from the next digit string;

- an optional digit string specifying a *precision* which specifies the maximum number of characters to be printed from a string;

- the character **l** specifying that a following **d, o, x,** or **u** corresponds to a long integer *arg*. (A capitalized conversion code accomplishes the same thing.)

- a character which indicates the type of conversion to be applied.

A field width or precision may be '*' instead of a digit string. In this case an integer *arg* supplies the field width or precision.

The conversion characters and their meanings are

dox The integer *arg* is converted to decimal, octal, or hexadecimal notation respectively.

c   The character *arg* is printed. Null characters are ignored.

s   *Arg* is taken to be a string (character pointer) and characters from the string are printed until a null character or until the number of characters indicated by the precision specification is reached; however if the precision is 0 or missing all characters up to a null are printed.

u   The unsigned integer *arg* is converted to decimal and printed (the result will be in the range 0 through 65535 on the LSI-11 for normal integers and 0 through 4294967295 for long integers).

%   Print a '%'; no argument is converted.

In no case does a non-existent or small field width cause truncation of a field; padding takes place only if the specified field width exceeds the actual width. Characters generated by *printf* are printed by PUTC(2).

Examples
To print a date and time in the form 'Sunday, July 3, 10:02', where *weekday* and *month* are pointers to null-terminated strings:

        printf("%s, %s %d, %02d:%02d", weekday, month, day, hour, min);

SEE ALSO
    putc(2), scanf(3)

BUGS
    Very wide fields (>128 characters) fail.

NAME
   puts, fputs — write a string to a device

SYNOPSIS
   puts(s)
   char *s;

   fputs(dev, s)
   int dev;
   char *s;

DESCRIPTION
   Puts writes the null-terminated string *s* on the output device CONSOLE and appends a newline character.

   Fputs writes the null-terminated string *s* on device *dev*.

   Neither routine writes the terminal null character. They return SYSERR if *dev* is invalid.

SEE ALSO
   gets(3), putc(3), printf(3), read(2), write(2)

BUGS
   Puts appends a newline, *fputs* does not; there is no good reason for this.

NAME

    qsort — quicker sort

SYNOPSIS

    qsort(base, nel, width, compar)

    char *base;

    int (*compar)();

DESCRIPTION

    Qsort is an implementation of the quicker-sort algorithm. The first argument is a pointer to the base of the data; the second is the number of elements; the third is the width of an element in bytes; the last is the name of the comparison routine to be called with two arguments which are pointers to the elements being compared. The routine must return an integer less than, equal to, or greater than 0 according as the first argument is to be considered less than, equal to, or greater than the second.

NAME

queue - q-structure predicates and list manipulation procedures

SYNOPSIS

#include <q.h>

int enqueue(proc, tail)
int dequeue(proc)
int firstid(head)
int firstkey(head)
int getfirst(head)
int getlast(tail)
int insert(proc, head, key)
int insertd(proc, head, key)
Bool isempty(head)
int lastkey(tail)
Bool nonempty(head)

int head, tail;
int proc;
int key;

DESCRIPTION

The *q* structure holds doubly-linked lists of processes, including lists of processes that are ready, sleeping, and waiting on a semaphore. These routines manipulate lists in the *q* structure as follows.

enqueue

Add a process to a FIFO list given the process id in argument *proc* and the *q* index of the tail of the list in argument *tail*. *Enqueue* returns argument *proc* to its caller.

dequeue

Remove a process from a list given the process id. The list on which the process is found need not be specified because it can be determined from the *q* structure. *Dequeue* will remove a process from both FIFO and ordered lists. It returns its argument to the caller.

firstid

Return the process id of the first process on a list given the *q* index of the list head in argument *head*.

firstkey

Return the integer key associated with the first entry on a list given the *q* index of the list in argument *head*.

getfirst

Remove the first process from a list and return its process id given the *q* index of the head of the list in argument *head*. *Getfirst* returns EMPTY if the list is empty, and a process id otherwise.

getlast

Remove the last process on a list and return its process id given the *q* index of the tail of the list in argument *tail*. *Getlast* returns EMPTY if the list is empty, and a process id otherwise.

insert

Insert a process into an ordered list given the process id in argument *proc*, the *q* index of the head of the list in argument *head*, and an integer key for the process in argument *key*. Ordered lists are always ordered by increasing key values. *Insert* returns OK.

insertd

Insert a process in a delta list given the process id in argument *proc*, the *q* index of the head of the list in argument *head*, and an integer key in argument *key*. *Insertd* returns OK.

isempty

Return TRUE if there are no processes on a list, FALSE otherwise, given the *q* index of the head of the list in argument *head*.

lastkey

Return the key of the last process in a list given the *q* index of the tail of the list in argument *tail*.

nonempty

Return TRUE if there is at least one process on a list, FALSE otherwise, given the *q* index of the head of the list in argument *head*.

BUGS

Most of these routines do not check for valid arguments or valid lists. Also, they assume interrupts are disabled when called, and will corrupt the list structure if the caller fails to disable interrupts.

NAME

rand, srand — random number generator

SYNOPSIS

srand(seed)
int seed;

rand()

DESCRIPTION

Rand uses a multiplicative congruential random number generator with period 2^{32} to return successive pseudo-random numbers in the range from 0 to $2^{31}-1$.

The generator is reinitialized by calling *srand* with 1 as argument. It can be set to a random starting point by calling *srand* with whatever you like as argument.

BUGS

Rand does not provide mutual exclusion among calling processes. Thus, there is a small chance that two concurrent processes will receive the same value.

NAME

scanf, fscanf, sscanf — formatted input conversion

SYNOPSIS

scanf(format [, pointer] ...)
char *format;

fscanf(dev, format [, pointer] ...)
int dev;
char *format;

sscanf(s, format [, pointer] ...)
char *s, *format;

DESCRIPTION

Scanf reads from the standard input device *CONSOLE*. *Fscanf* reads from the named input *device*. *Sscanf* reads from the character string *s*. Each function reads characters, interprets them according to a format, and stores the results in its arguments. Each expects as arguments a control string *format,* described below, and a set of *pointer* arguments indicating where the converted input should be stored.

The control string usually contains conversion specifications, which are used to direct interpretation of input sequences. The control string may contain:

1. Blanks, tabs or newlines, which match optional white space in the input.

2. An ordinary character (not %) which must match the next character of the input stream.

3. Conversion specifications, consisting of the character %, an optional assignment suppressing character *, an optional numerical maximum field width, and a conversion character.

A conversion specification directs the conversion of the next input field; the result is placed in the variable pointed to by the corresponding argument, unless assignment suppression was indicated by *. An input field is defined as a string of non-space characters; it extends to the next inappropriate character or until the field width, if specified, is exhausted.

The conversion character indicates the interpretation of the input field; the corresponding pointer argument must usually be of a restricted type. The following conversion characters are legal:

%   a single '%' is expected in the input at this point; no assignment is done.

d   a decimal integer is expected; the corresponding argument should be an integer pointer.

o   an octal integer is expected; the corresponding argument should be an integer pointer.

x   a hexadecimal integer is expected; the corresponding argument should be an integer pointer.

s   a character string is expected; the corresponding argument should be a character pointer pointing to an array of characters large enough to accept the string and a terminating '\0', which will be added. The input field is terminated by a space character or a newline.

c   a character is expected; the corresponding argument should be a character pointer. The normal skip over space characters is suppressed in this case; to read the next non-space character, try '%1s'. If a field width is given, the corresponding argument should refer to a character array, and the indicated number of characters is read.

e f   a floating point number is expected; the next field is converted accordingly and stored through the corresponding argument, which should be a pointer to *float*. The input format for floating point numbers is an optionally signed string of digits possibly containing a decimal point, followed by an optional exponent field consisting of an E or e followed by an optionally signed integer.

[indicates a string not to be delimited by space characters. The left bracket is followed by a set of characters and a right bracket; the characters between the brackets define a set of characters making up the string. If the first character is not circumflex (^), the input field is all characters until the first character not in the set between the brackets; if the first character after the left bracket is circumflex (^), the input field is all characters until the first character which is in the remaining set of characters between the brackets. The corresponding argument must point to a character array.

The conversion characters **d, o** and **x** may be capitalized or preceded by l to indicate that a pointer to **long** rather than to **int** is in the argument list. Similarly, the conversion characters **e** or **f** may be capitalized or preceded by l to indicate a pointer to **double** rather than to **float**. The conversion characters **d, o** and **x** may be preceded by **h** to indicate a pointer to **short** rather than to **int**.

The *scanf* functions return the number of successfully matched and assigned input items. This can be used to decide how many input items were found. The constant **EOF** is returned upon end of input; note that this is different from 0, which means that no conversion was done; if conversion was intended, it was frustrated by an inappropriate character in the input.

For example, the call

        int i; float x; char name[50];
        scanf("%d%f%s", &i, &x, name);

with the input line

        25   54.32E−1 thompson

will assign to *i* the value 25, *x* the value 5.432, and *name* will contain *'thompson\0'*. Or,

> int i; float x; char name[50];
> scanf("%2d%f%*d%[1234567890]", &i, &x, name);

with input

> 56789 0123 56a72

will assign 56 to *i*, 789.0 to *x*, skip '0123', and place the string '56\0' in *name*. The next call to *getchar* will return 'a'.

SEE ALSO
getc(2), printf(3)

DIAGNOSTICS
The *scanf* functions return SYSERR on end of input, and a short count for missing or illegal data items.

BUGS
The success of literal matches and suppressed assignments is not directly determinable.

NAME

strcat, strncat, strcmp, strncmp, strcpy, strncpy, strlen, index, rindex — string operations

SYNOPSIS

char *strcat(s1, s2)
char *s1, *s2;

char *strncat(s1, s2, n)
char *s1, *s2;

strcmp(s1, s2)
char *s1, *s2;

strncmp(s1, s2, n)
char *s1, *s2;

char *strcpy(s1, s2)
char *s1, *s2;

char *strncpy(s1, s2, n)
char *s1, *s2;

strlen(s)
char *s;

char *index(s, c)
char *s, c;

char *rindex(s, c)
char *s, c;

DESCRIPTION

These functions operate on null-terminated strings. They do not check for overflow of any receiving string.

Strcat appends a copy of string *s2* to the end of string *s1*. *Strncat* copies at most *n* characters. Both return a pointer to the null-terminated result.

Strcmp compares its arguments and returns an integer greater than, equal to, or less than 0, according as *s1* is lexicographically greater than, equal to, or less than *s2*. *Strncmp* makes the same comparison but examines at most *n* characters.

Strcpy copies string *s2* to *s1*, stopping after the null character has been moved. *Strncpy* copies exactly *n* characters, truncating or null-padding *s2*; the target may not be null-terminated if the length of *s2* is *n* or more. Both return *s1*.

Strlen returns the number of non-null characters in *s*.

Index (*rindex*) returns a pointer to the first (last) occurrence of character *c* in string *s*, or zero if *c* does not occur in the string.

NAME
swab — swap bytes

SYNOPSIS
swab(from, to, nbytes)
char *from, *to;

DESCRIPTION
Swab copies *nbytes* bytes pointed to by *from* to the position pointed to by *to*, exchanging adjacent even and odd bytes. It is useful for carrying binary data between LSI 11's and other machines. *Nbytes* should be even.

SEE ALSO
hs2net(3) hl2net(3), net2hl(3), net2hs(3)

Section 4: Device Descriptions

This section of the manual describes the Xinu device drivers available on the distribution tape. Each device driver implements the device independent I/O routines *open*, *close*, *read*, *write*, *seek*, *getc*, *putc*, *control*, and *init*, for one physical or pseudo-device. While the intuitive meanings of these routines are the same across all devices, each driver defines specific, sometimes device dependent meaning to them. If a particular operation does not make sense for a given device, the driver may choose to return *SYSERR* or *OK* without taking further action.

NAME

ether — standard 10Mbps Ethernet network interface device driver (type eth)

SYNOPSIS

#include <deqna.h>
#include <ether.h>

read(device buffer, length)
write(device, buffer, length)
init(device)

DESCRIPTION

The *eth* device driver provides input and output for a 10 Mbps Ethernet local area network. The standard Xinu device name for Ethernet devices is *ETHER*.

Implemented on a Digital Equipment Corporation DEQNA (Digital Equipment Q-Bus Network Adapter), the *eth* driver handles DMA input and output at the physical network level, transmitting complete frames between user processes and the device.

The driver honors the following operations:

read(device buffer, length)

Reads one frame into *buffer*, copying no more than *length* characters. It returns the length of the frame read; the count includes the 14-octet header.

write(device, buffer, length)

Writes a frame of *length* characters found in *buffer*. It returns *OK* if the frame was acceptable, *SYSERR* otherwise. It it important to note that *buffer* must specify the address of a valid buffer allocated from GETBUF(2), and that the driver does not copy the contents of the buffer. The call to *write* will return once output has been started, but the buffer will be in use until the device finishes. The driver calls FREEBUF(2) to dispose of the buffer once the device finishes using it.

init(device)

Initializes the device and driver, including DEQNA setup packet processing. The driver sets the device to accept only those packets addressed directly to the devices' physical address and broadcast packets (all 1's address).

NOTES

Although the DEQNA supports chaining back-to-back operations on both input and output, the driver forces a context switch and a new call from READ(2) or WRITE(2) to restart I/O, and depends on the hardware to buffer packets from the Ethernet.

NAME

internet — IP-level Internet interface pseudo-device driver (types dgm, dg)

SYNOPSIS

#include <network.h>

read(device buffer, length)
write(device, buffer, length)
open(device, name)
close(device)
control(device, function, arg1)
init(device)

DESCRIPTION

The *dgm* and *dg* device drivers, which operate as a related pair, provide a network interface at the IP datagram level. They accept datagrams from user processes and send them out on the DARPA Internet, or receive datagrams from the Internet and deliver them to user processes. The standard Xinu device name for the datagram master pseudo-device is *INTERNET*, and the standard name for individual connection pseudo-devices is *DGRAM*.

The drivers cooperate so that users can initiate connection by calling OPEN(2) on the datagram master device. If successful, the call to OPEN(2) returns the device descriptor of a *dg* pseudo-device that can be used with READ(2) or WRITE(2) to transfer data. Finally, when finished with the connection, the user process calls CLOSE(2) on the *dg* device.

The *dgm* driver consists of routines that implement OPEN(2) and CONTROL(2), while the *dg* driver consists of routines for READ(2), WRITE(2), CLOSE(2), and CONTROL(2). Primitives READ(2) and WRITE(2) operate in one of two basic modes. Either they transfer data in Xinugram format complete with an address header, or they transfer just the data portion of the datagram.

open(device,name,mode)

Used with the master device to open a datagram pseudo-device. Name is a string that gives an IP address and UDP port number in the form *i1.i2.i3.i4:u*.

control(device,function,arg1)

Used with master device to set the default gateway for nonlocal IP datagram traffic. The only function supported is *DGM_GATE* which takes an IP address as an argument and sets the default gateway to that address.

Used with a *dg* pseudo-device to set the transfer mode. The valid operations include *DG_CLEAR*, which clears any UDP datagrams that happen to be in the receive queue, and *DG_SETMODE*, which sets the pseudo-device mode.

The mode argument composed of a word in which the first two bits control the transfer mode and sixth bit controls timeout. The symbolic constants for these bits are:

DG_NMODE (001) − Normal mode
DG_DMODE (002) − Data-only mode
DG_TMODE (040) − Timeout all reads

Note that timeout can be applied to either transfer mode.

read(device buffer, length)

Used with a *dg* pseudo-device to await the arrival of a UDP datagram and transfer it to the user in the form of a Xinugram.

write(device, buffer, length)

Used with a *dg* pseudo-device to transfer a xinugram into a UDP datagram and send it on the Internet.

close(device)

Closes a *dg* pseudo-device.

init(device)

When applied to *dg* pseudo-devices initializes each to mark it not in use.

NAME

namespace — syntactic namespace pseudo-device driver (type nam)

SYNOPSIS

#include <name.h>

open(device, name, mode)
init(device)

DESCRIPTION

The *nam* pseudo-device driver provides mapping of OPEN(2) calls to underlying devices based on name syntax. The standard Xinu name for the namespace device is *NAMESPACE*.

The *nam* driver provides two operations as follows:

open(device,name,mode)

Open a device given its name and access mode (see ACCESS(2) for an explanation of modes).

init(device)

Initialize the namespace by establishing a default interpretation for names.

NOTES

Although system calls MOUNT(2), UNMOUNT(2), NAMMAP(2), and NAMREPL(2) are intricate parts of the naming system, they are not included in the driver simply because they do not fit the read/write paradigm easily.

NAME
    rfilsys — remote file system pseudo-device driver (types rfm, rf)

SYNOPSIS
    #include <rfile.h>
    #include <fserver.h>

    read(device buffer, length)
    write(device, buffer, length)
    open(device, name, mode)
    close(device)
    control(device, function, arg1, arg2)
    init(device)
    seek(device,offset)

DESCRIPTION
    The *rfm* and *rf* pseudo-device drivers work as a pair to provide access to
    remote files using a Xinu remote file server across an Internet. There is one
    master remote file pseudo-device (type *rfm*) for a given remote server. When
    users open the master remote file pseudo-device, they pass it the name of a
    specific file and the access mode for that file. The call to OPEN(2) returns
    the device descriptor of a remote file pseudo-device (type *rf*) connected to the
    named file.

    Once opened, a user calls READ(2), WRITE(2), GETC(2), or PUTC(2), to
    transfer data between the user program and the remote file; they call SEEK(2)
    to position the file pointer. The user calls CLOSE(2) to disconnect from the
    file. Finally, users call CONTROL(2) on the master pseudo-device to test file
    access protections, remove files, or change file names.

    The standard Xinu device name for the remote file master pseudo-device is
    RFILSYS; the standard Xinu device name for individual remote file pseudo-
    devices is *RFILE*. The operations on these devices are defined by:

    open(device, name, mode)
            Opens a connection to a remote file given the file name and access
            mode, and returns the device descriptor used to access the file. See
            ACCESS(2) for valid file modes.

    read(device buffer, length)
            Transfers up to *length* bytes of data from a file to the user's *buffer*,
            and returns the number of bytes found or *EOF* if no more data
            remains in the file.

    write(device, buffer, length)
            Writes *length* bytes of data to a file from the user's *buffer*. File length
            extends automatically if needed.

    close(device)

Disconnect from a file, leaving it on secondary storage.

control(device, function, arg1, arg2)

Handles file manipulation other than data transfer. The possible functions are:

FLACCESS — test access (*arg1* is mode string).
FLREMOVE — remove file named by *arg1*.
FLRENAME — rename file named by *arg1* to *arg2*
FLCLEAR — clear the remote file datagram port

init(device)

When called with an *rf* device, initializes the pseudo-device data structures at system startup. Initializing the master pseudo-device has no effect.

seek(device,offset)

Positions the file to *offset* bytes from the beginning.

NAME
tty — general-purpose terminal I/O device driver (type tty)

SYNOPSIS
    #include <slu.h>
    #include <tty.h>

    read(device buffer, length)
    write(device, buffer, length)
    open(device, name)
    close(device)
    control(device, function, arg1, arg2)
    init(device)

DESCRIPTION
The *tty* device driver provides input and output for a full-duplex ascii terminal device. On most Xinu systems, device *CONSOLE* is of type tty.

Currently implemented on a Digital Equipment Corporation serial line unit (SLU) like that on the DLV11 and MXV11, the driver expects one interrupt per character on both input and output.

The *tty* driver operates in one of three modes, with switching between the modes determined dynamically. In *raw mode*, it passes incoming characters to the reading process without further processing. In *cbreak mode*, the driver honors XON-XOFF flow control, character echo, and mapping between carriage return and line feed. In *cooked mode* the driver behaves like cbreak mode, but also handles line editing with backspace and line kill keys. Characters are processed according to the driver mode when they arrive, and are placed in a queue from which upper-half routines extract them. Echoing, presentation of control characters, and editing are controlled by several fields in the driver control structure, and may be changed dynamically.

The upper-half routines behave as follows:

read(device,buffer,length)
Reads up to one line into the user's *buffer*, stopping on an END-OF-FILE or NEWLINE character, or after *length* characters have been supplied. As a special case, if *length* is zero, the driver reads whatever characters are available in the input buffer (possibly zero). In cooked mode, *read* blocks until a line has been typed.

write(device,buffer,length)
Writes *length* characters from the user's *buffer*, mapping CARRIAGE RETURN to NEWLINE as specified by field *ocrlf* of the driver control structure. Write may block if the output exceeds the currently available buffer space.

getc(device)

Reads a single character and returns it as the function value.

putc(device,char)

Writes character *char*.

open(device,name)

Returns *OK* if character string *name* is null, and *SYSERR* otherwise, taking no action except generating a return value.

close(device)

Returns *OK* without taking any action.

init(device)

Initializes the driver. Note: for historical reasons, device *CONSOLE* is initialized to cooked mode with echo, visual control character printing, and line editing enabled, while other devices are initialized to raw mode.

control(device,function)

Controls the driver and provides non-transfer operations. The valid functions are:

TCSETBRK − set the line into the "break" state.

TCRSTBRK − reset the line, turning off "break" state.

TCNEXTC − lookahead one character without reading it.

TCMODER − change the driver to raw mode.

TCMODEC − change the driver to cooked mode.

TCMODEK − change the driver to cbreak mode.

TCECHO − turn on character echo.

TCNOECHO − turn off character echo.

TCICHARS − return a count of characters in the input buffer.

DIAGNOSTICS

Character errors are reported by turning on the high-order bit of the character.

NOTES

The version 6 driver used buffer counts as exact requests; version 7 is line oriented. Error reporting should be improved.

Appendix 3

Summary of Protocol Formats

This appendix summarizes the network protocols used throughout the text, showing the packet layout in table form. The protocols described are:

- **ARP & RARP**, the DARPA Address Resolution protocols,

- **ETHERNET**, the Ethernet link-level frame protocol,

- **ELOAD**, the Xinu Ethernet downloader protocol

- **FS**, the Xinu Remote File System protocol,

- **ICMP**, the DARPA Internet Control Message Protocol,

- **IP**, the DARPA Internet datagram protocol,

- **PURPLE**, the Xinu serial-line downloader protocol

- **UDP**, the DARPA Internet User Datagram Protocol,

Unless otherwise indicated, all binary integer fields in protocol headers are sent in *network byte order* with the most-significant byte sent first and the least-significant byte sent last. The LSI 11 and VAX computers store binary data in memory such that the least-significant byte resides at the lowest memory location, forcing the operating system to reverse the byte order for binary data before sending it and after receiving it. A further complication arises with LSI 11 long integers (4-byte integers) because they are stored with words swapped and bytes within words swapped. Thus, to examine a packet in memory, one must know whether integers in the packet have been translated to the host's format. No problem arises from character data because the host order and network order agree.

The remainder of this appendix illustrates protocol formats with tables that show packets as a sequence of 32-bit longwords. The heading above each table lists the starting bit positions of fields in the header, counting bits from 0 on the left.

DARPA ARP and RARP Protocol Format

The DARPA Address Resolution Protocol (ARP) provides dynamic binding between an Internet address and a physical address. The client, who knows an Internet address, broadcasts a request. Each machine acts as a server, responding to requests for its IP address, and returning a reply that contains its physical address.

The Reverse Address Resolution Protocol (RARP) allows a machine to determine its Internet (IP) address knowing only its physical hardware address using the same packet format as ARP. The machine wishing to know its address broadcasts a request, and receives a reply from the server.

Unlike most protocols, ARP/RARP packets do not have a fixed-format header. Instead, the early header fields contain counts that specify lengths of succeeding fields. The example below shows the ARP/RARP packet format for Ethernet hardware addresses (6 octets long), and Internet protocol addresses (4 octets long).

0	8	16	31
HARDWARE		PROTOCOL	
HLEN	PLEN	OPERATION	
SENDER HA (octets 0-3)			
SENDER HA(octets 4-5)		SENDER IP (octets 0-1)	
SENDER IP (octets 2-3)		TARGET HA (octets 0-1)	
TARGET HA (octets 2-5)			
TARGET IP (octets 0-4)			

Field *HARDWARE* specifies a hardware interface type for which the sender seeks an answer.

Field *OPERATION* specifies an ARP request, ARP response, RARP request, or RARP response.

The sender supplies its hardware address and Internet address, if known, in fields *SENDER HA* and *SENDER IP*.

When making a request, the sender also supplies the target hardware address (RARP) or target protocol address (ARP), using fields *TARGET HA* and *TARGET IP*. A response carries both the target machine's hardware and IP addresses.

Ethernet Link-Level Protocol Format

The Ethernet, a local area packet-switched network, uses the following link-level packet format.

```
0                              16                              31
┌──────────────────────────────────────────────────────────────┐
│                      PREAMBLE (0-31)                           │
├──────────────────────────────────────────────────────────────┤
│                      PREAMBLE (32-63)                          │
├──────────────────────────────────────────────────────────────┤
│                 DESTINATION ADDRESS (0-31)                     │
├───────────────────────────────┬──────────────────────────────┤
│      DEST. ADDRESS (32-47)     │     SOURCE ADDRESS (0-15)     │
├───────────────────────────────┴──────────────────────────────┤
│                    SOURCE ADDRESS (16-47)                      │
├───────────────────────────────┬──────────────────────────────┤
│          PACKET TYPE           │      DATA (octets 0-1)        │
├───────────────────────────────┴──────────────────────────────┤
│                     DATA (octets 2-5)                          │
├──────────────────────────────────────────────────────────────┤
│                            . . .                               │
├──────────────────────────────────────────────────────────────┤
│                   DATA (up to octet 1522)                      │
├──────────────────────────────────────────────────────────────┤
│                        CRC CHECKSUM                            │
└──────────────────────────────────────────────────────────────┘
```

The *PREAMBLE* consists of 64 bits of alternating ones and zeros. Fields *DESTINATION* and *SOURCE* specify the 48-bit Ethernet physical address of the receiver and sender. The *PACKET TYPE* field contains a 16-bit integer code that describes the format of the *DATA* in the packet. Finally, field *CRC CHECKSUM* contains a 32-bit Cyclic Redundancy Code computed by the sender and checked by the receiver to ensure integrity of the packet contents.

Normally, hardware supplies the 64-bit preamble and 32-bit CRC Checksum fields. Thus, packets in memory consist of only four fields: a 48-bit destination address, a 48-bit source address, a 16-bit packet type, and data.

Xinu Ethernet Downloader (ELOAD) Protocol Format

Xinu software is cross-compiled and cross-linked on a large timesharing system and downloaded into a microcomputer for execution. The Ethernet downloader protocol provides quick downloading of memory images over an Ethernet. It has been designed for an environment where the large timesharing system supplies only UDP/IP even though the target microcomputer can read and write packets directly to the Ethernet. In particular, the target microcomputer responds to ARP requests, allowing the timesharing system to think of the micro as a running system.

Downloader messages arrive encapsulated in standard IP datagrams using UDP. The data field of the UDP datagram contains one downloader message, which has one of two forms (data packet or command packet). All packets except the last one contain data to be loaded into memory. Memory data packets have the following format.

0	16	31
ADDRESS	DATA LENGTH	
DATA (BYTES 0-3)		
. . .		

Field *ADDRESS* specifies the memory address at which the data should be placed, and field *DATA LENGTH* gives the count of data bytes that follow. The data must be sent in exactly the order in which it should appear in the target machine's memory; the downloading protocol does not change byte order.

The last packet sent by the downloader contains register values and a startup command in the following format.

0	16	31
COMMAND (-1)	DATA LENGTH	
REGISTER 0	REGISTER 1	
REGISTER 2	REGISTER 3	
REGISTER 4	REGISTER 5	
REGISTER 6	REGISTER 7	
REGISTER PS	DELAY	
START ADDRESS		

Field *COMMAND* contains the value −1, and is used to distinguish the command packet from data packets. Successive fields contain initial values for the machine registers, followed by an optional delay. If nonnegative, the downloader will delay for approximately the specified number of seconds and then execute the downloaded program. If field *DELAY* contains a negative value, the downloader halts the processor after setting the registers. Field *START ADDRESS* contains the program entry point address as set by the loader.

The current version of the Ethernet downloader sends acknowledgements back to the downloading process over the console serial line. The valid responses are listed below.

Character	Meaning
R	Ready (Sent when eload starts)
A	Positive Acknowledgment of packet receipt
N	Negative Acknowledgement (retransmit)

Using the serial line to synchronize makes the downloading code straightforward, but may introduce unnecessary delay depending on processor load. It also prohibits the downloader from directing an image to a machine for which it does not have a serial connection. In particular, there is no way for a machine to request downloading. A new version is planned that sends acknowledgements over the Ethernet.

Xinu File Server (FS) Protocol Format

The Xinu remote file client communicates with a stateless remote file server using the File Server Protocol. Every request is acknowledged by the server with a reply that uses the same format as requests. The packet format is shown below.

0	16	31
FILE POSITION		
CHARACTER COUNT	OPERATION CODE	
FILE NAME (octets 0-3)		
. . .		
FILE NAME (octets 76-79)		
DATA (octets 0-3)		
. . .		
DATA (octets 508-511)		

Each request uses field *FILE POSITION* to specify an offset into a file at which the requested operation takes place. Field *CHARACTER COUNT* specifies the number of bytes to be transferred, and field *OPERATION CODE* specifies the operation to be performed (e.g., read or write). Field *FILE NAME* contains a null-terminated file or directory name. Finally, field *DATA* is optional. If present, it contains the data transferred. A summary of allowable operations and the exact interpretation of fields for each is given below.

op code	operation	count	position	object name	data
0	open	mode	file size[1]	file name	—
1	close	—	—	file name	
2	read	# bytes	offset[3]	file name	data read[1]
3	write	# bytes	offset[3]	file name	data written[2]
4	unlink	—	—	file name	—
5	rename	—	—	old name	new name
6	make dir.	mode	—	dir. name	—
7	remove dir.	—	—	dir. name	—
8	check access	mode	—	file name	—
−1	error[1]	—	—	—	—

---

[1]Field used only in reply packets.
[2]Field used only in request packets.
[3]Requests specify the starting offset for a transfer; replies specify the file offset after the transfer.

DARPA ICMP Protocol Format

Gateways send DARPA Internet Control Protocol Messages (ICMP) to hosts when they detect illegal or inefficiently routed datagrams. Hosts sometimes send ICMP messages to other hosts as well. Each ICMP message travels in an IP datagram, and has a format that depends on the message being sent. ICMP echo request/reply messages have the following form.

0	8	16	31
TYPE	CODE	CHECKSUM	
IDENTIFICATION		SEQUENCE NUMBER	
DATA			
. . .			

Field *TYPE* contains 8 for echo request, 0 for echo reply. The *CODE* field is zero.

Field *CHECKSUM* contains the ones complement of a ones complement checksum for the message.

Fields *identification* and *sequence* contain an identifier and sequence number used by the client to match replies to requests.

The field listed as *DATA* is an optional, variable-length fields that contains data to be returned to the client.

Destination Unreachable

Gateways send ICMP *redirect* messages to request that a host change the way it routes packets. Redirect messages have the format shown below. The meaning of the fields should be self evident.

0	8	16	31
TYPE	CODE	CHECKSUM	
GATEWAY INTERNET ADDRESS			
INTERNET HRD. + 64 BYTES OF ORIGINAL DATAGRAM			

DARPA IP Protocol Format

The DARPA Internet is a datagram-based packet-switched network based on unreliable, best-effort delivery. The Internet Protocol (IP) specifies the format of packets (datagrams) as they travel across the Internet. It is summarized below.

0	4	8	16	19	24	31

VERS	LEN	TYPE OF SERVICE	TOTAL LENGTH		
IDENT			FLAGS	FRAGMENT OFFSET	
TIME		PROTO	HEADER CHECKSUM		
SOURCE IP ADDRESS					
DESTINATION IP ADDRESS					
OPTIONS					PADDING
DATA					
. . .					

The 4-bit *VERS* field specifies the IP protocol version being used. Senders and receivers use the version field to be sure they agree on the packet format and contents.

Field *LEN*, also 4 bits, gives the internet header length measured in 32-bit words. Without options, the header length is 5.

The *TYPE OF SERVICE* field specifies how the packet should be handled. It is broken down into five subfields as shown in following diagram.

PRECEDENCE	D	T	R	UNUSED

The three *PRECEDENCE* bits specify packet precedence, with values ranging from 0 (normal precedence) through 7 (network control). When set, the *D* bit specifies low delay, the *T* bit specifies low throughput, and the *R* bit specifies high reliability. However, it seldom makes sense to set all three.

The *TOTAL LENGTH* field gives the length of the IP datagram measured in octets, including the length of the header.

Fields *IDENT*, *FLAGS* and *FRAGMENT OFFSET* allow the Internet to fragment a datagram into small pieces and then reassemble it. The *IDENT* is a unique integer that identifies the datagram. The low-order 2 bits of the 3-bit *FLAGS* field specify whether the datagram may be fragmented, and whether this is the last fragment. For a fragment, field *FRAGMENT OFFSET* specifies where in the reassembled datagram this fragment belongs measured in units of 8 octets starting at offset zero.

The *TIME* field (time to live) specifies how long, in seconds, the datagram is allowed to remain in the Internet system. In practice, the field is decremented by 1 each time the header is processed (e.g., by a gateway). The datagram will be discarded when the count reaches zero.

Field *HEADER CHECKSUM* gives the 16-bit one's complement of the one's complement of all 16-bit words in the header. For purposes of computing the checksum, the checksum field is taken to be zero.

Fields *SOURCE IP ADDRESS* and *DESTINATION IP ADDRESS* contain the 32-bit Internet addresses of the datagram's sender and intended recipient.

Field *OPTIONS* following the destination address field are not required in every datagram. When present, the field is of variable length. Some options are one octet long; others consist of a 1-octet option, a 1-octet length, and a set of data octets for the option. In addition, the option octet is partitioned into a 1-bit copy flag, a 2-bit option class code, and the 5-bit option identifier. Options are used primarily for debugging and maintenance. Details can be found in Feinler *et. al.* [1985].

The final field of an IP header, labeled *PADDING* represents zero octets that may be needed to ensure that the Internet header extends to an exact multiple of 32 bits.

The field labeled *DATA* shows the beginning of the data area of the packet. The length of the data area can be computed from the *TOTAL LENGTH* of the datagram and the header length, found in field *LEN*.

Xinu PURPLE Downloading Protocol Format

The Xinu serial line downloader uses a two-step bootstrap. The final bootstrap phase consists of a sender program, executing on a timesharing system, and a receiver program, executing on the microcomputer. The two programs cooperate to deposit a memory image in the micro over a full duplex serial line. The data to be deposited is divided into packets, and each packet has a header and checksum in the following format.

0	16	31
ADDRESS	DATA LENGTH	
DATA WORDS		
. . .		

The last packet sent by the downloader contains register values and a startup command in the following format.

0	16	31
COMMAND (-1)	DATA LENGTH	
REGISTER 0	REGISTER 1	
REGISTER 2	REGISTER 3	
REGISTER 4	REGISTER 5	
REGISTER 6	REGISTER 7	
REGISTER PS	DELAY	
START ADDRESS		

Field *COMMAND* contains the value −1, to distinguish the command packet from normal data packets. Successive fields contain initial values for the machine registers, followed by an optional delay, *D*. If nonnegative, the downloader will delay for approximately *D* seconds and then branch to the downloaded program. If field *DELAY* contains a negative value, the downloader halts the processor after setting the registers. Field *START ADDRESS* contains the program entry point address as set by the loader.

Byte Order and Framing

Data is treated as a sequence of bytes in memory and deposited in the micro's memory just as it appears in the sender's memory. Thus, the sender has responsibility for ensuring that integers appear in the micro's byte order; the downloading protocol does not perform any mapping.

PURPLE frames all packets with a Start-Of-Header (SOH) character. All occurrences of the SOH character in the address length, or data fields are escaped by preceding them with the ESC character. Occurrences of ESC in the packet are also escaped (i.e., by sending two escapes).

The receiver acknowledges each packet and then deposits the data at the specified memory location. The micro sends an ACK for positive acknowledgement and a NAK is the packet was corrupted. The micro can always resynchronize by sending a NAK and waiting for a SOH.

DARPA UDP Protocol Format

The DARPA User Datagram Protocol, UDP, permits datagram communication between user processes. The format of UDP messages is shown below.

0	16	31

SOURCE PORT	DESTINATION PORT
LENGTH	UDP CHECKSUM
DATA (octets 0-3)	
. . .	

Fields *SOURCE PORT* and *DESTINATION PORT* contain the 16-bit integer UDP port numbers used to demultiplex datagrams among the processes waiting to receive them. The *SOURCE PORT* is optional. When used, it specifies the port to which replies should be sent; if not used, it should be zero.

Field *LENGTH* specifies the length in octets of the UDP message including the header and data (if present). Thus, the minimum value for *LENGTH* is eight, the length of the header alone.

The field labeled *DATA* is an optional field of arbitrary length containing user data.

Field *UDP CHECKSUM* contains the UDP message checksum, or zero if the checksum is omitted. To calculate the checksum, UDP prepends a pseudo header to the message and suffixes octets of zeros to pad to the next exact multiple of 16 bits. It then computes the 16-bit one's complement of one's complement of the pseudo header, the UDP header, and the data. During checksum computation, the checksum field is assumed to be zero. The pseudo header consists of 12 octets as shown in the table below.

0	8	16	31

SOURCE IP ADDRESS			
DESTINATION IP ADDRESS			
ZERO	PROTO	UDP LENGTH	

The fields of the pseudo header labeled *SOURCE IP ADDRESS* and *DESTINATION IP ADDRESS* contain the source and destination Internet addresses that will be used when sending the UDP message. Field *PROTO* contains the IP protocol type code, and the field labeled *UDP LENGTH* contains the length of the UDP datagram.

The rational for the pseudo header is that it provides a check on the IP datagram in which the message travels as well as the UDP message itself, to ensure against misrouted datagrams.

Bibliography

ABRAMSON, N. [1970], the ALOHA System — Another Alternative for Computer Communications, *Proceedings of the Fall Joint Computer Conference.*

ABRAMSON, N. and F. KUO (EDS.) [1973], *Computer Communication Networks,* Prentice Hall, Englewood Cliffs, New Jersey.

ANDREWS, D. W., and G. D. SHULTZ [1982], A Token-Ring Architecture for Local Area Networks: An Update, *Proceedings of Fall 82 COMPCON,* IEEE.

BALL, J. E., E. J. BURKE, I. GERTNER, K. A. LANTZ, and R. F. RASHID [1979], Perspectives on Message-Based Distributed Computing, *IEEE Computing Networking Symposium,* 46-51.

BIRRELL, A., and B. NELSON [February 1984], Implementing Remote Procedure Calls, *ACM Transactions on Computer Systems,* 2(1), 39-59.

BOGGS, D., J. SHOCH, E. TAFT, and R. METCALFE [April 1980], Pup: An Internetwork Architecture, *IEEE Transactions on Communications.*

BOURNE, S. R. [July-August 1978], The UNIX Shell, *Bell System Technical Journal,* 57(6), 1971-1990.

BROWN, M., N. KOLLING, and E. TAFT [Nov. 1985], The Alpine File System, *Transactions on Computer Systems,* 3(4), 261-293.

BROWNBRIDGE, D., L. MARSHALL, and B. RANDELL [December 1982], The Newcastle Connections or UNIXes of the World Unite!, *Software — Practice and Experience* 12(12), 1147-1162.

BRUNT, R. B. and D. E. TUFFS [January-March 1976], "A User-Oriented Approach to Control Languages," *Software — Practice and Experience,* 6(1), 93-108.

CALINGAERT, P. [1982], *Operating System Elements: A User Perspective,* Prentice-Hall, Englewood Cliffs, New Jersey.

CERF, V., and E. CAIN [October 1983], The DOD Internet Architecture Model, *Computer Networks.*

CERF, V., and R. KAHN [May 1974], A Protocol for Packet Network Interconnection, *IEEE Transactions of Communications,* Com-22(5).

CHERITON, D. R. [1983], Local Networking and Internetworking in the V-System, *Proceedings of the Eighth Data Communications Symposium.*

CHERITON, D. R. [April 1984], The V Kernel: A Software Base for Distributed Systems, *IEEE Software,* 1(2), 19-42.

CHERITON, D., and T. MANN [May 1984], "Uniform Access to Distributed Name Interpretation in the V-System," *Proceedings IEEE Fourth International Conference on Distributed Computing Systems,* 290-297.

CLARK, D. D. [July 1982], Name, Addresses, Ports, and Routes, *RFC 814,* USC Information Sciences Institute, Marina del Ray, California.

COMER, D. E. [1984], *Operating System Design — The XINU Approach,* Prentice-Hall, Englewood Cliffs, New Jersey.

COMER, D. E. [April 1986], The Costs and Benefits of a Teaching Laboratory for the Operating Systems Course, *Technical Report TR-CS-589,* Computer Science Department, Purdue University, West Lafayette, Indiana.

COTTON, I. [1979], Technologies for Local Area Computer Networks, *Proceedings of the Local Area Communications Network Symposium.*

CROFT, B., and J. GILMORE [September 1985], Bootstrap Protocol (BOOTP), *RFC 951,* USC Information Sciences Institute, Marina del Ray, California.

DALAL Y. K., and R. S. PRINTIS [1981], 48-Bit Absolute Internet and Ethernet Host Numbers, *Proceedings of the Seventh Data Communications Symposium.*

DEUTSCH, L. P., and E. A. TAFT [June 1980], Requirements for an Experimental Programming Environment, *Technical Report CSL-80-10* Xerox Palo Alto Research Center.

DIGITAL EQUIPMENT CORPORATION., INTEL CORPORATION, and XEROX CORPORATION [September 1980], *The Ethernet: A Local Area Network Data Link Layer and Physical Layer Specification.*

DION, J. [Oct. 1980], The Cambridge File Server, *Operating Systems Review,* 14(4), 26-35.

DRIVER, H., H. HOPEWELL, and J. IAQUINTO [September 1979], How the Gateway Regulates Information Control, *Data Communications.*

EDGE, S. W. [1979], Comparison of the Hop-by-Hop and Endpoint Approaches to Network Interconnection, in *Flow Control in Computer Networks,* J-L. GRANGE and M. GIEN (EDS.), North-Holland, Amsterdam, 359-373.

ENSLOW, P. [January 1978], What is a 'Distributed' Data Processing System? *Computer,* 13-21.

FALK, G. [1983], The Structure and Function of Network Protocols, in CHOU, W. (ED.), *Computer Communications, Volume I: Principles,* Prentice-Hall, Englewood Cliffs, New Jersey.

FARMER, W. D., and E. E. NEWHALL [1969], An Experimental Distributed Switching System to Handle Bursty Computer Traffic, *Proceedings of the ACM Symposium on Probabilistic Optimization of Data Communication Systems,* 1-33.

FEINLER, J., O. J. JACOBSEN, and M. STAHL [December 1985], *DDN Protocol Handbook Volume Two, DARPA Internet Protocols,* DDN Network Information Center, SRI International, 333 Ravenswood Avenue, Room EJ291, Menlo Park, California 94025.

FINLAYSON, R. [June 1984], Bootstrap Loading Using TFTP, *RFC 906,* USC Information Sciences Institute, Marina del Ray, California.

FINLAYSON, R., T. MANN, J. MOGUL, and M. THEIMER [June 1984], A Reverse Address Resolution Protocol, *RFC 903,* USC Information Sciences Institute, Marina del Ray, California.

FITZGERALD, R., and RASHID, R. [May 1986], The Integration of Virtual Memory Management and Interprocess Communication in Accent, *Transactions on Computer Systems,* 4(2), 147-177.

FRANK, H., and W. CHOU [1971], Routing in Computer Networks, *Networks,* 1(1), 99-112.

FRANK, H., and J. FRISCH [1971], *Communication, Transmission, and Transportation Networks,* Addison-Wesley, Reading Massachusetts.

FRANTA, W. R., and I. CHLAMTAC [1981], *Local Networks,* Lexington Books, Lexington, Massachusetts.

FRASER, W., and D. R. HANSON [Jan 1985], High-Level Language Facilities for Low-Level Services, *Proceedings Twelfth Annual ACM Symposium on Principles of Programming Languages,* 217-224.

FRIDRICH, M., and W. OLDER [December 1981], The Felix File Server, *Proceedings of the Eighth Symposium on Operating Systems Principles,* 37-46.

FULTZ, G. L., and L. KLEINROCK, [June 14-16, 1971], Adaptive Routing Techniques for Store-and-Forward Computer Communication Networks, presented at *IEEE International Conference on Communications,* Montreal.

GERLA, M., and L. KLEINROCK [April 1980], Flow Control: A Comparative Survey, *IEEE Transactions on Communications.*

GOLDBERG, A. [February 1983], The Influence of an Object-Oriented Language on the Programming Environment, *Proceedings of the 1983 ACM Computer Science Conference,* 35-54.

GOSLING, J. [January 1983], SUNDEW: A Distributed and Extensible Window System, *Proceedings of the Winter USENIX Technical Conference,* 98-103.

GRANGE, J-L., and M. GIEN (EDS.) [1979], *Flow Control in Computer Networks,* North-Holland, Amsterdam.

GREEN, P. E. (ED.) [1982], *Computer Network Architectures and Protocols,* Plenum Press, New York.

HINDEN, R., J. HAVERTY, and A. SHELTZER [September 1983], The DARPA Internet: Interconnecting Heterogeneous Computer Networks with Gateways, *Computer.*

HOARE, C. A. R. [Aug. 1978], Communicating Sequential Processes, *Communications of the ACM,* 21(8), 666-677.

HORNIG, C. [April 1984], A Standard for the Transmission of IP Datagrams over Ethernet Networks, *RFC 894,* USC Information Sciences Institute, Marina del Ray, California.

KAHN, R. [Nov. 1972], Resource-Sharing Computer Communications Networks, *Proceedings of the IEEE,* 60(11), 1397-1407.

KORN, D. [1983], KSH - A Shell Programming Language, *Proceedings Summer 1983 USENIX Conference,* Toronto, 191-202.

LAMPSON, B. W. [1985], Work in Progress, Digital Equipment Corporation Systems Research Center, California.

LAMPSON, B. W., M. PAUL, and H. J. SIEGERT (EDS.) [1981], *Distributed Systems - Architecture and Implementation (An Advanced Course),* Springer-Verlag, Berlin.

MCNAMARA, J. [1982], *Technical Aspects of Data Communications,* Digital Press, Digital Equipment Corporation, Bedford, Massachusetts.

MCQUILLAN, J. M., I. RICHER, and E. ROSEN [May 1980], The New Routing Algorithm for the ARPANET, *IEEE Transactions on Communications,* (COM-28), 711-719.

METCALFE, R. M., and D. R. BOGGS [July 1976], Ethernet: Distributed Packet Switching for Local Computer Networks, *Communications of the ACM,* 19(7), 395-404.

MILLER, C. K., and D. M. THOMPSON [March 1982], Making a Case for Token Passing in Local Networks, *Data Communications.*

MITCHELL, J., and J. DION [April 1982], A Comparison of two Network-Based File Servers, *Communications of the ACM,* 25(4), 233-245.

MOCKAPETRIS, P. [November 1983], Domain Names — Concepts and Facilities, *RFC 882,* USC Information Sciences Institute, Marina del Ray, California.

MOCKAPETRIS, P. [November 1983a], Domain Names — Implementation and Specification, *RFC 883,* USC Information Sciences Institute, Marina del Ray, California.

MOCKAPETRIS, P. [January 1986], Domain System Changes and Observations, *RFC 973,* USC Information Sciences Institute, Marina del Ray, California.

MULLENDER, S., and A. TANENBAUM [December 1985], A Distributed File Service Based on Optimistic Concurrency Control, *Proceedings ACM Symposium on Operating Systems Principles,* 51-62.

NAGLE, J. [January 1984], Congestion Control In IP/TCP Internetworks, *RFC 896,* USC Information Sciences Institute, Marina del Ray, California.

NEEDHAM, R. M. [1979], System Aspects of the Cambridge Ring, *Proceedings of the Seventh Symposium on Operating System Principles,* 82-85.

NELSON, J. [September 1983], 802: A Progress Report, *Datamation.*

OPPEN, D., and Y. DALAL [October 1981], The Clearinghouse: A Decentralized Agent for Locating Named Objects, Office Products Division, XEROX Corporation.

PARTRIDGE, C. [January 1986], Mail Routing and the Domain System, *RFC 974,* USC Information Sciences Institute, Marina del Ray, California.

PETERSON, L. [1985], *Defining and Naming the Fundamental Objects in a Distributed Message System,* Ph.D. Dissertation, Purdue University, West Lafayette, Indiana.

PETERSON, J., and A. SILBERSCHATZ [1983], *Operating System Concepts,* Addison-Wesley, Reading, Massachusetts.

PIERCE, J. R. [1972], Networks for Block Switching of Data, *Bell System Technical Journal,* 51.

PLUMMER, D. [November 1982], An Ethernet Address Resolution Protocol, or Converting Network Protocol Addresses to 48.bit Ethernet Address for Transmission on Ethernet Hardware, *RFC 826,* USC Information Sciences Institute, Marina del Ray, California.

POSTEL, J. B. [April 1980], Internetwork Protocol Approaches, *IEEE Transactions on Communications,* COM-28, 604-611.

POSTEL, J. B. [August 1980a], User Datagram Protocol *RFC 768,* USC Information Sciences Institute, Marina del Ray, California.

POSTEL, J. B. [1981], Internet Protocol, *RFC 791,* USC Information Sciences Institute, Marina del Ray, California.

POSTEL, J. B. [1981a], Internet Control Message Protocol, *RFC 792,* USC Information Sciences Institute, Marina del Ray, California.

POSTEL, J. B. [1983], Echo Protocol, *RFC 862,* USC Information Sciences Institute, Marina del Ray, California.

POSTEL, J. B., C. A. SUNSHINE, and D. CHEN [1981], The ARPA Internet Protocol, *Computer Networks.*

POSTEL, J. B., and J. REYNOLDS, [October 1984], Domain Requirements, *RFC 920,* USC Information Sciences Institute, Marina del Ray, California.

REYNOLDS, J., and J. POSTEL [December 1985], Assigned Numbers, *RFC 961,* USC Information Sciences Institute, Marina del Ray, California.

RITCHIE, D. M., and K. THOMPSON [July 1974], The UNIX Time-Sharing System, *Communications of the ACM,* 17(7), 365-375; revised and reprinted in *Bell System Technical Journal,* 57(6), [July-August 1978], 1905-1929.

ROSENTHAL, R. (ED.) [November 1982], *The Selection of Local Area Computer Networks,* National Bureau of Standards Special Publication 500-96.

SALTZER, J. [1978] Naming and Binding of Objects, *Operating Systems, An Advanced Course,* Springer-Verlag, 99-208.

SALTZER, J. [April 1982] Naming and Binding of Network Destinations, *International Symposium on Local Computer Networks,* IFIP/T.C.6, 311-317.

SALTZER, J., D. REED, and D. CLARK [November 1984], End-to-End Arguments in System Design, *ACM Transactions on Computer Systems,* 2(4), 277-288.

SHOCH, J. F. [1978], Internetwork Naming, Addressing, and Routing, *Proceedings of COMPCON.*

SHOCH, J. F., Y. DALAL, and D. REDELL [August 1982], Evolution of the Ethernet Local Computer Network, *Computer.*

SMITH D. C., C. IRBY, R. KIMBALL, B. VERPLANK, and E. HARSLEM [April 1982], Designing the Star User Interface, *Byte* 7(4), 242-282.

SNA [1975], *IBM System Network Architecture — General Information*, IBM System Development Division, Publications Center, Department E01, P.O. Box 12195, Research Triangle Park, North Carolina, 27709.

SOLOMON, M., L. LANDWEBER, and D. NEUHEGEN [1982], The CSNET Name Server, *Computer Networks* (6), 161-172.

STALLINGS, W. [1984], *Local Networks: An Introduction*, Macmillan Publishing Company, New York.

STALLINGS, W. [1985], *Data and Computer Communications*, Macmillan Publishing Company, New York.

STALLMAN, R. M. [1984], Emacs: The Extensible, Customizable Self-Documenting Display Editor, in *Interactive Programming Environments*, BARSTOW, D. R., H. E. SHROBE, and E. SANDEWALL (EDS.), McGraw-Hill Book Company, 559-570.

SWINEHART, D., G. MCDANIEL, and D. R. BOGGS [December 1979], WFS: A Simple Shared File System for a Distributed Environment, *Proceedings of the Seventh Symposium on Operating System Principles,* 9-17.

TANENBAUM, A. [1981], *Computer Networks: Toward Distributed Processing Systems,* Prentice-Hall, Englewood Cliffs, New Jersey.

TEITELMAN, W. [April 1984], A Tour Through Cedar, *IEEE Software,* 44-73.

TEITELMAN, W., and L. MASINTER [April 1981], The Interlisp Programming Environment. *IEEE Computer,* 14(4), 25-34.

TICHY, W., and Z. RUAN [June 1984], Towards a Distributed File System, *Proceedings of Summer 84 USENIX Conference,* Salt Lake City, Utah, 87-97.

WARD, A. A. [1980], TRIX: A Network-Oriented Operating System, *Proceedings of COMPCON,* 344-349.

WEINBERGER, P. J. [1985], The UNIX Eighth Edition Network File System, *Proceedings 1985 ACM Computer Science Conference,* 299-301.

WELCH, B., and J. OSTERHAUT [May 1986], Prefix Tables: A Simple Mechanism for Locating Files in a Distributed System, *Proceedings IEEE Sixth International Conference on Distributed Computing Systems,* 1845-189.

WILKES, M. V., and D. J. WHEELER [May 1979], The Cambridge Digital Communication Ring, *Proceedings Local Area Computer Network Symposium.*

UNGER, C. (ED.) [1975], Command Languages, *Proceedings IFIP Working Conference, 1974,* North_Holland, Amsterdam.

XEROX [1981], Internet Transport Protocols, *Report XSIS 028112,* Xerox Corporation, Office Products Division, Network Systems Administration Office, 3333 Coyote Hill Road, Palo Alto, California.

Index

Z